more praise for

Poverty or Development

"*Poverty or Development* is a trail-blazing contribution that shall be emulated by all those interested in reconciling theory and research with the shape the world is taking. Methodologically sound and rich in data, it is an invaluable resource for social scientists. Its various chapters are so expertly integrated that it is hard to tell it is an edited collection."

—Patricia Fernandez-Kelly,
Department of Sociology, Princeton University

"Unlike many studies, which read off local and regional changes as straightforward byproducts of the global restructuring of capitalism, this collection offers a series of carefully historicized case studies of local and regional development in the bi-national Gulf Coast region. The book underscores the critical importance of government action in supporting the interests of specific groups, economic sectors, and localities in a globalizing economy, supporting the conclusion that 'globalization' is very much an unfinished project."

—Michael Peter Smith,
Professor of Community Studies and Development,
University of California, Davis

"These careful studies of the impact of NAFTA slice the globalization project open to show its real consequences for people in the U.S. South and Southern Mexico. *Poverty or Development* examines these processes on the ground and goes beyond to propose ways in which globalization might itself be restructured to produce a more humane, egalitarian, and sustainable world society."

—Christopher Chase-Dunn,
Department of Sociology, Johns Hopkins University

Global Restructuring and Regional Transformations
in the U.S. South and the Mexican South

Poverty or Development

Richard Tardanico & Mark B. Rosenberg, EDITORS

ROUTLEDGE
New York & London

Published in 2000 by
Routledge
29 West 35th Street
New York, NY 10001

Published in Great Britain in 2000 by
Routledge
11 New Fetter Lane
London EC4P 4EE

Printed in the United States of America on acid-free paper
Design and typography: Jack Donner

Library of Congress Cataloging-in-Publication Data

Poverty or development : global restructuring and regional transformations
in the U.S. South and the Mexican South /
edited by Richard Tardanico and Mark B. Rosenberg.
p.   cm.
ISBN 0-415-92431-6 (hardcover). — ISBN 0-415-92432-4 (pbk.)
1. Southern States—Economic conditions—1945-   2. Mexico—Economic
conditions—1994-   3. International economic integration.   4. Southern States—
Commerce—Social aspects.   5. Mexico—Commerce—Social aspects.
I. Tardanico, Richard.   II. Rosenberg, Mark B.
HC107.A13P696   1999
338.975—dc21   99-20479
CIP

Contents

CONCLUSION

Acknowledgments

This book is the culmination of a research project made possible by the generous financial backing of the Andrew W. Mellon Foundation of New York. Work on the project was facilitated by the organizational support of the Florida-Mexico Institute and the Latin American and Caribbean Center—both at Florida International University—and the Center for Latin American Studies at the University of Florida. Our thanks to Terry McCoy and Chris Andrew of the University of Florida; Orlandina de Oliveira of El Colegio de México; Fernando Salmerón of the Centro de Investigación y Estudios Superiores en Antropología Social in Mexico City; and Roberto Santillán of the Instituto Tecnológico de Monterrey, for their invaluable participation at various stages of the project.

Many individuals at Florida International University contributed to the project. We are particularly indebted to Alisa Newman for her expert editing as well as her patience, stamina, and good cheer in bearing up under the seemingly never-ending revisions. We also thank Pedro Botta for producing the maps and Lidia Tuttle, Douglas Kincaid, Eduardo Gamarra, Kimberlee Mark, Adriana Jiménez, Nerlyn González, Teresita Marill, Raquel Jurado, and Tricia Juhn for carrying out myriad essential tasks. Finally, we acknowledge the support of Beverly White of the Office of the Governor of the State of Florida and our friend William Olivera of Campeche, Mexico.

OVERVIEW

Map 1.1
U.S. South and Mexican South

1

Two Souths
in the New Global Order[1]

Richard Tardanico and Mark B. Rosenberg

... in a process of world integration that, left in the hands of God, callously sacrifices millions of workers for the sake of efficiency, productivity, and benefits for the few—you the exploited of Chiapas, would be worse than exploited. You would be thrust aside, abandoned to your fate.

—*Carlos Fuentes, letter to Subcommander Marcos*
of the Zapatista Army of National Liberation

... the Sunbelt image receded before the growing awareness of what an Atlanta journalist described as "a lush suburban North Georgia, an economic wasteland in South Georgia, and a catch-basin in the City of Atlanta for the impoverished refugees from south of the fall line."

—*Numan V. Bartley*

What insights can be gained by comparing the ramifications of global restructuring and the North American Free Trade Agreement (NAFTA) for the Mexican South and the U.S. South? After all, the two regions occupy quite distinctive and unequal parts of the world. The Mexican South is the epitome of "Third World." It is a land of violent clashes between indigenous and Western culture, of conquest, subordination, and exploitation by outside forces. It is a land of profound underdevelopment, whose immense resources—human and natural—have been fodder for a centuries-long trajectory of "modernizing" projects: Iberian expansionism; Mexican independence; Euro-U.S. industrial revolution; Mexican nationalism; and globalization. Within the latter of these is a subproject, NAFTA, which binds together Mexico, the United States, and Canada in a neoliberal regime of denationalized, reciprocal regulation of trade, investment, and associated affairs.[2]

The combination of denationalization and reciprocity is the defining feature of the new global order's formal trade and investment blocs. Of these blocs, only NAFTA subsumes a geographic set of both advanced and under-developed national economies[3] (Anderson and Blackhurst 1993; Bhalla and Bhalla 1997; Bulmer-Thomas et al. 1994; El-Agraa 1997; Weintraub 1997; Cable and Henderson 1994; and see Table 1.1). Furthermore, it is the only market-integrating arrangement of any kind—including the nonreciprocal, highly restrictive accords remaining from the cold war's geopolitics of metro-politan relations with former colonies and neocolonies—that territorially jux-taposes the world's dominant national economy with an underdeveloped country. Arguably, then, no other market-integrating arrangement contains as polarized a division of labor as that which stretches across the NAFTA zone: from the global corporate command posts of Manhattan to the indigenous subsistence farming of Chiapas.

This is the crux of the message sent around the world by the Zapatista National Liberation Army. Its actions and words stress not only the exploita-tion of southern Mexico's indigenous peoples but also their marginalization from global and continental shifts that are "segmenting societies and linking up valuable functions, individuals, social groups, and territories, while exclud-ing others" (Castells et al. 1995–96, 53). The effects in southern Mexico are wide-ranging: from armed insurgency to changes in long-standing, pervasive

Table 1.1
Social and Economic Indicators: The NAFTA Countries

	U.S.	Canada	Mexico
Population (millions)	260.6	29.2	88.5
Gross Domestic Product (million $)	6,648,013	542,954	377,115
Exports of Goods & Services (million $)	836,415	190,101	53,607
Purchasing Power Parity Per Capita (U.S. = 100)	100	77.1	27.2
External Debt/Gross Domestic Product	2.0%	0.8%	32.0%
Income Distribution (ratio highest 20% to lowest 20%)[a]	9.0	7.1	13.5
Adult illiteracy	<5%	<5%	8%
Young-Adult Age Group in Tertiary Education	81%	103%[b]	14%
Years Life Expectancy at Birth	77	78	71

Source: World Bank (1996; 189, 191, 201, 211, 219).
[a] A higher number indicates greater inequality.
[b] As reported.

everyday problems such as poverty, alcohol and drug abuse, intrafamilial and community violence, religious and political factionalism, and out-migration (Castañeda 1996; Collier 1994; Conroy and West in this volume; Gilly 1997; Hernández Navarro 1998; Zermeño 1997). Indeed, the geographic distribution of any Mexican gains from supranationalized investment and production is being concentrated elsewhere in the nation. As Victor Bulmer-Thomas et al. observe:

> The contrast between a poor South and a rich North [in Mexico] is likely to increase as traditional agriculture declines in states such as Chiapas, Guerrero and Yucatán, while the growth of industry and services clusters around urban conglomerations in the [central and northern] states of Mexico, Nuevo León and Sonora. (1994, 206)

Thus, the Mexican South is NAFTA's most extreme territorial instance of underdevelopment, as well as economic displacement under continental and world restructuring.

Embedded in the upper to middle layers of NAFTA's continental division of labor is a swath of activities including the "New," or "Sunbelt," economy of the U.S. South. Within the upper layers are, for example, telecommunications in Atlanta, research and development in North Carolina's Research Triangle, and the aerospace industry in Houston. Retail megamarketing in Arkansas, the country music industry in Nashville, and Latin American commerce in Miami are among the other New South signatures. So too are lower-wage activities such as Mercedes-Benz assembly in Alabama and a safe and sanitized Mardi Gras, not in withering New Orleans but in upstart Orlando's Universal Studios. Clearly, such facets of the the New South's economy provide no basis for comparison with the Mexican South, whose economy remains mired deep within the world periphery.

Yet by no means has the U.S. South at large broken entirely free of its own legacies of underdevelopment. Of course, worsening inequality and infrastructural deterioration plague the United States on a national scale, and every part of the country contains areas where such problems are acute. The New South's progress, however, has combined with stagnation or regression elsewhere to close much of the economic and social gap between the U.S. South on the whole and the rest of the nation (Griffin and Doyle 1995; MDC 1996, 1998). Nonetheless, evidence of the Old South's legacies is widespread. Poverty in the U.S. South exceeds the national average. The region ranks as substandard in education, health, and public services. It contains a disproportionate share of the nation's low-wage labor, undercapitalized businesses, and branch manufacturing plants. And its government policies remain hampered by old-regime ideologies, institutions, and interests. These legacies are most entrenched in rural and small urban areas, African American inner cities across the urban spectrum, and the states of Mississippi, Louisiana, Arkansas, and West Virginia (Bremer 1997; Carlton 1995; Glasmeier and Leichenko in this volume; MDC 1996, 1998).

Some segments of the U.S. South are primed to flourish under North American and global restructuring, but others are not. Most vulnerable are those activities, groups, and places that represent modern-day continuity with the regional legacies of primary-commodity and/or labor-intensive production. For instance, the U.S. South's sugar producers have tenaciously defended their sizable government protections and subsidies in the face of market deregulation and NAFTA. The region's winter vegetable growers have lost substantial ground to their Mexican counterparts, and its citrus growers fear the same (Andrew and Spreen 1997; Griffith in this volume). The closing of Levi Strauss's apparel production plants across the U.S. South in 1999 epitomizes the region's vulnerability as "branch plant capital of the nation" (Glasmeier and Leichenko in this volume). Under new global and continental trade regimes the region will probably suffer an accelerated loss of labor-intensive manufacturing operations in products such as textiles, apparel, furniture, and auto parts to Mexico, the Caribbean Basin, and beyond (Gereffi in this volume; MDC 1996, 1998). The same fate would appear to await some of its lower-end business services, including data-processing. There will certainly be regional winners—quite conceivably, many more winners than losers. At issue, however, is the U.S. South's emerging grid of sectoral, social, and territorial winners and losers compared to those of other U.S. regions, to those of Canada and other rich nations, and to those of less-developed countries such as Mexico (see Conklin 1997).

In sum, southern Mexico and the southern United States do share commonalities that, while obviously complicated and attenuated by the former's location within an underdeveloped country and the latter's within a rich and powerful country, are intriguing as potential sources of insight into reorganized inequalities under globalization and NAFTA. The commonalities center on the histories and legacies of the two regions as labor-repressive producers of primary commodities. These histories and legacies are based on the exploitation of specific ethnic groups: indigenous peoples in southern Mexico, and Africans and African Americans in the U.S. South (see Wolf 1982, 140, 279–85, 337–39). Likewise relevant, though, is a crucial difference between the two regional cases: since the mid-twentieth century a large portion of the U.S. South's activities, groups, and places has experienced significant and even dramatic upward mobility within the global division of labor, while such mobility for the Mexican South has been minimal (see Collier 1994; Gilly 1997; and this volume's chapters by Conroy and West; Wilson and Kayne; Porter; Fox and Aranda; and Roberts and Tardanico). What policy insights might be gained from considering not only the regional similarities but also the regional differences, particularly in regard to post–World War II economic and social paths? Above all, what are the implications for the premise of neoliberal market integration that a shift from state-centric to market-centric policies is the most effective route to widely shared development?

The volume's focus on the Mexican South and the U.S. South lays groundwork for more comprehensive comparisons of North American regions under global restructuring and NAFTA. Such comparisons would involve regions in Mexico, the United States, and Canada whose fundamental conditions render them particularly vulnerable to world-scale and continental realignments, as well as those whose aggregate fortunes appear likely to fare decently or to improve (see Britton 1996; Conklin 1997; Hansen 1998; Noponen et al. 1993; Otero 1996). This agenda entails making comparisons across North America's set of rich and poor countries within the global division of labor, a task involving considerable methodological risk. The specific risk is that profoundly unequal positions in the world economy may amount to qualitative differences between cases that render comparisons logically skewed (i.e., "apples and oranges"). For example, a comparison of poverty across the chasm of rich and poor countries confronts major differences in political, economic, and sociocultural context. Yet, while cognizant of these problems, Bryan Roberts (1991) ventures a comparison of the "coping strategies" of poor urban households under politico-economic restructuring in Britain, the United States, and assorted Latin American nations. His study yields insights into similarities and differences in the responses of poor people to their plight under distinctive local/global and domestic conditions. Christophe Demaziere and Patricia Wilson (1996) follow the same lines in comparing contemporary transformations of political economy in Europe and Latin America. Their objective is to glean policy lessons from points of convergence and divergence across the developed and less-developed worlds. June Nash (1994) explores the worldwide range of social responses to economic displacement under globalization by comparing the actions (and inactions) of workers in rich and poor countries. Philip McMichael and his colleagues (1994) chart the effects of global restructuring for agricultural production across and within such countries, while Saskia Sassen (1994) does the same for inequalities between and within the world's cities.

Such scholarship exemplifies a comparative approach that, in seeking to understand the processes and consequences of global reconfiguration, does not shy from traversing developed and less-developed countries[4] (e.g., Locke and Thelen 1995; McMichael 1990; Wallerstein 1995). This volume adheres to that spirit in addressing the ramifications of global and North American restructuring for the Mexican South and the U.S. South. Their regional histories of labor-repressive, primary-commodity production dispose many of their economic sectors, social groups, and localities to acute problems of exploitation and displacement under continental and world-scale transformations. At the same time, the two regions are subsumed in contrasting national politico-economic conditions, which in turn position them at unequal rungs in the world division of labor. This includes the marked upward trajectory of much of the U.S. South's economy and society since World War II, versus the mix of circumscribed gains and worsened underdevelopment that characterizes the Mexican South. Given these similarities and differences, disentangling the regional webs of probable winners and losers in the Mexican South and the U.S. South as the new global order takes hold is a key task of the volume. So too is the laying out of policy results and lessons. This revolves around assessment of debate over the roles of state-centric versus market-centric policies in both the genesis and mitigation of their regional problems.

The Political Economy of Regions in Theoretical Perspective

The volume examines the Mexican South and the U.S. South from the perspective of a historically unfolding world division of labor whose inequalities are politico-economic and territorial. Territorial positions of dominance and subordination within the world division of labor embody not only nations but also the domestic and transborder regions upon which nations and blocs of nations are built.[5] A region is a territorial cluster of relations, interests, values, identities, resources, and capacities, relative to a global hierarchy of such clusters. Underpinning the relative positions of regions within this hierarchy are their comparative-historical modes of incorporation into the world division of labor. The most basic distinctions are whether regions were incorporated relatively early or late in the history of world capitalism; under their own aegis or colonial imposition; as producers at the higher or lower ends of the commodity, technology, skill, and wage spectrums; and under conditions favoring more or less developmentally oriented government machinery and more or less egalitarian social structures (Chase-Dunn 1998; Roberts 1994; Tilly 1992; Wallerstein 1979; Wolf 1982).

These distinctions are evident in the differing patterns and unequal positions of regional political economies within individual nations and the world at large. Among the fundamental differences and inequalities are:

- the economy's sectoral-technical composition, density of internal linkages, and extent of local ownership and control;
- class, ethnic, and gender distributions of wealth and power;
- the features of culture and ideology concerning social relations, capital accumulation, political regime, territorial identity, and supraterritorial connections; and
- the government's form of embeddedness in society, ties to government machinery elsewhere, organizational traits, and modes of action.

Not only do such ensembles reflect distinctive interplays of regional and extraregional forces but they also improve or diminish the comparative prospects of regions—including their economic sectors, government structures, social groups, and localities—as the organization of the world and national economies changes (Chase-Dunn 1998; Keating and Longlin 1997; Hollingsworth and Boyer 1997; Roberts 1994; Sassen 1994; Scott 1998; Tilly 1992; Wallerstein 1974; Wolf 1982).

For example, a historical consequence of differing local/extralocal alignments is that comparable sets of raw materials have gone untapped in some regions, been captured and exploited by outsiders in other regions, or been transformed into local industrialization in others. The local outcomes of each scenario have varied, in turn, according to further differences in alignments. Focusing on the industrializing cases, the transformations have involved larger or smaller production units, more or less dependence on outsiders, denser or looser production linkages, and more or less productivity, innovation, and sociopolitical equity. In addition, the differences have disposed regions to greater or lesser adaptability to changes in national and world circumstances. This has included variable political capacities to reshape local as well as extralocal terrains of economy and society or to accommodate their shifts, as in the politics of establishing or reorganizing national and international markets (see Tilly 1992).

Saskia Sassen interprets the contemporary aspects of such patterns in world-historical perspective. Sassen writes, "in each historical period, the world economy has consisted of a distinct combination of geographic areas, industries, and institutional arrangements" (1994, 2). She describes how the world economy's ongoing changes have bolstered the position of leading urban-institutional complexes and interests that produce and deploy the new order's key activities of high finance and advanced services, such as those located in New York City, Los Angeles, Toronto, and Mexico City within the NAFTA bloc. More generally she describes how the changes have recontoured relations among and activities within areas across nations and the world. She demonstrates their impact in altering the sectoral and sociospatial forms of prosperity in some places and reigniting prosperity under new forms in others, while excluding vast zones—including portions of otherwise prosperous territories—from the arenas of wealth. Sassen concludes, "We can think of these new developments as constituting new geographies of centrality (that cut across the old divide of poor/rich countries) and of marginality that have become increasingly evident in the less developed world and in the highly developed world as well" (1994, 4). It is within this framework that this volume considers the regional cases of the Mexican South and the U.S. South.

Delineating the boundaries of a regional political economy is no simple task, however. Criteria of physical geography do not necessarily coincide with political, cultural, economic, or social arrangements, each of which may have its own distinctive spatial features. What one group considers a region another group might not, a divergence potentially involving not only local but also local/supralocal divisions. What constitutes a region by certain criteria at one time, such as cultural fabric, economic organization, national politics, or geopolitics, might not at another time, as geographic constellations change. The boundaries of regions may become stronger or weaker and their interiors more or less cohesive.[6] And practically speaking, data usually correspond to politico-administrative units such as nations, subnational states, and metropolitan districts, rather than units demarcated by other standards. At issue, in any event, is the comparative political economy of regions (and subregions) in relation to the contemporary reorganization of the world's hierarchies of capital, technology, skill, trade, and subsidy. Working from this point of view, the volume's contributors examine the Mexican South and the U.S. South in terms of three comparative questions:

1. What politico-economic and social characteristics of regions—including links to broader distributions of wealth and power—are associated with their upward and downward mobility or resistance to displacement in the changing world division of labor?

2. What are the consequences of such mobility or resistance for sectoral, social, and geographic inequalities within regions?

3. What are the implications of these baseline characteristics, patterns of mobility or resistance, and changing inequalities for the longer-range, comparative prospects of regions in the new global order?

The Chapters

The chapters by Amy Glasmeier and Robin Leichenko on the U.S. South and Michael Conroy and Sarah Elizabeth West on the Mexican South provide overviews of the regional and global issues that inform the volume's subsequent case studies. Regarding the U.S. South, Glasmeier and Leichenko pursue the themes of structural and geographic inequality and government policy. They situate the southern United States within the nation's historical sweep of territorially uneven economic and social transformations and its present-day policy ramifications. Their analysis revolves around a central policy debate. The emergence of the "New South" since World War II is commonly portrayed as an outcome of promarket policies that have permitted businesses to operate with minimal regulatory restraint—the very policies often touted as the prescription for ailing economies in Mexico and other countries worldwide. To what extent have promarket policies indeed propelled the New South ahead, and could they be expected to do the same not only for lagging areas of the U.S. South but also for the Mexican South?

Turning to the Mexican South, Conroy and West depict a region that shared marginally in Mexico's federal economic and social interventionism during the postwar decades of rapid import-substitution industrialization (ISI),[7] which was concentrated in central and north-central Mexico, and then has suffered disproportionate drops in federal spending and private investment since economic crisis and neoliberal reform began in the 1980s. The authors chart notable diversity in development indicators across southern Mexico. Yet the plight of most of southern Mexico stands in stark contrast to the postwar upturn in most of the southern United States, if alongside the experience of the latter's other, predominately rural zones. Conroy and West enumerate a series of hypotheses on southern Mexico's contemporary development prospects under national neoliberal policy, globalization, and NAFTA.

The first two case studies, one by Gary Gereffi on Mexico-U.S. apparel production and the other by Patricia Wilson and Thea Kayne on export-assembly production in Yucatán, discuss the prospects of the U.S. South and the Mexican South with respect to the global and continental reorganization of manufacturing. Gereffi's emphasis on the sociogeographic revamping of the apparel industry's commodity chain—from the various stages of production to retailing—sets the background for Wilson and Kayne's assessment of federal and state government initiatives in one area of southern Mexico to attract export-assembly manufacturing investment in apparel and other industries. Gereffi's portrayal of the supranational reorganization of apparel production underlines today's economic dilemmas of developed and underdeveloped countries alike, including the particular vulnerabilities of the poorest areas in the United States and Mexico. Wilson and Kayne illustrate these issues by demonstrating the intrinsic limitations of export-assembly production as a development strategy, as well as the insufficiency of cheap production costs alone as an enticement to manufacturing capital.

David Griffith shifts the topic to South Florida's segment of the North American and global commodity chain of winter vegetables (such as tomatoes, watermelons, bell peppers, and cucumbers). Griffith links South Florida's production of winter vegetables to Mexico as well as Central America and the Caribbean by underscoring the long-run transnationalization and ethnic realignment of the regional industry's workforce. He documents the harsh labor and living conditions of this workforce. He also documents its unfolding interplay with low-wage employment in urban services, including Florida's tourism economy. Griffith relates these patterns to the near-term effects of NAFTA on social inequality in agriculture, not only in South Florida but also across the U.S. South, the United States at large, and Mexico.

Robert Porter extends the analysis of agricultural commodity chains and NAFTA to the arena of federal/provincial government policy in southern Mexico. He does so in terms of the socioeconomic importance of coffee production in southern Mexico and its changes under the reorganization of the nationwide economy. Coffee is a traditional export commodity in Mexico. Yet, as Porter tells us, Mexican coffee—much of which enters the United States through its southern ports of New Orleans, Port Everglades (Fort Lauderdale, Florida), and Miami—has taken on nontraditional features in carving out a new niche in the U.S. markets for gourmet coffee and ice cream. Porter dissects the coffee commodity chain as a way of analyzing changes in its structures of economic and political control, and the ramifications of both the changes and the variable aspects of local politics for economic development and social inequality in southern Mexico. His findings represent a departure from perspectives that regard market-oriented reform and globalization as either bringing nothing but displacement and loss to poor areas of the world such as southern Mexico, or else as triggering widely shared, trickle-down prosperity in such areas.

Complementing Porter's chapter is Jonathan Fox and Josefina Aranda's study of the consequences of Mexican federal policy reform for community politics and development in the southern state of Oaxaca. Fox and Aranda situate such reform within Mexico's political transition of the late 1980s and early 1990s. This transition accelerated and consolidated the federal government's measures of fiscal austerity, trade liberalization, market deregulation, and privatization of public enterprise. It also confronted the political repercussions of these measures. The presidency of Carlos Salinas de Gortari (1988–94) attempted to fend off emergent Rightist and grassroots challenges to both its authority and that of the ruling Partido Revolucionario Institucional (PRI). Fox and Aranda specifically examine one component of this attempt, the implementation of the Municipal Solidarity Funds project. Backed by the World Bank, the funds represent a "targeted antipoverty program" geared to small-scale, participatory rural development projects. The funds are part of a more comprehensive National Solidarity Program, which President Salinas orchestrated to bolster popular electoral support of the PRI-based federal regime by emphasizing local decisions over such projects. The objective, then, has been to co-opt, forestall, and neutralize popular discontent by circumventing the PRI's thicket of patronage in the allocation of development resources. Fox and Aranda focus on the significance of the funds for participatory decision making and local development in Oaxaca. Their conclusions converge with Porter's in stressing the role of local sociopolitical matrices in shaping the dynamics of citizenship and the allocation of tangible resources for rural grassroots development, even as in fundamental ways wealth and power become more concentrated domestically and supranationally.

Alma Young changes the topic from rural to urban economy, and from the Mexican South to the U.S. South, while emphasizing a recurrent theme in the volume: the still critical importance of government policy—including local policy—under global restructuring. By the early 1980s, the New Orleans port economy, though still among the U.S. leaders, had lost substantial ground to other Gulf and national ports. Local recognition of the port's languishing condition crystallized as the New Orleans economy contracted in the mid-1980s due to the collapse of world oil prices. Young details how, as the local economy tumbled, a modernizing regime gained the upper hand within a strategic governmental body, the Board of Commissioners of the Port of New Orleans. The new regime acted decisively to carry out a far-reaching, successful plan of revitalization. Young's analysis provokes questions about the circumstances under which such politically led revitalization can be implemented in other port economies; the degree to which, under stepped-up national and global competition, it would necessarily prove successful elsewhere; and its impact on local socioeconomic inequalities.

Bryan Roberts and Richard Tardanico encapsulate the volume's discussions of urban-regional change into an analysis of employment transformations in Mexican and U.S. cities rimming the Gulf of Mexico. These are among the cities that correspond to a binational, politico-commercial consortium established by the governors of the zone's Mexican and U.S. states in the context of NAFTA. Roberts and Tardanico contrast the economic and employment contours of the era of domestically oriented, high-volume manufacturing with those taking shape under present-day market deregulation and globalization. They also contrast two perspectives on contemporary urban labor markets: one predicting employment to become more concentrated in the upper and middle layers of professional, managerial-technical, and skilled occupations; the other predicting polarizing concentrations at the high end of professionals and the low end of semiskilled and unskilled workers, particularly in cities ranking high in the global division of labor. After additionally contrasting the starkly unequal baselines at which Mexico and the United States cross paths with global and continental restructuring, Roberts and Tardanico examine shifts in the social structures of employment in a sample of Mexican and U.S. Gulf cities. They conclude by addressing a question running throughout the volume: under what conditions might transnational realignments promote not only aggregate economic growth but also socioterritorial development and equity?

References

Anderson, Kym, and Richard Blackhurst. 1993. Introduction and Summary. In *Regional Integration and the Global Trading System*, eds. Kym Anderson and Richard Blackhurst. New York: St. Martin's Press.

Andrew, C. O., and T. H. Spreen. 1997. Global Groves: The Citrus Industries of Florida and Veracruz. *LACC Occasional Papers*. Miami: Latin American and Caribbean Center, Florida International University.

Barnes, William C., and Larry C. Ledebur. 1998. *The New Regional Economies: The U.S. Common Market and the Global Economy*. Thousand Oaks, Calif.: Sage Publications.

Bartley, Numan V. 1990. *The Creation of Modern Georgia*. 2d ed. Athens: University of Georgia Press.

Bhalla, A. S., and P. Bhalla. 1997. *Regional Blocs: Building Blocks or Stumbling Blocks?* New York: St. Martin's Press.

Bremer, Jennifer. 1997. Positioning the South in the New Global Economy. *Southern Growth* (spring).

Britton, John N. H., ed. 1996. *Canada and the Global Economy: The Geography of Structural and Technological Change*. Montreal and Kingston: McGill-Queen's University Press.

Bulmer-Thomas, Victor, Nikki Craske, and Mónica Serrano. 1994. Who Will Benefit? In *Mexico and the North American Free Trade Agreement: Who Will Benefit?*, eds. Victor Bulmer-Thomas, Niki Craske, and Mónica Serrano. New York: St. Martin's Press.

Cable, Vincent. 1994. Overview. In *Trade Blocs? The Future of Regional Integration*, eds. Vincent Cable and David Henderson. London: The Royal Institute of International Affairs.

Cable, Vincent, and David Henderson, eds. 1994. *Trade Blocs? The Future of Regional Integration*. London: The Royal Institute of International Affairs.

Carlton, David L. 1995. How American Is the American South? In *The South as an American Problem*, eds. Larry J. Griffin and Don H. Doyle. Athens: University of Georgia Press.

Castañeda, Jorge. 1996. Mexico's Circle of Misery. *Foreign Affairs* 75, no. 4.

Castells, Manuel, Sherjiro Yazawa, and Emma Kiselyova. 1995–96. Insurgents against the New Global Order: A Comparative Analysis of the Zapatistas in Mexico, the American Militia and Japan's Aum Shinyo. *Berkeley Journal of Sociology* 40.

Chase-Dunn, Christopher. 1998. *Global Formations*. 2d ed. rev. Lanham, Md.: Rowman & Littlefield.

Collier, George. 1994. *Basta! Land and the Zapatista Rebellion*. Oakland, Calif.: Food First.

Conklin, David W. 1997. NAFTA: Regional Impacts. In *The Political Economy of Regionalism*, eds. Michael Keating and John Longlin. London: Frank Cass.

Cox, Ronald W., and Daniel Skidmore-Hess. 1999. *U.S. Politics and the Global Economy: Corporate Power, Conservative Shift*. Boulder, Colo.: Lynne Rienner Publishers.

Demaziere, Christophe, and Patricia A. Wilson, eds. 1995. *Local Economic Development in Europe and the Americas*. London: Mansell.

El-Agraa, Ali M. 1997. Regional Trade Arrangements Worldwide. In *Economic Integration Worldwide*, by Ali M. El-Agraa et al. New York: St. Martin's Press.

Fox, Jonathan, and L. David Brown, eds. 1998. *The Struggle for Accountability: Grassroots Movements, NGOs, and the World Bank*. Cambridge, Mass.: MIT Press.

Fuentes, Carlos. 1996. *A New Time for Mexico*. Trans. by Marina Gutman Castañeda and the author. New York: Farrar, Straus, Giroux.

Galbraith, James K. 1998. *Created Unequal: The Crisis in American Pay*. New York: The Free Press.

Gereffi, Gary. 1994. Rethinking Development Theory: Insights from East Asia and Latin America. In *Comparative National Development: Society and Economy in the New Global Order*, eds. A. Douglas Kincaid and Alejandro Portes. Chapel Hill: University of North Carolina Press.

Gilly, Adolfo. 1997. *Chiapas: La razón ardiente*. México, D.F.: Era.

Griffin, Larry J., and Don H. Doyle, eds. 1995. *The South as an American Problem*. Athens: University of Georgia Press.

Hansen, Gordon H. 1998. Regional Adjustment to Trade Liberalization. *Regional Science and Urban Economics* 28, no. 4.

Hernández Navarro, Luis. 1998. The Escalation of the War in Chiapas. *NACLA Report on the Americas* 31, no. 5.

Hollingsworth, J. Rogers, and Robert Boyer, eds. 1997. *Contemporary Capitalism: The Embeddedness of Institutions.* Cambridge: Cambridge University Press.

Keating, Michael, and John Longlin, eds. 1997. *The Political Economy of Regionalism.* London: Frank Cass.

Locke, Richard M., and Kathleen Thelen. 1995. Apples and Oranges: Contextualized Comparisons and the Study of Comparative Labor Politics. *Politics & Society* 23, no. 3.

McMichael, Philip. 1990. Incorporating Comparison within a World-Historical Perspective: An Alternative Comparative Method. *American Sociological Review* 55, no. 3.

———, ed. 1994. *The Global Restructuring of Agro-Food Systems.* Ithaca, N.Y.: Cornell University Press.

MDC. 1996. *The State of the South.* Chapel Hill, N.C.: MDC, Inc.

———. 1998. *The State of the South.* Chapel Hill, N.C.: MDC, Inc.

Nash, June. 1994. Global Integration and Subsistence Insecurity. *American Anthropologist* 96, no. 1.

Noponen, Helzi, Julie Graham, and Ann R. Markusen, eds. 1993. *Trading Industries, Trading Regions: International Trade, American Industry, and Regional Economic Development.* New York: The Guilford Press.

Otero, Gerardo, ed. 1996. *Neoliberalism Revisited: Economic Restructuring and Mexico's Political Future.* Boulder, Colo.: Westview.

Raynolds, Laura. 1997. Restructuring National Agriculture, Agro-Food Trade, and Agrarian Livelihoods in the Caribbean. In *Globalising Food: Agrarian Questions and Global Restructuring,* eds. David Goodman and Michael Watts. London: Routledge.

Roberts, Bryan. 1991. Household Coping Strategies and Urban Poverty in a Comparative Perspective. In *Urban Life in Transition,* eds. Mark Gottdiener and Chris G. Pickvance. Newbury Park, Calif.: Sage Publications.

———. 1994. Urbanization, Development, and the Household. In *Comparative National Development: Society and Economy in the New Global Order,* eds. A. Douglas Kincaid and Alejandro Portes. Chapel Hill: University of North Carolina Press.

Sassen, Saskia. 1994. *Cities in a World Economy.* Thousand Oaks, Calif.: Pine Forge Press.

———. 1996. *Loss of Control? Sovereignty in an Age of Globalization.* New York: Columbia University Press.

Scott, Allen J. 1998. *Regions and the World Political Economy: The Coming Shape of Global Production, Competition, and Political Order.* Oxford: Oxford University Press.

Stallings, Barbara, ed. 1995. *Global Change, Regional Responses: The New International Context of Development.* Cambridge: Cambridge University Press.

Tilly, Charles. 1975. *From Mobilization to Revolution.* Lexington, Mass.: Addison-Wellesley.

———. 1984. *Big Structures, Large Processes, Huge Comparisons.* New York: Russell Sage Foundation.

————. 1992. *Coercion, Capital, and European States, AD 900–1992*. Cambridge, Mass.: Blackwell.

Wallerstein, Immanuel. 1974. *The Modern World-System: Capitalist Agriculture and the Origins of the European World-Economy in the Sixteenth Century*. New York: Academic Press.

————. 1979. *The Capitalist World-Economy*. Cambridge: Cambridge University Press.

————. 1995. *The End of Liberalism*. New York: The New Press.

Weintraub, Sidney. 1997. The North American Free Trade Agreement. In *Economic Integration Worldwide*, by Ali M. El-Agraa et al. New York: St. Martin's Press.

Winters, L. Allan. 1993. Expanding EC Membership and Association Accords. In *Regional Integration and the Global Trading System*, eds. Kym Anderson and Richard Blackhurst. New York: St. Martin's Press.

Wolf, Eric R. 1982. *Europe and the People Without History*. Berkeley and Los Angeles: University of California Press.

World Bank. 1996. *World Development Report*. New York: Oxford University Press.

Zermeño, Sergio. 1997. State, Society, and Dependent Neoliberalism in Mexico: The Case of the Chiapas Uprising. In *Politics, Social Change, and Economic Restructuring in Latin America*, eds. William C. Smith and Roberto Patricio Korzeniewicz. Coral Gables, Fla: North-South Center Press at the University of Miami; Boulder, Colo.: Lynne Rienner Publishers.

2

From Free-Market Rhetoric to Free-Market Reality

The Future of the U.S. South in an Era of Globalization

Amy K. Glasmeier and Robin M. Leichenko

The South is one of the fastest growing regions in the United States. By turning the region's long-standing dependence on low wages into an asset, the states of the U.S. South have created a business climate that emphasizes deregulation, low social overhead charges, and lax environmental and business standards. This so-called free-market approach has been touted as the appropriate development model for other developing countries and regions, and in the harsh climate of debt crisis and the eclipse of import-substitution economies, it has emerged as the policy standard for multilateral financial agencies and the developing world. The case of Mexico since the 1980s is a prime example. But how laissez-faire has the U.S. policy environment actually been and how replicable is the U.S. South's development experience for developing countries and regions, including Mexico and its southern zone?

This chapter demonstrates that vigorous government intervention, particularly in the form of infrastructure investments and trade protection, played a key role in the U.S. South's transformation. Beginning in the 1930s, political leaders in the South successfully garnered more than the region's share of national resources, which were then targeted toward investments intended to rectify differences in regional factor costs while maintaining the region's low-wage status. This strategy strengthened the region's appeal to firms in mature industries seeking to escape from high-cost, unionized locations in the industrial heartland. Simultaneously, traditional labor-intensive industries in the South, such as apparel and textiles, successfully sought tariff and quota protection from international competition. These two distinct processes fixed in place a base of low-wage, low-skilled industries.

While the postwar era of U.S. southern economic growth has been impressive, it has not brought prosperity to all of the region's residents. Minorities, children, and single-parent families have generally been marginal beneficiaries of the region's expansion. The same is true for the rural areas in which a large portion of the region's less advantaged residents reside. Such areas remain dominated by low-skilled, low-wage industry owned predominantly by firms headquartered outside the region.

As institutionalized in NAFTA and the World Trade Organization (WTO), the contemporary trend toward increasing trade liberalization raises interesting new problems for the region and challenges its ability to shake off its designation as a peripheral region in an industrialized nation (Glasmeier and Conroy 1994). Given its economic and cultural legacies, a large portion of the U.S. South's labor force is ill-prepared for international competition. The long-term consequence of further liberalization may be a serious marginalization of low-skilled workers. The spatial distribution of economic activity in the South suggests that such marginalization will be particularly significant for the rural areas in which low-skilled industries are concentrated. At the same time, urban industries employing low-skilled workers are likely to experience similar cost pressures as economic integration creates opportunities for firms to penetrate new markets and consolidate production across large geographic areas. Has the U.S. South made significant progress since World War II, and particularly since the advent of the "Sunbelt" era in the 1960s? The answer is yes. But has the South's progress prepared the entire region for the effects of greater global economic integration, or has it created new risks of further marginalizing the region's rural areas?

This chapter explores these questions by drawing upon both historical and contemporary evidence. The chapter's first section examines the history of the "Old South" from the Civil War through the post–World War II era, tracing the implications of slavery and cash-crop agriculture for the region's development. During this period, massive federal investments helped pull the region toward national norms and set the stage for the rise of the "New South," which is examined in the chapter's second part. Here we show that while the South has made significant progress, it still suffers from serious inequality in the distribution of wealth, education, and industrialization. We also examine the industrial structure of the South, noting the tendency for the region's industrial base to converge toward the national structure. Yet, our research also shows that at a deeper level the South is still the disproportionate locus of low-wage jobs in the United States. The implications of greater global economic integration are explored in the third part of the chapter. This section examines the impacts of post–World War II trade protectionism on southern industries and workers and considers the potential effects of increasingly liberalized trade. The concluding section briefly considers possible justifications for regional policy in an era of globalization.

Defining the South

Our definition of the "South" follows the U.S. Census definition, which includes the states of Alabama, Arkansas, Delaware, Florida, Georgia, Kentucky, Louisiana, Maryland, Mississippi, North Carolina, Oklahoma, South Carolina, Tennessee, Texas, Virginia, and West Virginia, as well as the District of Columbia.[1] We selected this regional definition for several reasons. First, it is conventional and thus allows us the greatest access to statistical information on the region. Second, the definition is historical and represents states involved either directly or indirectly in the Civil War. Third, the states that comprise the region have for most of their existence been considered peripheral to the industrialized North. Dependent upon the North for capital, technology, and skills, the South has until very recently been defined relative to the more industrialized portion of the United States. While there are core economies within the region, such as the major urban areas of Atlanta, Houston, Birmingham, and Miami, large portions of the South remain peripheral relative to both the region itself and the U.S. economy as a whole.

The Old South

Contemporary economic conditions in the U.S. South in many ways reflect the region's unique economic history. The pre–Civil War South was a plantation economy based on slavery. Even after the Civil War, slavery's legacies of low labor productivity, low wages, and under-capitalization directed the South's course of economic development. New forms of institutionalized discrimination emerged through Jim Crow laws, and political and economic power continued to be concentrated among white elite planters and businessmen. Other legacies of slavery included widespread poverty (for blacks and rural whites), poor health care, and minimal investment in education and infrastructure. Many of these legacies persist today.

In addition to the effects of slavery, the South's historical development in the post–Civil War era, particularly since the 1930s, has been heavily influenced by the activities of the federal government. The federal government was deeply involved in efforts to rebuild the region immediately following the Civil War. Reconstruction, which lasted from 1865 to 1877, came to be identified by the southern elite with excess and corruption (Schulman 1991). For southern white political leaders, the consequences of Reconstruction included distrust of the federal government and unwillingness to cooperate with federal social initiatives. Southern opposition and mistrust of the federal government lasted until the Depression era.

Beginning with the New Deal programs of the early 1930s, an uneasy alliance was established between the federal government and southern elites. While the latter embraced certain aspects of the programs, such as infrastructure spending, they explicitly rejected the New Deal's social aims. The federal role in the South greatly expanded during and after World War II with increased spending on military bases, weapons manufacturing, and physical infrastructure (Markusen 1987). However, the tension between federal goals and the aims of local white leaders continued, resulting by the early 1960s in a partial transformation of the region. The South's economy underwent industrialization and modernization, converging with the rest of the nation, but its social structure remained decidedly backward (Schulman 1991).

An understanding of the significance of the legacy of slavery and the role of the federal government provides a broader perspective for evaluating the South's gradual economic convergence in terms of wage and income levels after 1929. This convergence was not the result of neoclassical factor price equalization across regions, nor was it the outcome of intraregional structural shifts from agriculture to manufacturing (Borts and Stein 1964; Carlino and Mills 1993). Rather, it was driven by passage of federal minimum wage laws (Wright 1986) and enabled by massive levels of federal financing. The aggregate statistics also seem to suggest that the South's convergence toward national norms has helped all of the region's residents. But this has not been the case. Inequitable social conditions in the South have meant that despite interregional convergence, high levels of inequality within the region have persisted over time (Persky 1992).

Post–Civil War to World War II:
The South as an Export-Based Economy

Industrialization in the South proceeded rapidly after the Civil War—faster, in fact, than industrial growth in the North during this period (Schulman 1991; Wright 1986). The South's industrial development centered around the cotton production complex, involving fertilizers, cotton seed processing, and textiles. Other, less significant industries of this period included timber, lumber, and tobacco. Growth in textiles was fueled in part by the southward shift of the northern textile industry, a trend that began before 1900 and was nearly complete by the 1920s. As with all southern industrial growth, the driving forces behind this shift included very low wages, seemingly unlimited supplies of unskilled labor, low taxes, and virtually no business regulation (Braun 1991; Cobb 1993).

Slavery's legacy also shaped the spatial structure of the southern industrial economy. Because plantations were self-sufficient, southern cities did not act as commercial hubs. Instead, the region was dotted with small rural settlements that catered to local trade. Southern industrialization did not break this pattern but in fact reinforced it. Textile mills cropped up in small towns throughout the region, resulting in a highly decentralized pattern of small-city urbanization that persists to the present day (Lonsdale and Browning 1971).

Even infrastructure investments, long missing in the slave-era South, became oriented toward exploiting opportunities associated with cotton. Prior to the Civil War, part of the South's relative underdevelopment could be attributed to the lack of transportation infrastructure with which to move goods both within and outside the region. Thirty years after the war, a great deal of money was invested in the development of a railroad system. However, increased access did not result in economic diversification. Planters retained a strong incentive to control the labor market and to discourage other sources of economic development from evolving in the region.

The New Deal: The Beginning of the South's Transformation

The South's low productivity and lack of diversification exacerbated the regional economic impacts of the Depression of 1929. So devastating were the regional effects that southern legislators who had long eschewed any federal involvement in the region demanded federal action (Schulman 1991). Southern leaders retained sufficient autonomy, however, to control and channel that federal action to provide economic relief without disrupting the South's social structure. This ability of the southern political leadership to avoid issues of social welfare while using federal money to promote economic development is clearly demonstrated in the case of the federal Agricultural Adjustment Administration (AAA). The AAA succeeded in raising cotton prices and increasing productivity by reducing crop acreage and promoting mechanization. Nevertheless, it failed to protect the tenants' share rights (Schulman 1991). The AAA programs ultimately benefited southern planters by enlarging farm size through consolidation of smaller units. At the same time, the program displaced thousands of tenants and sharecroppers, marking the beginning of a long phase of southern rural out-migration.

Once the federal government became involved in the southern economy, elite control over the southern labor market proved to be short-lived. The establishment of a national minimum wage in 1938 through the Fair Labor Standards Act significantly diminished the South's ability to retain its status as the nation's low-wage region (Wright 1986). As labor became more expensive, southern manufacturing firms had to raise labor productivity, move away from very low-wage sectors, and pursue new employers to fill in the gaps created by the decline in traditional industries. From the late 1930s on, southern economic development boosters sought external capital to provide needed jobs (Cobb 1993). While still selling the region's low costs, southern boosters also used local capital subsidies, union bashing, and claims of abundant docile labor to entice manufacturers to set up shop in the South. These actions were further cemented by unprecedented actions by state governments to secure federal funding for infrastructure and military operations.

From the late 1930s on, the South lagged far behind in manufacturing relative to its share of national population. Policy makers in Washington and a few visionaries within the region recognized the need for further industrialization. By the end of the 1930s, the South contained more than 27% of the nation's population but only 17% of its manufacturing. Armed with these statistics, the federal government set about bringing industry south through infrastructure investment and federal grants. The Tennessee Valley Authority (TVA) played a major role in this pursuit of industry by providing communities with technical assistance for recruiting outside investment. The TVA used its considerable electrical power resources to fuel consumer demand. Perhaps more important than its assistance in attracting industry, the TVA's influence over federal dollars changed the industrial landscape of the region. TVA leaders pressed the federal government to locate large processing facilities in the South. This, combined with the development of new manufacturing methods that better utilized the region's resources, led to the creation of a technical community which had been missing until this point.

World War II to the 1960s: Building a Regional Economy
The real expansion of industrial activities in the South occurred during World War II. The war effort brought 23% of war-related manufacturing production to the South in the form of new plants, conversions of existing facilities, and expansions (Schulman 1991). From the 1940s on, southern legislators sought continued federal assistance in the form of infrastructure and additional military procurement expenditures. Southerners dominated key appropriations committees and ensured the South its fair share of federal dollars. To reduce long-standing poverty in the region, the federal government also awarded procurement contracts to firms willing to relocate to the South (Schulman 1991).

As noted earlier, the willingness to seek federal spending was a historical reversal of past southern policy. World War II marked the first time that southern politicians saw the benefits of using outside resources to industrialize the region. Until this point, southern political leaders had vetoed government welfare spending. They feared that such spending would attract outsiders and that subsidies would encourage low-wage workers to concentrate in the region. Defense spending and infrastructure investment had none of these flaws. Thus, with the steady hand and deep pockets of the federal government behind it, southern industrialization and modernization became a reality. A process of region building based on external capital had taken hold, and the South began its rise from the nation's low-wage region to a shining example of federal development capabilities.

The capstone of federal efforts to industrialize the South came with the completion of the federal highway system, which increased the accessibility of rural areas to industry. Southern industrialization had always had a rural bias. A study of industrial location in the South from 1920 to 1969 clearly demonstrates that manufacturing in that region continued to be a rural phenomenon (Lonsdale and Browning 1971). This decentralized pattern of development was significantly enhanced and accelerated by the road system.

By the end of the 1960s, the South was primed for an era of massive growth. Particularly in the postwar context of U.S. hegemony in the world economy and national civil rights legislation, federal aid had enabled the South to close much of the gap with the rest of the nation. Even so, high levels of inequality, widespread poverty, and racial segregation persisted. In the early 1970s, low wages, low taxes, the absence of unions, and a lax regulatory environment made the rural South the prime target for industries in search of lower costs.

The New South

Historically, the South has received attention because of its poverty, which has been seen as pure, complete, and inescapable. Since the Depression, federal authorities have used various policy measures to rectify the dramatic differences between southern residents' standard of living and the rest of the nation's. These efforts came mostly in the form of interventions designed to equalize factor costs across regions. As noted by one commentator, pavement symbolized progress (Schulman 1991). Fearful that a singular emphasis on reducing business costs would fail to rectify persistent deficits in the region's human and social capital, liberals in both Washington, D.C., and the South argued strongly for more radical efforts to democratize the region. Progressives warned that without political reform, development efforts would fail to achieve their goals.

Despite massive investments in roads and other infrastructure, standards of living vary across the South. In speaking of the development impact of Interstates 85 and 95—symbols of the New South that opened the region from Washington, D.C., through the Carolinas and on to Houston—author Bruce Schulman quoted the Southern Growth Policies Board (SGPB):

> Those two highways connected the Sunbelt South with the still poor southern region it overlaid. The roads exposed, in the words of the SGPB, the "twin pressures of growth at the top and poverty at the bottom," gripping the south of the 1970s and 1980s. "A flash flood of change," the Board lamented in 1986, "stranded" many southerners amid the rising tides of the Sunbelt boom. The torrent swept some into prosperity, primarily immigrants and educated, middle class natives. But poor, under-educated southerners found themselves "high, dry, and unemployed." (1991, 175)

By the late 1990s, conditions were little changed.

Population Growth Rates:
Impressive in the 1970s, Slower in the 1980s

The South's postwar meteoric rise is clearly seen in the region's population growth from 1960 to 1990. During this period, the South's population grew from 54 million to 85 million, making it the nation's most populated region. The bulk of the growth occurred in the 1970s, when population expanded by 20%. By the 1980s, the region's growth rate was more in line with the national average and was significantly less than that of the West, where for three decades population consistently grew by more than 20% (Table 2.1).

Viewing the South in aggregate obscures the fact that population growth in the region has been highly uneven across states. Just two states, Florida and Texas, were responsible for 53% of the region's growth. With the addition of Georgia and North Carolina, these four states account for almost two-thirds of the region's growth during the thirty-year period. Growth was far more modest in the remaining states. In the 1980s, population growth in ten of the region's seventeen states—Alabama, Arkansas, Kentucky, Louisiana,

Table 2.1
Percent Population Growth in the South and the Nation 1960–1990

	1980–1990	1970–1980	1960–1970
South	13.4	20.0	14.2
Nation	9.8	11.5	13.3

Source: Rural Conditions and Trends. 1993. *Economic Research of the U.S.* Vol. 4, no. 3. Washington, D.C.: U.S. Department of Agriculture.

Mississippi, Missouri, Oklahoma, Tennessee, and West Virginia—was below the national average; some states, such as West Virginia, experienced negative growth rates (Table 2.2).

Table 2.2
Share of Population Growth in the Region Attributable
to the Top Four States 1970–1990

Florida	6,146,508
Texas	5,787,855
Georgia	1,890,286
North Carolina	1,544,226
Total Regional Change	22,653,000
Four-State Share of Regional Change	68%

Source: Bureau of the Census, U.S. Department of Commerce. 1992. *State and Metropolitan Data Book 1992.* Washington, D.C.: U.S. Government Printing Office.

Incomes Converge, but Poverty Persists

The trend toward regional income convergence is cited as evidence of the South's transformation. Whereas thirty years ago median family income in the South was 20 percentage points below that of the rest of the nation, today the region has moved closer to the national average (Table 2.3). Despite the trend toward convergence, however, long-standing differences persist in the living conditions of whites and nonwhites in the South. Indeed, on the basis of indicators such as poverty and education, conditions for nonwhites have remained static or declined over the period between 1970 and 1990.

Table 2.3
Median Family Income in the South as a Percent of the National Average

1989	1979	1969
89	90	84

Source: Rural Conditions and Trends. 1993. *Economic Research of the U.S.* Vol. 4, no. 3. Washington, D.C.: U.S. Department of Agriculture.

As of 1990, the South's poverty level was more than 2 percentage points above the national average and was considerably in excess of other regions. Between 1970 and 1990, the poverty rate for whites increased marginally from 11.0 to 11.3%, while for blacks it decreased from 32.5 to 31.6%. This decline is little consolation, however, given that the poverty rate for the South's black population is almost three times higher than it is for whites.

Comparisons between blacks and whites highlight the interracial disparity that characterizes income in the region. Poverty rates in black families headed by women, for example, are three times that of white female-headed families. While the trend in poverty rates has been downward, the measure reveals persistently high levels of poverty and inequality in the region (see MDC 1996, 1998).

Education Levels Increase, but the South Still Lags behind the Nation

Despite the region's commitment to public education, the South continues to spend less per pupil than other regions. And yet, the South has made significant progress since the 1960s. During the last three decades, the number of people with less than a high school education has steadily declined as the share of population completing high school and college increases (Table 2.4). However, the South still has the greatest share of population without a high school education. The region also fares only marginally better than the Midwest with regard to the share of residents having a college education.

Table 2.4
Highest Education Attained by Persons Aged Twenty-five and Older 1970–1990: Percent in South/Percent National

Year	Less Than High School	High School	College
1990	1.16	.96	.92
1980	1.19	.90	.93
1970	1.17	.79	.70

Source: Rural Conditions and Trends. 1993. *Economic Research of the U.S.* Vol. 4, no. 3. Washington, D.C.: U.S. Department of Agriculture.

The low level of spending on education has been particularly cruel to southern blacks. Blacks in the South are significantly more likely to lack a high school education than blacks nationally (51.7 versus 48.4%). The educational gap—measured by the percentage of the population with a maximum of high school education—between southern blacks and southern whites is also significant (48 versus 54%; Table 2.5).

Table 2.5
Highest Education Level Attained by Persons Aged Twenty-five and Older 1970–1990: Percent Blacks in South/Percent Whites National

Year	Less Than High School	High School	College
1990	1.85	.86	.50
1980	1.76	.72	.47
1970	1.66	.46	.39

Source: Rural Conditions and Trends. 1993. *Economic Research of the U.S.* Vol. 4, no. 3. Washington, D.C.: U.S. Department of Agriculture.

The experience of southern blacks compared with southern whites (Table 2.6) is only marginally better when compared with the experience of blacks versus whites at the national level. Positive changes have been most prominent in the area of high school education among blacks, where a convergence of national and regional norms is occurring.

Table 2.6
Highest Education Level Attained by Persons Aged Twenty-five and Older 1970–1990: Percent Blacks in South/Percent Whites in South

Year	Less Than High School	High School	College
1990	1.60	.90	.52
1980	1.51	.78	.50
1970	1.49	.52	.41

Source: Rural Conditions and Trends. 1993. *Economic Research of the U.S.* Vol. 4, no. 3. Washington, D.C.: U.S. Department of Agriculture.

The lack of sufficient progress in education, particularly for minorities, has relegated a disproportionate share of blacks to marginal low-paying jobs in the region (see Lyson 1989). Black employment has also been concentrated in industries in decline not only in the South but also at the national level. Despite massive investment, the region's minority residents have made highly uneven progress.

The Rural South: Anachronism or Achilles' Heel?
The described indicators take on distinct form in the rural South, a portion of the region that by many measures has been left behind in an era of rapid growth. The South's rural areas are home to almost one-third of the region's residents. Levels of education among the rural population are, in aggregate, substantially below both regional and national levels and are even more disparate when broken down by race. Compared with southern rural whites, southern rural blacks are 50% less likely to have a college education, 20% less likely to have completed high school, and one and one-half times more likely to have less than a high school education.

Similar disparities emerge when we examine income and poverty rates for residents of the rural South in general and for its whites and blacks specifically (Lyson 1989). Real income levels are almost 30% less in rural than in urban areas, and the previous trend toward greater rural/urban income equality has reversed since the 1980s. Poverty levels in rural areas are 23% higher than in urban areas, and blacks in rural areas are twice as likely to live in poverty as the average rural resident.

The rural South depends heavily on low-skilled manufacturing jobs. As discussed in previous sections, this pattern of development resulted from a conscientious effort to industrialize the region in the context of slavery's legacies. In the next section, the structure of the region's industry and its changes over time will be examined. This analysis suggests that the South's industrial structure is converging with the nation's, a predictable trend given its increased percentage of the U.S. population. While in aggregate the South's industrial structure shares similarities with the nation's, the rural South is still quite distinct in its dependence upon low-wage manufacturing.

Industrial Structure: The South Converges with the Nation, Yet Its Dependence on External Ownership Endures

During the postwar period, the growth in the South's population has been accompanied by a transformation of the region's industrial base. As a result, the South has virtually come to mirror the national industrial structure in proportions of jobs in aggregate sectors, including agriculture, mining, construction, manufacturing, and services (Table 2.7).

Table 2.7
Percent Jobs by Sector for the Nation and the Region

Sector	The Nation	The South
Agriculture	3	3
Mining	1	1
Construction	6	7
Manufacturing	18	7
Services	73	72

Source: Rural Conditions and Trends. 1993. *Economic Research of the U.S.* Vol. 4, no. 3. Washington, D.C.: U.S. Department of Agriculture.

Yet these figures obscure an enduring characteristic of the region's industrial composition. The South is still burdened by a disproportionate share of the nation's low-wage industries, as suggested by a disaggregation of results and examination of the industrial structure based on weekly income by sector (Glickman and Glasmeier 1989).

The number of low-wage jobs has been declining as a share of national employment for more than four decades. Foreign competition, automation, and technological change reduced low-wage jobs in all industries as a share of national employment from 5% in 1969 to 3% in 1986. A similar trend was experienced in the South, where over the same period low-wage jobs declined from 7 to 4.3% (Glickman and Glasmeier 1989). However, the South still holds a very large share of all low-wage manufacturing jobs: 42% of its manufacturing jobs are considered low wage, compared to 29% of manufacturing jobs nationally. Just two industries—apparel and textiles—account for more than 10% of the nation's low-wage jobs, most of which are found in the South (see Gereffi in this volume). Although low-wage jobs declined both nationally and in the South, the region's share of the nation's total low-wage jobs increased from 44 to 48% between 1969 and 1986.

A further and perhaps more ominous problem for the South is the role of external ownership of manufacturing industry. From a relatively early stage the region has attracted branch plants of firms located in the nation's high-cost regions (Cobb 1993; Glasmeier et al. 1993b; Johnson 1988). Branch plant dominance is particularly evident in industries such as textiles, food processing, auto and auto-related manufacturing, and electronics. These branch plants were established to take advantage of the region's low wages and burgeoning market (Wheat 1986). Growing international competition places these plants at risk, given that firms can now find even lower-cost locations within reasonable geographic proximity of the South.

More recently, the South has been a prime recipient of foreign direct investment (FDI). Since the late 1970s, the South has accounted for about 43% of total FDI in the United States. A significant portion of that investment has been sectorally concentrated and restricted to a few locations. One-third of all FDI in the South in 1989 was in the chemicals industry, a trend that has persisted with a slight decline in share since 1977. Individual states' shares of FDI have also been influenced by investment in the chemical industry, which has been concentrated primarily in Texas and Louisiana. Texas claims almost 10% of the nation's total FDI. Other major recipients include Florida, Georgia, and North Carolina. Although South Carolina ranks lower by this measure, one in five of its workers is employed by a foreign firm.

What is the reason for the relative spatial concentration of FDI in the South? FDI tracks investment in manufacturing, which has maintained a southern tilt for the last twenty years (Table 2.8). Factors statistically correlated with FDI and manufacturing location include access to labor, the absence of unions, and the presence of growing markets. One of the few detailed survey-based studies of foreign firm location indicates that foreign firms choose southern locations for labor availability and cost reasons (Glickman and Glasmeier 1989). Foreign direct investment thus appears to replicate the locational behavior of domestic firms.

Another key facet of the modern South's industrial economy is the role played by defense spending. As noted earlier, a major impetus to southern industrialization was the relocation of defense munitions and hardware plants during World War II. This was accompanied by huge investments following the

Table 2.8
Foreign-Owned Property, Plants, and Equipment in Manufacturing Sector
1977–1989

Year	The South's Percent of National Total
1977	45%
1980	43%
1982	50%
1985	47%
1989	43%

Source: Bureau of Economic Analysis, U.S. Department of Commerce. 1977–1980, 1985, 1989. *Foreign Direct Investment in the United States.* Washington, D.C.: U.S. Government Printing Office.

placement of troops in the region. As late as the end of the 1980s, the South received almost 50% of all federal dollars for personnel maintenance, while the region's share of material shipments was far less (21%). Both troop placement and material production are spatially concentrated within the region. Big defense players include Florida, Georgia, Texas, and Virginia. Defense downsizing has been particularly painful in the first three states, where major weapons systems programs have been either drastically downsized or terminated.

As the South has integrated into the national economy, it has begun to shake off aspects of its dependent and peripheral past. In the 1980s, as firms became more cost-conscious, some major companies moved their corporate headquarters to a select set of southern locations. Notable relocations, such as the J. C. Penney Corporation's move to Dallas, Texas, have been prominently reported in regional news. But the number of such relocations has really been quite modest, and given the rationale for most firms (e.g., the search for substantially lower-cost locations), it does not appear that this additional facet of the southern economy is reversing past patterns of development. An examination of other indicators of integrated core-region development, including levels of research and development funds and the availability of venture capital, suggests the South still remains largely dependent on outside stimulation from the nation's core regions (Florida and Smith 1993; MDC 1998; National Science Foundation 1992; Wheeler 1990).

Prospects for the South during an Era of Globalization

Trade protection has been a critical element in the persistence of low-wage industries in the South. Under conditions of free trade, the region might have lost its labor-intensive industrial employment to lower-cost locations long ago. In many ways the roots of modern trade policy can be traced to regulations intended to protect southern agricultural and industrial interests from low-wage competition emanating from less-developed countries. Because of the power of southern legislators who dominated key agricultural committees in the House and Senate during the entire postwar period, southern industries—especially textiles and apparel—received significant trade protection through a series of initially bilateral and then multilateral trade agreements.

Until the 1950s, U.S. industrial interests received protection against low-cost imports; in the 1930s, Japan was among the first countries to face restrictions in exporting cotton textiles to the United States. In later years, particularly in the 1960s, the South successfully fought for protectionist policies that regulated virtually all types of textiles imports. And yet, no policy has effectively stemmed the flow of imports. Each policy action has led affected trading partners to shift product lines, production technologies, and location to circumvent the effects of the new regulations (Glasmeier et al. 1993a). Additionally, the policies did not carry sufficient sanctions to force the industry to modernize. Even if a country such as Japan restricted output through voluntary restraints, other countries' products flooded in to fill the vacuum.

The power of southern legislators to secure trade restraints has been tied directly to the importance of the textiles and apparel industries to individual state economies. In the 1950s, 20% or more of manufacturing employment in seven southern states was concentrated in apparel and textiles; in three states—Georgia, North Carolina, and South Carolina—the figure surpassed 50% (Finger and Harrison 1994). As recently as the late 1980s, apparel and textiles comprised at least 25% of the manufacturing base in Georgia and North and South Carolina. These three states alone are responsible for 30% of the nation's total employment in the two industries. Nonetheless, protection has its price: reliance on low-wage industries has made the region persistently vulnerable to competition from lower-cost locations.

Trade-Related Restructuring and Southern Economy

In the late 1970s, U.S. industries first began to feel the effects of trade-related job displacement (Revegna 1992; Tyson and Zysman 1988). Rising international competition in sectors such as automobiles, textiles, and electronics—many of which benefited from export promotion subsidies within foreign countries—in combination with unfavorable U.S. exchange rates contributed to the loss of nearly three million U.S. manufacturing jobs between 1979 and 1992 (Howes and Markusen 1993). The U.S. regions most affected by import competition were the Midwest and the Northeast, the traditional industrial heartland of the United States (Howes and Markusen 1993). From 1979 to 1992, the Northeast lost more than 30% of its manufacturing jobs, while the

Midwest lost more than 18%. Despite heavy job losses within the textile industry, the South remained surprisingly unaffected by trade-related restructuring, losing fewer than 3% of its manufacturing jobs during the same period (Howes and Markusen 1993).

As described above, trade protection for traditional southern industries has helped to spare the South from the most severe consequences of rising levels of competition from manufacturing imports. A study of the import sensitivity of U.S. regions found that among southern states in 1990, only those in the East-South Central region (Alabama, Kentucky, Mississippi, and Tennessee) were disproportionately vulnerable to import-related job losses (Shelburne and Bednarzik 1993). In 1990, although the East-South Central region contained only 7.5% of all U.S. manufacturing jobs, 9.9% of these jobs were vulnerable to import competition (Shelburne and Bednarzik 1993). Other southern regions, including the West-South Central and South Atlantic, contained a less than proportional number of import-sensitive jobs in 1990. The West-South Central region (Arkansas, Louisiana, Oklahoma, and Texas) contained 8.2% of manufacturing jobs, but only 6.1% of import-sensitive jobs. The South Atlantic region (all other southern states) contained 16.4% of U.S. manufacturing jobs and 16.1% of import-sensitive jobs (Shelburne and Bednarzik 1993).

Even within the NAFTA area, the South has been relatively shielded from international competition. A study of trade between the United States, Canada, and Mexico in 1983–1991 suggests that increasing levels of North American trade during this period had minimal impact on the economies of southern states (Hayward and Erickson 1995). Overall, trade with Mexico and Canada has had little effect on the South's economy in recent years, although falling trade barriers associated with NAFTA and WTO indicate near-term, pending changes.

Trade Liberalization and the Future of the South

Trade liberalization, as illustrated by both NAFTA and WTO, represents opportunities and challenges to communities in the southern United States. NAFTA has created the largest consumer market in the world, creating significant opportunities for some firms, plants, and industries. WTO, most notable for protecting the property rights of both intellectual and service activities, will also result in expanded markets around the globe. While NAFTA created a trade zone in which American, Canadian, and Mexican firms were privileged over other competitors, particularly those from Asia, WTO throws open the door to trade expansion for more than 120 countries around the world, many with lower costs and in some cases greater skills than selected groups and regions in the United States.

The near-term effects of further liberalized trade on the South are likely to be minimal and highly sector-specific. Both trade agreements have phase-in properties that prolong the time before the full effects of trade liberalization are felt. The near-term effects are likely to be especially disruptive, though, for sectors and regions that benefited from trade protection (Conroy and Glasmeier 1993; Glasmeier et al. 1993b). For example, in the apparel industry, at least somewhat protected by the Multi-Fiber Arrangement, competition from lower-cost countries is likely to precipitate job dislocation. In the South, this industry accounts for several hundred thousand jobs. Some U.S. firms will undoubtedly relocate production to take advantage of lower wage levels in Mexico (see Gereffi in this volume). Other domestic industries, such as furniture, also will experience new competition as foreign firms, previously hampered by high tariffs, enjoy tariff reductions associated with WTO's implementation. In the short run, however, these effects are likely to be limited.

In the medium term, the South's industry structure will face serious challenges from lower-cost locations around the world. The more capital-intensive industries, such as textiles and machinery, will be encouraged to change locations as markets mature in developing countries. Furthermore, relocation is likely to occur as interindustry linkages encourage constellations of supplier firms to move toward their primary customers. Industries such as textiles and auto parts are particularly mobile in the medium term.

Over the long term, the composition of the South's labor force may dictate the impacts of trade liberalization. Stated in terms of conventional factor endowments theory, trade liberalization should benefit those factors of production that are relatively abundant in the United States and should harm other factors. Because the United States has a relative abundance of skilled labor, trade liberalization is likely to increase both demand and wages for skilled workers (Wood 1994). For unskilled labor, rising levels of trade, particularly between the United States and lower-wage developing countries, will tend to reduce both demand and wages (Leamer 1992). Because the U.S. South contains a disproportionate number of the nation's unskilled workers, it may be especially vulnerable to the long-run negative effects of trade liberalization. Investment in human capital will raise both education and skill levels for southern workers and may thereby help the South avoid a return to its former peripheral status during this era of liberalized trade.

Reflections on the Need for Regional Policies in an Era of Globalization

The postwar development of the U.S. South provides a striking example of policies designed to invest in location, rather than people. The U.S. South's ascendancy occurred as, in the setting of U.S hegemony in the world economy and the cold war, the region garnered more than its fair share of federal subsidies. To the extent that the South was underendowed with subsidies and infrastructure, this action was necessary to equalize conditions across regions. Indeed, from the standpoint of the South's physical capital, one of its competitive advantages today is newer vintage capital stock compared to that found in the industrial heartland.

The author of a report by the Southern Growth Policies Board, *Half Way Home and a Long Way To Go* (Rosenfeld 1986), points out that the South's historic emphasis on building a low-cost business environment has resulted in poorly funded school and infrastructure systems. The region's basic human and social infrastructure will seriously impede its ability to compete globally (see MDC 1996, 1998). Furthermore, just when the region needs to make critical investments in human and physical capital, business will be hard-pressed to pay higher taxes due to increased price competition. In the long term, firms will face ample locational options in regions, nations, and communities that have better infrastructure. Rural areas of the South are particularly susceptible to this pressure.

In the long run, an almost exclusive emphasis on policies that rectify spatial cost disadvantages may be a serious impediment as the region faces increasing competition from locations around the world. In hindsight, policymakers from organizations such as the Southern Governors Conference and the Southern Growth Policies Board recognize that past actions have not prepared the region's residents for global competition. Major efforts to enhance the human capital component of the region are increasing. However, changing the quality of the skills in a region is a long-term process that takes considerable resources, commitment, and, most of all, patience.

The benefits of investments in people are difficult to capture within a limited geographic area. The most qualified people tend to migrate to locations that present the highest rates of return on investment. In the early part of this century, the U.S. South suffered from the out-migration of its most qualified residents. Only after substantial investment was made in the region's physical assets did skilled workers return to the area.

Is there a place for regional policies in an era of globalization? Clearly, globalization is a problem for both people and places: places are as disadvantaged as people. Consequently, there is some rationale for regional policies. Regions are economies based on an area's resource endowment; any development policy must work in conjunction with this endowment and in some cases, such as the U.S. South, in spite of it. A development program operational at the national level is not likely to be sensitive to local particularities.

By the same token, as the U.S. South demonstrates, strong national growth does not exclusively ensure the prospects for development of peripheral regions of advanced nations. Nevertheless, as we have tried to suggest, strong, stable national macroeconomic policies are a necessary prerequisite for successful regional policies.

The U.S. South became the nation's low-wage region in an era when borders were relatively rigid and international trade was a small portion of the national economy. The persistence of the region's low-wage status was intimately tied to the power of regional industrial interests to stave off international pressures for change. The composition of the South's political base is changing, however. Southern political leaders can no longer cater to a narrow band of agricultural and low-wage industrial interests. The region's political constituencies now include multinational corporations and staunch free-trade advocates. As legislative votes on WTO and NAFTA demonstrated, old southern power blocs have been unable to prevent the eventual opening of the U.S. market to low-cost imports.

The region's contemporary political complexion also includes strong advocacy for a smaller, less interventionist federal government—just at the time when the region's protectionist shackles are coming off. The South's historic low-tax stance, designed to maintain labor intensive industries, is likely to come back to haunt the region as lessening international trade restrictions force out low-skilled jobs and usher in demands for better-trained workers. The contradiction between the contemporary political rhetoric calling for less government and the region's long-standing dependence on huge infusions of resources from the federal government may precipitate a new crisis in the U.S. South, one not easily resolved when free-market rhetoric faces free-market reality.

References

Borts, George H., and Jerome L. Stein. 1964. *Economic Growth in a Free Market*. New York: Columbia University Press.

Braun, Denny. 1991. *The Rich Get Richer: The Rise of Income Inequality in the United States and the World*. Chicago: Nelson-Hall.

Carlino, Gerald A., and Leonard O. Mills. 1993. Are U.S. Regional Incomes Converging? *Journal of Monetary Economics* 32.

Cobb, James C. 1993. *The Selling of the South: The Southern Crusade for Industrial Development*. 2d ed. Urbana: University of Illinois Press.

Conroy, Michael E., and Amy K. Glasmeier. 1993. Unprecedented Disparities, Unparalleled Adjustment Needs: Winners and Losers on the NAFTA "Fast Track." *Journal of Interamerican Studies and World Affairs* 34, no. 4.

Finger, J. M., and A. Harrison. 1994. The MFA Paradox: More Protection and More

Trade? National Bureau of Economic Research Working Papers Series. Cambridge, Mass.: NBER, Inc.

Florida, Richard, and Donald F. Smith, Jr. 1993. Venture Capital Formation, Investment, and Regional Industrialization. *Annals of the Association of American Geographers* 83, no. 3.

Glasmeier, Amy K., Jeffery W. Thompson, and Amy Kays. 1993a. The Geography of Trade Policy: Trade Regimes and Location Decisions in the Textile and Apparel Complex. *Transactions of the Institute of British Geographers* 18.

———. 1993b. *When Low Wages Are Not Enough Anymore: The Implications of Globalization on Rural Branch Plants.* Final Report to the Appalachian Regional Commission, The Aspen Institute and The Economic Development Administration. Institute for Policy Research and Evaluation. Pennsylvania State University, University Park, Penn.

Glasmeier, Amy K., and Michael E. Conroy. 1994. *Global Squeeze on Rural America: Opportunities, Threats and Challenges of NAFTA and GATT.* Institute for Policy Research and Evaluation. Pennsylvania State University, University Park, Penn.

Glickman, Norman J., and Amy K. Glasmeier. 1989. The International Economy and the American South. In *Deindustrialization and Regional Economic Transformation: The Experience of the United States,* eds. Lloyd Rodwin and Hidehiko Sazanami. London: Allen and Unwin.

Hayward, David J., and Rodney A. Erickson. 1995. The North American Trade of U.S. States: A Comparative Analysis of Industrial Shipments 1983–1991. *International Regional Science Review* 18, no. 1.

Howes, Candace, and Ann R. Markusen. 1993. Trade, Industry, and Economic Development. In *Trading Industries, Trading Regions: International Trade, American Industry, and Regional Economic Development,* eds. Helzi Noponen, Julie Graham, and Ann R. Markusen. New York: The Guilford Press.

Johnson, Merrill L. 1988. *High-Technology Branch Plants as Labor-Oriented Industries in the United States South.* Report for U. S. Department of Commerce, Economic Development Administration. Washington, D.C.

Leamer, Edward E. 1992. Wage Effects of a U. S.-Mexico Free Trade Agreement. Working Paper no. 3991. Cambridge, Mass.: NBER.

Lonsdale, Richard E., and Clyde E. Browning. 1971. Rural-Urban Preferences of Southern Manufacturers. *Annals of the Association of American Geographers* 61, no. 2.

Lyson, Thomas. 1989. *Two Sides to the Sunbelt, the Growing Divergence between the Rural and the Urban South.* New York: Praeger Press.

Markusen, Ann, R. 1987. *Regions: The Economics and Politics of Territory.* Totowa, N.J. : Rowman and Littlefield.

MDC. 1996. *The State of the South.* Chapel Hill, N.C. : MDC, Inc.

———. 1998. *The State of the South.* Chapel Hill, N.C. : MDC, Inc.

National Science Foundation. 1992. *National Patterns of R&D Resources 1992.* Compiled by John Jankowski et al. Washington, D. C.: author, Surveys of Science Resources Series.

Persky, Joseph. 1992. Regional Competition, Convergence and Social Welfare—The U. S. Case. In *International Integration and Labour Market Organization*, eds. Alberto Castro, Philippe Mehaut, and Jill Rubery. London: Academic Press.

Revegna, Ana L. 1992. Exporting Jobs? The Impact of Import Competition on Employment and Wages in U.S. Manufacturing. *The Quarterly Journal of Economics* 107, no. 1.

Rosenfeld, S. 1986. *Halfway Home and a Long Way To Go: A Report to the Southern Growth Policies Board.* Research Triangle Park, N.C.: Southern Growth Policies Board.

Schulman, Bruce J. 1991. *From Cotton Belt to Sunbelt: Federal Policy, Economic Development, and the Transformation of the South 1938–1980.* New York: Oxford University Press.

Shelburne, Robert C., and Robert W. Bednarzik. 1993. Geographic Concentration of Trade-Sensitive Employment. *Monthly Labor Review* 116, no. 6.

Tyson, Laura D'Andrea, and John Zysman. 1988. Trade and Employment: An Overview of the Issues and Evidence. In *The Dynamics of Trade and Employment*, eds. Laura D'Andrea Tyson, William T. Dickens, and John Zysman. Cambridge, Mass.: Ballinger Publishing Company.

Wheat, Leonard F. 1986. The Determinants of 1963–1977 Regional Manufacturing Growth: Why the South and West Grow. *Journal of Regional Science* 26, no. 4.

Wheeler, James O. 1990. The New Corporate Landscape: America's Fastest Growing Private Companies. *Professional Geographer* 42, no. 4.

Wood, Adrian. 1994. *North-South Trade, Employment and Inequality: Changing Fortunes in a Skill-Driven World.* Oxford: Oxford University Press.

Wright, Gavin. 1986. *Old South, New South.* New York: Basic Books.

3

The Impact of NAFTA and the WTO on Chiapas and Southern Mexico

Hypotheses and Preliminary Evidence

Michael E. Conroy and Sarah Elizabeth West[1]

The Zapatista rebellion in Mexico's southern state of Chiapas was launched by its principal protagonists because of their perceptions of decades of neglect by the Mexican government. Zapatista leaders also linked the rebellion, which began on January 1, 1994, to the onset that same day of NAFTA. Considerable attention has been given to the specific social and economic conditions of Chiapas since the outbreak of the rebellion. However, notwithstanding the importance of the "regional question" in scholarship on the formation of modern Mexico (e.g., Katz 1988; Knight 1986; Reynolds 1970), insufficient attention has been paid to the broader question of whether whole regions of Mexico, and the southern region in particular, may endure new difficulties as a result of NAFTA and globalization.

Our purpose is to contribute to the literature that does examine contemporary Mexico's regional inequalities as a fundamental aspect of its relations with NAFTA and globalization (e.g., Bulmer-Thomas et al. 1994; Castañeda 1996; Collier 1995; Oliveira and García 1997). We ask whether NAFTA and, implicitly, the subsequent creation of the World Trade Organization (WTO) out of the Uruguay Round of the GATT negotiations, should be considered a basis for believing that southern Mexico will be damaged significantly by the newly liberalized and globalized economy. Will Mexico's South benefit from such political and economic restructuring as much as its central and northern regions? Or is southern Mexico destined to become a more distant periphery of the rest of a liberalized, globalized, expanding Mexico, either within its traditional framework or within some reconfigured version?

The chapter is necessarily an exercise in analysis, projection, and creative speculation, rather than a simple arithmetic projection of trends or a more sophisticated modeling exercise. It is deliberately provocative in its interpretation of events in and impinging on southern Mexico, for it seeks to stimulate further analysis of the regional future of this critical portion of Mexico and further exploration of the impacts of NAFTA upon less-developed regions throughout the accord's geographic extent. Its significance more broadly may relate to the important global question: How and to what extent is worldwide economic liberalization and its attendant globalization restructuring the geographical inclusion and exclusion of regions? Can we hope that these trends will lessen substantial disparities in development, or should we expect them to exacerbate preexisting disparities, especially when they are implemented in a context of dramatically reduced state programs for ameliorating such disparities?

We begin by describing the socioeconomic characteristics of the seven southern states of Mexico (which we will use as Mexico's effective "South"), emphasizing their underdevelopment relative to most of the rest of Mexico. We then ask whether Mexican government policy in the recent years of fiscal reform and structural adjustment has contributed to lessening or widening the gaps between these states and the rest of the nation. We then focus on the case of Chiapas, about which a vast amount has been written since the start of the uprising, asking whether an assessment of the government's predictions of positive NAFTA impact can shed light on the potential future of southern Mexico in general. We close by discussing a set of hypotheses that arise from the analysis and that suggest answers to questions about the future of southern Mexico under the assumption that current Mexican government policy continues.

Characteristics of Southern Mexico

The seven states defined as constituting Mexico's "South" are, in alphabetical order, Campeche, Chiapas, Oaxaca, Quintana Roo, Tabasco, Veracruz, and Yucatán (see Map 1.1). Together, they contain approximately 20% of the nation's population, but 75% of the indigenous population. They constitute Mexico's most culturally and biologically diverse region. And they contain a large proportion of Mexico's most impoverished population. They vary considerably among themselves (see Table 3.1).

Two of the seven states, Oaxaca and Chiapas, contain more than a third of the population of the Mexican South; they are also heavily indigenous and rural, with nearly 75% of their populations living in mountainous rural areas. They are, in this sense, the logical extensions of the Mayan highlands of

Table 3.1
Basic Demographic Characteristics of the Southern States (1990)

State	Population (000s)	Percent Indig.	Percent Rural	Infant Mort.
Campeche	528.8	18.3	37.9	68.8
Chiapas	3,203.9	23.6	73.6	99.0
Oaxaca	3,021.5	37.6	78.2	116.6
Quintana Roo	493.6	36.6	48.7	63.8
Tabasco	1,501.2	5.3	67.9	86.3
Veracruz	6,215.1	11.3	39.3	74.2
Yucatán	1,363.5	46.1	38.6	99.6
All South	16,327.6	28.9	66.3	n/a
Mexico	81,140.9	11.1	32.0	72.2

Source: Nacional Financiera (1993).

Guatemala. Oaxaca and Chiapas consistently rank among Mexico's poorest states, with infant mortality well above the national average. Two of the seven states, Campeche and Quintana Roo, consist of thinly populated areas, each with total populations of approximately 500,000 in 1990. They tend to be "outliers" in many ways, for their small populations are affected strongly by rapidly growing industries, tourism in Quintana Roo (home to the resorts of Cancún, Cozumel, and Playa del Carmen), and old-growth lumbering and fisheries in Campeche. The state of Yucatán shares the Yucatán Peninsula with them. It has the highest indigenous proportion of all the region but one of the lowest proportions of population in rural areas. The states of Tabasco and Veracruz are dominated by the production and refining of petroleum. The indigenous proportion of their populations is much smaller (5.3% and 11.3%, respectively) than in the other states.

The human development indices for the southern states (Table 3.2) are based on the standard techniques of the United Nations Development Program. These measures provide clearer evidence of the position of the southern states relative to the rest of Mexico. The differences across components of the human development indices also illustrate the development variation across the states.

Oaxaca and Chiapas have the lowest indicators of human development, far below the national average in every component: life expectancy; literacy levels; broader educational attainment; and state-level GDP per capita. Campeche and Quintana Roo display much higher levels of the index on virtually every component. Tabasco, Yucatán, and Veracruz are also below the national average; but, for a different reason in each case, they place well above Oaxaca and Chiapas. Tabasco has unusually high GDP per capita, reflecting

Table 3.2
Human Development Indicators (1990)

State	Human Dev. Index	Life Expect.	Literacy	Educ. Attain.	GDP/cap. PPP$ '89
All Mexico	0.804	n/a	n/a	n/a	n/a
Federal District	0.934	71.03	95.87	8.50	15,141
Quintana Roo	0.742	69.11	87.40	6.20	5,354
Campeche	0.735	71.35	84.39	5.35	4,750
Tabasco	0.698	68.36	87.14	5.62	9,328
Yucatán	0.596	70.17	83.99	5.19	3,973
Veracruz	0.462	67.63	81.62	5.05	3,737
Chiapas	0.209	67.22	69.61	3.94	2,820
Oaxaca	0.165	67.08	72.32	3.98	2,299

Source: Alarcón González and Zepeda Miramontes (1992).

the booming oil production industry. Yucatán, with a more urbanized population, has higher life expectancy and literacy than Oaxaca and Chiapas, but falls below the states ranked above it in the overall index because of lower income and educational levels.

The composition of production and employment in these states is concentrated overwhelmingly in agricultural and other primary production, such as petroleum and lumber extraction. Table 3.3 shows the very small proportions of the nation's manufacturing employment found in these states.

Table 3.3
Shares of Industrial Employment, Selected Sectors (1988)

State	Percent of EAP	Food Processing (31)	Textile and Apparel (32)	Wood Products (33)	Chemicals (35)	Stone, Clay, and Glass (36)
Federal District	12.3%	16.4%	20.5%	12.3%	26.2%	10.1%
Quintana Roo	0.7%	0.2%	0.0%	0.9%	0.5%	0.3%
Campeche	0.6%	0.7%	0.0%	0.3%	0.0%	0.3%
Tabasco	1.7%	1.1%	0.0%	0.3%	1.2%	0.5%
Yucatán	1.7%	2.4%	1.7%	1.1%	0.8%	1.6%
Veracruz	7.5%	0.8%	1.6%	2.7%	10.7%	2.7%
Chiapas	3.6%	1.4%	0.3%	3.1%	1.0%	1.0%
Oaxaca	3.2%	2.5%	0.2%	3.1%	1.8%	1.5%
All South	19.1%	9.1%	3.8%	11.5%	15.0%	7.9%

Source: SECOFI (1992). Includes all of the ISIC two-digit industries that encompass the largest proportions of manufacturing employment found in each state.

By comparing the percent of the national economically active population (EAP) with the proportion of employment in each industry found in each state, we can obtain a rough indication of the underrepresentation of manufacturing industries in these states. The number of cases in which these states have industry shares larger than their shares of EAP is limited to chemical production in Veracruz, food processing in Yucatán, and wood products in Quintana Roo. The region as a whole falls far short of self-sufficiency in each of the manufacturing sectors listed, which are the region's largest.

Table 3.4 demonstrates the relative levels of infrastructure in these states. Mexico's extensive electrification program has raised local access to electricity to near national levels in Tabasco and the three states of the Yucatán peninsula (Yucatán, Campeche, and Quintana Roo). Oaxaca, Chiapas, and Veracruz, however, fall far below the national average. Highway penetration is generally lower than the national average and is especially low in thinly populated Campeche and Quintana Roo. The adequacy of drinking-water systems is the worst in the most rural states: Tabasco, Veracruz, Oaxaca, and Chiapas.

One other set of indicators is available for characterizing the relative standard of living in southern Mexico. The Mexican National Council on Population (CONAPO) created a comprehensive impoverishment index (*índice de marginalización*) with which to evaluate the combined effect of nine separate indicators, including both income and educational variables and a variety of housing characteristics.[2] The resulting index was used to divide states into five categories of impoverishment: very low; low; medium; high; and very high. Table 3.5 shows the categories into which the cluster of seven southern states fell, compared with northern states and the Federal District.

Table 3.4
Infrastructure Indicators (1990)

State	Houses with Electricity		Hwys/M sq.km		Houses with Water	
	Percent	Rank	kms	Rank	Percent	Rank
All Mexico	87.5%	n/a	122.2	n/a	79.4%	n/a
Federal District	99.3%	1	108.2	26	96.3%	1
Quintana Roo	84.5%	24	97.6	27	88.6%	9
Campeche	85.3%	21	110.6	25	70.7%	25
Tabasco	85.2%	22	284.3	8	58.3%	30
Yucatán	90.4%	12	186.0	11	71.5%	24
Veracruz	74.4%	30	143.5	17	59.8%	28
Chiapas	66.9%	32	149.1	16	58.4%	29
Oaxaca	76.1%	29	118.0	23	58.1%	31

Source: List (1994).

Table 3.5
Clusters of States by Level of Impoverishment (1988)

Northern Border States	Impov. Index Level	Southern States	Impov. Index Level
Federal District	Very low	Quintana Roo	Medium
Nuevo León	Very low	Guerrero	High
Baja California	Very low	Campeche	High
Coahuila	Low	Yucatán	High
Tamaulipas	Low	Veracruz	Very high
Chihuahua	Low	Chiapas	Very high
Sonora	Low	Oaxaca	Very high

Source: CONAPO (1988).

The overall pattern is quite clear: the Federal District and the northern states fall into the categories of "very low" and "low" levels of relative impoverishment; all of the southern states, with the exception of Quintana Roo, fall into the "high" and "very high" levels of impoverishment.

Allocation of Mexican Government Spending to the South

What have been the spending patterns of the Mexican government relative to the states of the South? Have the government's programs tended to ameliorate or aggravate the South's impoverishment? West (1994) analyzes a set of measures of total government spending per capita for 1980–1981, prior to the onset of the Mexican debt crisis, and for 1988–1992, the first years of President Carlos Salinas de Gortari's *sexenio*. Her analysis also separates out the expenditures of Mexico's National Solidarity Program (PRONASOL) for separate consideration, because PRONASOL was much touted as the government's response to the possibility that policies of stabilization and liberalization would aggravate inequality, both among individuals and across regions (Consejo Consultativo 1990).

West finds (as shown in Table 3.6) that government spending per capita in price-adjusted pesos from 1988 to 1992 was clearly skewed toward those states with relatively *lower* indices of impoverishment. The relationship is not consistently monotonic; some states categorized as having "low" levels of impoverishment frequently received the lowest levels of federal expenditures. In general, however, federal expenditures per capita in the areas of "very high" impoverishment were only 30 to 40% of the levels in states with "very low" impoverishment according to the CONAPO index. For the five-year period, the cumulative expenditures in areas of "very high" impoverishment averaged 35% of the spending in the nation's wealthiest states. Residents of states in the

Table 3.6
Federal Expenditures by Level of Impoverishment
(per capita; in 1992 pesos)

Impoverishment Index Level	1988	1989	1990	1991	1992	1988–1992
Very low	990.35	1032.94	1256.10	1403.61	1003.06	5686.06
Low	295.14	255.69	314.24	316.62	282.47	1464.16
Medium	318.61	351.96	647.69	558.25	621.00	2497.51
High	541.43	426.06	471.57	427.21	503.88	2370.15
Very high	388.78	365.69	435.95	334.02	485.15	2009.59
All Mexico	505.58	481.77	591.32	561.02	457.02	2596.71

Source: West (1994).

"high" and "medium" levels of impoverishment fared little better. They received, on average, 42% of the levels channeled to the wealthiest states.

What were the implications for Mexico's South relative to national patterns of government expenditure? Table 3.7 shows, not surprisingly, that Mexican federal expenditures per capita nationwide dropped considerably, an average of 44%, between 1980–1981 and 1988–1992. When analyzed state-by-state and applied to the southern states, the geographic bias in this austerity becomes quite clear. To be sure, in both 1980–1981 and 1988–1992 spending levels varied significantly across the southern states. Nevertheless, all seven of the southern states suffered losses in federal expenditures that were greater than the national average. The average decline in the South was 74%, which is

Table 3.7
Federal Expenditures in the Southern States
(per capita, in 1992 pesos)

State	Total/Year 1980–1981	Total/Year 1988–1992	Percent Change	PRONASOL/Year 1988–1992
All Mexico	1473	819	−44%	69
Federal District	2376	1613	−32%	232
Quintana Roo	2954	722	−76%	130
Campeche	9752	3510	−64%	152
Tabasco	7780	843	−89%	22
Yucatán	859	467	−46%	124
Veracruz	2377	640	−73%	17
Chiapas	1809	217	−88%	75
Oaxaca	963	424	−56%	79
All South	3784	974	−74%	—

Source: West (1994).

30% greater than the national average. The worst cases in the South—Tabasco and Chiapas—suffered declines that were double the national average.

PRONASOL spending per capita from 1988 to 1992 also ran counter to what would be expected if it were directed to the neediest areas. Three of the southern states with the highest levels of development (Quintana Roo, Campeche, and Yucatán) obtained more than twice the national average per capita of PRONASOL allocations. In contrast, Tabasco and Veracruz received less than half the national average. The states ranked as the poorest in the nation by most standards—Chiapas and Oaxaca—received approximately the same amount as the national average. The absolute magnitude of these PRONASOL distributions, however, averaged less than 15% of total federal spending (West 1994, 41). Even if PRONASOL's funds had been channeled to the nation's neediest states, they would have done little to offset the biases built into the larger federal spending pattern.

Private and mixed-banking financial flows have similarly been biased against Mexico's South. Table 3.8 presents data that demonstrate this region's net outflows of savings to the rest of Mexico. The "index of redistribution" of regional savings can be interpreted to mean that only 63.1% of local savings in southern Mexico were returned in the form of loans to residents of the area. Even though it has the lowest contribution of savings among all the regions studied by Hernández Laos (1994), 36.9% of the savings of the South financed loans to borrowers in other regions.

In summary, the southern states of Mexico are not just the poorest in the Mexican federation; they are also states that have been singularly disadvantaged by the national fiscal reforms and structural adjustment since 1982.

Table 3.8
Financial Flows across Regions 1950–1990[a]

Region	(a) Deposits Taken In	(b) Loans Extended	Redistribution Index
Northeast	20.54	16.86	82.1
North	17.52	21.60	123.3
Gulf Region	9.58	6.50	67.8
North Central	5.30	3.13	59.1
East Central	8.05	5.63	69.9
Mexico City Valley	29.92	40.30	134.7
South and Southeast	4.09	2.58	63.1

Source: Hernández Laos (1994).
[a]Regional distribution of deposits and lending from private and mixed banks.

The Prospects for Chiapas

The historiography of the rebellion in Chiapas is immense and rich.[3] No portion of Mexico has been studied more thoroughly in such a short period of time. A consensus is emerging about the fundamental agrarian roots of the social and economic crisis behind the rebellion. The Mexican government, however, has made a concerted effort to counter the notion that liberalization, in general, and NAFTA, in particular, will create more unemployment and deeper poverty in the state.

In 1994, the Mexican Secretariat for Commerce and Industrial Development (SECOFI) produced rapidly a study of the potential impact of NAFTA upon Chiapas and released it with great fanfare (SECOFI 1994). The purpose of the study, as indicated in the press release and in comments by SECOFI Secretary Jaime Serra Puche, was to diagnose the problems of the economy of Chiapas, to identify those activities "capable of seeing great development," and to "identify those products from Chiapas for which there will be great demand" in the United States and Canada once NAFTA is fully implemented. The study concludes with a list of nineteen projects that the SECOFI secretary indicated would imply "five billion new pesos of investment [approximately $1.5 billion at the exchange rate of that time] and the creation of 14 thousand direct new jobs" in agriculture, fishing, forestry, and manufacturing.[4]

Perhaps one should not expect more from the SECOFI study than is reasonable. It was produced rapidly and for explicitly political purposes. It was offered in the context of accusations that NAFTA would further harm the poor farmers of the region. The SECOFI study, however, provides an example of the way in which the abstract promises of NAFTA have been applied to producers in the poorest and most distant corners of Mexico. What we offer here is a rereading and an analysis of the report.

According to the SECOFI report, 90% of income in Chiapas is generated from agriculture. Corn, beans, and sugarcane are the principal products in five of the state's nine agricultural zones. Coffee is the top product in two of the other four; and cattle in the remaining two. The report suggests that during the fifteen-year phase-in for many products, productivity in Chiapas could be increased dramatically. What the study provides, however, is official confirmation of the lack of competitiveness of current production. For corn, the report indicates that production of 5 tons per hectare would be necessary for international competitiveness, but current production is 2.2 tons per hectare. For sorghum, 5 tons per hectare is also needed, but current production is 3.3. For beans, a minimum of 1.2 is needed, but current production is only 0.63 tons per hectare. The study assures readers that the Agriculture Ministry "presently possesses the technology needed to increase productivity to competitive levels" (SECOFI 1994, 3–50). But, by the end of 1995, agricultural extension services in Mexico had virtually ceased to exist.

In manufacturing, according to the report, 98% of firms in Chiapas are microenterprises; no more than 0.2% could be considered large-scale firms. The most important manufacturing sector, in terms of both number of firms and number of employees, consists of the cornmeal (*nixtamal*) mills and the neighborhood tortilla factories (SECOFI 1994, 1–15). The report offers no general suggestions for expanding manufacturing production; but more than half of the "proposed projects" listed at the end of the report involve large-scale industrial processing of agricultural products.

From the SECOFI perspective, the benefits of NAFTA would begin in the form of reductions in the prices of goods for which tariffs had previously been imposed. It is asserted at the start of the document, but not demonstrated anywhere within it, that the prices of consumer goods will be reduced in Chiapas between 6.5 and 9.1% during the period of tariff reduction. It is further asserted that real incomes will rise by that same amount. The latter, of course, would occur only if no other changes were associated with levels of nominal income. Making the prediction all the more improbable is that the previous discussion had already admitted that corn prices—a crucial source of local income—would fall and that most other subsistence products weren't even close to being competitive.

Although the study contains appendices with impressive algebra purporting to demonstrate the predicted rise in incomes, nothing in the appendices in fact produces that result. Taking the most optimistic estimate mentioned above and stretching it over the entire fifteen-year period for tariff reduction, there would be six-tenths of 1% per year in increased real income, if nominal income did not fall. Just four months after the report was released, though, the peso collapsed and the prices of all imported products rose by 40%. By the end of 1995, national income in Mexico had fallen by an estimated 7.2%. The short-term consequences brutally contradict SECOFI's optimistic prognosis.

The investment projects that were the highlight of the press conference when the report was released are listed in an unnumbered appendix at the end of the document. The section is called Production Projects in Chiapas and the Free Trade Agreement. The range extends from mangos and other fruits to cattle, bananas, coffee, corn and beans, cashews, shrimp farming, flowers, tourism, textiles, forest products, and infrastructure (including highway work, shopping centers, and new bank buildings). For each of the projects there is a description of the situation in Chiapas, a brief discussion of the potential impact of NAFTA, and a description of the proposed project—complete in many instances with names and phone numbers of key players.

In the year following the release of the study, we inquired at SECOFI, at the offices of the state government of Chiapas, and at as many of the phone numbers provided in the report as functioned to find a single project among those that were listed which was in fact undertaken. To date there is no evidence that any of the projects—including a shopping mall linked to a proposed Wal-Mart and which was therefore susceptible to NAFTA benefits—has been initiated. Many of the projects have been postponed or abandoned because of the peso's subsequent collapse. Others were apparently never more than preliminary proposals listed for possible government financing. The change of administration that occurred on December 1, 1994, as Salinas de Gortari's term ended, the controversies surrounding the election of his successor President Ernesto Zedillo, and then the resignation of the governor of Chiapas also took their toll.

Our reinterpretation of this report on NAFTA's anticipated benefits for the specific case of Chiapas may illustrate the best-case scenario of what might have been hoped for in southern Mexico from trade liberalization, for it was the most hopeful stance the government was able to take. We offer, by way of conclusion, a number of alternative hypotheses on the future of southern Mexico under the expected conditions of a further opening of the Mexican economy to the world, liberalization of internal markets, and reduction of the government programs that, as legacies of the Mexican revolution, had purchased rural peace and stability through subsidies and other kinds of support for the nation's poorest regions.

Hypotheses on the Future of the Southern States of Mexico

Our discussion of these hypotheses draws on this volume's analysis of the U.S. South by Glasmeier and Leichenko. They provide evidence on the narrowing of the development gap between the southern United States and the rest of the nation since World War II. We begin with a stylized comparison between the history of the U.S. South and the history of the Mexican South as a further basis for predicting the future of Mexico's lagging areas.

By the early 1990s, most of the U.S. South enjoyed relatively rapid growth, substantially based on a low-wage and nonunionized labor force, complemented by massive federal intervention. The economy of the U.S. South was indeed converging with those of the nation's more advanced areas. This transition was, as Glasmeier and Leichenko argue, closely associated with large-scale federal government interventions on many levels. The strategy included subsidies to the cotton, textile, and tobacco industries, erosion of the real value and relevance of the minimum wage, dramatic reductions in the cost of overland transportation because of the federally subsidized interstate highway system, and disproportionate federal investment in the South after World War II, including the cold war's massive military expenditures for bases, procurements, and related military-industrial development favoring the region. The federal government forced upon the U.S. South a painful solution to the racial conflict that had long hindered investment in the region by northern and foreign firms. Policies of trade protection initially benefited the high-wage North; trade liberalization after 1980 favored the low-wage, low-tax South, as firms sought to maintain their dominance in the U.S. market by lowering their costs in the face of intensifying foreign competition. The result was massive movement of jobs from the North to the South in the U.S. economy.

Under present conditions in Mexico, which of the factors behind the growth of the U.S. South is likely to foster a parallel course of development for the Mexican South? Hypothesis 1 is that government spending in Mexico, as we have documented above, is not diminishing disparities; rather, it is exacerbating national regional inequalities, above all for the cluster of southern states.

Hypothesis 2 is that the rebellion in Chiapas has been misconstrued by many observers as a military confrontation that will be settled by the strongest force, obviously the Mexican Army. There is in fact more reason to believe that the rebellion in Chiapas is fundamentally a class and ethnic confrontation that is deepening, rather than diminishing. Ethnic confrontations have increased significantly since the start of the rebellion; land conflicts in Chiapas and the surrounding states are ever more frequently Indian-Ladino conflicts. And fragmentary evidence indicates that the highlands of Chiapas and Oaxaca are becoming more uniformly indigenous in ethnicity, while the cities are becoming more Ladino. There is little reason to believe that in the near future the almost uniformly Ladino Mexican political leadership will be able to cope effectively with the escalating indigenous ethnic pressures and calls for ethnic and territorial autonomy.

Hypothesis 3 is that, in sharp contrast with what occurred in the United States, there is little likelihood of massive improvement in the infrastructure of the Mexican southern states that is crucial if the region is to become more attractive for the location of production destined for U.S., Canadian, and Mexican national markets. Of the 4,000 kilometers of limited access superhighway constructed during the Salinas administration, only one 400-kilometer thread leads south from Mexico's geographic midline. Furthermore, that single road, from Puebla to Oaxaca, is just two lanes wide for most of the way, and the toll structure on those roads is so high that little overland freight transport uses it. This toll structure, in use nationwide on the newly built roads, reflects both the rent-seeking bid process used to draw private financing and the fact that most of the superhighways were financed by foreign capital under conditions of a currency that was 50% stronger than it now is. There is little likelihood of lower tolls in the near future.

Hypothesis 4 is that the negative agricultural implications of NAFTA for the vast majority of the farmers of southern Mexico, who produce rainfed grains and other low-value products, will be compounded by the ongoing reduction in government credit, extension services, and price guarantees. This process will further reduce the already-limited ability of locations in southern Mexico to provide the locally financed infrastructure, job training, and other services that are integral to establishing the minimal competitive conditions for attracting investment.

Hypothesis 5 is that as the U.S. South continues its accelerated growth and transformation relative to other parts of the U.S. economy, the region that will become U.S. South's periphery is northern Mexico. It is northern Mexico—more than central Mexico, which anchored the nation's industrialization during the import-substitution era—that is receiving the majority of the investment coming both from Mexican investors seeking to process and assemble goods for the U.S. market and from international investors developing complete production processes (see the chapters by Gereffi; Wilson and Kayne; and Roberts and Tardanico in this volume).

There are, nonetheless, some opportunities for Mexico's South. First, southern Mexico is the locus of the largest supply of what may become the nation's most scarce resource: water. Whether for industrial processes that require abundant water, such as textile and electronics manufacturing, or for expansion of agricultural production, the water in the areas to the north of a line through Mexico City is, according to officials of the National Water Commission, virtually totally subscribed. Indeed, it is often oversubscribed. Of course, southern Mexico's role as a politically and economically subordinate supplier of primary commodities to the national and world economies has been integral to its historical process of impoverishment. As our analysis indicates, only under some dramatically new set of politico-institutional arrangements emphasizing territorial and social redistribution of authority and wealth as well as environmental sustainability could southern Mexico's water supply become a strategic point of leverage for the region's economic and social upgrading.

Second, as Porter discusses in this volume, some of southern Mexico's small coffee producers have avoided economic displacement and gained some measure of prosperity by taking advantage of variable socioeconomic and political conditions across the region to strengthen their position in new export niches. The possible grassroots lessons—political and entrepreneurial—for bolstering the positions of small producers of a wide range of rural and urban commodities in southern Mexico should not be overlooked (see Fox and Aranda in this volume; Fox and Brown 1998).

Third, according to the chapter by Wilson and Kayne, Yucatán's geographic proximity to the U.S. South promises significant opportunities for air-shipped, export-assembly production. As they emphasize, however, these opportunities can be parlayed into local development only if complemented by substantial improvement in economic and social infrastructure that permits the area's firms to establish quality-based export niches, to deepen and widen their local economic linkages, and to create regional growth in more skilled, better-paid, and more stable employment.

Finally, integral to these and other opportunities is Mexico's ongoing political transformation. With the crumbling of the hegemony of the Partido Revolucionario Institucional and with initial efforts at meaningful decentralization of government functions (if not quite of authority and financial resources), this transformation bodes well for the more autonomous economic growth and the improvement in social welfare of areas lying outside the dominant poles of central and northern Mexico (see Fox and Aranda in this volume). The energy and adaptability of southern Mexico's people may surprise observers if decentralizing trends establish the institutional and infrastructural conditions that enable the populace to act independently and entrepreneurially.

References

Alarcón González, Diana, and Eduardo Zepeda Miramontes. 1992. *Liberación comercial, equidad, y desarrollo económico.* México, D.F.: Friedrich Ebert Stiftung.

Bulmer-Thomas, Victor, Nikki Craske, and Mónica Serrano. 1994. Who Will Benefit? In *Mexico and the North American Free Trade Agreement: Who Will Benefit?* eds. Victor Bulmer-Thomas, Nikki Craske, and Mónica Serrano. New York: St. Martin's Press.

Burbach, Roger, and Peter Rosset. 1994. Chiapas and the Crisis of Mexican Agriculture. Food First Working Paper. Oakland, Calif.: Food First, December.

Castañeda, Jorge. 1996. Mexico's Circle of Misery. *Foreign Affairs* 75, no. 4.

Collier, George A. 1995. The New Politics of Exclusion: Antecedents to the Rebellion in Mexico. *Dialectical Anthropology* (spring).

CONAPO. 1988. *Indicadores sobre fecundidad y marginación.* México, D.F.: Consejo Nacional de Población.

————. 1990. *Indicadores socioeconómicos e índice de marginación municipal 1990.* México, D.F.: Consejo Nacional de Población.

Consejo Consultativo del Programa Nacional de Solidaridad. 1990. *Combate a la pobreza: Lineamientos programáticos.* México, D.F.: PRONASOL.

Fox, Jonathan, and L. David Brown, eds. 1998. *The Struggle for Accountability: Grassroots Movements, NGOs, and the World Bank.* Cambridge, Mass.: MIT Press.

Hernández Laos, Enrique. 1994. *La desigualdad regional.* México, D.F.: Siglo XXI.

Hernández Navarro, Luis. 1998. The Escalation of the War in Chiapas. *NACLA Report on the Americas* 31, no. 5.

Katz, Friedrich, ed. 1988. *Riot, Rebellion, and Revolution: Rural Social Conflict in Mexico.* Princeton, N.J.: Princeton University Press.

Knight, Alan. 1986. *The Mexican Revolution.* 2 vols. Cambridge: Cambridge University Press.

List, Sven. 1994. El desarrollo regional de México: Una perspectiva histórica. Unpublished paper. Department of Economics, University of Texas at Austin.

Nacional Financiera. 1993. *La economía mexicana en cifras.* México, D.F.: Nacional Financiera.

Oliveira, Orlandina, and Brígida García. 1997. Mexico: Socioeconomic Transformation and Urban Labor Markets. In *Global Restructuring, Employment, and Social Inequality in Urban Latin America,* eds. Richard Tardanico and Rafael Menjívar Larín. Coral Gables, Fla.: the North-South Center at the University of Miami; Boulder, Colo.: Lynne Rienner Publishers.

Parra Vázquez, Manuel R., and Blanca M. Díaz Hernández, eds. 1996. *Los Altos de Chiapas: Agricultura y crisis rural.* San Cristóbal de las Casas, Mex.: El Colegio de la Frontera Sur.

Reynolds, Clark W. 1970. *The Mexican Economy: Twentieth-Century Structure and Growth.* New Haven: Yale University Press.

Russell, Philip L. 1995. *The Chiapas Rebellion.* Austin, Tex.: Mexico Resource Center.

Secretaría de Comercio y Fomento Industrial (SECOFI). 1992. *Programa de política industrial y comercio exterior.* México, D.F.: SECOFI.

————. 1994. *Evaluación del impacto del TLC en el estado de Chiapas.* México, D.F.: SECOFI.

Urbina Nandayapa, Arturo de Jesús. 1994. *Las razones de Chiapas: Causas, desarrollo, consecuencias, personajes, y perspectivas del alzamiento armado en los Altos de Chiapas.* México, D.F.: Editorial Pac.

West, Sarah Elizabeth. 1994. PRONASOL and Poverty in Mexico: Regional Changes in Federal Spending 1980–1992. MA Thesis Report, University of Texas at Austin.

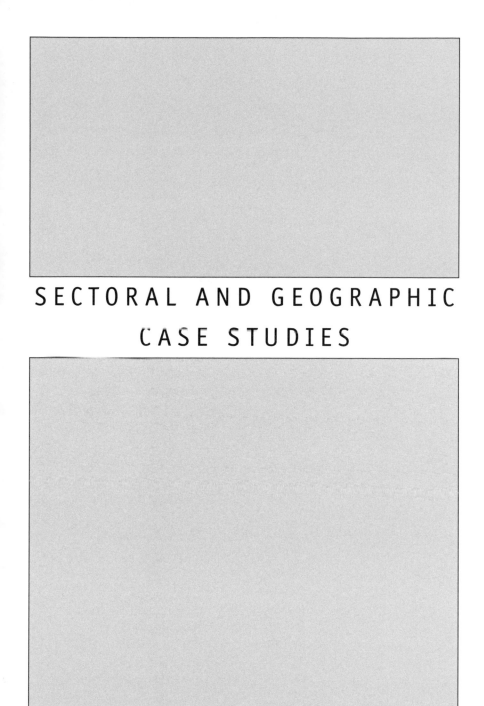

SECTORAL AND GEOGRAPHIC
CASE STUDIES

The Mexico-U.S. Apparel Connection

Economic Dualism and Transnational Networks

Gary Gereffi

The apparel industry captures many of the dilemmas and opportunities represented by the economic integration of Mexico and the United States, which has been accelerated by NAFTA. Although employment in the apparel sector has been steadily declining in the United States since the 1970s, there were still more than one million people employed in apparel jobs in 1991, and 85% of these people were considered production workers (OTA 1992, 189). By the end of 1994, the number of U.S. apparel industry employees had fallen to less than 800,000 (Finnie 1995b, 72). In Mexico, both apparel employment and apparel exports were booming in the 1980s and 1990s. This boom was fueled by abundant pools of low-cost labor working in assembly-oriented maquiladora plants, a series of sharp devaluations that made Mexican wage rates plunge ever lower by international standards, and a policy environment within Mexico that has dramatically liberalized the economy and promoted manufactured exports as a central plank of the country's new development strategy.

It should come as no surprise, therefore, that the apparel sector is one of the most contentious arenas for allegations by U.S. politicians and labor representatives who are concerned that Mexico is using NAFTA to take jobs away from the U.S. economy. Viewed from the Mexican side of the border, however, there are countercharges that U.S. companies are shamelessly exploiting Mexican workers by paying wages that are only one-tenth of those that prevail in U.S. textile and apparel plants.[1] Furthermore, the maquiladora sector is constrained by U.S. law from providing more than minimal local inputs (around 2–4% of the production costs in Mexico) because only U.S.-made inputs are exempt from tariff charges when the apparel items assembled in Mexico reenter the United States. Thus, the traditional maquiladora apparel sector is not considered to make a significant contribution to industrial development in Mexico through backward or forward linkages (Sklair 1993; Gereffi 1996).

In reality, the situation is far more complex than these stereotyped accounts suggest. First of all, the dynamics of global competition in the apparel sector force us to view U.S.-Mexican trade in a much broader context. Although Mexico's share of the U.S. apparel market has been growing rapidly, it is still dwarfed by Asian imports into the United States and is also surpassed by a considerable margin by the textile and apparel exports of the Caribbean and Central American nations. Second, within the United States and Mexico, textile and apparel production are highly concentrated in particular regions of each country. Both the labor impact and the possibilities for broader patterns of industrial development are mediated by the socioeconomic and institutional features of these production locales. Third, one cannot talk about the apparel industry without looking at its role within a broader apparel commodity chain that includes strategic linkages between raw material suppliers, fiber, textile and apparel firms, and the designers, distributors, and retailers of apparel goods. This commodity chain perspective is particularly critical in the North American context because the United States and Mexico have quite different strengths and weaknesses within the chain, which enhance the possibility for complementary forms of regional integration. Finally, just as countries and industries are misleading categories in analyzing global economic trends, so too do we need to challenge the centrality of firms as the key unit in contemporary trade and investment patterns. What is clearly emerging as a dominant economic form in the U.S.-Mexico textile and apparel complex are interfirm networks that join different kinds of companies in industrial clusters (or nodes) that span both country and industry boundaries. These North American networks, rather than the performance of individual firms, will be the key to the future competitiveness of Mexico and the United States in the global apparel industry.

The remainder of this chapter will elaborate on these points. It begins with a brief comparison of the U.S. and Mexican textile and apparel sectors, highlighting the profound differences that exist between them. The apparel commodity chain perspective is introduced to help us understand how the U.S. and Mexican economies are linked. This perspective also lays the groundwork for the contrasting roles of manufacturer- versus retailer-dominated networks in this sector. In assessing Mexico's comparative advantage as an apparel exporter, both labor costs and local industrial clusters built around specialized products are crucial in understanding Mexico's past trajectory and future prospects. Relevant comparisons include Asian as well as Caribbean Basin garment manufacturing nations. Following these economic and product-specific considerations, the role of state policy will be examined in order to determine the degree to which the U.S. and Mexican governments have been able to shape development outcomes to conform to national economic interests. Finally, several network initiatives in the U.S.-Mexican apparel commodity chain will be identified. These projects are intended to strengthen North American competitiveness in global apparel trade, but their consequences are likely to produce different winners and losers in the various transborder and subnational economies within the region.

This last issue concerns the basic question that unites the various chapters of this volume: How do the distributional consequences of NAFTA affect the southern regions of the United States and Mexico? Specifically, this chapter argues that the textile and apparel sector will grow rapidly in North America during the foreseeable future. A significant proportion of apparel sourcing by U.S. firms is shifting from Asia to the Western Hemisphere in response to the rising costs, logistical complexities, and increased political uncertainty connected with trans-Pacific trade, along with the lure of the newly established North American free-trade area. The main "winners" in this shift, however, will be subnational economies: the manufacturing districts in the U.S. South, where U.S. textile firms and producers of standardized apparel items remain concentrated; Miami, which has benefited from expanded trade with apparel suppliers in the Caribbean region; and northern Mexico, where most of Mexico's apparel and textile production capability is located. The southern part of Mexico is not likely to share in this bonanza. It is too remote from the U.S. border and the main population centers in Mexico to have large numbers of workers in export-oriented maquiladora plants for the apparel sector, nor are there any important centers of textile production in the region. Thus, while the dynamics of the apparel commodity chain are pulling the U.S. South and northern Mexico closer together, they are pushing northern and southern Mexico further apart.

Economic Dualism in the Mexican and U.S. Apparel Industries

The Mexican and U.S. textile and apparel sectors are a study in contrasts, including fundamental polarities within and between these two economies (see Chart 4.1). The most dynamic part of Mexico's apparel industry is its export-oriented maquiladora plants, which grew at about 10% annually during the late 1980s and even more rapidly in the 1990s. These factories

Chart 4.1
A Comparison of the U.S. and Mexican Apparel Sectors

United States	Mexico
Structure of industry and market Despite many years of intense import competition, a relatively large number of mostly small apparel firms continue to manufacture in the United States, many in New York, California, and the Southeast. In part, this is because rapid, flexible response to market shifts can compensate for higher direct production costs—especially in fashion-sensitive clothing—in this highly labor-intensive industry.	Although maquila plants can produce basic apparel products at costs well under U.S. costs, the Mexican industry is weak overall compared with successful Asian producers. Countries like China can undercut Mexico's costs at the low end, while manufacturers in more advanced Asian countries (e.g., Hong Kong) can supply better cost/quality combinations for fashion-sensitive goods. Domestically oriented Mexican apparel firms have had great difficulty meeting Asian competition since the lowering of import barriers.
Blue- and gray-collar labor force Large U.S. cities continue to provide pools of workers, many of them immigrants, willing to work for low wages under sweatshop conditions.	In principle, nearly unlimited; apparel firms often provide the first industrial jobs held by workers from rural areas.
Technical and managerial labor force Technical labor (as opposed to design) not particularly important, but management is critical for "Quick Response" strategies.	Poor productivity and quality in much of the industry reflect poor organization and management.
Labor relations Industry largely nonunion in the Southeast. Strong unions particularly in New York City have engaged in a lengthly effort to retain jobs and improve working conditions.	Low union coverage because of small size of domestic shops.
Availability of materials, components, and other inputs to production Many U.S. textile firms are low-cost producers, but because textiles trade internationally in large volumes, a local textile industry does not confer a great deal of advantage in apparel. Much the same is true for production equipment.	Mexico's textile industry is generally uncompetitive. Maquila producers get almost all their cloth from the United States, in part because this has been a condition for favorable tariff treatment.

United States (cont.)	Mexico (cont.)

Infrastructure (transportation, communications, etc.)

Good transport and communications, including computer links—a requirement for Quick Response.

Problems the greatest for small, independent firms and least for those tightly linked with U.S. apparel manufacturers or retailers.

Government policies

Extensive structure of import quotas within the framework of the Multifiber Arrangement (MFA), coupled with relatively high tariffs, have provided considerable protection for U.S. production. At the same time, because duties are only levied on foreign value-added, offshore assembly in Mexico and the Caribbean has been encouraged.

While Mexico's exports to the United States are in principle governed by bilateral quotas, in practice almost any apparel items from Mexico can enter in almost any quantity.

The future

U.S. apparel employment has been declining since the early 1970s and now stands at something under a million. Many of these jobs have been preserved through business strategies keyed to responsive customer service. To the extent that U.S. firms continue to implement such strategies effectively, they will remain viable against competition from both Mexico and the Far East. But if companies see NAFTA as meaning easy access to low-wage labor, they may forsake innovative strategies and simply move investments south of the border. Moreover, continuing U.S. trade restrictions on imports from third countries could lead to greater Asian investment in the Mexican apparel industry.

Mexico's export-oriented apparel sector continues to expand. NAFTA has accelerated this expansion by reducing or eliminating tariffs on Mexican goods. Most of the export-oriented plants currently do sewing on fabric cut in the U.S. because this qualifies the product for more lenient tariff treatment. With NAFTA, manual cutting for Mexican assembly has been moving south of the border, although companies with heavy automated cutting probably do not relocate those operations.

Source: Office of Technology Assessment (1992, 16).

based on a mass-production logic—i.e., very long runs of standardized items are sold throughout the year, with plant operations designed to minimize skill requirements and accommodate a high-turnover workforce. The maquiladoras assemble basic, commodity-like garments (blue jeans, underwear, and work clothes) in direct competition with many U.S. plants that face much higher sewing and cutting costs (see the chapters by Wilson and Kayne and by Roberts and Tardanico in this volume).

The nonmaquila part of Mexico's apparel industry, by contrast, includes many small firms that make cheap clothing of poor quality for sale in the domestic market. These firms are incapable of exporting into the United States. Informal distribution channels are a primary retail outlet for Mexico's domestic apparel producers. The main informal channels are the *tianguis* (bazaars that often travel daily from one part of the city to another), street vendors, and sprawling markets of small shops that account for more than one-third of Mexico's apparel retail sales, including substantial amounts of imported, resold, and counterfeit goods (Harris 1995, 100–1).

The United States has its own form of economic dualism within the apparel sector. On the one hand, there are companies that produce high volumes of standardized or basic clothing, such as blue jeans and work clothes (Levi Strauss, VF Corporation), underwear (Fruit of the Loom, Sara Lee), and men's dress shirts (Phillips-Van Heusen). These firms tend to have large, vertically integrated U.S. manufacturing plants, in addition to extensive networks of offshore production contractors in Mexico, the Caribbean Basin, and Asia. U.S. manufacturers of standardized apparel have been able to maintain a domestic production base in large part because automation (computerized cutting), modular manufacturing techniques, and work reorganization (so-called Quick Response strategies, aimed at greater flexibility and responsiveness to market demand) have helped offset higher relative wages (OTA 1992, ch. 9; Finnie 1995b). This segment of the U.S. apparel industry is concentrated in Texas (especially El Paso) and the southeastern United States (especially North and South Carolina and Georgia) (see Roberts and Tardanico in this volume).

In the fashion-oriented segment of the apparel market,[2] on the other hand, which includes items like women's outerwear, sweaters, and children's clothing, U.S. producers are far weaker and imports prevail. The firms that make fashion-oriented apparel typically are small sweatshops employing immigrant workers, using the traditional "bundle" method of assembly, and are primarily located around New York City and Los Angeles. Production in the fashion segment takes place near major retail markets and styling centers because of the continuing importance of design in apparel. Miami also has a burgeoning apparel sector, which focuses to a large degree on correcting defects, finishing, and providing ancillary services for 807-type apparel imports from Caribbean Basin countries.

Despite the presence of fashion-oriented garment production in several U.S. cities, U.S. retailers and popular designers (like Liz Claiborne, Donna Karan, Ralph Lauren, and Tommy Hilfiger) import large amounts of women's and men's fashion apparel from Asia. In 1994, the trade deficit of the United States in apparel was $32.8 billion ($38.4 billion in imports versus $5.6 billion in exports), while in textiles the trade deficit was only $2.8 billion ($9.2 billion in imports versus $6.4 billion in exports) (Finnie 1995a, 98). Nearly 40% of U.S. textile and apparel imports in 1994 came from four East Asian nations: China; Hong Kong; Taiwan; and South Korea. Imports from Mexico and the Dominican Republic, the two largest Latin American apparel exporters, are less than 10% of the U.S. total (see Table 4.1).

If one takes a closer look at these trade statistics, several important subpatterns emerge. First, China has consolidated its position as the dominant apparel supplier to the U.S. market, even though the rate of growth of Chinese imports has been curbed substantially by tough new quota agreements imposed by the United States.[3] Second, Hong Kong, Taiwan, and South Korea are all losing ground in terms of their share of the U.S. apparel market. This trend, due to relatively high labor costs in these East Asian nations and unfavorable exchange rates, appears irreversible. Third, Mexico and the Dominican Republic, along with Canada, are the fastest growing suppliers of textiles and clothing to the U.S. market, with average annual growth rates of 25% between 1983 and 1994. This growth in trade for Mexico and Canada will be accelerated by NAFTA, and the Dominican Republic is likely to continue to expand its presence in the U.S. market as well, especially if some form of NAFTA parity with Caribbean Basin Initiative countries is reached. Finally, it should be noted that the share of the top ten suppliers to the U.S. market decreased from nearly 70% in 1983 to just over 50% in 1994. This proliferation of new suppliers in the global apparel industry implies not only a much more intense competitive environment but also significant new opportunities for Mexico.

The North American Apparel Commodity Chain: Localization and Linkages

To get a better picture of the domestic implications for Mexico and the United States regarding these shifts in global trade, we need to look at the different segments of each country's apparel commodity chain.[4] If one envisions the complete apparel commodity chain as encompassing raw materials, yarn and synthetic fibers, textiles, apparel, and the distribution of apparel to retailers

Table 4.1
Top Ten Suppliers[a] of MFA Textiles and Clothing to the USA, 1983–1994

Countries	Rank 1989	Rank 1993	1983	1989	1994	% Share 1994	Average Annual % Change, 1993–1994
China							
Value (US$ mn)	3	1	913	3127	4931	12.3	16.6
Volume (mn sme)	1	1	657	1682	2042	11.8	10.9
Unit Price (US$/sme)			1.39	1.86	2.41		
Hong Kong							
Value (US$ mn)	1	2	2038	3686	4405	11	7.3
Volume (mn sme)	4	4	799	957	1023	5.9	2.3
Unit Price (US$/sme)			2.55	3.85	4.31		
Taiwan							
Value (US$ mn)	2	3	1757	3242	2830	7.1	4.4
Volume (mn sme)	2	3	992	1378	1237	7.2	2
Unit Price (US$/sme)			1.77	2.35	2.29		
South Korea							
Value (US$ mn)	4	4	1448	2939	2449	6.1	4.9
Volume (mn sme)	3	6	816	1058	864	5	0.5
Unit Price (US$/sme)			1.77	2.78	2.83		
Mexico							
Value (US$ mn)	10	5	173	647	1897	4.7	24.3
Volume (mn sme)	6	5	155	432	864	5.7	18.2
Unit Price (US$/sme)			1.77	1.5	2.83		
Dominican Republic							
Value (US$ mn)	9	6	139	667	1618	4	25
Volume (mn sme)	13	10	69	269	608	3.5	21.9
Unit Price (US$/sme)			2.01	2.48	2.66		
India							
Value (US$ mn)	7	7	292	743	1520	3.8	16.2
Volume (mn sme)	7	8	145	377	677	3.9	15
Unit Price (US$/sme)			2.01	1.97	2.25		
Philippines							
Value (US$ mn)	6	8	283	898	1457	3.6	16.1
Volume (mn sme)	10	11	160	361	534	3.1	11.6
Unit Price (US$/sme)			1.77	2.49	2.73		
Canada							
Value (US$ mn)	n/a	9	n/a	417	1317	3.3	25.9[b]
Volume (mn sme)	n/a	2	n/a	640	1318	7.6	15.5[b]
Unit Price (US$/sme)			n/a	0.65	1		
Italy							
Value (US$mn)	n/a	10	n/a	1033	1272	3.2	4.3[b]
Volume (mn sme)	n/a	15	n/a	226	250	1.4	2.0[b]
Unit Price (US$/sme)			n/a	4.57	5.09		
Top Ten Suppliers							
Value (% of all imports)			66[c]	60	53		9
Volume (% of all imports)			59[c]	54	46		8.8
All Imports							
Value (US$ mn)			10612	26749	39988	100	12.8
Volume (mn sme)			6443	12144	17286	100	9.4
Unit Price (US$/sme)			1.64	2.2	2.31		

Notes: sme = square meters equivalent; mn = millions. [a]Ranked according to value of imports in 1994. [b]1989–1994. [c]Top 8 suppliers. *Source:* Khanna (1996), based on U.S. official statistics.

(Appelbaum and Gereffi 1994), then the Mexican and U.S. commodity chains are quite distinct. Mexico has several large, reasonably successful synthetic fiber companies (like Akra of Grupo Alfa, Cydsa, and Celanese Mexicana), a multitude of maquiladora firms that export apparel products to the United States, and a reasonably strong retail sector that is beginning to fashion a number of strategies alliances with U.S. counterparts (e.g., Liverpool and Kmart, Aurrerá/Cifra and Wal-Mart, Comercial Mexicana and Price Club).

The weakest link in the Mexican production chain, by far, is the textile segment. The vast majority of Mexico's textile companies are undercapitalized, technologically backward, and inefficient, and they produce goods of poor quality. Most of Mexico's textile production is centered in the states of Puebla, Tlaxcala, Jalisco, Nuevo León, and Coahuila, while the maquiladora factories in the apparel sector are heavily concentrated in border cities such as Ciudad Juárez, Nuevo Laredo, and Tijuana, although a growing number of maquiladoras have shifted to interior locations in Mexico (Botella et al. 1991; Mandelbaum 1992; Wilson 1992).

By contrast, the United States is strong in synthetic fibers, textiles, and retailing, but limited in its garment production capability. The United States has a half-dozen giant, highly capital-intensive chemical firms like DuPont, Hoechst/Celanese, and Monsanto that dominate this segment. In textiles, there are about three hundred moderately capital-intensive companies in the United States. Most of the big textile firms like Burlington Industries, Milliken & Company, Cone Mills, Guilford Mills, and Fieldcrest Cannon are concentrated in and around North Carolina, and they are major producers of cotton as well as synthetic fabrics (Lande 1991). In retailing, a tremendous concentration has occurred among the biggest discounters, department stores, and specialty chains in the United States. Some analysts assert that the top ten retailers (including companies like Wal-Mart, Price Costco, May Department Stores, and The Limited) will account for nearly 50% of U.S. apparel sales by the year 2000 (KSA 1992). One of the reasons for this increased concentration is that U.S. retailing has become technology-intensive. Companies have spent hundreds of millions of dollars to set up electronic data interchange networks that allow them to implement Quick Response systems for automatic and continuous replenishment of certain stock items, thereby pushing inventory burdens upstream to the apparel suppliers and textile firms. Consolidation at the retail end of the apparel commodity chain has given a handful of big U.S. buyers substantial control over how and where the sourcing of garment production for the U.S. market takes place (Gereffi 1994).

The Mexican apparel commodity chain appears to be strongest where the U.S. chain is relatively weak: garment production. While at a general level this statement is true, the picture is far from simple. The relative strengths and organizational features of the different segments of the Mexican apparel commodity chain have evolved over time (see Figure 4.1). During Mexico's extended period of import-substituting industrialization from the 1920s until the 1970s, apparel production was centered in Mexico City and oriented primarily to the domestic market. Initially the upstream products in the apparel commodity chain were imported by immigrant traders, primarily of Lebanese and Jewish origin, who upon arriving in Mexico established themselves as textile wholesalers. Mexico City's garment district, where hundreds of wholesale outlets are clustered within a few square blocks in the downtown area, served as the national distribution center for wholesalers, retailers, and manufacturers alike. As rapid urban growth drove up land rents and the urban workforce was lured to new industries with more attractive wages and working conditions, production began to move outside of the city center, and industry clusters in outlying regions started to emerge.[5]

Industry clusters in the Mexican garment industry form a hub-and-spoke pattern, with wholesale distributors concentrated in Mexico City and agglomerations of specialized producers located in outlying regions. These industry clusters tend to develop very distinct product profiles at the regional level. Some of the most notable garment manufacturing clusters in Mexico include:

- *Children's outerwear:* Aguascalientes, capital of the state of the same name. This state's share of national employment in children's outerwear was 44% in 1985.

- *Uniforms:* Aguascalientes is a center for industrial uniform production in Mexico; in 1985, the state accounted for 23% of national employment in uniform production.

- *Women's intimate apparel and underwear:* Naucalpan (State of Mexico). The state's share of national employment in women's intimate apparel in 1985 was 41%, and its share in other underwear was 35%.

- *Sweaters:* Chinconcuac (State of Mexico), Moroleón (Guanajuato), and Tlaxcala (capital of the state of Tlaxcala). These three small communities specialize in the production of sweaters in Mexico. The contribution of their respective states to national sweater employment in 1985 was: State of Mexico (16%); Guanajuato (15%); and Tlaxcala (11%).

- *Shirts:* Monterrey (Nuevo León) and Tehuacán (Puebla). These cities became the leaders for shirt production in Mexico, displacing Mexico City from its traditional preeminence in this sector. Nuevo León accounted for 20% of national shirt-making employment in 1985 (down from 35% in 1970) and Puebla for 12%. Some claim the Tehuacán cluster's share of national shirt production is now closer to 50% (Hanson 1991, 8–9).

Figure 4.1
The Mexican Apparel Commodity Chain

Development Strategy	Raw Material ▲	Fiber ▲	Textile ▲			Apparel ▲			Retail ▲
	Raw Material	Fiber	Textile production	Fabric selection	Fabric purchase	Garment design	Pre-assembly	Garment assembly	Retail
	Wool, cotton silk, and petrochemicals	Natural and manmade fibers							Department stores / Specialty stores / Discount chains
Import Substitution Industrialization 1920s–1950s	Importers		Immigrant wholesale traders		Apparel manufacturers				Mexican retailers
Import Substitution Industrialization 1960s–1970s	Importers and Mexican fiber and textile companies		Wholesale traders (Mexico City)		Regional industry clusters				Mexican retailers
Export Promotion (Maquiladoras) 1980s–1990s	U.S. fiber and textile firms		U.S. clients (buyers and manufacturers)					Mexican contractors	U.S. retailers
North American Free Trade Agreement 1994–present	North American fiber and textile firms		North American clients and integrating firms/package providers (U.S., Mexican and Asian)					Mexican and Caribbean Basin contractors	North American retailers

These specialized clusters of garment producers in Mexico are frequently supported by a second type of cluster, the satellite community of subcontractors, which undertakes assembly for the larger manufacturing centers. Mexico City supports the largest concentration of satellite clusters, including the densely packed communities of Nezahuacóyotl and Almoloya del Río in the State of Mexico, but most of the outlying regional manufacturing centers also sustain at least a few satellites (such as San Martín Texmelucan for shirt production in Puebla and San Miguel el Alto for sweaters in Jalisco).

Mexico's apparel commodity chain suffered a variety of shocks with the onset of radical trade liberalization in the mid-1980s. The response of the Mexican economy to trade liberalization has been unbalanced, with imports expanding much more rapidly than exports. Imports for consumption have cut deeply into the market share of local apparel firms, while export growth has been concentrated in the maquiladora sector with few backward and forward linkages to the domestic economy. For garments, trade liberalization began to take effect in early 1988. Since then, garment imports have flooded the domestic market in Mexico. Total apparel imports in Mexico grew from $30 million in 1987 to $220 million in 1989, and then skyrocketed to $1.05 billion by 1994. Between 1989 and 1992, imports of woven apparel goods increased more than fivefold (from 440 million new pesos to 2.4 billion new pesos), while imports of knit apparel goods more than tripled (from 220 million new pesos to 720 million new pesos) (INEGI 1993, 82–83).

The opening to trade has permitted Mexico to expand its portfolio of international garment suppliers. The U.S. share of Mexican garment imports fell from nearly 90% in 1985 to 65% in 1992. The second most active participant in the Mexican market was Hong Kong, with 17% of total apparel imports in 1992 (INEGI 1993, 82–83). In all likelihood, many of these Hong Kong goods were produced in China and sent to Mexico by Hong Kong export traders. Mexican garment industry representatives have suggested that well over half of U.S. apparel exports to Mexico also are manufactured in Asia and merely distributed by U.S. buyers based in New York, Los Angeles, and Dallas (Hanson 1991, 46).

The maquiladora sector has benefited most dramatically from Mexico's opening to trade. Between 1986 and 1991, employment in the maquiladora apparel sector increased from 25,300 to 45,700 workers (OTA 1992, 182), and since 1985 much of the employment growth in maquiladoras has taken place in the interior of Mexico. By 1992, nearly 60% of the 51,800 people employed in apparel maquiladoras were located away from the border. These interior plants were also larger, with an average of 160 employees compared to 125 employees in the border factories (American Chamber of Commerce of Mexico 1992, 12, 14). Mexico's textile and apparel exports to the United States from the maquiladoras more than quadrupled from $335 million in 1987 to nearly $1.6 billion in 1994. Furthermore, the growth of garment exports in the maquila sector has been much faster than nonmaquila exports, as evidenced by the fact that Mexico's maquila exports rose from two-thirds of its garment total in 1987 to more than 80% of these exports in 1994 (see Table 4.2).

From a regional perspective, Mexico is competing for the U.S. market most directly with the Caribbean Basin Initiative (CBI) countries. In 1994, the total apparel exports (maquila and nonmaquila trade combined) from CBI countries was more than double Mexico's total: $4.6 billion versus $1.9 billion (Table 4.2). The leading CBI apparel exporter was the Dominican Republic ($1.6 billion), which actually had a higher level of garment exports than Mexico in the early 1990s before Mexico pulled ahead in 1994. The other leading CBI apparel exporters are: Costa Rica ($690 million); Honduras ($650 million); Guatemala ($610 million); Jamaica ($450 million); and El Salvador ($420 million) (see Table 4.3).

Mexico and Canada have lower unit prices for their textile and apparel exports than any of the CBI countries. This figure tends to reflect the mix of products that each country exports, rather than the actual production costs associated with this sector. For example, when we compare Mexico and Canada in terms of their ten leading export items to the United States under the trade categories established in the Multifiber Arrangement (MFA), we see that Mexico exports finished garments while Canada gives a greater emphasis to items that require more capital-intensive production processes, such as yarns, textiles, and carpets (see Table 4.4). A comparison of Mexico and the CBI countries in terms of their apparel exports to the United States shows that there tends to be a very high overlap in terms of their leading export items: cotton trousers; cotton underwear; cotton knit and nonknit shirts; and man-made fiber brassieres (see Tables 4.4 and 4.5).

However, when we compare the unit price for a particular item across countries, we see that Mexico is generally a higher cost supplier than the CBI countries. The unit price for men's and boys' cotton trousers (MFA category 347), for example, is $6.50 per pair in Mexico, $6.06 in the Dominican Republic, $5.74 in Costa Rica, $5.11 in Honduras, and $2.80 in El Salvador (see Table 4.6). The same general pattern holds for cotton trousers for women and girls (348), except that we find a slightly different ordering and mix of countries. Hong Kong is in the top spot (instead of in third place as for men's and boys' trousers), with Turkey, Colombia, and Israel being newcomers to the top ten list (see Table 4.7). These changes reflect the role of special U.S. bilateral quota agreements with diverse economies. In order to explain these price hierarchies and the development trade-offs they imply, we need to look in greater detail at the nature of the maquiladora strategy followed in the region.

Table 4.2

U.S. General Imports of Textiles and Apparel, Total and 807 Trade (9802) by Mexico and Caribbean Basin Initiative (CBI) Countries, 1987–1994

Year	Total Textile and Apparel Imports (US$ mn)	807/9802 Trade (US$ mn)	807/9802 Trade as a Share of Total Imports (percent)
World			
1987	23,659	1,425	6
1988	23,539	1,802	8
1989	26,749	2,137	8
1990	27,936	2,294	8
1991	29,040	3,021	10
1992	34,110	3,954	12
1993	36,079	4,814	13
1994	39,988	5,799	15
Mexico			
1987	495	335	68
1988	565	406	72
1989	647	492	76
1990	678	497	73
1991	879	662	75
1992	1,117	885	79
1993	1,372	1,104	80
1994	1,897	1,568	83
CBI Countries			
1987	1,125	894	79
1988	1,474	1,148	78
1989	1,801	1,377	76
1990	2,025	1,487	73
1991	2,590	1,975	76
1992	3,358	2,550	76
1993	4,064	3,134	77
1994	4,596	3,592	78

Note: mn = millions

Source: USITC (1995).

Table 4.3
U.S. General Imports of Textiles and Apparel
by North American and Caribbean Basin Initiative Suppliers,[a] 1990–1994

	1990 Value (US$ mn)	1990 Unit Price (US$/sme)	1991 Value (US$ mn)	1991 Unit Price (US$/sme)	1992 Value (US$ mn)	1992 Unit Price (US$/sme)	1993 Value (US$ mn)	1993 Unit Price (US$/sme)	1994 Value (US$ mn)	1994 Unit Price (US$/sme)
NAFTA Countries										
Mexico	678	1.5	879	1.55	1,117	1.86	1,372	1.84	1,897	1.94
Canada	483	0.62	600	0.68	823	0.84	1,020	0.91	1,317	1
CBI Countries										
Dominican Republic	723	2.51	958	2.64	1,256	2.62	1,458	2.66	1,618	2.66
Costa Rica	388	2.79	446	2.65	596	2.76	659	2.62	694	2.44
Honduras	118	2.27	202	2.38	370	2.94	508	3.22	649	2.95
Guatemala	206	2.19	350	2.61	474	2.8	565	2.91	612	3.14
Jamaica	238	2.51	255	2.43	296	2.21	391	2.43	455	2.25
El Salvador	70	1.21	107	1.53	183	2.03	268	2.03	421	2.09
Panama	63	3.15	63	3.50	51	3.64	42	2.80	31	2.21
Haiti	167	1.64	152	1.57	65	1.81	96	1.92	30	1.76
Nicaragua	0	N/A	1	N/A	3	3.00	11	2.75	29	3.63
Other	52	2.26	56	1.81	64	2.00	66	2.20	57	2.04
Total CBI Countries	2,025	2.32	2,590	2.42	3,358	2.59	4,064	2.63	4,596	2.59

Notes: sme = square meters equivalent; mn = millions.
[a]Ranked according to value of imports in 1994.
Source: USITC (1995).

Table 4.4
Mexico and Canada—
Top Ten U.S. Textile and Apparel Imports by MFA Category, 1994

NAFTA Country	MFA Category	Description	Value (US$ mn)	Unit Price (US$/sme)
Mexico	347	Cotton trousers mb	373	5.23
	348	Cotton trousers wgi	229	4.72
	639	MMF knit shirts wgi	132	3.64
	649	MMF brassieres	121	8.04
	338	Cotton knit shirts mb	66	4.55
	352	Cotton underwear	56	1.28
	670	MMF flat goods	54	3.44
	652	MMF underwear	54	1.12
	638	MMF knit shirts mb	52	1.82
	339	Cotton knit shirts wgi	51	7.94
Canada	665	MMF floor coverings	103	9.01
	443	Wool suits mb	91	25.96
	229	Cotton/MMF special purpose	90	0.27
	600	Textured filament yarn	85	0.54
	659	Other MMF apparel	67	3.34
	222	Cotton/MMF knit fabric	57	0.82
	339	Cotton knit shirts wgi	51	13.42
	348	Cotton trousers wgi	49	6.63
	347	Cotton trousers mb	42	9.44
	629	Other MMF staple/ filament fabric	40	1.99

Notes: sme = square meters equivalent; mn = millions; MMF = man-made fiber; mb = men's and boys'; wgi = women's, girls' and infants'.

Source: USITC (1995).

Table 4.5
Caribbean Basin Initiative Countries—
Top Five U.S. Textile and Apparel Imports by MFA Category, 1994

CBI Country	MFA Category	Description	Value (US$ mn)	Unit Price (US$/sme)
Dominican Republic	347	Cotton trousers mb	369	4.88
	649	MMF brassieres	129	7.06
	348	Cotton trousers wgi	123	4.17
	352	Cotton underwear	115	0.9
	647	MMF trousers	104	5.32
Costa Rica	347	Cotton trousers mb	160	4.62
	352	Cotton underwear	84	0.78
	649	MMF brassieres	71	6.36
	340	Cotton nonknit shirts wgi	55	4.45
	348	Cotton trousers wgi	50	4.64
Honduras	347	Cotton trousers mb	94	4.12
	340	Cotton nonknit shirts mb	83	3.97
	338	Cotton knit shirts mb	80	5.79
	339	Cotton knit shirts wgi	68	6.3
	348	Cotton trousers wgi	67	2.75
Guatemala	340	Cotton nonknit shirts mb	87	3.26
	347	Cotton trousers mb	76	4.58
	348	Cotton trousers wgi	73	3.91
	338	Cotton knit shirts mb	46	7.1
	435	Wool coats wgi	31	5.1
Jamaica	352	Cotton underwear	120	1.33
	632	MMF hosiery	103	3.85
	338	Cotton knit shirts mb	39	4.28
	340	Cotton nonknit shirts mb	35	3.99
	649	MMF brassieres	28	5.89
El Salvador	339	Cotton knit shirts wgi	50	5.59
	348	Cotton trousers wgi	48	2.88
	340	Cotton nonknit shirts mb	48	2.66
	338	Cotton knit shirts mb	41	3.47
	352	Cotton underwear	25	0.95

Notes: sme = square meters equivalent; mn = millions; MMF = man-made fiber; mb = men's and boys';
wgi = women's, girls' and infants'.
Source: USITC (1995).

Table 4.6 Top Ten Suppliersa of Men's and Boys' Cotton Trousers (category 347) to the USA, 1983–1994

	1983 Average Import			1989 Average Import			1994 Average Import		
	Value (US$ mn)	Price, US$ (per pair of cotton trousers)	Share of U.S. Imports (percent)	Value (US$ mn)	Price, US$ (per pair of cotton trousers)	Share of U.S. Imports (percent)	Value (US$ mn)	Price, US$ (per pair of cotton trousers)	Share of U.S. Imports (percent)
1. Mexico	14.2	3.73	4	109.4	5.15	9	373.1	6.50	17
2. Dominican Republic	6.8	3.88	2	136.6	5.52	12	368.8	6.06	17
3. Hong Kong	143.1	5.83	40	202.1	8.20	17	233.6	7.84	11
4. Costa Rica	3.8	5.93	1	54.1	5.60	5	160.2	5.74	7
5. China	43.3	3.37	12	110.4	6.75	9	101.5	6.46	5
6. Honduras	n/a	n/a	n/a	15.5	3.15	1	93.9	5.11	4
7. Guatemala	n/a	n/a	n/a	23.2	3.32	2	76.5	5.69	3
8. Philippines	16.8	5.5	5	73.9	6.76	6	70.0	5.96	3
9. Bangladesh	n/a	n/a	n/a	19.1	3.49	2	66.6	5.20	3
10. Indonesia	8.2	1.81	2	49.8	6.63	4	45.3	7.06	2
All U.S. imports	355.1	4.79	100	1,169.5	5.93	100	2,201.2	6.13	100

Table 4.7 Top Ten Suppliersa of Women's and Girls' Cotton Trousers (category 348) to the USA, 1983–1994

	1983 Average Import			1989 Average Import			1994 Average Import		
	Value (US$ mn)	Price, US$ (per pair of cotton trousers)	Share of U.S. Imports (percent)	Value (US$ mn)	Price, US$ (per pair of cotton trousers)	Share of U.S. Imports (percent)	Value (US$ mn)	Price, US$ (per pair of cotton trousers)	Share of U.S. Imports (percent)
1. Hong Kong	294.7	5.17	46	424.7	8.06	29	396.9	7.42	19
2. Mexico	13.3	3.56	2	67.7	5.06	5	229.2	5.86	11
3. Dominican Republic	3.8	2.91	1	40.1	4.23	3	122.5	5.18	6
4. Turkey	0.4	2.56	0	60.7	3.61	4	90.4	4.19	4
5. China	70.7	3.1	11	89.7	6.66	6	77.4	7.29	4
6. Guatemala	n/a	n/a	n/a	28.6	3.48	2	73.1	4.86	4
7. Philippines	18.7	3.64	3	31.4	6.19	2	67.9	5.93	3
8. Honduras	n/a	n/a	n/a	1.2	3.23	0	67.0	3.41	3
9. Colombia	0.1	2.2	0	24	5.63	2	55.8	6.46	3
10. Israel	n/a	n/a	n/a	13.6	8.17	1	52.4	6.04	3
All U.S. Imports	636.5	4.46	100	1448.3	5.83	100	2051.8	5.67	100

Notes for Tables 4.5 and 4.6: mn = millions. aRanked according to value of imports in 1994.
Source for Tables 4.5 and 4.6: Khanna (1996), based on U.S. official statistics.

Apparel Maquiladoras: The Low Road to Export Competitiveness

Export-oriented assembly in Latin America is centered in Mexico and the Caribbean Basin because of these countries' low wages and proximity to the U.S. market, where more than 90% of their exports are sold. Virtually all of the export-processing zone (EPZ) production in the region is of a very low value-added nature, which is a direct result of U.S. policy. Under U.S. tariff schedule provision HTS 9802.00.80 (formerly Clause 807), enterprises operating in EPZs have an incentive to minimize locally purchased inputs because only U.S.-made components are exempt from import duties when the finished product is shipped back to the United States. This constitutes a major impediment to increasing the integration between the activities in the zones and the local economy, and it limits the usefulness of EPZs as stepping stones to higher stages of industrialization.

Mexico's maquiladora industry, established in 1965, is made up of assembly plants (known as maquilas) that mainly use U.S. components to make goods for export to the U.S. market. In 1994, the maquiladora industry generated almost $6 billion in foreign revenue and employed 600,000 Mexicans (Burns 1995, 40). Until the past decade, Mexico's maquiladora plants typified low value-added assembly, with virtually no backward linkages. For apparel maquiladoras located on the border, the value added by local materials (including packaging) was just 0.6% of total production costs in 1992, compared with local value added of 5.6% for the apparel maquiladoras located in the interior of Mexico (American Chamber of Commerce of Mexico 1992, 16). Prior to the passage of NAFTA, maquila firms had virtually no backward linkages to domestic textile producers or forward linkages to retail stores in Mexico. Furthermore, these Mexican plants were the most vulnerable to direct competition from lower-cost CBI apparel suppliers.

Caribbean Basin venues have become favored locales for export-oriented assembly in Latin America. By the early 1990s, EPZs were a leading source of exports and manufacturing employment in various Caribbean nations. The Dominican Republic is a prime example. There are 430 companies employing 164,000 workers in the country's thirty free-trade zones; three-quarters of the firms are involved in textiles and apparel (Burns 1995, 39). In terms of employment, the Dominican Republic is the fourth largest EPZ economy in the world (the fifth if China's Special Economic Zones are included). The Dominican Republic has an especially large dependence on EPZs, whose share of official manufacturing employment on the island increased from 23% in 1981 to 56% in 1989. By this latter year, EPZs generated more than 20% of the Dominican Republic's total foreign exchange earnings (Kaplinsky

1993, 1855–56). U.S. investors account for more than half (54%) of the companies operating in the zones, followed by firms from the Dominican Republic (22%), South Korea (11%), and Taiwan (3%) (UNCTAD 1994, 90).

Caribbean EPZs have developed highly specialized export niches, such as underwear. The Dominican Republic, Costa Rica, Honduras, and El Salvador together supply more than 40% of all U.S. underwear imports.[6] Mexico and the CBI nations are viewed by U.S. apparel transnationals, such as Fruit of the Loom (the largest U.S. producer of men's and boys' underwear) and Sara Lee Corporation (the world's leading hosiery supplier, with brands like Hanes and L'Eggs), as part of "a trans-American alliance to take on Asian underwear manufacturers in world markets" (Coleman 1995a, B1). The rules-of-origin clauses in NAFTA have introduced a stricter logic of regional integration by limiting duty-free access to the U.S. market only to products that originate within the region. This is part of an all-out effort to reduce the impact of Asian imports of intermediate as well as finished goods in North American markets. Consensus for protectionism is undermined, however, by the fact that Mexico benefits more from the new rules than the CBI producers, and textile firms more than apparel companies.

The U.S. government, in an effort to close earlier loopholes, announced in March 1995 that it would put quota restrictions on imports of boxer shorts, briefs, undershirts, panties, and slips to force CBI underwear manufacturers to shift from their heavy use of 807 programs, which offer duty breaks for apparel made from U.S. and foreign fabric cut in the United States, to 807A programs, which provide tariff benefits and almost unlimited quotas for apparel made offshore from fabric both cut *and* formed in the United States (Finnie 1995a, 100). This heavy-handed measure to squeeze out foreign textile imports has generated complaints by some U.S. apparel companies, who want the freedom to choose their own fabrics. According to Laura Jones, the executive director of the U.S. Association for Importers of Textiles and Apparel in New York, "By mandating the use of American fabric, the government is setting the U.S. apparel industry against the U.S. textile industry. That's not what their job is about. That's a total perversion favoring one industry over another." Vertically integrated apparel manufacturers like Fruit of the Loom, however, with five plants and 4,000 workers in North Carolina, knits all its fabrics and sews more than 90% of its underwear domestically.[7] Thus, it supports a tough U.S. stance and wants to restrict Asian fabric imports into the Caribbean. According to Ronald Sorini, the senior vice president for international development and government relations at Fruit of the Loom's Chicago headquarters and a former chief U.S. textile negotiator, "What the quotas do is prevent subsidized fabrics from India, Pakistan, and

China from going to the Caribbean as a backdoor into the U.S. market" (Coleman 1995a, B3).

Labor also is beginning to implement more assertive strategies for dealing with U.S. apparel manufacturers in the Caribbean. Take the case of the Gap, a prominent U.S. apparel firm that acquires a substantial portion of its clothing from Central America. Mandarin, a contractor in El Salvador that makes clothes for the Gap, fired 350 workers when a union was formed to protest abysmal working conditions such as fourteen-hour workdays, subpoverty wages, and sexual abuse. The Gap, like a number of other U.S. apparel firms, has established much-touted corporate codes of conduct that require contract shops with whom it does business to abide by their countries' labor laws. When abuses are exposed, the typical response by a U.S. company is to rescind its contract with the offending factory, thereby throwing garment workers out of their jobs. In a meeting with Gap management, ousted employees from Mandarin in El Salvador demanded the reinstatement of the 350 workers who were fired for union organizing, an end to mandatory overtime so the younger girls could go to school, and pay for overtime work ("Sweating for the Gap" 1995). This kind of confrontation, which is being repeated elsewhere in the Americas and Asia, is forcing U.S. apparel firms to expand their notion of corporate responsibility and use their leverage as major buyers to play a more active role in improving working conditions in the Third World.

While EPZs in Mexico and the Caribbean have been associated with undeniable gains in employment and foreign-exchange earnings, these benefits are offset by a picture of job growth contingent on falling real wages and a decline in local purchasing power. In Mexico, the real minimum wage in 1989 was less than one-half (47%) of its 1980 level, and in El Salvador, workers in 1989 earned just 36% of what they did at the beginning of the decade (IDB 1990, 28). These trends exacerbate the polarization between the rich and the poor in Latin America, where close to 50% of the population lives in poverty, with 25% considered destitute.

The rivalry among neighboring EPZs to offer transnational companies the lowest wages fosters a perverse strategy of "competitive devaluation," whereby currency depreciations are viewed as a means to increase international competitiveness (Kaplinsky 1993). Export growth in the Dominican Republic's EPZs skyrocketed after a sharp depreciation of its currency against the dollar in 1985; similarly, Mexico's export expansion was facilitated by recurrent devaluations of the Mexican peso, most recently in 1994–1995. Devaluations heighten already substantial wage differences in the region. Hourly compensation rates for apparel workers in the early 1990s were $1.08 in Mexico, $0.88

in Costa Rica, $0.64 in the Dominican Republic, and $0.48 in Honduras, compared to $8.13 in the United States (ILO 1995, 35–36). Although it may make sense for a single country to devalue its currency in order to attract users of unskilled labor to their production sites, the advantages of this strategy evaporate quickly when other nations simultaneously engage in wage-depressing devaluations, which lower local standards of living while doing nothing to improve productivity.

The Emergence of Transnational Networks

During the presidency of Carlos Salinas (1988–1994), the Mexican government was committed to enhancing the competitiveness of Mexican industry through free trade. This policy of commercial openness was the defining characteristic of the Salinas administration. Since the 1980s, the Mexican government has shifted its relationship to the private sector from regulation and control to promoting industrial competitiveness through cooperation and dialogue.[8] Although the Mexican state was clearly reducing its role in the economy, a move long called for by those in the private sector, there nonetheless arose strong criticism by many domestic companies that viewed the economy as opening too fast, causing foreign corporations to be the main beneficiaries of Salinas's policies.

The Salinas government was quite well informed about the situation of the textile and apparel industry. In 1992, Mexico's Ministry of Trade and Industrial Development established the Program to Promote Competitiveness and Internationalization of the Textile and Apparel Industries (SECOFI 1992). This initiative grew out of a series of meetings with industry representatives in which both sides agreed on many of the principal problems in the areas of foreign trade, technology, industrial organization, and financing. The reform measures proposed in the government program included: reforming Mexico's customs system with the active involvement of the private sector to eliminate or reduce contraband; identifying sources of unfair competitive practices in the areas of trade and taxes; providing firms with financial incentives to acquire needed market information, technology and outside expertise to improve productivity and expand exports; and stimulating the creation of modern forms of industrial organization with an eye toward facilitating vertical and horizontal integration in the textile production chain. This plan for the textile and apparel industries became a model for public-private sector cooperation within the Salinas government, and it was extended to thirty-six other industrial sectors in the last two years of the administration.

Given the consensus among industry experts that the textile sector is the weakest link in the Mexican apparel chain, the key question is: Who will be the main "organizing agents" in modernizing Mexico's apparel commodity chain? The notion of organizing agents is used here to refer to those firms, foreign and domestic, that could enhance the competitiveness of the apparel commodity chain in Mexico through backward or forward linkages with major producers and retailers. The assessment of Kurt Salmon Associates (KSA), a leading U.S. consulting firm in the soft-goods area, is that NAFTA will result in the creation of 90,000 new jobs in the apparel sector in Mexico, primarily for export, by the late 1990s. Substantial new investments will be made by Mexican, U.S., and Far Eastern apparel and textile manufacturers. KSA estimates that current players will make 15% of the apparel investments and 25% of the textile investments, compared to 15% and 10%, respectively, for new Mexican investors, and 30% and 25% for East Asian investors. U.S. and Canadian investors will account for the balance—40%—of both the apparel and textile investments (Reed 1993).

Potential organizing agents, located in every segment of the commodity chain, have already begun to undertake such investments in Mexico: fibers (Celanese Mexicana, Cydsa, DuPont); textiles (Burlington Industries, Guilford Mills, Cone Mills, Grupo Kalach, Grupo Saba); apparel (Sara Lee, VF Corporation, Levi Strauss); and retailers (J.C. Penney, Sears, Kmart-Liverpool, Wal-Mart-Cifra). There are substantial differences in the scope and content of these varied attempts at vertical and horizontal integration in the Mexican economy, but one commonality is that the role of state policies is dramatically reduced when interfirm linkages are the solution of choice for enhancing international competitiveness, especially when these linkages cross national boundaries, as they are prone to do in textiles and apparel.

The Mexico-U.S. apparel connection actually is made up of two quite different types of economic networks. First, there are the *manufacturer-centered networks* that dominate Mexico's traditional maquiladora sector. Mexican export-oriented assembly plants are organically linked and completely subordinate to U.S. textile and apparel producers in these networks. These manufacturers tend to be large, vertically integrated, and rooted in the U.S. South. Many of the leading textile firms are headquartered in North Carolina and include: Burlington Industries, the second largest U.S. textile company with 1994 sales of $2.1 billion, 23,600 employees, and forty-one manufacturing plants in nine U.S. states, plus three plants in Mexico; Cone Mills, the world's largest supplier of denim fabric, with sales of $810 million in 1994; and Guilford Mills, with 1994 sales of $700 million (Finnie 1995a).

These textile firms are closely connected to many of the largest U.S. apparel manufacturers, such as privately owned Levi Strauss and Company, the world's largest apparel firm with sales of $6.1 billion in 1994; VF Corporation, the world's largest publicly held apparel company with 1994 sales of $5 billion and a 30% share of the U.S. jeans market (including a large number of popular brands such as Lee, Wrangler, and Rustler); and Fruit of the Loom, which has 1994 sales of $2.3 billion and a 40% share of the U.S. men's and boys' underwear market (Finnie 1995b). All of these U.S. textile and apparel manufacturers have extensive production networks linking the U.S. South with Mexico.

Reports indicate that U.S. transnational textile and fiber companies are taking steps to control strategic nodes of Mexico's apparel commodity chain. In 1992, Cone Mills of Greensboro, North Carolina, the world's largest producer of denim fabrics, purchased a 50% stake in Compañía Industrial de Parras S.A. (CIPSA), one of Mexico's largest textile firms. These two companies formed a joint venture, called Parras-Cone, which has set up Mexico's largest denim-making factory in the La Laguna region of Coahuila in northern Mexico (Finnie 1995a, 118–19). This plant, which is expected to help Coahuila triple its production of denim during the late 1990s, will provide much of the denim used in Mexico's cotton trousers assembly plants. Cone is the largest denim supplier to Levi Strauss and Company, the world's leading manufacturer of jeans, which has a number of twin plants in the El Paso/Ciudad Juárez area. Thus, there is a strong cotton connection between textile production centers in Coahuila and numerous apparel plants on either side of the Mexico-Texas border.

One of the newest ventures is the effort by Guilford Mills, also of Greensboro, North Carolina, to create a "Textile City" near Cuernavaca, about 40 miles south of Mexico City. Guilford Mills, Alfa (Mexico's largest industrial enterprise), and DuPont, among others, will join forces to create a mammoth industrial park for the textile and apparel industries, complete with a training center and a demonstration apparel factory (Coleman 1995b). Since Guilford is a leading manufacturer of fabrics using man-made filament yarns (nylon, rayon, and acetate), and both DuPont and Alfa make the synthetic fibers used in these yarns, this venture in central Mexico has a different raw material base than the cotton textile complexes in northern Mexico. U.S. transnationals, in conjunction with large Mexican partners, thus are preparing to do battle with Asian and CBI exporting nations in order to gain a more stable and profitable share of the North American apparel market. This kind of competition through networks is likely to mark the face of the apparel commodity chain in North America for decades to come.

Along with these manufacturer-centered transnational networks, the apparel commodity chain in Mexico is also being transformed by a new wave of *retailer-centered networks*. Discount retail chains such as Wal-Mart, Kmart, and Price Club, and department stores such as J.C. Penney and Sears have expanded rapidly in Mexico during the past several years. These retailer-centered chains play a double role: they constitute a pipeline for the delivery of imported consumer goods into the heart of the Mexican economy, and they also have the capability to purchase and deliver Mexican-made goods to external markets where these retail chains have stores, especially the United States. In this buyer-driven commodity chain, local firms develop the commercial ties with foreign buyers needed to move from the maquiladora system of low-wage assembly based on imported inputs to the "package supplier," specification-contracting role typical of the East Asian apparel exporters (Gereffi 1995; Gereffi and Hempel 1996).

Despite its current recession, the lure of Mexico's nearly 100 million consumers, half of whom are under the age of twenty, has proved irresistible for U.S. retailers. Spurred by NAFTA, the Americanization of Mexican retailing is in full swing. Sears Roebuck, for years the largest department store chain in Mexico, is being joined by other prominent U.S. department stores (such as J.C. Penney, Dillard, and Saks Fifth Avenue). More significant is the incursion of giant U.S. discount chains which augment retail consolidation by establishing joint ventures with Mexican partners: Wal-Mart, the largest retailer in the United States, and Cifra, Mexico's biggest retailing organization, have announced a 50–50 partnership; strategic alliances have also been formed between Kmart and Liverpool, and Price Club and Comercial Mexicana, along with other international retail companies (see Table 4.8)

Table 4.8
Mexican Retailer Partnerships with U.S. Retailers

U.S. Company	Mexican Partner	Number of Stores Opened in Mexico[a]
Wal-Mart	Cifra	67
Price Club	Comercial Mexicana	2
Fleming	Gigante	7
Kmart	Liverpool	2
JC Penney	None	0
Dillards	Melvin Simon, Fondo Opción	0
FW Woolworth	None	0
Burlington Coat Factory	None	1
Saks Fifth Avenue	None	0

[a]As of March 1995.
Source: Harris (1995).

Although the ambitious expansion plans of U.S. retailers may be put on hold or slowed somewhat because of Mexico's current slump, two longer term implications of the U.S. retail invasion are likely to be quite significant. First, Mexico's informal distribution outlets, made up primarily of street markets, have been the dominant retail channel for many consumer items, including about one-third of all apparel sales. Giant U.S. discount chains, like Wal-Mart or Price Club, are likely to erode sales first and foremost in the informal sector, with negative consequences for employment and income among these small vendors. Second, the relocation of U.S. retailers to Mexico may increase the incentive to establish local supplier networks for buyer-driven commodity chains. In this way, U.S. retailers could provide a kind of tutelage for the Mexican firms from which they order goods similar to that which has long prevailed in U.S. buyer-driven commodity chains in Asia (Gereffi 1994, 1995).

Implications for the U.S. South and the Mexican South

The creation of new production and trade networks between the United States and Mexico in textiles and apparel is linking the U.S. South and the northern and central regions of Mexico ever more tightly together. The U.S. South is in a position to become the coordinating hub of the North American apparel commodity chain. North Carolina and Texas are the nerve centers of the manufacturer-centered U.S.-Mexico networks. North Carolina is of central importance because it is the headquarters for most of the big U.S. textile plants, many of which are making new investments in Mexico. When NAFTA becomes fully implemented, U.S. textile companies expect to be able to supply Mexican apparel plants duty free from textile production centers located inside Mexico. Texas is important as the main U.S. production site of Levi Strauss and a number of other large U.S. apparel manufacturers, although other states in the U.S. South (such as North Carolina, South Carolina, and Georgia) also have major apparel production facilities.

The U.S. South also plays a critical role in the retailer-centered apparel networks emerging in Mexico. Wal-Mart, the largest retailer in the world with sales of $67 billion and 2,440 stores in 1993, is headquartered in Bentonville, Arkansas. J.C. Penney, the largest department store and the sixth largest retailer in the United States, with sales of $19 billion and 2,300 stores in 1993, is headquartered in Dallas, Texas. Dillard, another one of the top thirty U.S. retailers with sales of more than $5 billion in 1993, is headquartered in Little Rock, Arkansas (Warfield et al. 1995). Wal-Mart, J.C. Penney, and Dillard have all formed joint ventures with retail partners in Mexico in the 1990s and stand to benefit greatly both by selling to Mexico and by sourcing apparel items from Mexico.

Unlike the apparel maquiladoras, which assemble garments from inputs supplied by U.S. manufacturers, the sourcing networks of U.S. retailers in Mexico will have to rely on the purchase of finished apparel items, made in many industries within Mexico's preexisting garment manufacturing clusters for shirts, sweaters, underwear, outerwear, and so on. Central and northern Mexico are important to these retailer-centered networks from both demand and supply points of view. U.S. retailers will open new stores in Mexico's largest cities first—Mexico City, Guadalajara, Monterrey, and Puebla. These four cities account for 40% of Mexico's retail sales of apparel items (Harris 1995, 95) and are close to Mexico's traditional specialized clusters of garment producers in the central and northern parts of the country. Thus, the retailer-centered networks, if they can adapt the techniques utilized in Asia's highly successful form of specification contracting (Gereffi 1995), will have a greater opportunity to encourage the development of small and medium-sized enterprises in Mexico.

The lead firms in these manufacturer-centered and retailer-centered networks in the North American apparel commodity chain are in a position to play a direct role in upgrading Mexican domestic industry. U.S. textile manufacturers are entering into production joint ventures with Mexican counterparts to build large textile complexes in northern and central Mexico to supply local apparel plants. U.S. apparel manufacturers also provide both the technology and incentives for their Mexican affiliates to meet international competition. The next step would be for the U.S. retailers that are going into Mexico to play a similar role in upgrading local supplier networks. There is some evidence that this is already happening. The Banco Nacional de Comercio Exterior, a government bank to promote foreign trade, has established a Vendor Certification Program that evaluates small and medium Mexican enterprises that wish to become suppliers for U.S. retail chains. About four hundred suppliers, mainly in the food and beverages sector, have already been approved, and three hundred of these suppliers are exporting. Less than two dozen textile and apparel companies had received a positive evaluation by 1994.[9]

The U.S. South, while it will retain a considerable amount of textile and apparel production facilities, is upgrading its role to a more technology-intensive and commercially oriented node in the North American commodity chain. The Textile/Clothing Technology Corporation (TC[2]), located in Raleigh, North Carolina, has developed computerized programs that reduce cycle times for apparel design, production, and delivery from twenty to forty-five weeks to an astonishing forty-eight hours (Finnie 1995b, 75). This requires designers, manufacturers, and retailers to have access to the same data simultaneously, but it increases the importance of belonging to Quick Response networks in the industry. These networks can easily span national boundaries in geographically proximate countries like Mexico, the United States, and Canada, and they would act as a disincentive to long-distance supply networks such as those established in Asia.

With the rapid expansion of U.S. apparel imports from Caribbean Basin nations since the late 1980s (see Table 4.2), Miami's role in the North American commodity chain has become more important (see Roberts and Tardanico in this volume). Unlike Mexico, the CBI nations have no textile production centers. Much of the fabric cutting for garments sewn in CBI countries is done in Miami. In addition, Miami has developed a large "remake" industry that repairs defective garments arriving from the Caribbean before they reach their final U.S. retail destination. Despite their recent success, CBI countries are concerned that Mexico is now in a position to gain at their expense. Following the passage of NAFTA, some apparel production has already been relocated from CBI countries to Mexico. Furthermore, the peso's sharp devaluation at the end of 1994 made Mexican exports cheaper in terms of U.S. dollars, causing U.S. imports of textiles and apparel from Mexico to jump 32% in March 1995 alone. Both the American Apparel Manufacturers Association and the American Textile Manufacturers' Institute are lobbying in favor of a bill that would give Caribbean nations trade benefits equivalent to those now enjoyed by Mexico under NAFTA. The position being adopted by the U.S. government, however, is that Caribbean trade parity with Mexico will only occur when the $780 million in annual tariff revenues received on apparel items imported from the twenty-four CBI nations can be replaced from another source (Finnie 1995a, 99–102). Until then, Mexico remains the world's fastest growing source of apparel supply to the U.S. market.

The southern part of Mexico is a loser in this transition in relative, if not absolute, terms. It is not losing jobs in the apparel sector, but it is not gaining them either. Yucatán, the only state in southern Mexico with a significant potential to expand its garment production capability because of relatively large population and its proximity to Miami, had only 2% of Mexico's apparel employees in the late 1980s, and the average size of the state's 425 garment factories was very small, just 6.5 workers per plant (INEGI 1993, 32; see Wilson and Kayne in this volume). These Yucatán microenterprises are tiny compared to the 160 employees in Mexico's typical apparel maquiladoras located in the interior of the country. In 1992, Yucatán had less than 1% of Mexico's 500,000 maquiladora employees. By contrast, the northern state of Chihuahua (which includes Ciudad Juárez, located across from El Paso,

Texas) had one-third of Mexico's total maquiladora workforce, and Baja California Norte (located next to San Diego, California) had another 20% (American Chamber of Commerce of Mexico 1992, 13–14). Thus, Mexico's South has no place to fit in the North American apparel commodity chain. What northern Mexico can't produce, Caribbean nations will.

The northern and central regions of Mexico are tied to the U.S. South by the production and trade networks being established by large U.S. fiber, textile, and apparel firms. Big U.S. retailers also are establishing new sourcing networks in Mexico for export as well as sale within the Mexican market, but these supply chains are close to the U.S. border or to the major population centers of Mexico. The CBI countries supplement Mexico as a low-wage alternative for apparel sourcing to the United States, which has strengthened Miami's position as a service node in the apparel sector but does not help the Mexican South. In the end, the high road to export competitiveness for Mexico will be to shift out of the maquiladora assembly business and engage in more integrated manufacturing of standardized garments using local textiles and fibers (such as is envisioned in the new "Textile City") or to move to the more lucrative fashion-oriented segment of the apparel commodity chain being vacated by established Asian suppliers. In either scenario, southern Mexico appears destined to be a bystander.

References

American Chamber of Commerce of Mexico. 1992. Maquiladora Statistics. *Review of Trade and Industry (with the Maquiladora Newsletter)* [fourth quarter].

Appelbaum, Richard P., and Gary Gereffi. 1994. Power and Profits in the Apparel Commodity Chain. In *Global Production: The Apparel Industry in the Pacific Rim*, eds. Edna Bonacich, Lucie Cheng, Norma Chinchilla, Nora Hamilton, and Paul Ong. Philadelphia, Penn.: Temple University Press.

Botella C., Ovidio, Enrique García C., and José Giral B. 1991. Textiles: Mexican Perspective. In *U.S.-Mexican Industrial Integration: The Road to Free Trade*, ed. Sidney Weintraub. Boulder, Colo.: Westview Press.

Burns, Gail. 1995. Free-Trade Zones: Global Overview and Future Prospects. *Industry, Trade, and Technology Review* (Sept.).

Coleman, Zach. 1995a. UnderWar. *Winston-Salem Journal*, Aug. 7.

———. 1995b. Textile City: Guilford Mills Prepares for Industrial Park in Mexico. *Winston-Salem Journal*, Nov. 4.

Finnie, Trevor A. 1995a. Outlook for the U.S. Textile Industry. *Textile Outlook International* 61.

———. 1995b. Outlook for the U.S. Apparel Industry. *Textile Outlook International* 62.

Gereffi, Gary. 1994. The Organization of Buyer-Driven Global Commodity Chains: How U.S. Retailers Shape Overseas Production Networks. In *Commodity*

Chains and Global Capitalism, eds. Gary Gereffi and Miguel Korzeniewicz. Westport, Conn. and London: Praeger.

————. 1995. Global Production Systems and Third World Development. In *Global Change, Regional Response: The New International Context of Development*, ed. Barbara Stallings. New York: Cambridge University Press.

————. 1996. Mexico's "Old" and "New" *Maquiladora* Industries: Contrasting Approaches to North American Integration. In *Neoliberalism Revisited: Economic Restructuring and Mexico's Political Future*, ed. Gerardo Otero. Boulder, Colo.: Westview.

Gereffi, Gary, and Lynn Hempel. 1996. Latin America in the Global Economy: Running Faster to Stay in Place. *NACLA Report on the Americas* 29, no. 4.

Hanson, Gordon H. 1991. U.S.-Mexico Free Trade and the Mexican Garment Industry. Unpublished report prepared for the Bureau of International Labor Affairs, U.S. Department of Labor (Sept.).

Harris, Randolph J. 1995. Apparel Retailing in Mexico. *Textile Outlook International* 59.

Instituto Nacional de Estadística Geográfica e Informática (INEGI). 1993. *La industria textil y del vestido en México*. México, D.F.: INEGI.

Inter-American Development Bank (IDB). 1990. *Economic and Social Progress in Latin America*. Washington, D.C.: IDB.

International Labor Organization (ILO). 1995. *Recent Developments in the Clothing Industry*. Geneva: ILO.

Kaplinsky, Raphael. 1993. Export-Processing Zones in the Dominican Republic: Transforming Manufactures into Commodities. *World Development* 21, no. 11.

Khanna, Sri Ram. 1996. Trends in U.S. and EU Textile and Clothing Imports. *Textile Outlook International* 63.

Kurt Salmon Associates (KSA). 1992. Dancing with Juggernauts. *The KSA Perspective* (Jan.).

Lande, Stephen L. 1991. Textiles: U.S. Perspective. In *U.S.-Mexican Industrial Integration: The Road to Free Trade*, ed. Sidney Weintraub. Boulder, Colo.: Westview Press.

Mandelbaum, Judah. 1992. Competitiveness of the Mexican Textile Chain. *Textile Outlook International* 44.

Office of Technology Assessment (OTA), U.S. Congress. 1992. *U.S.-Mexico Trade: Pulling Together or Pulling Apart?* ITE-545. Washington, D.C.: U.S. Government Printing Office.

Reed, William A. 1993. Sourcing and Marketing in Mexico. Excerpts from a speech delivered at Kurt Salmon Associates' Soft Goods Breakfast, New York, June 15.

Secretaría de Comercio y Fomento Industrial (SECOFI). 1992. *Programa para promover la competitividad e internacionalización de la industria textil y de la confección*. México, D.F.: Secretaría de Comercio y Fomento Industrial.

Sklair, Leslie. 1993. *Assembling for Development: The Maquila Industry in Mexico and the United States* (updated and expanded edition). La Jolla: Center for U.S.-Mexican Studies, University of California at San Diego.

Sweating for the Gap in Central America. 1995. *Sweatshop Watch* 1, no. 1.

United Nations Conference on Trade and Development (UNCTAD). 1994. *World Investment Report 1994: Transnational Corporations, Employment and the Workplace.* Geneva: UNCTAD.

U.S. International Trade Commission (USITC). 1995. *U.S. Imports of Textiles and Apparel Under the Multifiber Arrangement: Annual Report for 1994,* USITC Publication 2884. Washington, D.C.: USITC.

Warfield, Carol, Mary Barry, and Dorothy Cavendar. 1995. Apparel Retailing in the USA-Part 1. *Textile Outlook International* 58.

Wilson, Patricia A. 1992. *Exports and Local Development: Mexico's New Maquiladoras.* Austin: University of Texas Press.

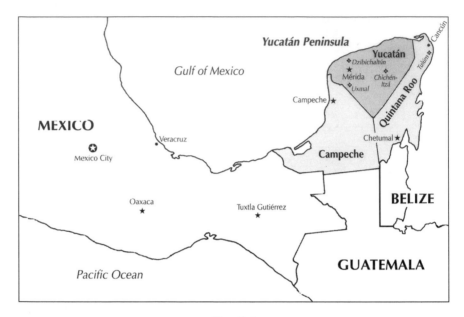

Map 5.1
Yucatán State and Peninsula
❖   Archaeological Site

Local Economic Development and Transnational Restructuring

The Case of Export-Assembly Manufacturing in Yucatán

Patricia A. Wilson and Thea Kayne

Localities around the world are scrambling to avoid being marginalized in a rapidly restructuring global economy. Low-wage localities are jumping on the bandwagon of global assembly, or trying to do so, as they search for new roles in the international economy. But very few of the successful cases have been able to emulate the Asian "tigers" in using export-assembly industry as a launching pad for local advancement to higher rungs in the global commodity ladder of manufacturing production. Mexico's northern border region has been the country's primary site of export-assembly industry, or maquiladoras. In a context of abrupt national deindustrialization of employment since the early 1980s, the northern border region has made large gains in direct employment in the maquiladoras, as, given Mexico's sharp loss of import-substitution manufacturing firms and jobs, the geographic weight of the country's manufacturing activities has shifted from its central to northern zone (Oliveira and García 1997). This shift notwithstanding, the northern border region has been notably unsuccessful in spawning a locally owned manufacturing base. In fact, as the maquiladora industry along the border has become more sophisticated with the introduction of advanced flexible technology, its previously minimal degree of integration with the local economy has declined even further (Roberts and Tardanico in this volume; Wilson 1992).

With NAFTA, a new geographic strategy for maquiladoras has become possible. NAFTA regulations allow gradually increasing sales by maquiladoras to Mexico's internal market. In the year 2001, when the maquiladoras will gain unlimited access to the Mexican market, the maquiladora rubric itself will become obsolete, and the sector's plants will begin to function under the same rules as other plants. Responding to the combination of this change and new North American content requirements, the far-sighted maquiladoras have already seen the desirability of creating responsive local supplier bases to enhance their competitiveness in supplying the Mexican and U.S. markets. These maquiladoras are nonetheless a distinct minority, both along the border and in the nation's interior.

In the state of Yucatán, which has attracted a small but steady sector of mainly traditional low-technology maquiladoras, there is very little recognition of NAFTA as either threat or opportunity. Only the most modern plants are gearing up for competition in the integrated North American market, while lagging, labor-intensive plants face increasing competition from cheaper labor sites in Central America. For Yucatán to develop a dynamic internal economy and to prosper from international trade, it must move beyond its position as a low-wage mecca by establishing some quality-oriented niche.

Economic Development in Yucatán: An Overview

The Yucatán Peninsula, famous as a center of both ancient and contemporary Mayan culture, includes the states of Yucatán, Campeche, and Quintana Roo. Since the Spanish conquest in the sixteenth century, when the city of Mérida became the seat of regional colonial government, Yucatán has dominated the peninsula politically and economically. The state of Yucatán has more than double the population of its peninsular neighbors and has the highest levels of infrastructural and industrial development. The state is also the regional center for government, medical, legal, and educational services. In all three states, the tertiary economy (commerce and services) is the principal source of employment. Tourism is a vital source of revenue for Quintana Roo, particularly around Cancún and Cozumel. Fishing and petroleum extraction are key economic activities in Campeche. In Yucatán state, 47% of jobs are concentrated in commerce and services, with some 25% of employment generated by manufacturing and 27% by agriculture (see Table 5.1). Yucatán's main exports are honey, henequen (now contributing 18% of all export value), concentrated orange juice, apparel, stone items, marine products, furniture, and hammocks (INEGI 1993).

Yucatán provides a contemporary story of conscious state policy to revitalize a declining local economy by reinserting it in the global economy on the basis of cheap manufacturing labor. The state government launched a controversial international publicity campaign in the 1980s to lure U.S. investors with advertisements of labor costs below one dollar an hour. This policy can claim some success, especially in attracting maquiladoras that produce for and buy from plants in the southeastern United States. Yet, the number of

Table 5.1
Distribution of Economically Active Population in Yucatán by Sectors, 1990

		No. Employed
Primary Sector	27.0%	
Agriculture, livestock, hunting, fishing		110,057
Total		**110,057**
Secondary Sector	24.5%	
Mining		451
Oil and gas production		534
Manufacturing industry		62,986
(Maquiladora industry)		(3,423)
Electricity and water		3,095
Construction		32,866
Total		**99,896**
Tertiary Sector	46.5%	
Commerce		56,103
Communications and transportation		14,640
Financial services		6,142
Public administration and defense		13,451
Social and community services		35,896
Professional and technical services		5,963
Restaurant and hotel services		13,587
Personal services and maintenance		43,552
Total		**189,334**
Other	2.0%	8,050
Total Economically Active Population		**407,337**

Source: INEGI (1993).

maquiladoras in Yucatán remains modest, despite studies by the international consulting firms Ernst & Young and Plant Location International that rank the state among the 10 most competitive regions in the world for direct foreign investment (INBC 1994b, 3). Moreover, the benefits to the local population have been limited.

Since the late 1800s, the henequen industry has shaped both economic structure and development strategy in Yucatán. The production and export of henequen, a fibrous plant used to make twine and rope, generated vast wealth for the local elite and represented a significant source of foreign exchange for the national economy. Based on a large pool of cheap agricultural labor, Yucatán depended heavily on henequen exports to the U.S. and Europe. By the 1970s, however, international competition in the fiber industry and the development of plastics and synthetic rope precipitated the decline of henequen production.

In the early 1980s, Yucatán faced a clear need for economic restructuring through an alternative development strategy. Federal and state planners sought to revive the economy by exploiting the state's comparative advantages in tourism and industry. Since Yucatán was already more industrialized than neighboring Campeche and Quintana Roo, the new phase of development policy focused on marketing the state as the industrial frontier of the Yucatán Peninsula.

The recruitment of maquiladoras has been a key element of the effort to integrate Yucatán into the international production system. What follows is an analysis of the history of the maquiladora program in Yucatán and its impact on local economic development (see Appendices 5.1 and 5.2). How is the growth of the maquiladora industry affecting the state economy in terms of employment, technological advancement, and linkages with local business? What role does the state play in the context of free trade and regional economic integration? And how can local policy foster development that benefits the Yucatecan population?

The Maquiladora Industry in Yucatán

Although maquiladoras emerged as part of the Border Industrialization Program in the mid-1960s and have long been associated with the northern border region, maquiladoras have also existed in Mexico's interior since the early 1970s (Sklair 1989, 139–46). By 1973, most restrictions limiting the geographical location of maquiladoras had been removed, and in 1974 there reportedly were eighty-three plants in states other than those along the northern border. The recession of 1974–1975 reduced this number to forty-one. Yucatán was among the first interior states to house maquiladoras; as early as 1972, there were two plants in Mérida. These two plants, however, apparently did not survive the subsequent recession. As part of the more recent campaign to attract export-platform manufacturing, 1980 is now recognized as the year when the first maquiladora opened in Yucatán (Cruz Pacheco 1993, 30); Ormex, a manufacturer of orthodontic material and a subsidiary of Ormco Corporation of Glendora, California, opened in Yucatán in March 1980 and was the state's sole maquiladora until 1985. The largest growth spurt in Yucatán's export-assembly industry came at the end of the 1980s (see Table 5.2).

The maquiladora industry that has developed in Yucatán thus far consists of approximately twenty-seven plants. Among these are assemblers of apparel (41%), jewelry (19%), and sporting goods (11%). Additional plants assemble marine products, orthodontic materials, and metal components. All ten of

Table 5.2
Evolution of Yucatán Maquila Industry, 1980–1994

Year	No. of Plants	No. of Employees	Average No. of Employees
1980	1	n/a	n/a
1985	3	n/a	n/a
1986	4	374	94
1987	10	897	90
1988	12	1,624	135
1989	12	2,173	181
1990	26	3,423	132
1991	32	4,400	138
1992	31	4,929	159
1993	26	5,100	196
1994[a]	27	5,532[a]	205

[a]As of April 1994.
Source: Cruz Pacheco (1993); and INEGI (1994).

the apparel plants opened between 1985 and 1993, and the five jewelry manufacturers began operating between 1989 and 1991. The single electronics plant arrived in 1992. Plant size varies widely: one metal mechanics company has only eight employees, while the largest maquiladora in Yucatán—a subsidiary of Maidenform—employs 1,210 people in two plants. Yucatán maquiladoras tend to be medium-sized businesses, averaging 196 employees. The apparel plants are larger, with an average of 298 employees per plant (see Table 5.3). Overall, 74% of the plants are foreign owned, the majority by U.S. parent companies; Canada, Italy, and Hong Kong are represented by three of the garment assembly plants. Since 1991, local companies have been allowed to apply for partial maquiladora status. According to the Federal Secretariat of Commercial and Industrial Development (SECOFI), seven Yucatecan companies have since obtained permits to operate as maquiladoras.

The Roles of the Public and Private Sectors

Both the state and federal governments have promoted the growth of export-platform manufacturing in Yucatán. As part of a strategy of national industrial decentralization, federal legislation passed on August 15, 1983, encouraged the location of maquiladoras outside the country's principal manufacturing centers, providing incentives such as allowing the sale of up to 40% of interior maquiladora production on the domestic market. The 1984 Regional Program of Henequen Reorganization and Integrated Development, designed by the federal government and Yucatán state agencies, aimed at

Table 5.3
Characteristics of Yucatán Maquiladoras by Sector, 1993–1994

Sector	No. of Plants	% Foreign Owned	Average No. of Employees per Plant	Average % Female Workers
Apparel	11	64	298	84
Jewelry	5	100	158	48
Sporting Goods	3	50	114	n/a
Orthodontic Material	2	58	175	80
Electronics	1	100	340	65
Other	5	n/a	40	n/a

Source: Survey by authors, July 1994; and SECOFI (1994).

diversifying the state's economy while establishing alternative sources of employment for displaced henequen workers. Capitalizing on Yucatán's strategic location near the United States (closer to the U.S. southeastern seaboard than to the U.S.-Mexico border) and the low cost of labor, the plan promoted export-oriented manufacturing. It anticipated that, in addition to generating local employment, the maquiladoras would stimulate the growth and diversification of local industry, exerting a multiplier effect on the structure of the state economy through linkages with local suppliers.

Private capital also played a key role in developing the maquiladora program. Between 1984 and 1987, groups of local investors joined forces with government agencies in planning the construction of infrastructure for maquiladoras. The so-called Grupo Yucatán, comprised of twenty Yucatecan entrepreneurs and backed by national banks such as Nacional Financiera and Banco de Comercio Exterior, helped to finance infrastructure projects (Castilla and Torres 1994, 291; Sklair 1989, 153). Anticipating an influx of new plants, the public and private sectors invested heavily in the development of industrial parks, which came to occupy more than 1,600 acres (Mexican Investment Board 1994, 22–23).

Three industrial parks in Yucatán are equipped with full infrastructure. The Felipe Carrillo Puerto Industrial Park and the Yucatán Industrial Park accommodate several plants on the outskirts of Mérida, and Yukalpeten Industrial Park, designed for marine-related industry, is situated 6 kilometers from downtown Progreso, the regional port. The ACIM complex, which lies just outside the Mérida airport and is the newest of Yucatán's parks, still lacks some services.

In an effort to decentralize local manufacturing, Yucatán's Department of Industrial and Commercial Development has planned to add industrial sites elsewhere in the state. A park containing a women's apparel assembly plant is located in the eastern city of Valladolid, and two garment assembly plants are currently operating in Motul. According to Arturo López Alonzo, director of the state's international trade promotion activities, plans are also underway to construct an industrial park in Izamal. However, 90% of Yucatán's maquiladoras are concentrated in the municipality of Mérida (INEGI 1993, 350).

Yucatán's Maquiladora Economy in National Perspective

Yucatán's maquiladoras are "traditional," defined by Wilson (1992) and Gereffi (1992) as predominantly labor-intensive operations with a high proportion of female workers, low worker productivity, and low wages. Table 5.4 shows the low level of value added per worker (a measure of productivity) in Yucatán's maquiladoras compared to those in other regions of Mexico. The table also shows the high percentage of female line workers and the low earnings per worker compared to maquiladoras elsewhere in the country. Yucatán falls into Mexico's lowest wage tier. Nationwide, the average hourly wage for Mexican manufacturing workers was $2.17 in 1991, roughly twice that of Yucatán's export-platform workers.

By far the single largest group of employees in these plants is young women. As of April 1994, 5,532 people were employed by Yucatán maquiladoras, 64%

Table 5.4
Yucatán Maquiladora Industry in National Perspective[a]

	No. Plants	No. Employed[b]	No. Line Workers	% Female (of Line Workers)	Valued Added[c]	Valued Added per Worker	Wages Paid to Workers[d]	Wages per Workers
Baja California Norte	745	116,745	96,220	54	1,252,949	13.0	83,208	864.8
Chihuahua	308	174,809	141,425	59	395,768	2.8	97,687	690.7
Tamaulipas	298	103,762	82,737	62	1,180,203	14.3	75,806	916.2
Sonora	177	45,659	36,865	57	417,051	11.3	26,114	708.4
Coahuila	175	50,401	42,586	60	372,452	8.7	29,694	697.3
Nuevo León	84	23,339	19,128	61	278,766	14.6	12,946	676.8
Durango	53	8,694	7,758	72	56,733	7.3	4,260	549.1
Jalisco	42	9,204	6,950	69	215,491	31.0	6,285	904.3
México	30	3,753	2,959	74	59,208	20.0	2,250	760.4
Yucatán	27	5,532	4,658	76	30,529	6.6	2,379	510.9
Nation	2,059	568,530	464,270	60	6,001,630	12.92	3,448,727	763.6

[a]Data for number of plants, employees, line workers, % female, and wages are from April 1994.
[b]Includes technical and administrative employees as well as workers.
[c]Data for value added are the total from January–April 1994. Wages paid and value added are in thousands of new pesos.
[d]Amount is the average total of new pesos, April 1994.
Source: INEGI (1994).

of whom were women. The figure rises to 76% when only line workers, as opposed to technical and administrative personnel, are considered (INEGI 1994, 18). These rates are considerably higher than the national averages of 49% for employees in general and 60% for line workers only.

The high percentage of female workers reflects the predominance of apparel plants in Yucatán. The contribution of apparel plants to Mexico's nationwide maquiladora industry declined from 25% in 1975 to 15% in 1987 (Anderson 1990, 106). In Yucatán, however, apparel plants represent 41% of all maquiladoras and appear to be increasing in proportion. Six of the ten apparel maquiladoras in the state have opened within the last five years. Whereas the apparel sector accounts for only some 9% of total maquiladora employment nationwide, it represents nearly 60% of Yucatán's total maquiladora jobs (INEGI 1994). In Mexico and internationally, this sector is well known for having an above average share of women workers.

Yucatán's maquiladoras are essentially an export enclave. While they create local jobs and infuse foreign exchange into the state economy, they otherwise remain unconnected to local or national industry. The use of domestic inputs, which was expected to be higher in Yucatán than the northern border zone because of the distance between the former and U.S. suppliers, is just as low in Yucatán as along the northern border. Statewide, 99% of maquiladora inputs are imported, primarily from the United States (INEGI 1994, 30).

In our survey of fifteen Yucatán export-assembly plants (see Table 5.5 and Appendix 5.1), the majority indicated that inputs are purchased in the United States; 40% obtain most of their production materials from Florida, South Carolina, and other U.S. southern states. Industria Textil Maya, one of three 100% Mexican-owned apparel plants, receives all of the cloth for its production of women's clothing from North Carolina. Balmex, an intimate apparel maquiladora with headquarters in Winston-Salem, North Carolina, also relies on imports from that U.S. state. The one Hong Kong-owned apparel producer obtains cloth from Florida and South Carolina. A Yucatecan subsidiary of a sporting goods and hunting accessories manufacturer based in San Antonio, Texas, imports particle board and plastic from several U.S. southern states. And three of the five Yucatán jewelry plants have headquarters in Florida and receive some or most of their metal and gems from that state. Only one of the fifteen companies surveyed is currently subcontracting with other local firms.

Given the state's geographical isolation from Mexico's leading supplier clusters in Monterrey, Guadalajara, and Mexico City, several plant managers reported that it is much less expensive, more efficient, and more convenient for the plants to import production supplies. Mérida's number of potential

Table 5.5
Characteristics of Fifteen Yucatán Maquiladoras Surveyed, by Sector

Sector	No. of Plants	% Foreign Owned	Average No. of Employees per Plant	Average % Female Line Workers
Apparel	7	90	372	84
Jewelry	4	100	156	48
Sporting Goods	1	100	55	n/a
Orthodontic Material	2	58	175	80
Electronics	1	100	340	65

Source: Survey conducted July 1994 by authors.

suppliers is minuscule, and packaging material and office supplies are virtually the only locally available products that maquiladoras use.

Technologically, few Yucatán maquiladoras can be considered "flexible" producers (see Wilson 1992). Computer-controlled production machinery is rare across the board. However, the soft side of flexible production is somewhat more visible. Of the fifteen maquiladoras surveyed, four have workers performing more than one job (i.e., multiskilling). Ten of the firms surveyed use statistical process control, and eight rely on just-in-time inventory (with inputs coming from the United States via air transport).

The demands of international competition require increasing emphasis on quality, and all the firms surveyed indicated that workers were incorporated to some extent in the quality-control process. There is a disparity, though, between the rhetoric and the reality of quality control. While some companies are actively integrating workers at all levels into this aspect of production, the efforts of others appear superficial.[1] Quality control is of particular importance in the jewelry sector, where production adds a relatively high amount of value. This sector in Yucatán employs an average of 48% women, slightly less than the national average for maquiladoras overall.

The two plants that manufacture orthodontic material best exemplify Yucatán's flexible producers. Ormex, the state's oldest maquiladora, has substantially expanded its production since it began operations. This plant is the only offshore manufacturing facility of its California parent company. Workers in the Mérida plant rotate through the production process and are organized into committees responsible for diagnosing and evaluating problems. These committees change members every six months. The company has had such success with its quality control system that its output, 40% of which is exported to Europe, bypasses quality assessment in the company's U.S. headquarters and is sent directly overseas.

The second maquiladora in this sector, Reytek, manufactures dental crowns and bridges and has been in operation since 1987. Seventy percent of the Reytek plant's production is exported to the U.S. and Europe, while 30% is sold to dentists in the Mérida area. The plant's production is extremely rapid and efficient. Orders for products from U.S. dentists are filled and sent by overnight air service within three days. Workers are incorporated in problem diagnosis, machinery maintenance, and quality circles similar to those at Ormex. There is substantial investment in worker training, and product quality exceeds U.S. industry standards. The Reytek plant has grown rapidly and appears poised to meet the challenges of increasing North American market integration and global competition.

Sociodemographic Impact of the Maquiladoras

Maquiladoras tend not to employ heads of households, male or female. According to Yucatecan social scientist Luis Ramírez Carrillo, the income generated in maquiladora jobs generally benefits the workers themselves but not other family members. The women employed in export-assembly firms usually stop working after a relatively short period of time, without having acquired substantive training that can later be applied to other jobs. Since workers do not typically stay in export-assembly employment into middle age, such work has not dramatically affected family roles or dynamics (Ramírez interview with author).

Such employment does not seem to be a pull factor for urban migration, either. The state of Yucatán's population is highly urban. In 1990, 41% of its 1.4 million people lived in Mérida, up from 28% in 1970 and 36% in 1980. The percentage of people living in cities with populations greater than 10,000 grew from 38 to 52% between 1970 and 1980. By 1990, although the average annual urban growth rate had slowed compared to the previous decade, 58% of the state's population lived in large cities (INEGI 1993; Reyes Pérez 1994, 68–69).

Mérida is by far the most populous city in the state, with more than ten times the population of the next largest city, Tizimin. It is, however, difficult to correlate the state's contemporary pattern of urbanization directly to the growth of the maquila industry. The majority of the sector's workers live in Mérida and surrounding communities. They do not commute from rural areas for work, nor do they seem to move to Mérida specifically in search of export-assembly employment. The small size of Yucatán's maquiladora industry has restricted its local demographic impact. This situation contrasts with that of the northern border zone, where migration is integrally tied to the maquiladora boom (Ramírez interview with author; Roberts and Tardanico in this volume; Sklair 1989, 156–66).

Assessment of the Current Maquiladora Program

The growth of Yucatán's export-platform industry during the past decade has not proceeded without setbacks. Despite heavy investments in infrastructure, the industry remains deficient in this respect. Industrial Polygon, one of the first local parks constructed to accommodate maquiladoras, closed shortly after the installation of several plants. Three of the five companies in the Polygon canceled activity in the state altogether, apparently because of inadequate infrastructure and poor utility service. The park's other two plants relocated elsewhere in the Mérida area. Indeed, at least half the maquiladoras operating in the state of Yucatán are located outside the industrial parks. All of the jewelry plants and several other small plants have chosen stand-alone, central urban locations. At least nine of the maquiladoras that came to Yucatán in the late 1980s are no longer operating in the state. All but one of the electronics manufacturers, initially an important group for the state's economy, have closed. And at least twenty companies that have been granted maquiladora status in Yucatán have, for unknown reasons, declined to locate there (Castilla and Torres 1994, 293–94).

There are several drawbacks to operating in Yucatán. Despite the low cost of labor and proximity to the United States, the state's business setting is not hospitable for many companies. Two of the drawbacks most frequently cited by plant managers are the high cost of telecommunications and electricity and poor transportation facilities. The distance between the industrial parks and the outlying communities where most workers live is a cause of absenteeism and employee turnover. Although state officials boast of Yucatán's low employee turnover rate relative to the rate on Mexico's northern border, every one of the seven plant managers interviewed in the Yucatán Industrial Park complained of high absenteeism and/or turnover and the inadequacy of transportation for workers. Some companies are providing workers with transportation funds as an incentive to decrease absenteeism.

The Port of Progreso, 34 kilometers north of Mérida, was expected to be of great value to the state in supporting both tourism and international trade. It has two maneuvering terminals, one with a depth of 16 feet, the other 24 feet. According to plant managers and economic analysts, however, such depth is inadequate for large ships, and the port must be improved before it can be internationally competitive. Most plants rely exclusively on air transport. Here too, although development officials tout the short travel time to cities in the U.S. South, Yucatán appears unprepared for large volumes of business travel. Currently, only one airline flies from Mérida to Miami and New Orleans, and two airlines fly to Houston.

Another hindrance for some companies is the 2% payroll tax on Yucatecan maquiladoras. Other Mexican state governments also levy this tax, but border states such as Baja California Norte allow deferment of payroll taxes for several years in order to encourage foreign investment. The Yucatán Maquiladora Association has been lobbying the state government to reduce or renegotiate the tax (Alpizar interview with author).

For some companies, Yucatán is indeed a propitious location. Most of the managers interviewed are essentially content with the state's business conditions and said they would choose Yucatán again. The area is clearly less saturated with maquiladoras than the northern border zone, and Yucatán's labor force is cheaper, less mobile, and less politically organized. (Only one maquiladora in the state is unionized.) The state is also a more convenient location for companies with headquarters in the U.S. South, where eight of the fifteen plants surveyed have parent companies. Four Yucatán maquiladoras have parent companies in Florida (two in Miami, one in Ellenton, and one in Sunrise/Fort Lauderdale). Four others are based in Atlanta, North Carolina, and Texas (Houston and San Antonio). Foreign and Mexican managers also cite the cultural and physical attractions of the Yucatán Peninsula, as well as Mérida's high quality of life, as advantages to locating in the state. Indeed, several maquiladoras appear to be thriving in Yucatán. David Alpizar, president of the Yucatán Maquiladora Association, cautions that a future local boom in the industry like that of the late 1980s remains uncertain. In the meantime, however, the existing plants are committed to remaining in Yucatán and plan on expanding their local activities.

A clear failure of the local maquiladora program has been in employing displaced henequen workers. The plants do not appear to be alleviating the important problem of rural unemployment, and there is no indication that a notable percentage of their employees were previously employed by the henequen industry (Castilla and Torres 1994, 303). The plants do provide jobs, but they can hardly be relied upon to resolve the state's unemployment problems. Maquiladoras account for only 9% of all manufacturing jobs in Yucatán, compared to 11% of the nation's total manufacturing employment and 26% in the northern border states (Gereffi 1994, 3).

The industry is also of limited benefit in employing the technicians and professionals graduating from Yucatán universities. In 1989, 54% of Yucatán's maquiladora employees in managerial positions were Mexican, and of these, 70% were from Yucatán state (Ramírez 1993). Apparently, however, the small number of maquiladoras in the area has been unable to absorb a significant percentage of the state's technical and professional graduates (Roberts and Tardanico in this volume). The plants are not supporting or stimulating wider local industrial development. Their greatest economic contribution remains the generation of foreign exchange.

The Yucatán State Government's Role in International Trade Promotion

In recent years, the Yucatán state government has broadened the scope of its export-led development strategy, expanding its efforts to market the area as a strategic center for a wide range of international businesses. The Yucatán International Business Development Center, which opened in January 1994, advertises the area as a prime investment site for foreign businesses interested in taking advantage of the NAFTA-based increase in trade opportunities. Located in the Yucatán Industrial Park, the business center serves as the headquarters of a state effort to globalize the Yucatán economy by promoting local international business contacts and foreign trade. Jointly funded by the State of Yucatán, local universities, and Mexico's National Science and Technology Council, the center functions as a branch of the state office of commercial and industrial development. It evolved partly as a result of cooperation with a wide variety of U.S. economic development initiatives.

The center has focused its promotional activities on the U.S. South. It has signed an accord with the Beacon Council of Miami, Florida (a nonprofit organization promoting economic development in South Florida), agreeing to cooperative projects involving business networking, matchmaking, trade missions, joint ventures, and technology transfers. Agreements are also being developed with city authorities in Miami and Tampa, Florida, and in Mobile, Alabama. At least ten other cities in Florida, Illinois, Mississippi, Louisiana, and South Carolina have expressed interest in collaborating with the center (INBC 1994a).

The center intends to provide potential foreign investors with virtually any needed service, from "business culture" counseling to assistance in navigating local government requirements. Its facility maintains a database of potential local joint venture partners and assists international companies with importing, exporting, trade-show participation, distribution, licensing, and subcontracting. The facility office also includes an incubator program[2] designed to promote economic development through support for upgraded local technology. Small, nascent technology-based companies, Mexican or foreign, are provided with low-rent space and office services in addition to the center's other services. The incubator program currently houses one company and has space available for twenty-four businesses. It is a member of the U.S. National Association of Business Incubators and the Mexican Association of Business Incubators and Industrial Parks.

Small-Business Assistance

A salient feature of the Yucatán economy is the predominance of small-scale enterprise. *Microenterprises*—defined by the Federal Secretariat of Commercial and Industrial Development (SECOFI) as those employing fifteen people or less and having net annual sales below $300,000—are the vast majority of the state's manufacturing industry. In 1988, 92% of Yucatán's nearly 4,000 industrial establishments were microbusinesses. ("Small" enterprises are defined as those employing up to one hundred people and having net annual sales not greater than $3 million. "Medium-sized" enterprises employ no more than two hundred and fifty people and have net annual sales of no more than $6.5 million.) Microfirms in Yucatán provide 33% of all local manufacturing employment, but only 11% of manufacturing wages. In contrast, the seventeen large manufacturing firms (representing only 0.5% of the total manufacturing sector) contribute 40% of manufacturing wages. Together, small and medium-sized businesses constitute 7.5% of local firms, providing 43% of employment and 49% of manufacturing wages in the area (INEGI 1993).

For both foreign and Mexican micro- to medium-sized enterprises in Yucatán, the state branch of SECOFI provides the primary source of technical assistance and counseling. Its local representatives are currently working with several groups of microbusinesses in Mérida and rural areas. One group of rural entrepreneurs, who produce shoes, is developing a sales catalog and plans to begin exporting to Costa Rica. Another group of twenty-four microbusinesses is banding together to apply jointly for a federal loan. Manuel Pereira, a SECOFI small-business counselor, believes that Yucatán's smaller enterprises will gradually benefit from free trade through increased access to markets and inputs. However, he emphasizes that local business attitudes and technological capabilities need to advance and that small entrepreneurs must become better organized and more reliant on modern production methods.

NAFTA's Anticipated Impact on Yucatán Maquiladoras

Most of the export-platform plant managers surveyed in Yucatán (73%) expect that NAFTA will have little or no effect on their businesses. Most of them recognize the likelihood of increasing competition, particularly for cheap labor, but they do not regard North American market integration as a threat. Twenty-seven percent predicted that NAFTA will be positive in the long term for southeast Mexico and the country as a whole. Several managers reported that NAFTA has facilitated the importing of inputs and decreased the amount of paperwork and the weight of bureaucratic regulations that were previous obstacles to trade. None of those interviewed expressed negative opinions concerning NAFTA or worried about its impact.

For the "new" maquiladoras, NAFTA will bring expanded opportunities for lucrative participation in the integrated North American market. Managers of the more modern export-platform plants in Yucatán are well aware of the ramifications of free trade for their businesses and believe that they are prepared for successful international competition. The future for the older-style plants, on the other hand, appears less promising. Insofar as wage rates eventually rise in Mexico, the plants for whom cheap labor is the sole motivation for being in Yucatán may be forced to close or move to neighboring low-wage countries. According to Alpizar, some foreign companies already prefer Central American locations to Mexico. "It is of little value for the state to generate grand campaigns promoting the image of Yucatán as a site for maquiladora location if the costs of production are high compared to those in Central America," he points out. "Guatemala and Honduras, in addition to Costa Rica, are now obtaining maquiladora contracts originally destined for Yucatán" (Alpizar interview with author).

Conclusions and Implications for Public Policy

If Yucatán is to parlay international trade into a dynamic local economy, then it must move beyond its current position as a low-wage mecca. Select segments of manufacturing in Yucatán, particularly some maquiladoras, are using relatively advanced technology and flexible production systems. Although the Yucatán economy is not yet anchored in export-platform activities, these hold the greatest potential to lead the local economy to an export model based on advances in technology, skill, income, and living standards. Nevertheless, progress in this direction will be possible only if the plants broaden their local transaction networks and increase their local economic linkages (see Wilson 1992).

Yucatán ranks low on the global commodity chain (Gereffi 1994, and in this volume). Its maquiladoras are not creating local supplier networks, and a government policy based on recruiting foreign companies without facilitating their connection to the local economy will do little to promote regional development. Compared to Mexico's northern frontier, Yucatán is at a major disadvantage in supplying the domestic market, which is concentrated in Mexico City, Guadalajara, and Monterrey. The minority of Yucatecan maquiladoras that target the integrated North American market should be cultivated by the government with the goal of upgrading local infrastructure, technology, skills, and linkages. As long as Yucatán's foreign companies emphasize low wages and low-skill jobs, the state's manufacturing industry will remain mired in traditional export-processing. It will also run the distinct risk of losing ground to other low-wage, low-skill locales in the Americas and worldwide.

Appendix 5.1
Maquiladoras in Yucatán

Apparel

Balmex*
Createx*
Doulton de México*
Industrias Mayafiel
Industrias Oxford de Mérida*
Industria Textil Maya*
Manufactura de Ropa Meridana
Manufactura de Especializadas de Exportación
Ning Bo Ace Mexican Apparel
Produce Mexico*
Vogue Dessous*

Electronics

Grupo Ravelli Electronics*

Jewelry

Dinastía Mexicana
Industrias Goldmex*
Joyas de Exportación*
Manotec*
Plainco*

Orthodontic Material

Ormex*
Reytek International*

Sporting Goods

Artículos de Caza San Angelo*
Mexgloves
Saxon de Yucatán

Textile

Milltex

Others

Ladcomex (metal components)
Manufactura Internacional Marina (fiberglass yachts)
Perfiles Cominssa (drapes)
Tiburón de Tierra (marine products)

*Surveyed by authors, July 1994.
Sources: INEGI (1994) and Yucatán Department of Industrial and Commercial Development.

Secretariat of Commerce and Industrial Development (SECOFI)

Lic. Raúl Bandala, Yucatán Office Director
Ing. Manuel Pereira, Industry Manager
Ing. Jesús Carrillo, Commerce Manager
Licda. Lorena Vera, Manager of Economic and Statistical Analysis

Yucatán Department of Industrial and Commercial Development

Ing. Arturo López, Director of International Trade Promotion

Yucatán International Business Development Center/Business Incubator

Ing. Arturo López, Director
Licda. Nancy Conroy, International Relations Director

Yucatán Maquiladora Association

David Alpizar, President
Lic. Román Zavaletta, Manager

Secretariat of Social Development (SEDESOL)

Lic. Raúl Casares, Yucatán Regional Delegate

National Solidarity Program (PRONASOL)

Ing. Rubén Leirana, State Coordinator

Autonomous University of Yucatán

Lic. Raúl Vela, Professor of Economics
Dr. Luis Ramírez, Coordinator: Centro de Investigaciones Regionales,
    Unidad de Ciencias Sociales
Lic. José Torres, Lecturer in International Trade
Lic. Carlos Sosa, Lecturer in Economics and Public Administration

References

Anderson, Joan B. 1990. Maquiladoras in the Apparel Industry. In *The Maquiladora Industry: Economic Solution or Problem?* ed. Khosrow Fatemi. New York: Praeger Publishers.

Castilla Ramos, Beatriz, and Beatriz Torres Góngora. 1994. Un nuevo impulso a la industria maquiladora. In *Yucatán: De cara al siglo XXI*, eds. José Luis Sierra and G. de Jesús Huchim. Mérida, Yucatán: Compañía Editorial de la Península.

Cruz Pacheco, Jesús. 1993. Desarrollo histórico de las maquiladoras en Yucatán. *Cuadernos de economía* 40. Mérida: Universidad Autónoma de Yucatán.

Department of Industrial and Commercial Development, State of Yucatán. 1993. *Yucatán: The New Frontier for Business.* Mérida, Yucatán: Department of Industrial and Commercial Development.

Gereffi, Gary. 1992. Mexico's Maquiladora Industries and North American Integration. In *North America Without Borders?* ed. Stephen Randall. Calgary: University of Calgary Press.

———1994. Mexico's Maquiladoras in the Context of Economic Globalization. Unpublished paper. Department of Sociology, Duke University, North Carolina.

Glasmeier, Amy, Amy Kays, and Jeffery Thompson. 1993. *When Low Wages Are Not Enough Anymore: The Implications of Globalization on Rural Branch Plants.* Final Report to the Appalachian Regional Commission, the Aspen Institute, and the Economic Development Administration. Institute for Policy Research and Evaluation, Pennsylvania State University.

Instituto Nacional de Estadística Geográfica e Informática (INEGI). 1993. *Yucatán Statistical Yearbook.* Mérida, Yucatán: INEGI.

———. 1994. *Estadística de la industria maquiladora de exportación.* Mérida, Yucatán.

International Business Development Center (INBC). 1994a. *Business Center Newsletter.* Mérida, Yucatán: INBC.

———. 1994b. *Yucatán Development Update.* Mérida, Yucatán: INBC.

Mexican Investment Board. 1994. *Economic Overview of the State of Yucatán.* Mérida: Department of Industrial and Commercial Development, State of Yucatán.

Oliveira, Orlandina de, and Brigida Garcia. 1997. Mexico: Socioeconomic Transformation and Urban Labor Movements. In *Global Restructuring, Employment, and Social Inequality in Urban Latin America*, eds. Richard Tardanico and Rafael Menjívar Larín. Coral Gables, Fla.: The North-South Center at the University of Miami; Boulder, Colo.: Lynn Rienner Publishers.

Ramírez, Luis Alfonso. 1993. El escenario de la industrialización en Yucatán. *Comercio Exterior*, February.

Reyes Pérez, Jorge. 1994. La dinámica del desarrollo urbano reciente. In *Yucatán: De cara al siglo XXI.* eds. José Luis Sierra and G. de Jesús Huchim. Mérida, Yucatán: Compañía Editorial de la Península.

Secretaría de Comercio y Fomento Industrial (SECOFI). 1994. *Programa de política industrial y comercio exterior*. México, D.F.: SECOFI.

Sklair, Leslie. 1989. *Assembling for Development*. Boston: Unwin Hyman.

Wilson, Patricia A. 1992. *Exports and Local Development: Mexico's New Maquiladoras*. Austin: University of Texas Press.

———. 1994. Maquiladoras and NAFTA: The Great Divide. Unpublished paper. Department of Community and Regional Planning, University of Texas at Austin.

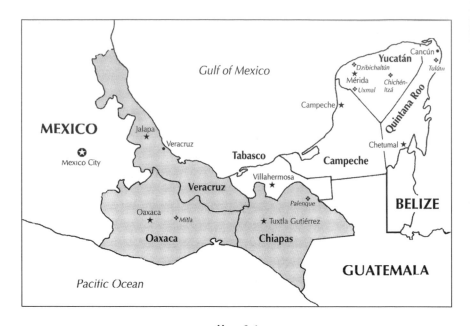

Map 6.1
States of Veracruz, Oaxaca, and Chiapas
❖   Archaeological Site

6

Politico-Economic Restructuring and Mexico's Small Coffee Farmers

Robert Porter

Economic crisis and neoliberal reforms have transformed rural Mexico since the 1980s. In this setting, economic restructuring in Mexico's coffee sector is affecting more than three million people, mostly in poor indigenous communities scattered throughout the country's mountainous coffee-growing areas, especially in the southern states of Chiapas, Veracruz, and Oaxaca. What will neoliberal reform and globalization mean for the hundreds of thousands of small coffee farmers and their families in these areas, as well as for their development prospects in general?

Mexico's coffee sector has undergone dramatic changes since the 1980s, as market reforms and new institutional frameworks replaced older forms of state intervention. Mexico provides an excellent example of the effects of changing patterns of global trade on small farmers, because 92% of its coffee producers are small farmers who hold no more than 5 hectares of land. Of particular concern are the constraints on, as well as opportunities for, small farmers under the restructuring of agricultural markets and how small coffee farmers have responded to changing circumstances.

Not only manufacturing but also agriculture in Mexico has been profoundly reoriented, filling new export market niches during the last decade or so. Mexican coffee, although a traditional export crop, exemplifies this tendency. Mexican coffee has found a niche in the growing U.S. specialty (gourmet) coffee market, providing, for instance, quality beans for Starbucks Coffee Company and the flavoring for Ben & Jerry's coffee-flavored ice creams. Such market niches for high-quality, high-value products are a feature of globalization, as changing consumption patterns reshape commodity chains[1] (McMichael 1995; Talbot 1997; Smith 1996).

A commodity chain approach (Gereffi and Korzeniewicz 1994) offers valuable insights into not only the constraints on but also the opportunities for small coffee farmers and their producer unions. Where along the coffee commodity chain can producer unions gain control from private intermediaries? Where does corporate control limit their opportunities? How does the restructuring of state, national, and subnational institutions affect control over different nodes of a commodity chain? The prospects of small farmers under economic restructuring are intimately related to their ability to scale up the coffee commodity chain and to capitalize their producer unions. Focusing on who controls which stages of a commodity chain sheds light on who is winning and who is losing under pro-market reforms.

I organize this chapter as follows: First, I present an overview of the international coffee economy, with special attention to the commodity chains associated with the Mexican case. Second, I examine government macroeconomic and sectoral policies that have influenced Mexico's coffee growers, with emphasis on the shifting institutional setting of Mexico's coffee sector and its impact on small farmers. Third, I compare the role of coffee producer unions across Mexico's variable local contexts to explain divergent consequences of market reforms for small farmers. Finally, I conclude by assessing the theoretical implications of the case of Mexican coffee for the distributional consequences of economic market-oriented reforms and international market integration.

My most basic finding is that the impact of economic restructuring on small coffee producers has not been uniform. Paradoxically, market reforms and institutional restructuring have created opportunities for some small coffee farmers even as most have faced severe hardships. Unexpectedly, the reforms implemented in certain southern Mexican states have opened up opportunities for some coffee producer unions, creating the political space for public-private cooperation. Moreover, producer unions in less favorable climates have managed to succeed under market reforms, owing to the unions' flexible and innovative strategies. Such strategies shed light on how other small coffee farmers may be able to overcome collective action problems, scale up commodity chains, and survive in increasingly competitive markets.

Mexico and the International Coffee Market

The International Coffee Agreement (ICA) in Mexico 1980–1989

Mexico, along with almost all other major coffee-producing and coffee-consuming countries, participated in the International Coffee Agreement from 1962 to 1989. The International Coffee Organization (ICO), based in

London, monitored ICA's activities, which included stabilizing prices through restricting the supply of coffee on the world market. The ICO used export quotas as its major instrument to restrict supply, and prices for the ICA years generally fluctuated between $120 and $140 per 100 lbs. of coffee, considered a decent return for coffee growers.

ICA worked reasonably well from 1980 to 1989. The average price of Mexican prime-washed coffee for these ten years was $138.56 per 100 lbs. Graph 6.1 illustrates the robust coffee prices of 1980–1989 in contrast to 1990–1993, when coffee prices dropped to dangerously low levels for small coffee producers.

During the 1980s, Mexico produced 5.5% of the world's total coffee production, 4.5% of the world's coffee exports, and 4.6% of the total value of world coffee exports. Mexico emerged during this period as the world's fourth largest producing country and fifth largest coffee exporter. The country's coffee producing area grew by 70%, reaching 678,075 hectares by the decade's end. Mexico became the second largest exporter of the "other milds" variety of arabica coffee, which enjoyed increasing favor in world markets. Mexico's yields, however, remained low compared with those of most other coffee producing countries, averaging 11.90 *quintales* (46 kg.) per hectare.

Graph 6.1
Price of Mexican Prime Washed Coffee on N.Y. Futures Market

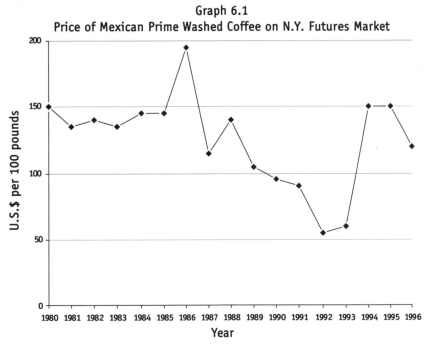

Source: International Coffee Organization (1996).

*The Collapse of ICA Export Quotas and the International Coffee Crisis
1990–1993*

While ICA worked reasonably well to stabilize international coffee prices, dis-agreements over export quotas and the growing popularity of free-trade poli-cies led to the agreement's abrogation in July 1989. An immediate result was a drop in prices, which devastated hundreds of thousands of smallholder coffee growers. The average monthly price of coffee dropped from $120 per 100 lbs. in June 1989 to $87.56 per 100 lbs. in July 1989. From 1990 to 1993, average yearly prices were $75.66 per 100 lbs., a 45% decrease from the 1980–1989 period. During the early 1990s these prices fell below many Mexican coffee growers' production costs of roughly $85 per 100 lbs., thus adversely affecting their livelihoods (Hernández and Celis 1994; García 1993). Graph 6.2 shows how the price drop affected Mexican coffee's foreign-exchange earnings.

The impact of this downswing was most severe for Mexico's small coffee farmers, who actually receive prices much lower than the price of green coffee on the international market. This is because small farmers are often forced to sell their coffee as raw, unprocessed beans to larger growers who process and resell the coffee to exporters. These larger coffee estate owners pay smallhold-ers roughly 13% of the international market price for their unprocessed, raw

Graph 6.2
Value of Mexican Green Coffee Exports

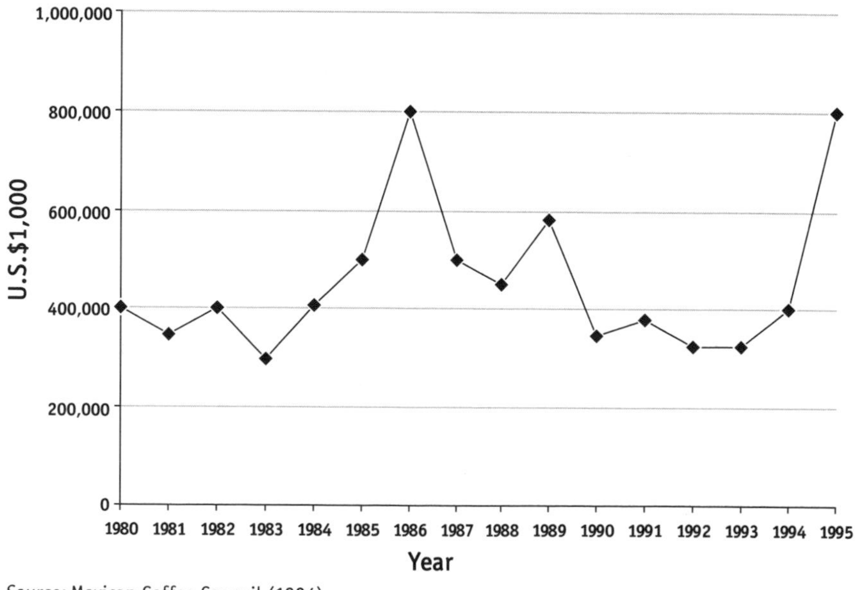

Source: Mexican Coffee Council (1994).

coffee.[2] Hence the incomes of small coffee farmers decreased markedly during the coffee crisis years (1990–1993), as the buyers of their beans reacted to changes in the world market by lowering prices for raw coffee. Because of their low yields, furthermore, many smallholders were unable to increase quantity to offset lower prices, as did larger growers. According to Neil Harvey (1996, 192), "small coffee producers suffered a 70 percent drop in income during this period." In desperation, many smallholders abandoned their coffee plots and migrated out of coffee regions (Hoffman 1992; García 1993). Others faced the challenge by diversifying their income strategies, shifting production into other crops or activities (Martínez Quezada 1995; Villafuerte Solís 1993).

Rebounding Coffee Prices 1994–1996

Mexican coffee export earnings started to rebound in 1994 because of rising prices, which increased by 107% over the previous year's average. The country's export revenues skyrocketed from $396 million in 1994 to $766 million in 1995, the second highest amount of coffee export earnings in Mexico's history. The average yearly price rose from $75.66 per 100 lbs. in 1990–1993 to $137.15 in 1994–1996, similar to the average during the ICA years.

Although Mexico's drastic devaluation of the peso in December 1994 made the country's coffee exports more competitive, high inflation and increasing costs for credit and fertilizers offset the potential gains from increased coffee prices, especially for small farmers. Due to their huge debts and low level of capitalization, most smallholder producer unions were much less able than larger growers to take advantage of the more favorable market conditions of the mid-1990s.

Mexico's Coffee Commodity Chain

Mexican coffee growers often receive as little as 30 cents a pound for coffee that is sold for $7–8 a pound to U.S. consumers, a price differential strongly related to control over the processing, roasting, and marketing of coffee beans (Griswold 1991). Coffee passes through a complex commodity chain from the time the coffee cherries are harvested until it reaches our cups. While transnational corporations such as Nestlé and General Foods continue to control much of the roasting, marketing, and final processing stages of the chain, smallholders have steadily gained control over various other nodes, including prior processing and financing. They have also challenged transnationals' monopoly over marketing and distribution within the growing specialty market.

Some important transactions take place prior to the harvesting of coffee, including the provision of credit and fertilizer. The prices that smallholders pay for these inputs play a key role in their final profit margins. In the past, large coffee growers often controlled these inputs and sold them to small coffee farmers at quite expensive prices. This was an area where the Mexican state intervened from 1973 to 1989, subsidizing inputs for roughly one-third of small producers during much of this period. As the state's role in the coffee sector has vastly diminished in the 1990s, input prices have skyrocketed for coffee growers.

Once farmers have obtained needed inputs and the coffee is harvested, a complex chain of agro-industrial processing begins. The first stage is called *wet-processing*. Immediately after harvesting the beans, smallholders separate the fleshy, red cherry from the bean inside by passing the coffee through a hand-driven depulper, usually located on the coffee farm or in a nearby community. Coffee cherries must be depulped as soon as possible (within twenty-four hours) after harvest, or else they begin to decompose. The coffee beans are then washed in fermentation tanks, a process that is important in determining the final quality of the bean. After washing, the beans are spread out on concrete patios for drying; depending on weather conditions, drying takes about a week.

After wet-processing, temporary storage, and transportation of the coffee to a regional collection center, the beans are ready for the next stage in the chain, called *dry-processing*, which requires more expensive machinery and larger agro-industrial units. During dry-processing, the thin, dry parchment skin that still covers the (now dry) coffee bean is removed by machinery, after which the beans are classified and sorted (also by machine) for sale. Once the beans are sorted, bagged, and ready for sale, they have reached the green coffee stage, which is how coffee is bought and sold on the international market.

Comparative prices received in 1995 for coffee as it was processed at different stages illustrate the importance of gaining control over these stages of the commodity chain. Small coffee farmers received only 3 pesos per kilo for unprocessed coffee cherries (*cereza* coffee), compared to 15 pesos per kilo for wet-processed coffee (*pergamino* coffee) and 22 pesos for dry-processed, or green coffee (Martínez 1995). Gaining control over these stages of the commodity chain means more income for small coffee farmers and less for private intermediaries.

Unlike the relatively inexpensive machinery required to wet-process coffee, the dry-processing centers require huge start-up costs. In 1993, for example, a regional coffee producer union in Guerrero projected that its new coffee-processing plant would cost $1.5 million (Lee 1993). Without collective action and the formation of larger producer unions, it is impossible for small coffee farmers to integrate vertically and sell their coffee at higher stages in the commodity chain. Gaining control of the dry-processing stage of the commodity chain has been a major hurdle for smallholders acting collectively.

Once coffee has been processed as green coffee, it is usually sold to exporters, or directly"to importers via sales contracts. The coffee is transported again, now from the dry-processing center to a railroad or dock, and most of it is shipped to the United States. Once the coffee arrives in consuming countries, it is bought by brokers who distribute it to roasters and retailers.

The roasting stage of the coffee commodity chain requires sophisticated techniques and expensive machinery and is almost totally controlled by consuming countries. In 1991, for example, only 10% of Mexican coffee was ground and roasted in Mexico. Since 40% of the value added for coffee occurs during grinding and roasting, this is a formidable barrier to small coffee farmers (Carlsen 1991; Smith 1996).

Processing the raw beans into instant coffee adds another 50% to the value of coffee. Within Mexico, since the 1960s transnational corporations have set up instant processing plants to be close to the raw material source (Talbot 1997). The level of technology required for processing green to instant coffee, however, is out of reach of most small coffee growers in Mexico, unless they form larger, vertically integrated enterprises such as regional producer unions. An instant coffee plant being constructed by such a union in Chiapas, for instance, is projected to cost $10 million, which only a large organization could finance (Heinegg and Ferroggiano 1996).

Changing consumption patterns are affecting Mexico's coffee sector. One of the characteristics of the new international coffee market since the collapse of ICA in 1989 has been the rapid growth of specialty, or gourmet, coffee consumption. As of 1997, the specialty coffee market had increased its share of the total U.S. coffee market to 35%, and it is still growing.[3] The meteoric rise of Starbucks Coffee Company illustrates this pattern within the United States (Smith 1996). This market niche is well suited for countries producing the highest quality arabica coffees, such as Colombia, Mexico, and Costa Rica. Certain regions within these countries are renowned for the high quality of their arabica coffee, a reputation that favorably positions them in the growing specialty market.

The organic-coffee market niche is also growing in consuming countries, allowing smallholders another point of entry into the lucrative international coffee trade (Griswold and Ward 1996). By 1994, organic coffee had captured 2 to 3% of the U.S. coffee market and is expected to increase its share to 5% by 1999. Mexico emerged as the world's leading organic-coffee exporter in the 1980s, with independent producer unions playing the key role within this growing niche.

Although Mexican producer unions are making only minor inroads into coffee roasting and instant coffee production, they are gradually gaining control over other stages of the commodity chain, allowing them to reap more of the value added. Since the early 1980s, one of the major strategies of Mexico's growing independent coffee producers' movement has been to gain control over more of these stages, especially processing, marketing, distribution, and finance. Numerous producer unions in Mexico's coffee regions now wet- and dry-process their own coffee, as well as market it abroad and finance production with their own credit unions. The growth of the specialty coffee market in the United States has created opportunities for small farmers to market their coffee directly to roasters, cutting out importers and distributors and improving smallholder incomes. The strategies of these producer unions may hold lessons for the thousands of still unorganized coffee farmers scattered throughout the mountains of southern Mexico.

Coffee Production Systems: Smallholders versus Large Estates

Although small farmers predominate, smallholder and large-estate production are Mexico's two general types of coffee farming. Larger coffee plantations, such as in the Soconusco region of Chiapas, are based on monocultural planting patterns, including intensive use of chemical fertilizers and pesticides (Villafuerte Solís 1993). These plantations hire seasonal workers from nearby highland areas, where labor is usually abundant. During the 1996 harvest, about 350,000 laborers worked on Mexico's coffee plantations (Paz Paredes 1995).

These coffee plantations usually have processing facilities as part of their vertically integrated operations. Large producers have access to credit through private banks and establish marketing arrangements with private brokers and traders. A mere 441 large coffee estates, half of them from Chiapas, produce a sizable share of Mexico's coffee crop. Less than 0.5% of Mexico's coffee growers produce roughly a third of the total coffee crop (Hernández 1991; Darling 1991).

Most of Mexico's small coffee farms are worked by family labor on small plots in highland areas. These coffee-producing families usually intercrop coffee trees with shade trees of various types, often banana or citrus. Most of these smallholders have diversified household economic strategies, combining subsistence corn production with their major cash crop: coffee. The concentration of small farmers in Mexico's coffee sector is striking in comparison with other coffee-producing countries, such as Brazil and Colombia. The prevalence of very small farms (< 5 hectares) as a percentage of total coffee farms is higher in Mexico (92%) than in any other Latin American country (Rice and Ward 1996; Hernández 1991) (see Table 6.1). Moreover, roughly two-thirds of producers

Table 6.1
Mexican Coffee Producers and Land Area Stratified by Plot Size

Coffee Plot Size (Hectares)	Producers	%	Coffee Land Area (Hectares)	%
0.1–2.0	203,924	70.18	258,330	33.88
2.1–5.0	64,330	22.14	227,816	29.88
5.1–10.00	16,928	5.83	128,133	16.80
10.01–20	4,049	1.39	61,538	8.07
20.01–50	902	0.31	28,765	3.77
50.01–100	256	0.09	18,971	2.49
100.01 +	185	0.06	38,940	5.11
Total	290,514	100	762,493	100

Source: INMECAFE (1992); Lorena Paz Paredes (1995).

working the smallest coffee plots (< 2 hectares) are ethnically indigenous; they are among the poorest of Mexico's rural poor.

Smallholders and large estates are often located within the same coffee region. In this setting, coffee estate owners often finance smallholders, or process and market their coffee, reaping the benefits of control over these stages of the commodity chain. Since most plantation owners are *Ladinos*, ethnic cleavages overlap class divisions within Mexico's coffee regions. Moreover, many of these larger coffee plantation owners in Chiapas, Oaxaca, and Veracruz exert substantial political clout within their respective states.

There is little variation in these distributions of small and large producers among Mexico's three most important coffee-producing states (Chiapas, Veracruz, and Oaxaca), as seen in Table 6.2. On the one hand, coffee farmers with plots smaller than five hectares make up 91% of all producers in Chiapas, 94% in Veracruz, and 89% in Oaxaca. On the other hand, growers with more than 20 hectares make up less than 1% of all coffee producers in each state. One of the few comparative differences is the greater portion of large estates (> 50 hectares) in Chiapas, where large growers form 0.28% of the total, compared with only 0.05% in Veracruz and 0.15% in Oaxaca. Chiapas's large estates also cover a larger proportion of this state's total coffee-growing area (14.5%) compared to Veracruz (2.5%) or Oaxaca (7.7%).

Government Policy in the Mexican Coffee Sector

The Mexican Coffee Institute (INMECAFE)
During the administration of Luis Echeverría (1970–1976), the government's role in the coffee sector changed markedly. In the context of massive waves of

Table 6.2

Coffee Producers and Coffee Land Area in Chiapas, Veracruz, and Oaxaca
Stratified by Plot Size

Coffee Plot Size	Chiapas		Veracruz		Oaxaca	
	Producers	Coffee Land Area (Ha.)	Producers	Coffee Land Area (Ha.)	Producers	Coffee Land Area (Ha.)
0.1–2.0	48,762 (66.1%)	66,725 (29.2%)	48,397 (71.9%)	59,309 (38.9%)	34,224 (61.9%)	47,757 (27.4%)
2.01–5	18,248 (24.7%)	65,149 (28.5%)	14,891 (22.1%)	52,013 (34.1%)	15,001 (27.1%)	54,707 (31.4%)
5.01–10	5,102 (6.91%)	38,709 (16.9%)	3,132 (4.65%)	22,993 (15.0%)	4,709 (8.52%)	35,828 (20.6%)
10.01–20	1,202 (1.63%)	17,803 (7.79%)	586 (0.87%)	8,994 (5.89%)	1,130 (2.04%)	17,466 (10.0%)
20.01–50	208 (0.28%)	6,703 (2.93%)	181 (0.26%)	5,637 (3.69%)	139 (0.25%)	4,612 (2.65%)
50.01–100	104 (0.14%)	7,945 (3.48%)	29 (0.04%)	1,959 (1.28%)	52 (0.09%)	4,002 (2.30%)
100+	116 (0.15%)	25,190 (11.0%)	11 (0.01%)	1,908 (1.25%)	36 (0.06%)	9,392 (5.41%)
Total	73,742 (100%)	228,254 (100%)	67,227 (100%)	152,457 (100%)	55,291 (100%)	173,765 (100%)

Source: INMECAFE (1992).

peasant mobilizations throughout the country, Echeverría challenged the hold of rural bosses in many indigenous coffee-producing regions through federal intervention based on increasing the powers of INMECAFE. This federal agency's role was widened from technical advising to regulating coffee production and marketing, as well as promoting productivity through access to credit. INMECAFE began to work with the National Bank for Rural Credit (BANRURAL) and the state-owned fertilizer agency (FERTIMEX) to provide cheap credit and fertilizer for Mexico's small coffee growers.

Small producers were organized into Unions of Economic Production and Marketing (UEPCs), which represented the federal government's attempt to incorporate small coffee farmers into the Mexican state's corporatist structure. Coffee farmers organized into UEPCs often received credit in kind (subsidized fertilizers) and repaid it with part of their coffee harvest. Coffee farmers participating in UEPCs were automatically affiliated with the National Campesino Confederation's (CNC) Federation of Coffee Producers.

Although its performance varied across the country's coffee regions, INMECAFE's role in providing credit, purchasing coffee at guaranteed prices, and setting up processing centers drove out many private intermediaries.

Large exporters, in fact, became principal opponents of INMECAFE, as it cut into their monopoly over coffee-processing and marketing. Indeed, INMECAFE purchased a substantial share of total coffee harvests from the early 1970s well into the 1980s, although this share dropped sharply during the period of economic crisis and neoliberal reform. This downward trend is depicted in Graph 6.3.

During its period of expanded powers, INMECAFE penetrated various nodes of the coffee commodity chain previously controlled by private middlemen, providing alternative channels whereby smallholders could reap more of the value added from coffee production. Regarding processing, for example, INMECAFE gave credit to smallholders so that they could purchase their own wet-processing machinery, including manual depulpers, fermentation tanks, and cement patios for drying beans in the sun. The agency also dry-processed smallholders' coffee at large INMECAFE-owned processing centers set up throughout Mexico's coffee regions. Finally, INMECAFE exported Mexican coffee abroad.

Macroeconomic policies also influenced the conditions of Mexico's coffee growers. During the 1980s, the peso depreciated in real terms, which helped Mexican exporters across the board, including the coffee sector. Moreover,

Graph 6.3
Percent of Mexican Coffee Purchased by Public Sector (INMECAFE)

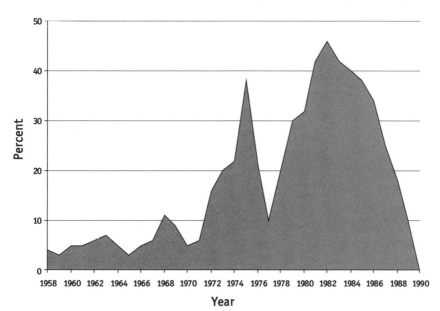

Source: Compiled from data in Nolasco (1985) and CMC (1994).

two key agricultural inputs, credit and fertilizer, were subsidized by the government during this period. BANRURAL provided small coffee farmers with loans below commercial interest rates, and FERTIMEX subsidized fertilizer prices for Mexico's agricultural producers in general. The combination of favorable world prices, a depreciated peso, and subsidized inputs favored the coffee sector as a whole during the 1980s.

While state penetration into the coffee sector improved the livelihoods of many smallholders, neoliberal technocrats increasingly perceived state agricultural agencies, such as INMECAFE, as inefficient during the economic crises of the 1980s. Once Mexico joined the General Agreement on Tariffs and Trade (GATT) in 1986, the administration of Miguel de la Madrid (1982–1988) deepened the liberalization of agriculture. Many state-run companies, such as FERTIMEX, the state tobacco firm (TABAMEX), and the state's sugar refineries (AZUCAR), were privatized.

The economic crisis and neoliberal reforms of the 1980s adversely affected Mexico's small coffee farmers, many of whom began mobilizing against INMECAFE. The agency became a unifying target for sit-ins, marches, and demonstrations. Accusations of corruption also weakened the agency's position. By 1989, small coffee farmers were among the many voices favoring the dissolution of INMECAFE.

The Critical Juncture in the Mexican Coffee Sector: The Collapse of ICA, the Dissolution of INMECAFE in 1989, and the Aftermath

The administration of Carlos Salinas de Gortari (1988–1994) accelerated the liberalization of Mexican agriculture. Michael Foley writes that in 1990

> tariffs on most [agricultural] products were dropped, subsidies on inputs (including credit) were withdrawn or sharply reduced, and the guarantee price was eliminated for all crops but maize and beans. The government's crop insurance program, Anagsa, was abolished, and the rural development bank, Banrural, announced that it would no longer service commercial growers and would target loans, at market rates, only to peasant growers whose operations were judged profitable. (1995, 62)

Cut loose from state tutelage, small producers throughout Mexican agriculture found themselves faced with foreign competition precisely when prices for their inputs were increasing and prices for their crops were decreasing.

In the coffee sector, at the same time that ICA was abrogated in 1989, the Salinas government abruptly dissolved INMECAFE, creating a vacuum for small coffee producers. Their incomes dropped, because no public sector agencies were created to fill the credit and fertilizer void. An immediate consequence was increasing debt and even bankruptcy for thousands of small-holders. As Neil Harvey observes:

> Most coffee producers were caught in a cycle of debt and poverty. Unable to repay loans because of the fall in prices and income, they became ineligible for new loans. The accumulation of debt in this sector reached approximately $270 million by the end of 1993. In these conditions thousands of small growers . . . abandoned production in the 1989–1993 period (1996, 1192).

Coffee farming inputs, such as chemical fertilizers and pesticides, became more expensive than the profits earned from low coffee prices. An overvalued exchange rate exacerbated this situation, raising the price of imported inputs while lowering the price of exported coffee. The immediate losers in the price drop were the small producers, who, because of their small plots and low yields, were unable to compensate for lower prices by increasing production like the larger growers.

The state's withdrawal from the coffee sector meant that the purchasing, financing, processing, and marketing stages of the commodity chain formerly handled by INMECAFE would now have to be taken over by producer unions or would revert back to the private sector. A struggle for control of these stages of the commodity chain ensued. Transnational corporations responded by vertically integrating into the production end of the commodity chain. Coffee purchasers working directly for Nestlé and General Foods brokers, for example, began displacing local intermediaries at the purchasing stage in the commodity chain (Cristina Renard 1992).

Transnational corporations, especially Nestlé, have also increased their control over the processing and marketing of instant and decaffeinated coffee within Mexico. This form of backward integration by transnationals threatens Mexico's own coffee industry as well as producers, who fear that U.S. corporations will begin using cheaper Brazilian coffee when producing instant coffee for sale in the Mexican market. Since coffee transnational corporations (even after NAFTA) do not have to display country of origin labels, there is no way that Mexico can know what percent of the domestic instant coffee consumed is made with Mexican coffee (Cristina Renard 1992; Smith 1996).

On the other hand, producer unions began vertically integrating their unions from the bottom up, scaling up the commodity chain from the opposite direction of transnational corporations. These producer unions lack the administrative experience of transnationals and large growers/ exporters, who have years of experience marketing coffee internationally. Nevertheless, some producer unions took advantage of market opportunities and scaled up the commodity chain.

Competition also erupted over who would control the infrastructure that INMECAFE decided to transfer to coffee growers during its withdrawal. While the government at first offered to transfer INMECAFE's sixty-five dry-processing centers to independent and government-affiliated smallholders, much of this infrastructure (12% of the nation's total) never reached these groups. Or, alternatively, in many cases this agro-industrial infrastructure was handed over to less efficient government-affiliated producer unions, thus bypassing the independent producer unions.

Another consequence of INMECAFE's withdrawal and the drop in world coffee prices was a shift in smallholder household production strategies. Women and children in smallholder families began working more on coffee plots, affecting labor patterns within the family as well as opportunities for children to go to school. Another response was to shift production into corn, which required clearing large areas of land using slash-and-burn cultivation, often causing ecological damage. Finally, young men and women throughout the coffee regions opted to migrate, heading for the agribusiness fields of northern Mexico and the U.S. border states (Velázquez and Hoffman 1995; García 1993).

Solidarity Poverty Programs Target Coffee Smallholders

In 1989, President Salinas created an antipoverty program called the National Solidarity Program (PRONASOL), which increased the decision-making roles of states and municipalities. This program came about because, ironically, neoliberal policies were hurting the same groups whose votes were becoming increasingly important to the official Partido Revolucionario Institucional (PRI) as competition intensified in Mexico's electoral system (Bruhn 1996; Dresser 1991; Fox and Aranda in this volume). One of the primary targets of PRONASOL has been small coffee farmers, 60% of whom are classified as living in extreme poverty and 62% of whom belong to indigenous groups (Fox 1994a). Carlos Rojas, the first director of PRONASOL, was extremely sympathetic to the plight of coffee farmers and became a key ally of independent producer unions during the Salinas administration (Hernández and Celis 1994).

Because so many coffee farmers are indigenous peoples, Mexico's National Indigenous Institute (INI) implemented most of the PRONASOL programs targeting small coffee farmers. In the past, INI suffered from organizational corruption, although a reformist current has led the agency in recent years. The Salinas administration greatly increased INI's budget, breathing new life into this agency. INI's growth in an era of privatization and fiscal austerity illustrates the kind of institutional restructuring the PRI perceived as necessary for political survival during neoliberal reforms.

In 1990, SEDESOL, the agency in charge of PRONASOL, began financing INI's Regional Solidarity Funds, which targeted producers with coffee plots smaller than 10 hectares in marginalized coffee regions. Solidarity's Aid to Coffee Production program was made up of a series of subprograms, designed to assist coffee farmers at various stages of the production process. These subprograms included collection and marketing, production assistance, direct credits, harvesting and transportation, organic-coffee projects, technical assistance, and terrace construction, among others.

In order to administer the Regional Solidarity Funds, and eventually to transfer implementation directly to producer organizations, the Salinas government created the National Operating Group, which consisted of state and regional operating groups. This new institution was to be made up of representatives of producer organizations (both official and independent), as well as INI officials who managed the Regional Solidarity Funds. "Co-responsibility" between state agencies and producer unions was the theme stressed by federal reformists.

The National Coffee Council

In 1993, the Salinas presidency created a federal government agency called the National Coffee Council (CMC). The CMC, which is a more top-down agency than INI and controlled by the Ministry of Agriculture and Water Resources (SARH), illustrates the inter-organizational conflicts within the new institutional framework emerging in Mexico's coffee sector. SARH, along with the Foreign Trade Bank (BANCOMEXT), focuses on increasing coffee production, whereas INI perceives its role as cushioning indigenous smallholders from the shocks of economic restructuring (Hernández and Celis 1994).

Tensions between the INI and SARH blocs ripple throughout Mexico's coffee-producing states, affecting policy implementation at various levels. Moreover, there are different interests within each of these blocs. Within INI, for example, there are, on the one hand, factions working to improve the conditions of indigenous coffee growers and, on the other hand, corrupt INI officials derailing federal programs through their control over regional INI centers. Within the National Coffee Council, progressive as well as reactionary governors control the state coffee councils, which play a minor role in all coffee-producing states except Oaxaca.

President Ernesto Zedillo (1994–2000) added coffee to the nine basic agricultural commodities that qualify for the national agricultural support program, PROCAMPO, which reflects continued commitment by the federal government to cushion the worst shocks of Mexico's neoliberal reforms in the countryside. This is in the PRI's own interest, as the rural vote in southern states, once taken for granted, is becoming increasingly important and less predictable. Faced with the dilemma of maintaining one-party rule while implementing neoliberal policies that are devastating the livelihoods of Mexico's rural poor, the federal government has gradually changed the organizational framework that regulates the coffee sector. It was within this changing framework that coffee producer unions mobilized and bargained with state agencies between 1989 and 1996.

Smallholders, Collective Action, and the New Coffee Producer Movement in Mexico

A new peasant movement emerged in Mexico in the 1980s, with small coffee producers as its most organized sector. Most smallholders suffered as ICA collapsed and the state withdrew from the coffee sector. Nevertheless, some coffee growers managed to take advantage of shifting international and national conditions, forming independent coffee producer unions and scaling up the coffee commodity chain. In the very same international and national context, variable subnational contexts emerged, creating political opportunities for some smallholders while limiting opportunities for others. Such subnational variation, along with differing strategic choices and degrees of cohesiveness of coffee producer unions, explains why some small coffee producers weathered the worst coffee crisis in Mexico's history (1990–1993) while others did not.

This section compares the political opportunity structures that took shape in Oaxaca, Chiapas, and Veracruz during this time. What margins of maneuverability were available for independent coffee producer unions in these locations? What strategies did coffee producer unions pursue within these margins? The answers to these questions shed light on the configurations of winners and losers within Mexico's coffee sector under economic restructuring since the 1980s.

Small Coffee Producers: Government-Affiliated (CNC) Producer Unions versus Independent Producer Unions (CNOC)

Given Mexico's historical commitment to *campesinos*, most small coffee producers are lumped into a category called the "social sector," which is distinguished from the private sector. Traditionally, most small coffee farmers in the social sector were either unorganized or belonged to local branches of the Federation of Coffee Producers of the National Campesino Confederation (CNC). Most of the CNC-affiliated organizations, part of Mexico's state corporatism, are widely regarded as inefficient and corrupt. Today, about 90,000 coffee producers, 31% of all Mexican coffee growers, are affiliated with the CNC's National Federation of Coffee Producers.

Within the social sector, however, fundamental changes occurred throughout Mexico's coffee regions in the 1980s. New, autonomous organizations emerged, challenging the Mexican state's monopoly over this rural constituency. Beginning with widespread mobilizations against INMECAFE for higher coffee prices, independent smallholders formed their own National Network of Coffee Producer Organizations (CNOC) by 1989. This independent federation then mushroomed, organizing 71,126 coffee producers, 25% of the total, by 1996.

Faced with this challenge, the federal government tried, unsuccessfully, to reinvigorate the CNC's National Federation of Coffee Producers. Salinas's attempts at *cenestroika*, however, came up against years of frustration on the part of small coffee farmers, many of whom were tired of government corruption and inefficiency. In some coffee producer states, such as Oaxaca, a massive shift occurred, in which coffee producers formerly organized into UEPCs and affiliated with the CNC switched over to independent coffee producer unions. In other states, however, such as Veracruz, governors working with a historically strong and well-established CNC narrowed the possibilities for independent producer unions.

Economic Restructuring and Small Coffee Farmers: Explaining Divergent Outcomes in Chiapas, Oaxaca, and Veracruz

Table 6.3 illustrates the relationship between more and less favorable subnational institutional contexts and the strength of independent producer unions. The argument is that the combination of a favorable institutional context combined with strong producer unions should promote the livelihoods of small farmers than other cases. Even so, as we shall see below, these are only tendencies. Other factors, especially external linkages and the strength of CNC producer groups, mediate the fate of independent coffee producer unions. Nevertheless, the tendency remains. Thus, most Oaxacan small farmers weathered the coffee crisis much more smoothly than their counterparts in Chiapas and Veracruz.

Oaxaca

Oaxaca is the state where small coffee farmers, especially those belonging to independent producer unions, have had the most success. Its moderate governor, Heladio Ramírez (1986–1992), and his successor, Diódoro Carrasco Altamiro (1992–1998), created a favorable institutional context for coffee producer organizations to bargain with the state government. During the

Table 6.3

Relationship Between Subnational Institutional Context and Strength of Coffee Producer Unions[4]

	Chiapas	Veracruz	Oaxaca
Institutional Context	Less Favorable	Medium	More Favorable
Strength of Independent Producer Unions	Medium	Weak	Strong

withdrawal of INMECAFE in 1989, Governor Ramírez created a state coffee council, which soon became the key institution shaping Oaxacan coffee policy. Independent small producers mobilized, forming a statewide federation of small producers (CEPCO) and gained inclusion, including voting power, within this new institution. Through negotiations with the state governor, CEPCO managed to gain control over some of the agro-industrial infrastructure, including dry-processing plants and warehouses, which INMECAFE was transferring to producer unions as it withdrew from the coffee sector.

The ability of 23,000 smallholders (42% of all Oaxacan coffee farmers) to organize into a unified state-level network (CEPCO) was partly the result of the strong regional coffee producer unions formed in the early 1980s. In turn, the antecedents of these producer unions lie in earlier social struggles. As Fox (1994b) explains, "Oaxaca's rapidly growing coffee-producer movement of the 1990s . . . traces its roots back to the food council movement" of the early 1980s, where peasant groups took control over government food distribution programs. Regional producer unions emerged from this experience, uniting coffee farmers from isolated communities and increasing their bargaining power. These regional unions remained small enough (from a few hundred to a few thousand members) to maintain close contact with their social base, fostering grassroots participation.

Another factor explaining the success of CEPCO is its moderate and pragmatic approach to negotiating with the Oaxacan state government. CEPCO focused on production issues, leaving electoral and partisan debates aside, which created some common ground between state agencies and producer unions. Oaxaca's state coffee council and producer unions were able to work together to solve many concrete issues for small coffee farmers. The combination of a moderate governor working with moderate producer unions was a winning mix for small coffee farmers in Oaxaca.[5]

The Solidarity programs for smallholders in Oaxaca's coffee regions were originally implemented by regional INI centers scattered throughout the state's multiple coffee regions. The presence of active regional organizations served as a check on corruption and inefficiency within many of these regional INI centers, as coffee producer unions were given some say in how projects and programs were implemented. This was part of the government's commitment to coresponsibility between coffee producer unions and government agencies implementing Solidarity poverty programs. Since the state governor and his successor were reformists, there was little serious opposition blocking federal programs from reaching coffee regions. On the contrary, a comparatively high level of cooperation characterized federal-state relations in terms of implementing Solidarity programs in Oaxaca's coffee regions (see Fox and Aranda in this volume).

During the Salinas administration, many of Oaxaca's regional producer unions were able to consolidate their organizations by reinvesting credits received from Solidarity programs into diverse projects, such as self-managed credit unions, organic-coffee programs, and higher quality agro-industrial machinery. Organized producers were granted Solidarity credits each year, receiving amounts indexed to repayment rates for credits received the prior year. Oaxaca had the highest repayment rates of these Solidarity loans of all coffee-producing states. By reinvesting funds received from the federal government, Oaxaca's coffee producers gained control over higher stages of the coffee commodity chain. Many of the projects created with Solidarity funds increased the quality of coffee grown by Oaxacan producer unions, allowing smallholders to compete more effectively in international market niches.

Oaxaca is home to one of the richest coffee-producing areas in Mexico, the Pluma Hidalgo region. An independent regional producer union based in this region, the Union of Indigenous Communities–100 Years of Solitude, has worked through the Aztec Harvests marketing and distributional arm of the CNOC to export its coffee directly to the United States.[6] This is the kind of coffee that can compete very well in the growing specialty coffee market niche in the United States, and these producers have taken full advantage of this opportunity. Moreover, even the reformist governor of Oaxaca, Diódoro Carrasco Altamiro, was involved in promoting the UCI–100 Years of Solitude producer union, providing contacts with the Specialty Coffee Association of America, a key group of coffee importers, distributors, and roasters in the United States. A reformist governor working with an independent producer union illustrates the kind of public-private cooperation that characterizes Oaxaca's coffee sector.

Opposition within Oaxaca did come, however, from rural bosses entrenched in some of the state's coffee-producing regions. These rural bosses, who perceive Oaxaca's reformist governors as weakening their monopoly on the lucrative coffee trade, blocked implementation of federal programs in some of the regional INI centers, especially those regions where producer unions were weak or nonexistent.[7] Nonetheless, as the state coffee council consolidated in Oaxaca in the early 1990s, its regional coffee council structure began to supplant INI regional centers in implementing federal Solidarity projects. Since Oaxaca's governor is also the head of the state coffee council, this was basically a victory for an alliance between state reformists and independent producer unions against rural bosses and some of their local allies.

While all Oaxacan smallholders benefit from access to the state coffee council, the independent unions organized under CEPCO's umbrella have been much more successful than some of the CNC producer unions in improving the livelihoods of their members. Independent unions, for example, have much higher repayment rates for INI-Solidarity loans than government-affiliated unions, which allows them to capitalize their organizations more. The pioneer organic-coffee producer union in Mexico is an independent regional organization in Oaxaca,[8] as are most other producer unions with organic-coffee projects. Government-affiliated unions have been much less innovative and flexible.

Chiapas

In Chiapas, Mexico's most important coffee-producing state and home to the largest number of small coffee farmers (some 74,000), the political context of the 1980s and much of the 1990s was quite different than Oaxaca's. Hard-line governors Castellanos Domínguez (1983–1988) and González Garrido (1988–1993) were unsympathetic to the demands of independent coffee producer unions (Harvey 1992, 1996). Unlike Oaxaca, where Governor Ramírez created the Oaxacan state coffee council in 1989 (the same year as INMECAFE's withdrawal), it wasn't until 1993 that an underfunded and ineffectual state coffee council emerged in Chiapas. In the interim, many Chiapan smallholders were left on their own. The level of productivity of Chiapas's small coffee producers fell by 35% during this period (Harvey 1996, 192; Darlington 1995).

Within Chiapas, conflicts emerged between federal reformists who were sympathetic to the plight of small coffee farmers and more conservative state governors. In 1993, for example, three top INI officials working with the Solidarity program were jailed in this conflict-ridden state. Hard-line governors, backed by a traditional oligarchy of landowners and ranchers, derailed federal Solidarity programs at the implementation stage by capturing state agencies. This gave small coffee growers in Chiapas less access to credit for building agro-industrial infrastructure and consolidating their unions, weakening their ability to scale up the coffee commodity chain and compete in international markets.

Unlike in Oaxaca, coffee producers in Chiapas formed their state-level federation of coffee producers much later, losing the opportunity to gain concessions from INMECAFE during the 1989 conjuncture. This state network, called COOPCAFE, has since grown to about 10,000 members dispersed among thirty different coffee producer organizations. Unlike CEPCO, however, COOPCAFE is internally divided, which weakens its bargaining power.[9] Although the state also has some successful, and independent, regional producer unions—such as the La Selva Union of Ejidos, the Majomut Union of Ejidos, and the Indigenous Producers from the Sierra Madre of Motozintla (ISMAM)—not all these regional organizations are affiliated with COOPCAFE (Harvey 1992; Martínez Quezada 1995; Heinegg and Ferroggiaro 1996). ISMAM, for instance, one of Chiapas's most successful independent regional producer unions, is not a member of COOPCAFE. Unlike Oaxaca, where nearly 50% of all small producers are affiliated with CEPCO, in Chiapas only 32% of coffee growers form part of COOPCAFE.[10] Internal divisions within Chiapas's coffee producer movement have created a more fragmented coalition facing a more repressive state government.

The few examples where producer unions managed to benefit their members in Chiapas are all groups that have found market niches abroad. These producers also forged alliances with federal reformists, checking the power of hard-line state governors. For example, the La Selva Union of Ejidos had personal contacts with President Salinas and other top officials. This union was able to tap into the organic-coffee market, as were the Majomut Union of Ejidos and ISMAM producer organizations. Coffee farmers belonging to these unions, unlike others within Chiapas, received Solidarity programs and projects with less interference. These regional producer organizations also had external linkages with fair-trade organizations as well as support from the Inter-American Foundation.[11]

The La Selva Union of Ejidos in Chiapas has been one of the major producer unions benefiting from the Aztec Harvests marketing strategy of the CNOC, which is based on exporting high-quality coffee directly to small- and medium-sized roasters, cutting out importers and distributors. Because of the high quality of its coffee and this unique marketing strategy, this organization was able to succeed despite being based in an area very close to the Zapatista uprising. Its experience contrasts with the situation of the majority of Chiapas's small coffee growers, who were unable to invest in their coffee plots and were forced to migrate out of coffee regions or to diversify into subsistence corn production.

Veracruz

Veracruz's institutional context was more favorable than the polarized situation of Chiapas, but not as favorable as Oaxaca's. Veracruz governor Dante Delgado (1988–1992) was more moderate than his contemporaries in Chiapas, but he did block federal resources from reaching independent producer unions, channeling these resources instead to CNC coffee producer unions. His successor, Patricio Chirinos (1992–1998), continued this policy (Hoffman 1992; Velázquez and Hoffman 1995; Olvera 1991, 1994; Celis 1991). While it is rational from the perspective of Veracruz's governors, who have to respond to the strength of a powerful CNC constituency in their state, the relationship between the government and producers has not been nearly as mutually beneficial in Veracruz as it has been in Oaxaca. Complicating the situation in Veracruz were frosts that hit some coffee regions in 1989, further devastating small coffee farmers.

Unlike Oaxaca, independent producer unions in Veracruz are more divided and have been unable to form a state-level federation to increase their bargaining power. The largest independent regional producer union in Veracruz, the Veracruz Coffee Producers Union (UPCV), includes only 2,400 members out of a total of about 67,300 coffee growers in the state. The largest independent regional unions in Veracruz, the UPCV, the General Union of Workers, Peasants and Popular Sectors (UGOCP), and the Independent Central for Rural Workers and Peasants (CIOAC), are ideologically at odds with each other. While the UPVC adopted a more productivist, negotiating strategy, the UGOCP and CIOAC were more confrontational, adopting mobilization strategies (Velázquez and Hoffman 1995). Yet, these two latter groups were also divided, belonging to different national-level peasant confederations, thereby complicating alliances with moderate, productivist-oriented organizations like the UPCV as well as with each other.

Because some of the largest independent regional producer unions within Veracruz are openly affiliated with leftist parties, unlike the case of CEPCO in Oaxaca, the political stakes are higher for Veracruz's governors in supporting these independent producer unions. Electoral and party politics have fragmented the producer union movement in Veracruz, driving a wedge between the independent and official blocs of small producer unions. In Veracruz, for instance, much of INMECAFE's agro-industrial infrastructure passed into the hands of the private sector or to less efficient government-affiliated producer unions. The combination of a strong CNC and a more radical challenge from independent producer unions closed off the political center in Veracruz, which has been the basis for compromise in Oaxaca.

Although the Veracruz state government also blocked access to Solidarity funds for some independent producer groups, this was less frequent than in Chiapas. The UPCV, for example, was able to mobilize producers and gain access to an emergency program for coffee farmers affected by the adverse weather conditions in 1989. In regions where coffee producers are well organized, their unions have been able to integrate into regional operating groups and oversee implementation of federal programs. In many of Veracruz's indigenous regions, however, small producers remain unorganized, and some INI bureaucrats have misused funds targeted at indigenous smallholders (Olvera 1994, 62). Unlike in Oaxaca, where a new institutional structure (state/regional coffee councils) leveled the playing field at the implementation stage, the lack of new institutions in Veracruz allowed INI to capture more of the regional agencies responsible for implementing federal programs.

The CIOAC regional producer union, based in the fertile Huatusco coffee region of Veracruz, illustrates the way that regional producer unions located in areas of higher-quality coffee can benefit from gaining access to market niches. The Huatusco-based union, like the La Selva Union of Ejidos from Chiapas and the UCI–100 Years of Solitude producer union from Oaxaca, has been one of the major beneficiaries of the work of Aztec Harvests in the United States. With help from the national-level CNOC, the CIOAC producer union in Huatusco was able to sell its high-quality coffee to the growing specialty coffee niche in the United States, even as other Veracruz coffee growers were migrating out of coffee regions because of low market prices.

Overall, the Veracruz state government was much less forthcoming with resources for the multiple projects proposed by the independent small coffee producer unions than were governments in Oaxaca. Unlike their Oaxacan counterparts, Veracruz's governors are more constrained in their ability to work with independent producer organizations openly affiliated with leftist parties. In Oaxaca, a rising tide lifted all boats, as new institutions benefited small coffee farmers across the board, albeit to different degrees. In Veracruz, on the other hand, governors channeled resources toward the CNC, which helped some producers but partially marginalized others. While faring better than growers in Chiapas, smallholders in Veracruz did not achieve the degree of public-private cooperation found in Oaxaca.

Conclusion

Promarket reforms, although detrimental to many smallholders, paradoxically have created opportunities for some coffee producer unions to appropriate control over key nodes of the commodity chain, strengthening their ability to compete in new market niches. Public-private cooperation within the coffee sector, exemplified in the Oaxacan case, has facilitated this process. Some regional producer unions have also succeeded in less favorable institutional contexts, such as Chiapas, through flexible and innovative strategies.

These kinds of regional producer unions may hold key answers to how small farmers in general can survive in increasingly competitive global markets. Given the importance of flexibility in today's (post-Fordist) agricultural export markets (Raynolds 1994, 146), regionally based enterprises may have advantages over larger-sized national and international firms. Smaller-scale coffee producer unions, for example, can respond more quickly to market signals than state-run giants such as INMECAFE. Thanks to their connection to their social base, democratic producer unions can use the social capital of their members to motivate higher levels of participation. Communication channels and learning processes are much more fluid in these kinds of coffee producer organizations. For instance, while democratic coffee producer unions could convince members to change traditional labor patterns to take advantage of the growing niche for organic coffee, INMECAFE never succeeded in persuading coffee producers to change their labor patterns and increase productivity on their coffee plots (Nestel 1995; Nolasco 1985). INMECAFE lacked the close contact between leadership and social base that democratic producer unions have, a resource that fosters the flexibility needed in competitive markets.

One of the principal questions regarding the role of small producer unions is their ability to institutionalize this flexibility. As advisors of these unions become increasingly specialized in the intricacies of coffee marketing, there is a tendency for leadership and base to move apart, weakening the informational flows and channels of participation that are the lifeblood of flexible organizations. This will be a key challenge facing many of the producer unions that have succeeded under market-centric reforms.

Unfortunately for Mexico, most smallholders remain unorganized or are organized in less efficient and less democratic CNC producer unions. This is why the real losers of economic restructuring remain small coffee farmers, who are so vulnerable to shifts in global markets. Mexico's new coffee producer movement, however, has managed to organize nearly 25% of the country's coffee growers. The strategies of the regional producer unions that are the building blocks of this movement point to possible pathways for the remaining smallholders to compete successfully in changing global markets.

References

Bruhn, Kathleen. 1996. Social Spending and Political Support: The "Lessons" of the National Solidarity Program in Mexico. *Comparative Politics* 28, no. 2.

Celis, Fernando. 1991. UPCV: Del cambio de terreno al fortalecimiento de una organización democrática. In *Cafeteleros: La construcción de la autonomía*, ed. Luis Hernández. México, D.F.: Servicio de Apoyo Local, A.C.

Carlsen, Laura. 1991. Changes Brewing: Coffee Sector Adjusts to Diminishing State Role. *Business Mexico* (Apr.).

Cristina Renard, María. 1992. El café en el Tratado de Libre Comercio. *Cuadernos Agrarios* 4.

Darling, Juanita. 1991. Mexico's Coffee Crisis. *Los Angeles Times*, Dec. 8.

Darlington, Shasta. 1995. Wake Up and Smell the Coffee. *Business Mexico* 5, no. 7.

Dresser, Denise. 1991. *Neopopulist Solutions to Neoliberal Problems: Mexico's National Solidarity Program*. La Jolla: Center for U.S.-Mexican Studies, University of California at San Diego.

Foley, Michael. 1995. Privatizing the Countryside: The Mexican Peasant Movement and Neoliberal Reforms. *Latin American Perspectives* 84, no. 1.

Fox, Jonathan. 1994a. Targeting the Poorest: The Rule of the National Indigenous Institute in Mexico's Solidarity Program. In *Transforming State-Society Relations in Mexico*, eds. Wayne Cornelius, Ann Craig, and Jonathan Fox. La Jolla: Center for U.S.-Mexican Studies, University of California.

———. 1994b. Fighting the Odds: Grassroots Participation in Mexico's Community Food Councils. In *Inquiry at the Grassroots*, eds. William Glade and Charles Reilly. Arlington, Va.: Inter-American Foundation.

García, Arturo. 1993. Reality in the Campo. *Business Mexico* 3, no. 8.

Gereffi, Gary, and Miguel Korzeniewicz, eds. 1994. *Commodity Chains and Global Capitalism*. Westport, Conn. and London: Praeger.

Griswold, David. 1991. Mexico's Small Coffee Farmers: Looking Out for the Farmer. *Café Olé Magazine* (Nov.).

Griswold, David, and Justin Ward. 1996. Mexico's Mistaken Coffee Policy. *Journal of Commerce* (Nov. 6).

Harvey, Neil. 1992. La unión de uniones de Chiapas y los retos políticos del desarrollo de base. In *Autonomía y nuevos sujetos sociales en el desarrollo rural*, eds. Julio Moguel, Carlota Botey, and Luis Hernández. México, D.F.: Siglo XXI.

———. 1996. Rural Reforms and the Zapatista Rebellion: Chiapas. In *Neoliberalism Revisited: Economic Restructuring and Mexico's Political Future*, ed. Gerardo Otero. Boulder, Colo.: Westview Press.

Heinegg, Ayo, and Karen M. Ferroggiaro. 1996. *Inter-American Foundation Strategy in the Mexican Coffee Sector: A Case Study of ISMAM*. Unpublished manuscript.

Hernández Navarro, Luis, and Fernando Celis Callejas. 1994. Solidarity and the New Campesino Movements: The Case of Coffee Production. In *Transforming State-Society Relations in Mexico*, eds. Wayne Cornelius, Ann Craig, and Jonathan Fox. La Jolla: Center for U.S.-Mexican Studies, University of California at San Diego.

Hernández Navarro, Luis, ed. 1991. *Cafeteleros: La construcción de la autonomía*. México, D.F.: Servicio de Apoyo Local, A.C.

Hoffman, Odile. 1992. Renovación de los actores sociales en el campo: Un ejemplo en el sector cafetelero en Veracruz. *Estudios Sociológicos* 10, no. 30.

INMECAFE (Mexican Coffee Institute). 1992. Coffee Statistics. Xalapa, México.

International Coffee Organization (ICO). 1996. Mexico Prime Washed Coffee on the N.Y. Futures Market.

Inter-American Foundation (IAF). 1996. The Small Farmer Portfolio of the Inter-American Foundation in Mexico 1988–1994. Arlington, Va.: IAF.

Lee, Steven. 1993. Harvest of Blame: Mexican Farmers Fear Free-Trade Pact. *Dallas Morning News*, Feb. 21.

Martínez, Raciel. 1995. Oaxaca Will Export Some 756 Tons of Coffee to the United States. *Report of the Specialty Coffee Association of America*. Long Beach, Calif.

Martínez Quezada, Alvaro. 1995. *Crisis del café y estrategias campesinas: El caso de la Unión de Ejidos Majomut en los Altos de Chiapas*. México, D.F.: Chapingo Autonomous University.

McMichael, Phillip, ed. 1995. *Agro-food System Restructuring in the Late Twentieth Century: Comparative and Global Perspectives*. Ithaca, N.Y.: Cornell University.

Mexican Coffee Council (CMC). 1994. *Base de datos estadísticos en materia de café*. Mexico, D.F.

Nestel, David. 1995. Coffee in Mexico: International Market, Agricultural Landscape and Ecology. *Ecological Economics* 15.

Nolasco, Margarita, ed. 1985. *Café y sociedad en México*. México, D.F.: Centro de Ecodesarrollo.

Olvera, Alberto. 1991. Las luchas de los caficultores veracruzanos: La experiencia de la Unión de Productores de Café de Veracruz. In *Cafeteleros: La construcción de la autonomía*. Luis Hernández et al., eds. México, D.F.: Servicio de Apoyo Local, A.C.

———. 1994. Neocorporativismo y democracia en la transformación institucional de la cafecultura: El caso de Veracruz. *Cuadernos Agrarios* 10.

Paz Paredes, Lorena. 1995. Una mirada al período de crisis de la cafecultura mexicana. Recuento de políticas oficiales y respuestas campesinas. *Cuadernos Agrarios* 11–12.

Porter, Robert M. Forthcoming. State, Market, and Mexico's New Peasant Movement: The Case of Coffee Producers 1980–1996. Ph.D. dissertation. Department of Political Science, University of California at Santa Barbara.

Raynolds, Laura. 1994. Institutionalizing Flexibility: A Comparative Analysis of Fordist and Post-Fordist Models of Third World Agro-Export Production. In *Commodity Chains and Global Capitalism*, eds. Gary Gereffi and Miguel Korzeniewicz. Westport, Conn. and London: Praeger.

Rice, Robert, and Justin Ward. 1996. Conservation, Coffee and Commerce in the Western Hemisphere. Smithsonian Migratory Bird Center and Natural Resources Defense Council White Paper. Washington, D.C.: Smithsonian Migratory Bird Center.

Singelmann, Peter, ed. 1995. *Mexican Sugarcane Growers: Economic Restructuring and Political Options.* La Jolla: Center for U.S.-Mexican Studies, University of California at San Diego.

Smith, Michael D. 1996. The Empire Filters Back: Consumption, Production, and the Politics of Starbucks Coffee. *Urban Geography* 17, no. 6.

Snyder, Richard. Forthcoming. After the State Withdraws: Neoliberalism and the Politics of Reregulation in Mexico. Ph.D. dissertation. Department of Political Science, University of California at Berkeley.

Talbot, John M. 1997. The Struggle for Control of a Commodity Chain: Instant Coffee from Latin America. *Latin American Research Review* 32, no. 2.

Velázquez, Emilia, and Odile Hoffman. 1995. Las organizaciones campesinas de los años noventa ante un viejo dilema: La vinculación entre lo político y lo económico. Unpublished manuscript.

Villafuerte Solís, Daniel, ed. 1993. *El café en la frontera sur: La producción y los productores de Soconusco, Chiapas.* México, D.F.: Instituto Chiapaneco de Cultura.

Zendejas, Sergio, and Peter de Vries, eds. 1995. *Rural Transformations Seen from Below: Regional and Local Perspectives from Western Mexico.* La Jolla: Center for U.S. Mexican Studies, University of California at San Diego.

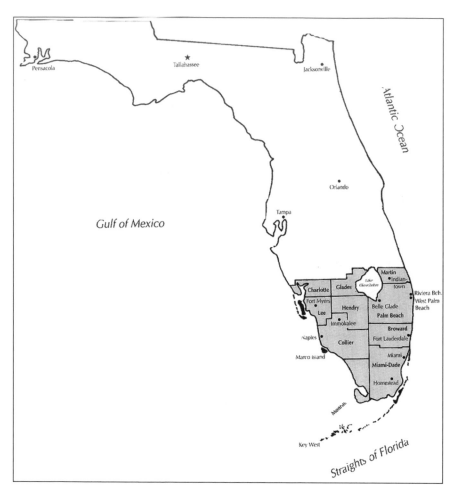

Map 7.1
South Florida

7

Work and Immigration

Winter Vegetable Production in South Florida

David Griffith

South Florida has become one of the most internationalized zones in the United States. Miami-Dade County's percentage of foreign-born residents has surpassed even New York City's in recent years. Miami's Little Havana and Little Haiti reflect the growth of Caribbean populations in South Florida, yet new immigrants from Mexico, the Dominican Republic, El Salvador, Guatemala, and other parts of Central America and the Caribbean continue to shape neighborhoods all the way from Homestead, south of Miami, to West Palm Beach and Riviera Beach to the north (see Map 7.1).

South Florida's inland cities mirror the ethnic mix of the coastal metropolis. During winter harvests, Mexicans, Chicanos, Haitians, Quiché,[1] and others form neighborhoods in inland communities like Belle Glade, Immokalee, and Indiantown.[2] These neighborhoods usually emerge either alongside or within poor neighborhoods that are home to other minorities, primarily African Americans. They tend to be located near public housing and public services complexes and isolated from the more affluent (and generally white) sections of the inland communities. Similarly, South Florida's coastal strips are socially, culturally, and economically distinct from the more inland sections of coastal cities and inland rural areas. From time to time, South Florida newspapers contrast the squalid rural ghettoes of Belle Glade and Immokalee with the glimmering yacht basins and celebrated wealth of Palm Beach and Marco Island.

Connecting the incredibly rich and incredibly poor areas of South Florida is a disquieting, apartheid-like symbiosis similar to those socioeconomic relations elaborated in Third World peasant studies of the past thirty years. Since the late 1960s, much social scientific inquiry concerning Latin American and

Caribbean peasants has suggested that peasant communities exist as labor reserves, absorbing the costs of reproducing workers for local and U.S. labor markets (Collins 1988; de Janvry 1983; Dinerman 1978; Goldring 1990; Griffith 1983; Mines 1996). Relying on small plots of land, raising a few head of livestock, engaging in limited cash cropping and cottage industries, or migrating to take advantage of extralocal economic opportunities, peasant households provided their own food and other necessities while sending surplus workers to work for wages outside their villages. In Mexico, Rodolfo Stavenhagen (1965) labeled this phenomenon "internal colonialism." This characterization replaced the political neutrality of folk-urban continuums and diffusion-of-innovation studies with an emphasis on the political and economic subordination of the Mexican peasantry, and, derivatively, the peasantries of many other countries as well. Parallel studies depicted transformations of peasant communities as consequences of social contexts in which cheap food products and subsidized labor were needed for urban and industrial development. In many communities, merchants influenced peasant production decisions by simultaneously promoting the consumer goods of industrialized countries and taking payments in key commodities such as coffee, bananas, potatoes, tobacco, and sugar. These developments quickly tied peasants into urban, national, and international markets in ways that exposed them to the whims of international tastes, political decisions, and economic cycles.

The next wave of studies built upon these insights by placing peasant communities in the context of the relations between rich and poor countries within an increasingly complex global division of labor (Sanderson 1985; Nash and Fernández 1983). According to this approach, both economic and social transnationalism are creating demands for more and cheaper consumer products (including food), more reliable and faster technologies of communication, improved transportation systems, and more complex methods of conferring legal status on the peoples of the world. These processes have made the world's borders simultaneously more and less important to the lived experiences of those who occupy subordinate positions in the international division of labor. On the one hand, ethnic identities—which are often fused (or confused) with nationality—have become more politicized, as migrants not only cross international borders but also enter ethnically mixed neighborhoods and labor markets in recipient countries. For example, a study of immigrant adjustment and ethnicity in South Florida reports that Haitian immigrants are far more active in the politics of Haiti than in local U.S. politics (Richman 1994; Griffith and Stepick 1994; Chafee 1994). On the other hand, acquiring full citizenship status or asylum as a political refugee has become more difficult in many developed countries. Many national governments have increased the range of legal statuses that individuals may obtain, allowing resident "nonimmigrants" to work in various countries without receiving the full benefits of citizenship (Griffith et al. 1994).

National governments have reinforced the increasing transnational mobility of capital and people by crafting economic agreements, such as NAFTA, and other symbols of multinational unity, such as GATT and the European Union. NAFTA essentially rubber-stamps the complex economic and social integration that has characterized Mexico-U.S. relations for the past century. In so doing, NAFTA may contribute to transnational and domestic economic, social, and territorial requirements, but it does not promise to diminish the structural inequalities that divide the two countries (Heppel and Torres 1996a, 1996b).

Mexican labor has been an integral part of certain U.S. regional and sectoral economies for well over a century, a condition that has been little reduced by border patrols, NAFTA, or policy initiatives, such as the 1986 Immigration Reform and Control Act or California's Proposition 187. The use of Mexican labor in U.S. agriculture, particularly perishable crop agriculture, has been common in the southwestern U.S. since late in the last century, and in the eastern U.S. since the 1950s. Like other low-wage, unskilled labor markets, however, perishable crop agriculture has always suffered from high labor turnover due to the seasonality of the work, occupational injury, and other factors, such as housing and supervision problems. Over time, Mexican migrant networks constructed around farmwork have accessed different employment and income opportunities both within Mexico and the United States. Consequently, recent studies of U.S. agriculture and other rural industries, such as poultry and meat packing, have documented rapid changes in the gender and ethnic compositions of their labor forces (Griffith 1993; Griffith and Kissam 1995; Smith 1991; Stull et al. 1995).

In this setting, researchers are also documenting the growth of transnational families and communities that are ever more skilled at conducting business and social transactions across international boundaries (Basch et al. 1994; Goldring 1990; Rouse 1992). These transactions include child sharing, gift exchange, communication assistance, and financial services, a list that suggests ingenuity and desperation. Such arrangements commonly reflect new opportunities, yet they also reflect poverty, the breakup of families and communities, high levels of stress and uncertainty, and feelings of frustration and guilt. On balance, they are, as June Nash (1993) points out, distressing signs of widening and deepening insecurity facing subsistence agriculture, fishing, cottage industry, and other household-based incomes. Thus, while many observers celebrate transnationalism as a creative force, others regard it—at least under current institutional conditions—as principally a generator of socioeconomic polarization on a world scale.

Whether involving new opportunities, desperate measures, or both, the lives of low-income immigrant families and communities tend to revolve around strategies to reduce consumption costs and obtain multiple income sources. Neighborhoods throughout South Florida and the countries of Latin America and the Caribbean bear the scars of such activities. For instance, housing strategies represent one of the most common ways for immigrants to reduce consumption (Fitchen 1992; Griffith and Kissam 1995; Mahler 1995). Strategies include: crowding into small rooms and dwellings, such as garages and utility sheds; sharing space in shifts; rotating among homeless shelters and low-cost rooming houses and motels; living with relatives; and accepting employer-provided housing. These practices result in increased competition for public space and services within low-income neighborhoods; reduced security; increased exposure to crime, building hazards, and public health risks; and deteriorating housing stock.[3]

Among poor immigrants, new sources of income come from opportunities within migrant networks and between new and old immigrants. Among these opportunities are charging for translation and other cultural brokerage services; engaging in various levels of labor referral or labor contracting; and charging for transportation to shopping, medical clinics, and government services. In her study of Salvadorans on Long Island, New York, Mahler (1995) found that more experienced immigrants often took advantage of those with less experience by providing over-priced housing, as well as courier and telecommunications services to keep migrants in contact with their families in El Salvador. Richman (1994) found that Haitian immigrants in West Palm Beach, Florida, similar to Salvadorans, established successful enterprises devoted to maintaining communication and material connections between Haiti and Florida as well as supplying Haitians with products and services. Griffith and Kissam (1995) documented two common ways that immigrant farmworkers derive income from other immigrants. First, "anchor households," consisting of boarding households established by elder (often female) members of families, provide temporary housing for groups of friends and kin in migrant staging areas, at the same time that they provide rental income to older and more experienced immigrants who have learned the dynamics of local housing markets. Second, farm labor contractors often construct artificial networks of farmworkers from whose paychecks they deduct not only room and board but also other expenses for items such as cigarettes and liquor.

Engaging in multiple livelihoods may be most prevalent in rural settings. In such locales, seasonal employment, the opportunities for scrounging food, small-scale gardening and animal husbandry, fishing, gathering, hunting, and the like combine with generally lower housing costs both to attract the working poor and encourage them to engage in multiple income-earning endeavors (Amato 1996). Often isolated, rural areas also provide opportunities for the development of transportation services, itinerant merchandising, and other small-scale, entrepreneurial initiatives. Immigrants in the South Florida agricultural producing areas have been successful as "pinhookers," small crews that negotiate with growers directly for the last vegetables in a field, picking the produce that remains after the main harvests and selling the ripe vegetables to local stores or on street corners.

Against this backdrop, this chapter examines housing and labor market practices in the South Florida winter vegetable industry. For at least the past fifty years, this industry has had important labor links with Mexico and other Latin American and Caribbean countries, which in turn have influenced the composition of the labor supply in agriculture and other rural industries across the U.S. Southeast and the Eastern Seaboard. During the November 1997 debates over fast-track authority for President Clinton, the *Miami Herald*, citing opposition primarily from agricultural interests, reported, "Florida is a key battleground in Clinton's struggle to win Congress' approval to cut new trade deals around the globe" (Oct. 31, 1997, 18A). An analysis of South Florida agriculture, then, is crucial to understanding the ways in which broad political economic trends are likely to affect local settings. The internal dynamics of local labor and housing markets, social problems, trade relationships, and other political-economic dimensions of these settings are often overlooked by economic analyses that examine national employment statistics, trade deficits, and other data that are too broadly aggregated to recognize regional or local processes of dislocation.[4]

This chapter's ultimate purpose is to raise questions about the long-term impact of NAFTA on agricultural labor relations in South Florida.[5] It reports that labor relations in South Florida agriculture have developed in such a way that labor will not be a significant constraining factor on future production decisions. However, competition for markets for fresh vegetables, particularly those affected by NAFTA, will likely constrain future production without taking into consideration taste, quality, or other factors appreciated by consumers of Florida produce. Florida growers continue to produce high volumes of tomatoes, citrus, and other fruits and vegetables preferred by North American consumers. Acreage fell in 1995–1996, but overall it has increased notably since the beginning of the decade, continuing to generate high demand for what appears to be an inexhaustible supply of workers from Mexico, Central America, and the Caribbean.

South Florida Agriculture: An Overview

A partial list of the vegetables produced in South Florida includes tomatoes, watermelons, bell peppers, cucumbers, squash, Irish potatoes, sweet corn, bush and pole beans, celery, cabbage, leafy vegetables, and Chinese vegetables. Production is dominated by corporate and family farms, most of which specialize in vegetables. Some of the larger firms have diversified into citrus, but few have integrated livestock into their enterprise mix. Production is oriented almost entirely toward a fresh wholesale market. In 1989, prior to NAFTA, crops achieved values of between $1 billion and $1.5 billion annually (FASS 1990). Tomatoes that are picked green and gassed to a pinkish color occupy the most acreage (around 33,000), followed by green peppers (17,000 acres), cucumbers (around 9,000 acres), and squash (around 8,000 acres). By the mid-1980s, these figures had grown to 49,000 acres of tomatoes (+48%), 21,700 acres of bell peppers (+27%), 13,500 acres of cucumbers (+53%), and 12,500 acres of squash (+56%). Between the 1994–1995 and 1995–1996 seasons these figures fell slightly, but were still considerably higher than plantings at the end of the 1980s.

Ethnicity

Along with growers, who tend to be white, six ethnic groups make up most of South Florida's farm labor market: (1) Mexicans/Mexican Americans; (2) Guatemalans/Central Americans; (3) African Americans; (4) Haitians; (5) Cubans; and (6) British West Indians, primarily from Jamaica.

Mexicans/Mexican Americans

Mexicans and Mexican Americans, recruited into Florida agriculture primarily through network ties to South Texas Chicano families (Broidy 1987), have represented an increasing share of South Florida's new immigrant agricultural labor force since the 1950s. Today they represent its largest ethnic group (NAWS 1997). Especially since the 1960s, the growth of the Florida tourist economy and associated urban and coastal development, coupled with civil rights legislation and the increasing empowerment of native minorities, drew English-speaking minorities out of the Florida farm labor market (Griffith and Kissam 1995; Hudson 1979). Florida citrus and vegetable growers turned to South Texas for new workers, finding Mexican and Chicano families, many of whom were former *bracero,* workers, who had been displaced as growers mechanized cotton cultivation. Through network ties and diffuse information links between Mexico, California, the U.S. Southwest, Texas, and Florida, Mexicans migrate to Florida annually for the winter vegetable and citrus harvests. Many of the earlier Texas-based Chicano immigrants, once the children of farmworkers, have settled out of the migrant stream into inland communities, such as Immokalee and Indiantown. Others have established themselves as farm labor contractors and other culture brokers, pinhookers, foremen, or supervisors. New immigrant groups of indigenous Mexicans have begun to show up in South Florida agriculture in recent years, primarily Mixtec and Zapotec workers from southern Mexico with farm experience in California.[6]

Guatemalans and Central Americans

The Guatemalans and other Central Americans in South Florida are primarily refugees from northwestern Guatemala and from the refugee camps of Chiapas and other parts of southern Mexico. Most arrived during the late 1970s and early 1980s. Guatemalans predominate among Central Americans in the agricultural labor force. While many Central Americans have been granted political asylum, a substantial (though unknown) proportion remains undocumented. According to a random-sample survey of low-wage workers conducted in 1990 in Immokalee, 33% of the Guatemalans had received work authorization after applying for political asylum, 43% were undocumented, and the remainder were legalized under the amnesty and Special Agricultural Worker (SAW) provisions of the Immigration Reform and Control Act (Griffith et al. 1990).

African Americans

Most of the African Americans in South Florida's labor markets occupy low-income positions. However, this group's presence in the farm labor market has diminished since the arrival of Mexicans and Mexican Americans in the 1950s. Historically, African Americans have been particularly susceptible to such labor control mechanisms as debt peonage and vagrancy laws; Florida proved resistant to federal laws against peonage well into this century (Daniel 1972). Studies comparing African Americans in South Florida and elsewhere to other ethnic groups have documented qualitatively distinct network relations within the African American community. These networks are based primarily on ties established through mothers, rather than through work, immigration, and village or neighborhood residence (Wilson and Martin 1982; Model 1985). This contrasts with the artificial networks of farm labor contractors (FLCs) common among young Latino males. Notwithstanding the access to public-sector job opportunities that distinguishes African American opportunity structures from those of Latin American and Cuban immigrants, racism and prejudice continue to relegate most African Americans to the low end of the labor market.

Haitians

Haitians in South Florida represent a diverse group, differentiated by class background based on the conditions under which they fled Haiti. Earlier arrivals tend to be more affluent than later ones. The most well-known and concentrated migrations occurred during the late 1970s and early 1980s, when Haitian boat people fled the Duvalier regime in large numbers (Stepick and Portes 1986; Stepick and Stepick 1990). Haitians are concentrated in coastal urban pockets from Dade to Palm Beach Counties, as well as in inland communities such as Belle Glade, Indiantown, and Immokalee. Many of the latest arrivals find work in agriculture around Belle Glade and Immokalee during the winter, following crews up the eastern seaboard during the summer.

Cubans

Cubans have entered Florida in a number of waves. The first three waves identified by Portes and Mozo (1985) began after the onset of the Cuban revolution in December 1959. These waves consisted mainly of upper- and middle-class families who used their capital and entrepreneurial backgrounds to establish an ethnic enclave in Miami, coming to wield considerable local political power and economic influence (Portes and Bach 1985; Portes and Mozo 1985; Pedraza-Bailey 1985). The fourth wave consisted primarily of *marielitos* from the 1980 Mariel boat lift, when Fidel Castro allowed anyone who wanted to cross to the Florida Keys by boat, emptying prisons and mental institutions into the exodus at the same time. These Cubans were not, by and large, well-received by the established Cuban population in Miami and have remained marginalized economically and politically. In agriculture, Cuban women have been the backbone of some fruit and vegetable packing, but they tend not to work in harvesting.

British West Indians

British West Indies agricultural workers are confined almost exclusively to the sugarcane industry, imported within the legal provisions of the H2a program[7] and housed in the towns between Pahokee and Moore Haven, along the southern rim of Lake Okeechobee. Eighty percent of the sugar workers are from Jamaica, with the remainder coming from Barbados, Dominica,

St. Vincent, and St. Lucia (Griffith 1986a, 1986b; Wood and McCoy 1985). Due to increasing lawsuits against growers regarding nonpayment of wages brought by the Florida Rural Legal Services, the H2a program was phased out in 1992. There are substantial populations of British West Indians in other parts of South Florida, primarily Miami, but they have not been major suppliers of farm labor.

General Labor Force Characteristics

Nine of the ten counties that comprise South Florida—Broward, Charlotte, Collier, Dade, Glades, Hendry, Lee, Martin, and Palm Beach (the tenth, Monroe, is composed primarily of the Everglades and the Florida Keys)—contain more than one-third of the state's labor force; generally, too, they have lower unemployment rates than the rest of the state. During the late 1980s, unemployment ranged from a low of 3.6% in Lee County to a high of 11.7% in nearby Hendry County, a predominantly agricultural area. The distinction between the two counties held across the region: counties with large urban areas had lower unemployment rates than rural counties.

The industries most frequently cited as competing with vegetable producers for labor are construction, tourism, landscaping and nurseries, garbage collection and recycling (including scavenging), and other agriculture, primarily the citrus industry. With the exception of the citrus industry, most of these industries relate to South Florida's rapid population growth. Farmworker jobs usually require few skills and pay poorly.

The importance of agriculture as a source of jobs and income varies from county to county. Agriculture is most important in Hendry and Glades Counties, where it accounts for more jobs than other industry sectors. It is also a major employer in counties such as Collier (with a ratio of agricultural to service-sector jobs of 1:1.3), Martin (1:5.6), Palm Beach (1:6.4) and Lee (1:10.4). The ratios of agricultural to construction and manufacturing jobs are even higher, since these make up smaller proportions of all jobs. In Dade, Broward, and Charlotte Counties, the ratio of agricultural to service-sector jobs surpasses 1:15, yet agriculture remains a crucial seasonal employer for many low-wage workers. In January 1997, Florida agriculture provided 82,800 jobs, 14,800 of which were seasonal.

The System of Production

South Florida vegetable producers usually specialize in vegetables as opposed to other agricultural commodities, with most producing more than one crop. A common enterprise mix is that of staked tomatoes with bell and jalapeño peppers, followed by cucumbers and squash. More elaborate operations may include eggplants, sweet corn, onions, leafy vegetables, Chinese vegetables, and other greens.

Until the 1989–1990 Christmas freeze, pepper producers had seen a "streak of record pepper crops" in ten of the previous fourteen years (FASS 1991, 37), and tomato producers had seen increasing values since the 1984–1985 season. Cucumber producers had their lowest annual yield since 1973–1974, and squash production was the lowest since 1975–1976. Production statistics show staked tomatoes as the clear leader in terms of vegetable production in South Florida, with 26,975 acres in 1988–1989, compared to 13,650 acres of green peppers, 7,600 of cucumbers, and 4,900 of squash (FASS 1990). Even compared to other vegetables not listed here, such as Irish potatoes, leafy vegetables, and melons, tomatoes emerge as the industry leader. Throughout Florida, in fact, tomatoes generate the most value for vegetable producers—around one-third of all value. By the 1995–1996 season, tomato production had grown to 45,500 acres, up by 69%.

Two facets of tomato production are notable. First, in 1987, dominance in tomato production shifted from the Florida's east coast to the southwest, or from Dade to Collier County. At the same time that southwestern Florida production emerged as the new leader, Dade County producers began displacing ground tomatoes with staked culture techniques, thereby increasing yields. Staked acreage increased from 1,200 acres in 1987–1988 to 5,750 in 1989–1990; at the same time, ground acreage fell from 7,950 to 50 acres. Neither the immigration reforms of the late 1980s and early 1990s nor the threat of NAFTA seem to have had any impact on planting decisions; production statistics indicate that trends were not interrupted from the mid-1980s to the mid-1990s. Similar observations can be made for citrus, which expanded greatly during this period.

While squash and cucumbers are not nearly such key crops in South Florida, they play an important role in keeping land and labor crews employed in production between tomato and green pepper production. They are also important "backup" crops during years when weather conditions cause losses of tomatoes or peppers. According to local cooperative extension personnel, growers explored more diversified cropping strategies in the wake of the 1989 freeze.

Production and Marketing

South Florida vegetable growers produce exclusively for a "fresh market," usually packing their produce themselves and selling to wholesale dealers who, in turn, ship to points across the United States. Where South Florida produce is sold depends primarily on competition from other domestic and foreign producers. During most of January and February, South Florida is the only domestic producer of tomatoes, competing with Mexico and other foreign producers; obviously, this accounts for the opposition of Florida tomato growers to NAFTA. During most of the winter, Florida tomatoes dominate eastern U.S. markets. Later, during the end of the harvest period—just before California producers harvest their first tomato crop—South Florida growers have access to the entire U.S. market, but at that time they experience difficulty filling orders. Pepper producers report similar marketing behaviors.

Vegetable producers have been extremely active in the general food market. Product branding remains primitive; although most growers stamp their names on the sides of their shipping boxes, none claim to have brand recognition comparable to Dole pineapples or Chiquita bananas. Even so, Florida produce enters the market by means of a multifaceted marketing strategy. Besides the efforts of individual firms, the Florida Fruit and Vegetable Association and other growers associations, such as the Florida Tomato Committee and the Florida Tomato Exchange, have maintained an active role in marketing Florida produce.

In 1990, for example, in addition to their opposition to NAFTA, Florida tomato growers attempted to boycott pinhookers. Pinhookers, who usually are Mexicans or of Mexican ancestry, use crews assembled from networks of family and friends to negotiate directly with growers for vegetables remaining in fields. These crews harvest the remaining crop and sell the produce themselves through open market channels or by trucking the produce to points as close as restaurants along the coasts or as distant as markets in Atlanta. The boycott against pinhookers originated with growers' fears that pinhookers were becoming too competitive, especially those who were trucking produce outside of Florida. Other fears derived from quality-control issues, since pinhookers tend not to have the packing facilities for washing tomatoes. According to one grower interviewed during our study: "When somebody in Atlanta gets sick from some pinhooker's tomatoes, they aren't going to blame pinhookers. They're going to blame *Florida* tomato growers." The boycott failed, however, primarily because smaller growers still rely on pinhookers for the sale of produce that would otherwise rot in the field. Months after the boycott was in effect, farmers throughout South Florida posted signs at their gates proclaiming, "Pinhookers Welcome."

Agricultural Labor

Until World War II, most of South Florida's agricultural labor was supplied by African Americans. Debt peonage, vagrancy laws, and other mechanisms of labor control assured growers a steady supply of labor during the early years of Florida agriculture (Daniel 1972). As African Americans entered wartime industries and the military, Florida agricultural producers began importing workers from the Bahamas and elsewhere in the Caribbean to supplement those African Americans who remained. This labor-importing program, known as the British West Indies Temporary Alien Labor Program (U.S. Congress 1978), built upon earlier uses of immigrant workers supplied through labor brokers in the Northeast (particularly New York City), and long-standing trade relations between Florida, Latin America, and the Caribbean. While the British West Indies program eventually was restricted to Florida sugar production, the practice of looking overseas for labor has not remained confined to the sugar industry.

Between World War II and the 1960s, South Florida vegetable production continued to depend primarily on African American workers, with sporadic use of foreign-born workers from a variety of countries. In the 1950s, French Canadians worked in the vegetable fields, and the first Hispanic workers began coming to South Florida from Texas. The latter signaled the beginning of the current Mexican dominance of South Florida vegetable production. Between 1956 and the mid-1970s, the proportion of Mexican workers grew in relation to all other ethnic groups. This ethnic change occurred not only in the harvest labor force but also in farm labor contracting as well. Today, by all accounts, South Florida vegetable workers are primarily Mexicans and Mexican Americans with direct lineal kinship ties to Texas, the Río Grande valley, and traditional labor-exporting states in Mexico, such as Nuevo León and Michoacán. Despite the Mexican majority, however, significant numbers of African American, Haitian, Central American, Cuban, and Puerto Rican workers also work in vegetables and occupy positions as farm labor contractors.

Thirty-Five Years of Florida Agriculture (1956–1991)

This section analyzes three phases of Florida's agricultural labor: 1956–1978; 1978–1986; and 1986–present. These phases reflect social and political developments that have had major consequences for growers, labor intermediaries (such as FLCs), farmworkers, and the overall structure and viability of Florida agriculture. The period between 1956 and 1978 was marked not only by the growth of Mexican migrant labor but also by great strides in farm mechanization, the end of the Bracero program (1964), the Farm Labor Contractor Registration Act (1972–1974), the Civil Rights movement, and U.S. involvement in Vietnam. The period of 1978–1986 encompassed passage of the Migrant and Seasonal Agricultural Protection Act, along with the entry of waves of Haitian boat people, Central American refugees, and Cuban *marielitos* into South Florida. These new immigrants reconfigured the ethnic complexion of the farm labor market, exerting a particularly lasting influence on packing and processing. Finally, a third phase began with the 1986 Immigration Reform and Control Act.

Phase I: The Mexicanization of Florida Farm Labor 1956–1978

By the 1950s, only two of the major cropping systems of South Florida agriculture—sugarcane and vegetables—had established themselves as viable economic industries with significant potential for growth. Citrus production was as yet important only in Central Florida (where it remains anchored, despite some fledgling development in Hendry and Lee Counties), and ornamental horticulture, including flower production, was not yet commercially significant. The vegetable and sugar industries, however, were well established as South Florida entered the second half of the 1950s.

In 1956, when Florida's total labor force surpassed one million people for the first time in history, the first Latino family appeared in Immokalee, seeking farmwork. Most Florida farmworkers, as noted above, were African Americans; as late as 1970, African Americans comprised 56 percent of the Florida farm labor force (Polopolus and Emerson 1975), with Mexicans making up only 6.4 percent of all farmworkers and the remainder comprised of growers' family members and others. In the last years of the 1950s, conditions in the fields and associated living conditions can easily be called to mind by remembering the widely publicized, nationally broadcast film by Edward Murrow, *Harvest of Shame*, much of which was filmed in and around Immokalee. That film depicted morning labor market negotiations, known as "shape-ups," not too different from those seen today in Immokalee. It showed abysmal living conditions, harsh disciplinary measures, and scenes suggesting the importance of housing, crew leadership, and transportation in controlling workers' labor time. Florida farmworkers and crew leaders were portrayed as predominantly black and white. The film's narrator remarked of an early scene:

> This scene is not taking place in the Congo, it has nothing to do with Johannesburg or Cape Town, it is not Nyasaland or Nigeria. This is Florida. These are citizens of the United States in 1960. This is a shape-up for migrant workers. . . . This is the way humans who harvest the food for the best fed people in the world get hired. One farmer looked at this and said, "We used to own our slaves, now we just rent them." (Barry 1990, 37)

By the end of the 1960s, several social developments set the stage for the influx of Mexicans and Mexican Americans into Florida agriculture. First, the

Civil Rights movement and the increasing U.S. military involvement in Vietnam aroused sympathy and organizing efforts among minorities, women, young people, and antiwar protesters. Second, the end of the Bracero program in 1964 and the growth of César Chávez's United Farm Workers movement furthered the general increased interest in organized labor among farmworkers.[8] The third factor setting the stage for Mexican migration was Florida's rapid tourist development, spurred by the construction of Disney World. Fourth, the beginnings of a national demographic shift to the Sunbelt was accelerated in Florida by massive federal investment in the space program and the associated growth of economy and population along Florida's east coast. Finally, the Cuban revolution removed Cuba from the competitive arena in agriculture (due to the U.S.-imposed economic embargo). The exodus from Cuba also yielded capital, technical expertise, and expanded markets for Florida growers.[9]

Phase II: Labor Force Restructuring 1978–1986

Influxes of Haitian, Guatemalan, and Cuban economic and political refugees into Florida from the late 1970s to the mid-1980s combined with the maturation of Mexican and Mexican American networks emanating out of South Texas to reconfigure South Florida's low-wage labor force by ethnicity, legal status, and experience in the U.S. labor market. By the late 1970s and early 1980s, Mexican crew leaders were assembling crews in Immokalee and Haitians were working the sweet corn harvests around Belle Glade. These two ethnic groups had already established footholds in the South Florida farm labor market.

During this period, sugar companies came under pressure from the U.S. Department of Labor and Florida Rural Legal Services to recruit Haitian and Cuban refugees instead of importing Jamaican workers. This pressure suggests that South Florida's labor markets were experiencing labor surpluses. Along with Cubans and Haitians, Guatemalans were entering South Florida labor markets at this time, swelling the potential agricultural labor pool. The growth and complexity of the farm labor force intersected with wider market conditions in agriculture to restrict farm wages to the legislated minimum wage. It is in this context of labor surplus that South Florida's labor force became differentiated by ethnicity, legal status, and experience. It is also the background for considering Phase III (1986–1991) of Florida's agricultural labor, based on information collected from a sample of eighteen growers, eighteen labor intermediaries, eighty-eight workers, and other observers of South Florida's vegetable production. The following section concludes with a brief consideration of NAFTA's probable impact on tomato production since the 1989–1991 research period.

Phase III: From Immigration Reform to Free Trade

The Grower Sample

South Florida's vegetable growers commonly own more than one farm and grow more than one commodity. The eighteen-grower sample used in this study represents 40 to 50% of all such growers in the region. South Florida agriculture is dominated by closely held family farm corporations. The eleven farms that are organized into corporations have more land on average than the seven farms that are not so organized (2,524 acres versus roughly 900 acres), although the gap between the two groups narrows considerably when the two outliers are removed (1,782 versus 1,036 acres) (see Table 7.1). Corporate organization is often accomplished for tax purposes, and therefore does not necessarily reflect distinct organizational differences. Thus, family farms predominate, and those in the sample are primarily vegetable farmers.

Table 7.1
Selected Features of Growers in the Sample

	County	Major Crop	Acreage[a]	Structure	Number of Vegetable Workers[b]
1.	Collier	Pepper	450	IP	75–150
2.	Collier	Tomato	9,200	Corp	400–500
3.	Collier	Tomato	1,620	FF	300
4.	Collier	Tomato	1,500	FF/Corp	500
5.	Hendry	Tomato & Pepper	200	FF/Corp	45–136
6.	Collier	Tomato	2,650	Corp	250
7.	Palm Beach	Pepper	700	FF/Corp	200
8.	Palm Beach	Pepper	1,360	FF	200
9.	Palm Beach	Tomato	4,915	FF/Corp	300–400
10.	Collier	Tomato	1,200	Corp	n.d.
11.	Lee	Tomato	1,600	Corp	100–225
12.	Collier	Tomato	1,380	FF	150–300
13.	Collier	Tomato	825	Corp	300
14.	Collier	Tomato	706	FF	370
15.	Collier	Tomato	2,450	Corp	400–500
16.	Collier/ Hendry	Tomato	700	FF	100
17.	Collier	Tomato	n.d.	FF/Corp	1,485
18.	Collier	Tomato	80	IP	64–71

IP = individual proprietor; Corp = corporation; FF = family farm. [a] Refers to total farm acreage.
[b]During peak of harvest.

Source: Griffith and Camposeco (1989–1991).

Four growers plant citrus along with vegetables, and all but three of the growers interviewed produce the four major vegetables of southwestern and southeastern Florida: tomatoes, various peppers, cucumbers, and squash. Only one grower in the sample raises cattle commercially, and among the citrus-producing growers, winter vegetable production accounts for more acreage than any other commodity.

Politically, the issues of environment, urban sprawl, and NAFTA overshadow growers' concerns with labor recruitment and utilization. Indeed, in the face of increased input costs, government regulation, and the specter of free trade, labor is one area where growers still exercise substantial control. It is, along with environmental concerns, also one of the two primary areas of contention surrounding the ratification and institution of NAFTA, and thus a key area in which to examine aspects of competitiveness.

Use of Farm Labor Contractors (FLCs)

Foremost among South Florida vegetable producers' labor practices is their use of farm labor contractors. Without exception, all growers interviewed use FLCs, although the specific character of their use varies. Some growers delegate complete control over labor relations to FLCs, while others work alongside FLCs in partnership-type arrangements. A major issue in grower relations with FLCs concerns the extent to which the relationship is fully or partially subcontractual, or the extent to which growers are directly involved in labor recruitment, employee record keeping, and supervision. A question about subcontracting farm operations elicited the following responses:

> "It's hard to subcontract labor. You can do it, but there's no supervision."

> "We've been subcontracting labor for the past three to four years. The crew leaders like it that way. He's running his own business. That relieves us of paperwork, but we pay extra for it."

> "Five years ago the crew leader used to be more of a subcontractor. Now he's treated more like an employee."

Variation exists in the use of FLCs. Only one grower reported subcontracting nearly all components of labor relations. More commonly, the larger firms have their own personnel directors who deal with FLCs on a daily basis, jointly managing and addressing labor issues, while the smaller growers work alongside the FLCs in their fields, also managing workers. In either case, FLCs provide valuable cultural and linguistic brokerage functions in addition to recruiting, transporting, and supervising workers.

Crew Size and Composition

According to growers, crew sizes have dwindled over the past fifteen to twenty years. This trend has been driven by legislation passed during the 1970s that altered farm labor practices—the Farm Labor Contractor Registration Act (FLCRA) and the Migrant and Seasonal Agricultural Worker Protection Act (MSPA)—combined with aggressive efforts by rural legal services to enforce these laws. As a result, FLCs have become more accountable to laws governing the transport and housing of workers and informing them of their legal rights, including pay levels, methods of payment, and other charges they incur while on the job. Most obviously, crew sizes decreased because restrictions on transporting workers led to more cars, vans, and trucks augmenting school bus-sized means of transport. Ironically, this trend facilitated mobility within the rural United States in general, enabling some farmworkers to branch out into other regions and other economic sectors. Less obviously, crew sizes decreased because, under the new conditions, smaller crews are easier to manage. This is especially the case when labor management involves not only task assignment and direct supervision but also recruitment, linguistic and cultural brokerage functions, and labor reliability issues.[10]

Smaller crew sizes may also be related to the growth of labor contracting as a way for entrepreneurial farmworkers to improve their economic positions. One of the complaints about FLCs, discussed in more detail below, is that there are too many "nickel contractors" whose only function is to assemble, for a fee, small crews of eight to twelve workers for work with larger FLCs.

Today's crews typically range in size from twelve to eighty workers, with most growers working between five and eight crews. As late as 1985, by contrast, crews ran as high as two hundred and fifty individuals. Internally, crews are organized by field walkers, who operate like foremen beneath the crew leader. In the case of "supercontractors" (Hepple and Amendola 1991), the crew leader may be working for a larger FLC. However large or small the crews, these days a grower's interaction with his or her field workers is always a *mediated* interaction, cushioned by the cultural practices and social relations that exist between the FLC, crew leader, field walker, and crew members. Growers in South Florida rarely "know" their seasonal workers independently of the crew leader. This lack of intimacy allows growers the luxury of overlooking or ignoring many of the farmworkers' more pressing problems. This applies, in particular, to housing.

Housing Issues

Worker housing constitutes a key differentiating feature among growers. Housing for workers varies from farm to farm depending on location, crop, and how much farm owners and managers need or desire stability in their labor force. Along the coast, zoning restrictions prevent growers from building migrant worker housing, a situation compounded by the area's rising construction and housing costs. It is therefore likely that southeastern Florida's growers will continue transferring the responsibilities of housing workers to FLCs and the workers themselves, as is common in southwestern Florida. This will continue the additional trend of housing farmworkers further from the coastal production centers, turning inland communities like Belle Glade and Indiantown into ever-larger labor reserves, and thus increasing the time farmworkers spend riding to and from work. Since it is not customary to pay agricultural workers for time spent traveling to and from work, this trend reduces their hourly wages. In addition, when workers have to pay for their own housing, their earnings are effectively reduced by around 25%, thus contributing to labor turnover (Taylor et al. 1997).

Some growers use housing as a means of stabilizing their labor forces. Building new farmworker housing may lay the groundwork for eventually applying for certification to import temporary foreign workers in the H2a program, which requires worker housing. The link between increased housing development and the H2a program was noted by some growers who hoped that citrus growers moving into South Florida would utilize the H2a program to reduce the competition for labor between vegetable and citrus growers.

Those growers who provide no housing to workers report, first, that workers are exceptionally destructive toward housing and, second, that government regulations regarding housing are too strict and sometimes contradictory. Failing to provide workers with housing has not resulted in either labor shortages or compensatory wages rates. Even so, those growers who provide no housing tend to suffer from higher labor turnover during harvest peaks, when they are forced to experiment with wage rates (offering slightly higher piece rates) and payment systems (frequency of payment) to secure an adequate supply of workers.

Wages and Systems of Payment

Two methods of paying farmworkers operate in South Florida: (1) payment according to a standard piece rate that varies little from farm to farm; or (2) payment by hourly wage, in almost all cases the minimum wage, plus a piece rate of one-third to one-quarter of the standard piece rate. A minority of growers pay only hourly wages.

While the wage rates are quite uniform, payment methods vary by idiosyncratic practice. During the season, many growers experiment with frequency of payment, with combining wages and piece rates, and with the piece rates by themselves. Some growers report dealing with labor shortages by first raising piece rates; if labor supplies fail to improve, growers may reduce the rate itself and change from a weekly payment schedule to paying workers daily, which workers prefer. Such examples indicate that farm labor relations are negotiated daily.

Payment systems changed on some farms in recent years, with more growers paying weekly instead of daily for most of the year. These changes are related to the growing practice of keeping records on individual farmworkers as opposed to leaving this responsibility to crew leaders. This practice raises an interesting issue pertaining to the FLC system and the relations between growers and FLCs. Specifically, it is likely that the shift from paying FLCs a single check for the entire crew to paying workers individually occurred because of questions concerning the FLCs' tax-withholding practices. Under the old system, FLCs could (and did, judging from lawsuits) claim that they were withholding taxes from workers and keep the amount withheld, or they could negotiate different wage rates with growers than those actually offered to workers. Two factors encouraged growers to assume the responsibility of paying workers individually. First, a number of growers interviewed—in Florida and elsewhere (Heppel and Amendola 1991; Griffith 1988)—clearly feared the aggressive legal action by rural legal services against FLCs and against growers as joint employers. Although these legal activities have been exaggerated in grower lore, the few cases that resulted in fines against growers were well publicized. Second, the persistent, wider negative publicity directed toward unscrupulous FLC pay practices probably also led more growers to begin assuming responsibility for paying workers in order to avoid investigations by state or federal labor officials.

This change in payment system signals an altered relationship between growers and FLCs, effectively reducing the FLCs' role from that of labor contractors to labor supervisors/managers and employees. Only one of the eighteen growers interviewed reported moving in the opposite direction—from using FLCs as foremen to subcontracting more of the work to them. In this case, the grower was an extremely large firm with supercontractors, who were entrusted with keeping payroll records and who themselves hired a number of registered FLCs as foremen, field walkers, and the like. Absorbing the responsibility for paying workers also offers growers more opportunity to experiment with payment systems, frequency of payment, and wage rates. Hence, they can directly witness the extent to which these aspects of production are related (or unrelated) to productivity, labor quality, and the health and welfare of their employees.

Grower Perceptions of Farmworkers

Those growers who work closely with farmworkers offer firm opinions about such factors as the effects of ethnicity, legal status, and length of time in the United States on worker productivity, docility, and reliability. Many studies have found that U.S. demand for farmworkers is characterized by a growing preference for Spanish-speaking labor (Griffith and Kissam 1995; NAWS 1996). During our interviews, a question about different ethnic groups having different attitudes toward farmwork elicited statements such as:

> "The Spanish will work, but Haitians have learned the system. There are too many giveaway programs."

> "Ninety-five percent of the crews are Spanish speakers: Mexicans, Texans, Guatemalans. Five percent of the crew are Haitians, but we do not like to deal with Haitians any more; there is a language barrier. Most of the crews are men, very few women. . . . For H-2 workers, we prefer Central Americans, Mexicans, Guatemalans—not islanders from the Caribbean."

> "The labor force used to be all Mexican. Also, now, the Haitians are leaving the fields, for tourist industry jobs. African Americans don't want to work . . . they're on welfare. Haitians have to do it [designated tasks] their way. Mexicans do it like you want them to. Haitians make a scene in the field if you don't like what they are doing. You have to beat them up or they'll beat you up. They'll tear up the stakes and then tear up the field."

> "Latins understand farmwork. They come from farming backgrounds, they understand how to treat the land. If they're laying sod they know enough to put the green side up. Guatemalans know how to work the land because they work it themselves back home."

> "People from the U.S. don't work. It's degrading to them. Haitians no longer want to work. They get here, get legal, and leave for the motels and restaurants. They're going for the air conditioning. Clean, cool environments. We lost a crew of Haitians to the Marriott."

> "Your average healthy Mexican can make more money in the field than in the packing house. In the packing house, women make the best graders. They're more conscientious."

Labor Intermediaries

Types of Labor Intermediaries

Labor intermediaries can be either company foremen, who work directly for companies, or FLCs, who supply and supervise labor. These are two distinct groups. Generally, foremen are middle-class, white or African American men who come from either farming or professional backgrounds, such as positions with the Job Service, the employment branch of the U.S. Department of Labor's Employment and Training Administration. They are familiar with registering FLCs, with state and federal labor regulations, and with the dynamics of the labor process itself. Others come from previous positions in agriculture, from rural industries, or from farming backgrounds themselves.

Far more common than foremen are FLCs. They are distinct from crew leaders who, although perhaps registered as FLCs, in practice act as supervisors and oversee a number of crews. An FLC, however, assembles crews, hires and supervises crew leaders and field supervisors, and occupies a crucial intermediate position between farmworkers and growers.

Farm Labor Contracting: General Characteristics

Throughout the United States, farm labor contracting is often a family tradition originating in the Mexican American and Chicano farmworking families of California and the lower Río Grande valley (Vandeman 1988). The migration into Florida of Spanish-speaking farmworkers during the 1950s and 1960s provided opportunities for enterprising farmworkers who possessed the cultural, linguistic, and social skills to establish themselves as small, nickel contractors. Many of them gradually parlayed these skills into building complex transportation, labor supervision, and housing operations. It is common for FLCs to respond to questions about their background in labor contracting by citing family involvement:

> "I was born and raised in Florida; I worked in a cotton gin many years. I've been in agriculture many years: in Texas I was a crew leader. My father was a crew leader; he did a little [contracting], but now he is a supervisor."

> "Family business—my father did it."

> "My father, uncle, grandfather were all crew leaders. I was born into it. The whole family (four men) work in the business."

> "Since 1980 I have been a crew leader in Florida. Immokalee, Clewiston. My father is here. He was a crew leader, but my bothers and sisters are not in farm labor."

Some FLCs and crew leaders, however, worked their way into labor contracting directly through fieldwork:

> "I started as a tomato picker in 1975. I started to be a foreman in 1980. I was born in Brownsville, Texas. My family came from Molcuino, Mexico. I came to Florida in 1975."

"I have been a crew leader for thirty-five years; I came from Edinburg, Texas, in 1950, where my family were farmers. I have a son working with me."

"In 1986 I registered as FLC. I was working as farmworker before. Summertime I go with my crew to Tennessee. I am from Guanajuato, Mexico.

"I was a peasant in Mexico. Texas was the first place I worked as farmworker. I came to Florida 1988. I am a field walker or foreman."

"My father was just a farmworker. I come from New York. My father is from Guadalajara. My mother is from Texas. I was working in oranges and I have been in Immokalee thirty-six years. I am alone."

"I came to Immokalee seventeen years ago as a labor contractor, seventeen years ago. I came from Hebronville, Texas. I was a farmworker there."

"I started one year ago. I was in Naples. I was a foreman. For eighteen years I was a farmworker in Florida. I am from Texas. I came from Mexico."

"I was born in Robstown, Texas. There I was in construction work. I am Texan. I am working as a crew leader in Immokalee, but I take people to Charlotte City, Florida. I have been a crew leader seven years. I was a foreman before that."

Table 7.2 further reflects the different personal histories of involvement in farm labor contracting.

Opportunities for becoming an FLC still exist; indeed, a chief complaint among labor contractors in South Florida today is that there are too many of them, creating intense competition against one another for workers. Crew sizes are normally thirty to forty workers, but can go as high as seventy. Nevertheless, as pointed out above, crew sizes have decreased since the mid-1980s, having peaked at two hundred and fifty to three hundred workers per crew. Shrinking crew sizes may underlie the growth of crew leadership positions that current FLCs complain about, since more crews of smaller size create opportunities for farmworkers to become field walkers, crew supervisors, or "nickel contractors." This gives farmworkers supervisory experience, a prerequisite for becoming a crew leader.

Along with the daily interactions of FLCs with crews and growers come several other responsibilities, some of which FLCs share with growers. Ultimately, growers and FLCs are jointly responsible for serious problems, especially those involving pay and occupational injury. Yet, FLCs, crew leaders, and field walkers assume full responsibility for day-to-day problems. In the

Table 7.2
Selected Characteristics of Labor Intermediaries (N = 18)

Type	Years of Experience	No. of Workers Peak[b]	No. of Workers Low[b]	No. of Summer Crews[b]	Migrant Destinations
1. FM[a]	5	400	15	9	None
2. FM	12	1,485	85	27	VA SC MD PA
3. FLC	n.d.	71	12	4	used to/quit
4. FLC	n.d.	50	30	4	none
5. FLC	25	60–100	30	1	GA
6. FLC	n.d.	315	100–150	7–8	AL
7. CL	6	105	40–50	n.d.	AL
8. CL	5	36–50	24	1	none
9. CL	11	110–112	30	3–4	SC
10. FLC	35	215–265	109–129	3–4	none
11. FLC	5	40	24	n.d.	TN
12. CL	3	280–320	130	n.d.	none
13. FLC	36	156	156	n.d.	none
14. FLC	17	210	120	2	none
15. CL	1	35–40	25	1	none
16. FLC	11	120	45	2	VA MD
17. FLC	12	90–100	72	n.d.	N. FL
18. CL	2	24	18	2	none

[a]FM = foreman; CL = crew leader; FLC = farm labor contractor. [b]Some double-counting occurs in terms of crew sizes, since FLCs tend to use the same crews for different crops.
Source: Griffith and Camposeco (1989–1991).

field, for example, a typical method of disciplining workers is simply to order the worker to leave the field, which is particularly harsh when the field is located as far as 20 miles from the farmworkers' living quarters. A less harsh approach is to refuse to "punch the ticket" (i.e., the card that is used to keep track of a worker's productivity and to reckon his or her pay). This can happen when the worker brings bruised fruits or vegetables to the truck. Both actions involve direct confrontations with farmworkers, which, witnessed by other farmworkers, can either strain relations with the entire crew or further enhance a crew leader's power.

Crew Compositions and FLC Preferences for Specific Types of Workers

Through close, daily interaction with workers, crew leaders and FLCs observe the changing compositions and attitudes of different kinds of farmworkers. Crew compositions reflect the Mexicanization of much of the rural labor force across the United States, particularly in agriculture. All but one crew leader, a Guatemalan with a fully Guatemalan crew, said that his or her crew was composed almost entirely or mostly of Mexican workers.

Regarding the gender composition of the crews, FLCs agree that men predominate; the women in the crews tend to be married or related to male crew members. Single males—those unaccompanied by their families—are most common, and dormitory-style housing, rooming houses, and crowded apartments with unrelated men living together are common sights throughout the inland towns of Immokalee, Belle Glade, and Indiantown. The declining use of Haitians and African Americans in the farm labor force has been offset by increasing use of Central Americans, primarily Guatemalans, as well as indigenous workers from Mexico, a process documented in California as well (Zabin et al. 1993). Still, Mexican workers remain the pillar of the labor force. Like growers, FLCs tend to cite the high productivity of single male Mexican workers, who emerge from FLC discourse as the cream of the farm labor supply. A question about preferences for specific types of workers yielded statements such as:

> "Mexican workers are here to work hard—if you need a lot of workers one day, a lot picked, use Mexicans. Otherwise, use Guatemalans, who exercise more care with the fruit."

> "I prefer Mexicans because they speak Spanish and are from my country. I trust them."

> "[I prefer] Mexicans. [They are] faster and good hard workers."

> "Mexicans: they know the work. The Guatemalans and Haitians don't follow the instructions."

> "[I prefer] Guatemalans and Mexicans—they do not complain."

> "I work with any kind of people, but I am more confident with Mexicans. There is a network between them."

The most obvious themes are those of productivity and experience with the work, yet some statements reflect cultural instead of economic attributes: language use; trust; confidence; and region of origin. There are also references to "dedication," "following instructions," and "lack of complaints." Together, such statements suggest that an FLC's profile of a good worker includes not only hard work but also a certain submissiveness or docility with regard to the crew leader's authority. Good workers do not question crew leader decisions; they understand and execute instructions quickly and accurately. Unquestioned relations are enhanced by hiring workers whom FLCs trust, who speak the FLC's native language, and so on. In short, most FLCs hire workers from their own cultural background.

Recruitment and Field Supervision

There are well-known shape-up areas throughout South Florida where large numbers of workers gather to wait for FLC buses daily. These places bustle in the early morning and are the most common sites of recruitment and daily negotiation over wages and working conditions. A few FLCs interviewed use a more direct recruiting method than the morning shape-up, trying to keep crews together by picking up workers at their living quarters. Others use housing as a way of recruiting workers and keeping crews stable over time, renting units only to those who work for them. Overall, recruitment relies heavily on traditional and informal techniques (shape-ups and networks), and almost never on formal agencies such as private employment agencies, the U.S. Employment Service, growers' associations, or other formal channels, such as newspaper advertisements. Indirectly, however, both the U.S. Employment Service and growers' associations do become involved in farm labor recruiting. The former register FLCs; the latter operate Agricultural ID centers that issue "white cards" (*tarjetas blancas*) to farmworkers, which indicate that work authorization forms have been properly filled out. Otherwise, state agencies and their formal channels have little direct impact on the daily business of assembling crews.

Crew assembly practices vary throughout the season, just as wages and payment systems change with labor supply. Early in the season (October, November), FLCs are more selective in hiring than in mid-December, when labor supply and demand are more in balance. Under conditions of perceived shortages of labor, "screening" is likely to consist of little more than refusing work to known "troublemakers." Of course, this implies a largely subjective component to screening. During labor surpluses, FLCs check documents and select the workers they prefer for subjective and objective reasons (including factors such as youth and gender and whether they are Mexican or from another Spanish-speaking background). Such screenings diminish as labor supply tightens.

Field supervision consists of staying with workers throughout the day and transporting them between activities and fields. Field walkers and crew leaders, many of whom have close kinship and friendship ties with a "core" of crew members, tend to maintain the pace of work, as well as order, through direct interaction with workers, leaving the system vulnerable to the idiosyncrasies of supervisors. Supervisory styles range from abusive to affective;

workers themselves demonstrate a great deal of sensitivity to stylistic differences in supervision and often base their decisions to quit on the poor supervisory skills of some field walkers. There are no formal grievance procedures in the fields—that is, no internal channels for appealing a decision by a field walker, crew leader, or FLC. Workers' ability to complain ultimately depends on personal relations with crew leaders, while the FLC relies on the fact that workers are generally interchangeable to enforce rules and orders. Crews generally do not include networks of friends and kin who will collectively challenge a crew leader's authority.

Government Regulation of Farm Labor Contracting

Accounts of infamous FLC abuses have motivated many key pieces of farm labor legislation and cases brought to court. Relations between FLCs and government agencies are, at best, uneasy and mistrustful, and growers and FLCs alike have reported instances of what they see as government persecution. The U.S. Department of Transportation routinely fined FLCs for insurance and safety violations in January 1991, an action FLCs viewed as unfair. Other government agencies particularly disliked by FLCs are the Wage and Hour Division of the U.S. Department of Labor, housing inspection authorities, and the Immigration and Naturalization Service, despised by FLCs and growers who rely heavily on unauthorized workers. FLCs convey a sense of being harassed by government agencies that act in the name of the safety and rights of labor. Animosity toward government agencies on the part of growers and FLCs tends to converge in response to new laws governing immigration (particularly employer sanctions) and the minimum wage, as well as laws designed to keep workers informed of their rights.

Farmworkers

Demographic Characteristics of South Florida Vegetable Farm Workers

The sample of eighty-eight farmworkers interviewed during the 1990–1991 season conforms to the emerging national profile of U.S. farmworkers (e.g., Hepple and Amendola 1991; Mines and Anzaldua 1982; Griffith et al. 1990; Polopulus and Emerson 1975; Griffith and Kissam 1995; NAWS 1997). Nearly half (49%) are Mexican or Mexican American, 20% are Guatemalan, and the remaining 30% are Haitian and African American.

Besides the predominance of Mexicans/Mexican Americans in the sample, the farmworkers can be characterized as highly mobile, relatively new immigrants, underemployed, young, working in a number of locations and for a number of employers or FLCs during the course of a year, and relatively inexperienced in the U.S. farm labor market. Seventy-eight percent were born outside of the United States, 91% are male, 53% are single, two-thirds rent their living space, and one-fifth live in employer-provided housing. The workers range in age from seventeen to fifty-eight, with a mean age of thirty-one, and are paid between $2.66 and $8.12 per hour, with a mean hourly wage of $4.62.

In addition to being primarily young, male, and foreign born, most workers live with three or four other farmworkers in rented housing. Less than 20% of the sample reside in South Florida with any of their children, more than 80% leave the area after the harvests, nearly 13% were in Mexico immediately prior to moving to South Florida, and at least 75% reside in other states or countries during some portion of the year.

These figures testify to a largely transient labor force attracted to the United States and South Florida for work as opposed to family or other noneconomic reasons. The foreign-born vary by their experience in the United States, an important factor when considering wages. More than one-third entered the United States since the passage of the 1986 Immigration Reform and Control Act (IRCA), and nearly half entered the farm labor market since then. This finding supports the conclusion, in line with a number of other studies (Bach and Brill 1990; Griffith et al. 1991), that IRCA may have contributed to increased flows of migrants. Seasonal agricultural workers (SAWs) can now cross the border with more ease, and with each return trip spread more labor market information to fellow workers about *el norte* (Massey et al. 1987).

Patterns of Farmwork: Crops and Tasks

Farmworkers rarely specialize in a single crop or task. The sampled farmworkers name five crops in which they are currently working and list ten tasks. During the previous year, however, the farmworkers gained experience in more than twenty-five different crops and twenty tasks. The tasks ranged from harvesting (the most common) to more skilled work with irrigation systems and pinhooking. Crops mentioned included a wide variety of leafy and other vegetables, fruit-and-nut tree crops, berries, melons, and tobacco. The distribution of crops and tasks over the survey sample was uneven, with the tomato harvests being the most important. Farmworkers typically move from preharvest to harvest to postharvest activities during the course of a year. Thus, while fewer than 20% of the workers listed tasks other than harvesting as their current task, this is probably more a result of the time of year of the survey (the harvest season) than an accurate reflection of the experience of South Florida farmworkers.

Physical and Social Conditions of Work

A short series of questions about the physical conditions of the fields revealed relatively little variation in workers' responses. Most workers reported having water to drink (99%), water to wash with (88%), and toilets (78%) at the fields. Very few farmworkers (less than 5%) reported having to pay for rides to the fields, only 4% reported having to pay for equipment such as gloves, and no farmworkers said that they had to pay any kind of kickback or fee to get the job. Further, only 4% of all farmworkers felt that the tasks they were assigned or the crops they worked in jeopardized their health enough for them to quit. This does not mean that farmworkers had no complaints about specific field conditions, tasks, or crops. In response to a question about crops that they quit, would liked to have quit, or would not like to work in again, slightly more than one-quarter of the workforce (27%) cited specific crops: 19% cited tomatoes; 5% said "any vegetables"; 2% cited citrus; and 1% cited flowers. A similar question about tasks elicited nearly the same percentage of complaints (28%), with harvesting most often cited as the task they would like to leave.

It is clear that the aspects of farm employment most germane to the workers involve not the physical conditions in the fields but the social conditions in the organization and supervision of work, including the nature of crew leadership and workers' relations with growers and farm labor contractors. Most farm labor recruitment, field supervision, and daily interaction with farmworkers is handled by FLCs as opposed to growers; in fact, fewer than 2% of the farmworkers stated that they worked for someone other than FLCs. The population is divided, however, over what might be called "loyalty"; 50% of the surveyed farmworkers work for a single FLC, while 44% work for more than one FLC. The remainder work directly for a grower, or for a combination of grower and FLC.

Some slight variations emerge when we compare these two groups. First, those who seem "loyal" to a single FLC are more likely to be either U.S.-born or Haitian, which implies that phenotypically black individuals will be more likely to work with a single FLC (34% of "loyal" farmworkers are phenotypically black, compared to 17% of the farmworkers who work for more than one FLC). This reflects the paucity of African American and Haitian FLCs relative to those of Mexican, Mexican American, or other Latino background, and suggests that phenotypically black workers have fewer alternative FLCs from which to choose.

Subtle differences between these two groups emerge in terms of experience in the labor market. Among foreign-born workers, those who work with more than one FLC are slightly more likely to have more than five years of experience in the U.S. labor market, while those who work for only one FLC are slightly more likely to have come to the U.S. only recently. This comparison suggests that farmworkers with more experience in the U.S. may acquire more independence from individual FLCs, and those with less experience in the United States are most likely to become dependent on a single FLC.

Wages, Benefits, and Factors Affecting Wage Rates

The wage rates and payments systems reported by the entire population of South Florida farmworkers agree, for the most part, with those reported by growers and labor intermediaries. Farmworkers reported earning average wages of more than the 1991 minimum wage ($4.62) for hourly tasks, with mean weekly incomes of around $175.00. Data about piece rates suggest that, for some workers, farmwork is potentially remunerative relative to other unskilled occupations, but that for other workers it is abysmally low paying. Numbers of buckets picked per day range from a high of 260 ($91.00 to $104.00, depending on the piece rate) to a low of 12 ($4.20 to $4.80), with the modal number being 150 ($52.50 to $60.00), the median 115 ($40.25 to $46.00), and the mean 117.11 ($40.98 to $46.84, sd=51.87). With the exception of those at the low extremes (one in five workers earns less than minimum wage), most workers seem to make more than minimum wage while working in South Florida vegetables.

Such variation encourages further analysis of the data. The farm labor market includes a number of job positions, with wide disparities between individuals at the high and low extremes of payment and work loads. Few dispute that farmwork can be high paying relative to competing economic sectors (e.g., food processing, hotel and restaurant work, landscaping). However, farmworkers' incomes are reduced by long periods of "wet time"—periods of little or no work. Because this chapter's research was conducted during the peak harvest season, few farmworkers reported earning less than minimum wage.

Examined more closely, however, the data reveal systematic differences between workers grouped according to experience and relative leverage in the U.S. labor market. Tables 7.3 and 7.4 show that the foreign born—who are among the most migratory—vary according to time spent in the United States and experience in the U.S. farm labor market, which in turn affects their earnings. The tables also show that wages vary by ethnic background, here deduced from the language spoken in the home, although this may reflect time and experience in the United States more than ethnicity per se.

These figures, particularly those presented in Table 7.4, are illuminating for other reasons as well. For example, the earnings of Haitians, who are known for their assertiveness regarding workers' rights in South Florida, are roughly

Table 7.3
Hourly and Weekly Income and Weekly Hours by Time Spent in the U.S.

Time in U.S.	Hourly Mean[a]	Weekly Mean[b]	Mean Hours[c]
U.S.-born	$5.50 (sd=1.45)	$200.17 (sd=94.04)	35 (sd=11.71)
Pre-1982	$4.87 (sd=1.26)	$215.90 (sd=40.82)	44 (sd=8.31)
1982–1986	$4.69 (sd=1.41)	$186.80 (sd=56.00)	43 (sd=10.39)
1987–1991	$3.97 (sd=.86)	$131.35 (sd=50.05)	35 (sd=11.66)

Analysis of Variance: [a]p = .024; [b]p = .001; [c]p = .047
Source: Griffith and Camposeco (1989–91).

Table 7.4
Mean Hourly Wages by Native Language Use in Home

Native Language	Mean Hourly Pay
English (n = 13)	$5.12 (sd = 1.35)
Spanish (n = 42)	$4.60 (sd = 1.27)
Creole (n = 13)	$5.13 (sd = 1.40)
Kanjobal, Chuj (n = 18)	$3.75 (sd = .43)

Analysis of Variance: p = .004; two cases deleted due to missing values.
Source: Griffith and Camposeco (1989–1991).

on par with those of U.S.-born workers. Conversely, the earnings of the Kanjobal- and Chuj-speakers from Guatemala, the newest immigrant groups in the region, are not only the lowest but also the least variable. It is not surprising, therefore, that Mexican workers are preferred to Haitians, and that Guatemalan workers are rapidly taking their place alongside the Mexicans.

Migration Patterns

The transience of farm labor underlies much of its quality as an occupation and accounts for a good deal of the demographic characteristics of farmworkers themselves. Seasonal work results in seasonally variable income, a seasonal need to migrate in search of work, or a seasonal opportunity for the foreign born to return to their home regions or to seek experience in other parts of the country or the world. Two comments on this issue are warranted here. First, in South Florida and elsewhere, it appears that some young (under twenty-five), male farmworkers view and experience the migrant way of life as those of us from a middle-class U.S. upbringing might view and experience summer camp. Consider the similarities: separation from parents and most other family members, dormitory-style room and board, daily outdoor activities, and farm labor contractors like camp counselors organizing, directing, and supervising activities. I do not mean to draw this comparison out too extensively. For one thing, these observations are not relevant to older farm-workers and to workers with families. For another, some aspects of farmwork (occupational hazards, dictatorial FLCs, and so on) clearly differentiate migrant farm labor camps from summer camps. Finally, I recognize the risk that such observations might deflect attention from the fundamental, wide-spread hardships of migrant farmwork. Nonetheless, among some young, male, single migrant farmworkers, this dimension does exist, a point that sug-gests comparative research on national, class, and ethnic patterns of life tran-sition and employment among young males.

A second, positive attribute of migrant farmwork is that it exposes young migrants and migrant families to new areas, broadening their horizons and experiences beyond the confines of the farm labor market. Pedraza-Bailey (1985) found that Mexican migrant farmworkers who settled out of the migrant stream in the northern regions of the U.S. Midwest acquired jobs that earned them more than the average standard of living among Mexicans and Mexican Americans living in the Río Grande valley. The long-term con-sequences of migration thus must be weighed against the hardships of migrant farmwork life.

Of course, most of the workers in this chapter migrate during the year to other farmwork jobs in the United States or back to their home countries. Among the foreign born, only 45% report never returning home; 12% return home every four or more years, and 21% every two to three years. A sizable proportion, 21%, are what we consider cyclical migrants, returning home every year. Most cyclical, 69%, are Mexican workers, while the other 31% are Haitians. In addition to such high international mobility, fully 83% of the farmworkers are migrants within the United States, working in other areas within Florida and/or other states. One-quarter of the population work only in Florida, while 35% work in two states, 25% in three states, and 13% in four or more states during a typical year. The farmworkers report having worked in seventy-eight different work locations in and outside of Florida, eighteen states, and four foreign countries during the year prior to survey. This again testifies to a highly mobile workforce, and confirms the idea that South Florida is both a labor-importing and labor-exporting region for the U.S. farm labor force. Most of the states were in the southeastern, eastern, and midwestern United States, although farmworkers also worked in California, Arizona, and Oregon. The farmwork locations immediately prior to working in South Florida vegetables are other parts of Florida (62%) and other southeastern states (11%), as well as west/southwestern (9%), mid-Atlantic (9%), midwestern (4%), and northeastern (4%) states.

Earlier it was mentioned that the workers in the sample had experience with more than twenty different crops. A typical "annual round" among South Florida vegetable workers is to work in vegetables throughout the year, moving from South Florida to the Palmetto/Ruskin area of Florida in late spring or early summer, then into Georgia or the Carolinas and on up into the vegetable harvests of the mid-Atlantic states, the Northeast, or midwestern locations such as Ohio or Michigan. The link between Florida and Texas, especially among Mexican nationals and Mexican Americans, remains durable as well. As discussed below, these internal and international migrations often accompany movement between sectors of the farm labor markets and between farm and nonfarmwork.

Nonfarmwork Experience

Growers' fears about IRCA concerned the movement of farmworkers into other low-wage sectors of the labor market, or the fear that legalization and increased "freedom" in the labor market from work authorization (that is, from SAW and post-1982 provisions of the law) will lead to higher exit rates from farmwork. This chapter's data suggest that leaving farmwork altogether is neither a common result of gaining experience in nonfarm jobs, nor a unidirectional movement. More than two-thirds of the sample had no experience outside of farmwork during the previous year. Yet, more than one-quarter of the workers (27%)—all of whom were working in agriculture during the time of the interview—had occupied positions outside agriculture sometime during the year prior to the interview. Obviously, these workers had moved back into farmwork from nonfarm occupations.

What were the nonfarm jobs? According to growers, the sectors of the economy most likely to compete with farmwork for workers were construction, tourism, and nurseries/landscaping. While not mentioned by growers, the food-processing sector (which includes vegetable packing, meat packing, and other kinds of food processing) was also a competitor for labor. To be sure, food processing can be considered merely another kind of farmwork, falling into the category of "agricultural services."

Employment outside of agriculture is commonly associated with migration. Some 45% of the sampled laborers work in nonfarm jobs outside of Florida, and many Mexican workers migrate from construction jobs in Texas to jobs in the Florida tomato harvest. Furthermore, some of the migrants working in Florida cross county lines as they move between farm and nonfarm jobs in their need to obtain multiple livelihoods.

Employment in nonfarm sectors varies by ethnicity. Haitians are the most likely to work outside agriculture, with 57% having some nonagricultural experience, mostly in tourism, compared to only 11% of Guatemalans. Even so, Burns (1993) found that landscape architectural firms in eastern Florida tapped into Guatemalan networks in Indiantown to secure labor for golf course construction, while Griffith and Kissan (1995) found poultry firms that recruited Guatemalan workers. Among both U.S.-born and Mexican/Chicano workers, around 28% have nonagricultural experience. The nature of this experience varies, and experience in nonagricultural sectors does not preclude employment in agriculture, as illustrated by the following vignettes:[11]

Rafael Olmo. Rafael entered the United States in 1988, at the age of fifteen, and began working a year later. With less than four years of experience in the U.S., he lived and worked in three states and two countries. From November 1989 to August 1990, he worked in North Carolina at a pork packing plant, until he decided to move back to his home in Veracruz, Mexico, for a three-month stay. Two days after New Year's Day 1991, Rafael moved to Brownsville, Texas, and found work as a manual laborer on a construction crew. This job lasted only a month, when a labor contractor he had met earlier told him of work in Palm Beach, Florida. This is where Rafael was working, picking cherry tomatoes, when we interviewed him.

Pierre Bastide. A Haitian who entered the U.S. in 1985, Pierre comes from a nonagricultural background in Haiti but entered the farm labor force as soon as he arrived. He came to the United States with his mother, and together they found work picking peppers around Immokalee. He suffered a back injury during the 1989–1990 harvest season and worked for a number of months in a packing house instead of in the fields. He worked seven days per week, earning around $170.00 weekly. By October 1990 he had recovered from his back injury enough to begin working in the fields again.

Miguel Hernández. Living with his two sons in a trailer in the labor camp of one of the largest vegetable producers on Florida's east coast, Miguel picks a variety of crops to assure a constant and varied supply of vegetables to the roadside stands operated by the farms. He came to the United States in 1987 but didn't begin working in agriculture until 1990, when, on the advice of his two sons, he left a construction job in Mission, Texas, to come to Florida for farmwork.

Pedro Martínez. Pedro left a job as an office worker in Mexico and entered the United States in 1990. He listed six separate jobs over the past year in the United States, including work in the tobacco harvest in North Carolina during the summer of 1990. In September he moved to Lantana, Florida,

and found work in a nursery—repotting plants, planting, and cleaning—
for a little over two weeks. In October he moved to Lake Worth and a job in
landscaping, working nearly a month until moving back to Lantana to sort
and grade cucumbers in a packing house for a month and ten days, when
he quit to enter the tomato harvest.

These cases indicate that decisions of migrants to move between the farm
and nonfarm sectors are conditioned by factors other than wages and working conditions, including occupational injury, network ties, and continued
migration between Mexico (or Haiti) and the United States. The specific
recruitment mechanisms, the dissemination of job market information, and
the locations of farmwork and nonfarm jobs enter into the rational calculus
of new immigrants and unskilled U.S. workers seeking employment. The
ways workers in such circumstances receive and act on job market information are creative and diverse. In one case in Brownsville, Texas, ads posted on
a restaurant wall told of work picking tomatoes in Virginia, giving the name
of a crew leader. Without knowing the crew leader, one individual said that he
called the crew leader and drove from Texas to Virginia the next day with fifteen other Mexicans. Combined with its reliance on a largely foreign-born,
migrant workforce, farmwork lends itself to such hastily planned excursions.
Not uncommonly, groups of ten to twenty young men will undertake a 2,000-
mile journey together on a moment's notice. Having arrived at the destination, the mostly young and unaccompanied male farmworkers are not likely
to pass up nonfarmwork if they are currently unemployed. Nor are they are
likely to pass up a chance to move back into farmwork if they perceive that the
picking is good, the piece rates promising, and the chance to earn more than
their current wages is high.

Conclusions

This chapter's observations suggest several trends in South Florida's agricultural workforce. Over the long term, there appears to be increasing use of
foreign-born, Spanish-speaking farmworkers; growth in farm labor contracting; a continuing tendency for growers and FLCs to recruit the newest of the
immigrant workforce; poor prospects for labor organizing; and remarkably
stable but generally low wages and rough working conditions. In the short
term, there appears to be an increase in the circulation of farmworkers among
U.S. southern, mid-Atlantic, northeastern, and midwestern vegetable farms
and an increase in their circulation between the farm and nonfarm sectors of
the economy; the movement of Haitians out of harvesting; the persistence of

pinhooking; and the raiding of agricultural labor markets by hotels, restaurants, landscaping firms, and nurseries in Florida's east and west coastal metropolises. These trends intersect with political and economic challenges to South Florida agriculture in the forms of NAFTA, stricter environmental regulation of water and run-off, and urban sprawl.

How is the continued unfolding of NAFTA liable to affect both farmworkers and farm ownership? The history of growers, FLCs, and farmworkers in South Florida is one of simultaneously resisting and adjusting to the terms of state intervention. Their responses to NAFTA seem no different. Organized resistance to NAFTA has come from growers' associations such as the Florida Fruit and Vegetable Association and the Florida Tomato Committee, whose representatives argue that free trade has already resulted in unfair trading practices by Mexican producers and the displacement of nearly half the vegetable producers of South Florida. Production statistics tell a somewhat different story, showing that acreage planted in tomatoes, cucumbers, squash, and other vegetables increased through the first half of the 1990s, but then dropped from the 337,850 acres planted in the 1994–1995 season to 323,200 acres in the 1995–1996 season, a decline of 4.3% (FASS 1997). If nearly half the growers have indeed gone out of business (a claim that individuals at the Florida Agricultural Statistical Service consider greatly exaggerated), it has had only a slight effect on plantings. This small impact suggests that NAFTA has caused increased capital concentration by pushing out the less competitive growers in what has become an international and interregional production system, in which companies produce in more than one country or more than one region of the United States. Several Florida agricultural firms already produce or help organize production on farms up and down the eastern seaboard and at some locations in California and Mexico (Griffith and Kissam 1995).

While these organizational changes are surely devastating to those family farmers who have been or will be driven out of business by free trade, it is unlikely that these developments will significantly alter farm labor relations in South Florida or in those regions of the eastern United States that South Florida communities supply with farm labor. Historically, the farm labor supply in Florida has adjusted to civil rights legislation, increased legal attention by Florida Rural Legal Services and government regulatory agencies, and immigration reform. Growers up and down the eastern seaboard and, increasingly, throughout the eastern U.S., often rely on the same FLCs that organize and supervise workers for Florida harvests. It is these individuals who organize the daily dynamics of the farm labor market and who are most responsible for labor recruitment and supervision; thus, it is these individuals

who exert the most powerful influence over the social and ethnic compositions of farm labor. Recently, FLCs (or simply LCs) have begun branching out
into other sectors of the economy, primarily food processing. At the same
time, they have begun tapping into networks of indigenous Mexican workers,
particularly Zapotec and Mixtec workers from southern Mexican regions that
are unlikely to benefit from NAFTA.

These trends build on four decades of integration between South Florida
and Mexico, dating back to the first families that entered Florida because of
developments such as the mechanization of cotton harvests and shifting cropping strategies throughout the southern and eastern United States. Today, the
Mexicanization of rural America is far advanced. Both agricultural and nonagricultural labor markets increasingly use workers from Mexico, Central
America, and the Caribbean. Labor relations are converging in ways coinciding with predictions that NAFTA would stimulate convergence between
Mexican and U.S. labor markets, perhaps raising labor standards in the former while lowering them in the latter. Small, isolated towns throughout my
adopted state of North Carolina now have *tiendas*, or shops, that not only
stock Mexican foods and fly Mexican flags but also provide translation and
international communication services to new immigrants to the region, serving as exchanges for housing and labor market information within and outside of agriculture. Entire rural neighborhoods and urban apartment
complexes throughout the state use Spanish as their principal language, and
cities and small towns are laced with aromas of hot corn oil and cumin. It is a
social, cultural, and demographic groundswell that preceded NAFTA, that
continued quietly and steadily through all the loud negotiations accompanying NAFTA's ratification, and that in the long run NAFTA is likely to reinforce.

References

Amato, Joseph. 1996. *To Call It Home: The New Immigrants of Southwestern Min-
    nesota.* Marshall, Minn.: Crossings Press.
Bach, Robert, and Howard Brill. 1990. The Impacts of the 1986 Immigration
    Reform and Control Act on the U.S. Labor Market and Economy. Final Report
    to the U.S. Department of Labor. Binghamton, N.Y.: SUNY Institute for Mul-
    ticulturalism and International Labor.
Barry, D. Marshall. 1990. *The Adverse Impact of Immigration on Florida's Farm-
    workers.* Occasional Paper No. 3. Center for Labor Research and Studies,
    Florida International University, Miami, Fla.
Basch, Linda, Nina Glick-Shiller, and Cristina Szanton Blanc. 1994. *Nations
    Unbound: Transnational Projects, Postcolonial Predicaments, and Deterritorial-
    ized Nation-States.* Langhorns, Penn.: Gordon and Breach.

Broidy, Elizabeth. 1987. Patterns of Household Immigration into South Texas. *International Migration Review* 21, no. 1.

Burns, Allan. 1993. *Maya in Exile.* Philadelphia: Temple University Press.

Chaffee, Sue. 1994. *The Survival Strategies of Haitian Immigrant Women.* MA thesis. Department of Sociology and Anthropology, Florida International University, Miami, Fla.

Collins, Jane. 1988. *Unseasonal Migrations: The Effects of Rural Labor Scarcity in Peru.* Princeton: Princeton University Press.

Daniel, Peter. 1972. *In the Shadow of Slavery: Debt Peonage in the South.* Champagne: University of Illinois Press.

De Janvry, Alain. 1983. *The Agrarian Question and Reformism in Latin America.* Baltimore: Johns Hopkins University Press.

Dinerman, Ina. 1978. Patterns of Adaptation Among Households of U.S. Bound Migrants from Michoacán, Mexico. *International Migration Review* 12, no. 4.

Fitchen, Janet. 1992. On the Edge of Homelessness: Rural Poverty and Housing Insecurity. *Rural Sociology* 57, no. 2.

Florida Agricultural Statistical Service (FASS). 1990. Florida Agriculture. Institute for Food and Agricultural Sciences, University of Florida, Gainesville, Fla.

———. 1991. Florida Agriculture. Institute for Food and Agricultural Sciences, University of Florida, Gainesville, Fla.

———. 1997. Florida Agriculture. Institute for Food and Agricultural Sciences, University of Florida, Gainesville, Fla.

Goldring, Luin. 1990. Development and Migration: A Comparative Analysis of Two Mexican Migrant Circuits. Working Paper 37. Washington, D.C.: Commission for the Study of International Migration and Cooperative Development.

Griffith, David. 1983. *The Promise of a Country: The Impact of the BWI Temporary Alien Labor Program on the Jamaican Peasantry.* Gainesville, Fla.: Ph.D. dissertation. Department of Anthropology, University of Florida at Gainesville.

———. 1986a. Peasants in Reserve: Temporary West Indian Labor in the U.S. Farm Labor Market. *International Migration Review* 20, no. 4.

———. 1986b. Social Organizational Obstacles to Capital Accumulation Among Returning Migrants: The British West Indies Temporary Labor Program. *Human Organization* 45, no. 1.

———. 1988. *Enhanced Recruitment Demonstration Project: Virginia and North Carolina Apple Harvests.* Technical report submitted to the Office of the Assistant Secretary of Policy, U.S. Department of Labor. Washington, D.C.

———. 1989. Consequences of Immigration Reform for Low-Wage Workers in the Southeastern U.S.: The Case of the Poultry Industry. *Urban Anthropology* 19, no. 1.

———. 1993. *Jones's Minimal: Low-Wage Labor in the United States.* Albany: State University of New York Press.

Griffith, David, and Jerónimo Camposeco. 1989–1991. *Labor Intermediary Survey.* Commission on Agricultural Workers.

Griffith, David, Ed Kissam, David Runsten, Ann García, and Jerónimo Camposeco.

1990. *Assessing the Availability and Productivity of U.S. Farm Labor Under Enhanced Recruitment, Wage, and Working Conditions: An Ethnographic Approach.* Second interim report to the Office of Policy, U.S. Department of Labor. Washington, D.C.

Griffith, David, Ed Kissam, David Runsten, Anna García, Jerónimo Camposeco, Manuel Valdez-Pizzini, and Max Pfeffer. 1991. *Farm Labor Supply Study.* Technical report produced for the U.S. Department of Labor.

Griffith, David, and Alex Stepick. 1994. Ethnicity and Allegiance: Forms of Capital and Transnationalism in Southern Florida. Paper presented to the Russell Sage Foundation, New York, N.Y.

Griffith, David, Monica Heppel, and Luis Torres. 1994. Labor Certification and Employment Practices in Selected Low-Wage/Low-Skill Occupations: An Analysis from Worker and Employer Perspectives. Technical Report prepared for the West Virginia Bureau of Employment Programs.

Griffith, David, and Ed Kissam. 1995. *Working Poor: Farmworkers in the United States.* Philadelphia: Temple University Press.

Heppel, Monica, and Luis Torres. 1996a. Maquiladoras and Migration. Policy Brief, Center for Inter-Cultural Education and Development, Georgetown University, Washington, D.C.

———. 1996b. Mexican Immigration to the United States After NAFTA. *Fletcher Forum of World Affairs* 20, no. 2.

Hepple, Monica, and Sandra Amendola, eds. 1991. *Immigration Reform and Perishable Crop Agriculture: Volumes I and II.* Washington, D.C.: Center for Immigration Studies.

Hudson, Bruce. 1979. *The Florida Citrus Labor Market.* Working Paper No. 35–79, Center for the Study of Human Resources, University of Texas at Austin.

Mahler, Sarah. 1995. The Dysfunctions of Transnationalism. Working Paper 73. Russell Sage Foundation, New York, NY.

Massey, Douglas, Rafael Alarcón, Jorge Durand, and Humberto González. 1987. *Return to Aztlan: The Social Process of International Migration from Western Mexico.* Berkeley and Los Angeles: University of California Press.

Mines, Richard, and Ricardo Anzaldua. 1982. *New Migrants vs. Old Migrants: Alternative Labor Market Structures in California Citrus.* Monograph 9, San Diego: University of California, U.S.-Mexican Relations.

Mines, Richard, Susan Gabbard, and Ruth Smartick. 1991. National Agricultural Worker Survey (NAWS). Washington, D.C.: U.S. Government Printing Office.

———. 1996. National Agricultural Worker Survey (NAWS). Washington, D.C.: U.S. Government Printing Office.

———. 1997. National Agricultural Worker Survey (NAWS). Washington, D.C.: U.S. Government Printing Office.

Model, Suzanne. 1985 A Comparative Perspective on the Ethnic Enclave: Blacks, Italians, and Jews in New York City. *International Migration Review* 19, no. 1.

Nash, June. 1993. *From Tanktown to High Tech.* Albany: State University of New York Press.

Nash, June, and M. Patricia Fernández-Kelley, eds. 1983. *Women, Men, and the New International Division of Labor.* Albany: State University of New York Press.

Pedraza-Bailey, Sylvia. 1985. Cuba's Exiles: Portrait of a Refugee Migration. *International Migration Review* 19, no. 1.

Polopolus, Leo, and Robert Emerson. 1975. Florida Agricultural Labor and Unemployment Insurance. Bulletin 767, Institute for Food and Agricultural Sciences, University of Florida, Gainesville, Fla.

Portes, Alejandro, and Rafael Mozo. 1985. The Political Adaptation Process of Cubans and Other Ethnic Minorities in the United States: A Preliminary Analysis. *International Migration Review* 19, no. 1.

Portes, Alejandro, and Robert Bach. 1985. *Latin Journey: Cuban and Mexican Immigrants in the United States.* Berkeley: University of California Press.

Richman, Karen. 1994. Entrepreneurs of Transnationalism: Haitian Communication Services in South Florida. Paper presented at the 1994 Annual Meeting of the Society for Applied Anthropology, Cancún, Mexico.

Rouse, Roger. 1992. Making Sense of Settlement. In *Towards a Transnational Perspective on Migration: Race, Class, Ethnicity and Nation Reconsidered,* eds. N. Glick-Schiller, L. Basch, and C. Blanc-Szanton. New York: Annals of the New York Academy of Sciences, No. 645.

Salley, George. 1983. *A History of the Florida Sugar Industry.* Clewiston, Fla.: Florida Sugar Cane League.

Sanderson, Steven, ed. 1985 *The Americas in the New International Division of Labor.* New York: Holmes & Meier Publishers, Inc.

Sassen-Koob, Saskia. 1989. New York's Informal Economy. In *The Informal Economy: Studies in Advanced and Less Developed Countries,* eds. Alejandro Portes, Alejandro M. Castells, and L. Benton. Baltimore: Johns Hopkins University Press.

Smith, Robert. 1991. The Mushroom Industry in Chester County, Pennsylvania. In *Immigration Reform and Perishable Crop Agriculture. Volume II: Case Studies,* eds. Monica Hepple and Sandra Amendola. Washington, D.C.: Center for Immigration Studies.

Stavenhagen, Rodolfo. 1965. Classes, Acculturation, and Internal Colonialism. In *Social Problems in Latin America,* ed. I. Horowitz. New York: Monthly Review Press.

Stepick, Alex, and Alejandro Portes. 1986. Flight into Despair: A Profile of Recent Haitian Refugees in South Florida. *International Migration Review* 20, no. 2.

Stepick, Alex, and Carol Dutton Stepick. 1990. People in the Shadows: Survey Research Among Haitians in Miami. *Human Organization* 49, no. 1.

Stull, Donald, M. Broadway, and D. Griffith. 1995. *Any Way They Cut It: Meat Processing and Small Town America.* Lawrence: University Press of Kansas.

Taylor, Edward, Philip Martin, and Michael Fix. 1997. *Poverty Amid Prosperity: Immigration and the Changing Faces of California Agriculture.* Lantham, MD: Urban Institute Press.

U.S. Congress. 1978. The West Indies (BWI) Temporary Alien Labor Program: 1943–1977. A study prepared for the Subcommittee on Immigration, Committee on the Judiciary, U.S. Senate, 95th Cong., 2d sess. Washington, D.C.: U.S. Government Printing Office.

Vandeman, Ann. 1988. Labor Contracting in California. Ph.D. dissertation, Department of Agricultural Economics, University of California, Berkeley, Cal.

Wilson, K., and W. Martin. 1982. Ethnic Enclaves: A Comparison of the Cuban and Black Economies in Miami. *American Journal of Sociology* 88.

Wood, Charles, and Terry McCoy. 1985. Migration, Remittances, and Development: A Study of Caribbean Cane Cutters in Florida. *International Migration Review* 19, no. 2.

Zabin, Carol, Michael Kearney, David Runsten, and Anna García. 1993. *Mixtec Migrants in California Agriculture: A New Cycle of Rural Poverty*. Davis, Cal.: California Institute for Rural Studies.

Politics of Decentralized Rural Poverty Programs

Local Government and Community Participation in Oaxaca[1]

Jonathan A. Fox and Josefina Aranda

Mexico is a key case for understanding the reform of rural development because it has become an international model for the rollback of state intervention in economy and society. The conventional view is that the Mexican state has withdrawn its heavy hand from regulating rural markets, property, and politics. We argue, in contrast, that the Mexican state's rural intervention continues in new forms, in some ways penetrating the countryside more deeply than before. This process is quite different from the patterns of rapid withdrawal that characterize the Mexican state's privatization of state-owned enterprises and international trade liberalization, for example. Compared with these "macro"-policy arenas, Mexico's reform of rural productive and distributive policies inherently involves much more decentralized and heterogeneous implementation, as well as large voting blocs important to the federal regime. During the administration of Carlos Salinas de Gortari (1988–1994), the state's managers considered the option of abrupt unilateral withdrawal from the countryside, but the political costs under growing electoral competition obliged them to attempt the creation of new pro-market public regulatory institutions (Cornelius et al. 1994). The state's rural reforms involved withdrawing with one hand, but "reintervening" with the other (Fox 1995).

To be successful in mitigating poverty, Mexico's promarket rural reforms require the state apparatus to operate with qualitatively higher levels of accountability than in the past. Yet Mexico's progress toward accountable governance—that is, accountability in the public institutions that enforce the "rules of the game" for market activity—has been highly uneven, across both policy arenas and geographic space. Many of Mexico's rural areas are characterized by weak civic movements for local democratic and accountable governance. Even where rural civic movements have broad, deep roots, they often lack the leverage needed to hold higher levels of government accountable (Fox 1996). Because of this unfavorable balance of power, the official project of streamlining and targeting the Mexican state's role in agricultural development and antipoverty efforts can be undermined by authoritarian elements deeply embedded in the state apparatus itself.

The context for restructuring the Mexican state's rural intervention was set after the debt crisis of 1982, when the state's managers recast its long-standing role in national economic development. The pattern of state withdrawal at the macrolevel involved little public institution building to occupy the resulting vacuum, as the inadequate regulation of the privatized banking system made painfully obvious. Distributive policy was a partial exception, falling largely under the heading of the National Solidarity Program (PRONASOL) (Cornelius et al. 1994).

In the short term, the Salinas administration's efforts to use PRONASOL's targeted antipoverty projects succeeded in buffering political conflicts driven by the social costs of economic reform—until the indigenous rebellion in Chiapas in 1994. The widespread sympathy for the rebellion among Mexico's rural poor showed that federal rural social programs were not necessarily having their intended political effect of controlling the countryside's potential threats to central authority. Much of the Salinas government's augmented funding for rural antipoverty programs did not reach its intended beneficiaries, and the spreading concept of "the right to have rights" weakened the impact of discretionary, clientelistic resource allocation. Under Zedillo, budget cuts and the dismantling of PRONASOL further weakened antipoverty programs. More generally, the increased public-sector accountability supposed to accompany market-friendly institution building lagged far behind the withdrawal of the federal state's earlier levers of intervention.

Against this backdrop, has the decentralization of rural programs increased their development effectiveness and public responsiveness? A particular problem of decentralized rural development programs is the typically limited capacity of local governments to improve policy outcomes. Rural local governments can be direct channels for targeted antipoverty programs because they ostensibly represent the poorest of the poor, but they are usually the poorest and institutionally weakest local governments.[2] Their capacity to represent the poorest citizens presents an even greater problem. Even if electoral politics are competitive at the national level, rural political maps are usually quite uneven, often dominated by entrenched authoritarian elites, perhaps dotted by enclaves of relatively democratic pluralism, with grey areas in between (Fox 1996). Official decentralization programs rarely take this heterogeneity into account. Researchers face the challenge of documenting generalizable patterns amidst inherently heterogeneous local development decision-making processes.[3] Our chapter examines the case of Oaxaca (see Map 6.1) from the standpoint of a decentralization program designed to strengthen local government and community decision making in the poorest areas of rural Mexico.

The recent wave of enthusiasm for decentralization has been encouraged by its conceptual compatibility with the decentralized mechanisms of productive resource allocation associated with free markets. In this view, decentralization becomes the appropriate mechanism for reforming the provision of public goods such as health, education, and targeted poverty-reduction programs. Nonetheless, *just as concentrated market power, rent-seeking, and other kinds of market failure can block the private sector's promised productive efficiency, authoritarian and/or bureaucratic concentrations of power at local and state levels can prevent decentralization from leading to increased public sector efficiency and accountability.* Our analysis suggests that devolution of project funding decision making to communities is not likely, by itself, to promote increased accountability.[4] The outcome is promising where local governments are *already* democratic and responsive to their citizens, as in much of the Mexican state of Oaxaca. Where these prior conditions do not hold, decentralization can actually reinforce authoritarian rule at the local level, as in the state of Chiapas (see Porter in this volume).[5]

The Mexican government has carried out a wide range of regional and local development programs since the early 1970s, but until recently federal agencies made the key decisions in those programs even at the most local levels. In 1989, the Mexican government began to channel significant amounts of resources to municipal governments. These resources were intended to fund development projects chosen by local communities, first under the multifaceted PRONASOL program and more recently under the banner of "New Federalism." The Municipal Funds program, like PRONASOL more generally, targeted the urban poor, peasant smallholders, and indigenous communities.[6] It was among the most decentralized of the various PRONASOL programs; others channeled their funding through local governments or social organizations, but key resource allocation decisions often remained in the hands of state or federal officials. By 1995, though, the Social Development Ministry reported that more than 90% of federal funds for regional development were channeled through state or local governments, at least 50% through municipal governments (*La Gaceta*, April 15, 1995 [SEDESOL]). The Municipal Funds program is the most important PRONASOL program to continue into the Zedillo presidency.[7]

PRONASOL was carried out against the background of growing numbers of rural Mexicans living in absolute poverty, in spite of macroeconomic stabilization in the early 1990s.[8] In an effort to target public works funding to the rural poor, the World Bank financed the Municipal Funds program as part of its $350 million Decentralization and Regional Development Project in the states of Oaxaca, Hidalgo, Chiapas, and Guerrero (1990–1995).[9] This chapter assesses the development impact of the local projects as well as the decision-making processes that led to their selection. Our field research focused on the state of Oaxaca. Of the four states funded by the World Bank loan, Oaxaca was the most likely to produce some positive results in terms of participatory decision making because of its unique system of local government; most jurisdictions are very small, responsive to indigenous communities, and relatively autonomous from higher levels of government.[10] The sample of local governments covers 9% of the state's 570 municipalities, stratified by region, relative size, and ethnicity. The empirical findings are representative for this state of three million people, but they cannot be generalized to states where local governance structures are different. However, the study highlights causal relationships relevant to other states, such as the importance of submunicipal governance structures for representing the rural poor.

The Municipal Funds program represents the confluence of two policy streams. The first is a series of innovations in the Mexican government's antipoverty programs during the previous two decades. Successive reform initiatives attempted to improve targeting and impact through varying combinations of community participation in project selection, job creation, community implementation, and oversight of projects.[11] This trend was paralleled by the second policy stream, involving the spread of autonomous organizations of low-income people, usually based on producer, consumer, village, or neighborhood associations. Societal participation in development decisions remained limited to project implementation at the local level. Poverty-reduction strategies generally excluded any role for civil society in policy formulation, though there were partial exceptions in a few regions and sectors. One case is the notable impact of the autonomous small coffee producers' movement on sectoral policy (see Porter in this volume, and Hernández and Celis 1994), and another is the National Indigenous Institute's Indigenous Peoples' Regional Development Funds (see Fox 1994). Only in these cases did the government allow social organizations to go beyond project implementation to participate in resource allocation decisions.

Uneven cycles of targeted federal antipoverty spending converged with a gradual process of administrative and constitutional reform to strengthen the municipality. After the amendment of Article 115 of the Mexican

Constitution in 1983 granted municipalities more responsibility for service delivery, town councils were created to decentralize municipal administration. This reform was only partial, however, since it did not match the new development responsibilities of municipalities with greater sources of revenue, especially in low-income rural areas.[12] Only in 1990 did the government's revenue-sharing formula begin to reduce its bias against poorer, rural states.[13] The Municipal Funds program involved a convergence of these twin trends of ostensibly more targeted social spending and municipal decentralization.

Program Implementation[14]

The Municipal Funds program proposes to devolve local project decision making to the municipal and community level. Its official goal is "to strengthen the autonomy of municipalities and to strengthen their capacity to respond to the community" (SEDESOL 1993a, 8). The Municipal Funds projects are instructed to follow PRONASOL's basic principles:

> respect for the communities and their decisions, support for organized social participation, co-responsibility in program operations, and honesty, transparency and efficiency in resource management. The direct executor of the projects will be, to the degree possible, the Solidarity Committee itself; the municipality will be responsible for seeing that the project is carried out in the terms approved by the Social Development [federal ministry] Delegation [state level office]. (SEDESOL 1993a, 11)

The state and federal governments set the amounts to be assigned to each municipality. The mayor and town council, together with representatives of the state government, then explain program operations and solicit proposals in each locality. The town council (*cabildo*) analyzes and selects proposals that comply with the Municipal Funds program guidelines. A municipal solidarity council is then formed, led by the mayor and including a representative of the state government, the local village delegates, or *agentes municipales* (representatives of outlying settlements, known as *agencias*), the municipal treasurer, the municipal councillor for public works, and representatives of the community-level solidarity committees ("to be democratically elected").[15]

In principle, municipal funds are to be spent on projects that "benefit the largest number of least favored residents" (SEDESOL 1993a, 14).[16] The specific program guidelines for project grants include community infrastructure and productive projects with potential positive social impact (in the form of loans for investment, though not for working capital).[17] Once the municipal council has been formed and the projects approved, an assembly in each community with a project elects a formal solidarity committee to take responsibility for its construction, operation, and maintenance. After the package of municipal project proposals is turned in to the regional offices of the Social Development Ministry for approval, up to 100% of project funds are transferred to the municipal authorities for deposit in a special account. Solidarity committees report project progress monthly to the municipal council, which in turn reports to the state government. Thus, while municipal funds devolve federal development funds to the local level, state governments decide how to allocate them among municipalities.

Allocating funds to poor states does not guarantee antipoverty targeting. The World Bank's loan agreement with the Mexican government did not specify that municipal funds should go to the poorest communities within each state. The agreement listed several criteria, including implementation capacity, need, and population size, but since they were not mutually consistent in terms of antipoverty targeting, in practice, the formulas were determined by each state government. Oaxaca Governor Heladio Ramírez (1986–1992) was atypical in that he distributed the funds relatively equally to each municipality. This amounted to M$50 million per municipality (almost $17,000), plus M$2 million extra budgeted per submunicipal agency.[18] Ramírez's apparently arbitrary formula gave the program an appropriately rural bias in Oaxaca, though the total amount for all projects in most municipalities was below the ceiling established for any *one* project in the national guidelines cited above.[19] Oaxaca's relatively clear allocation criteria contrasted with the lack of consistency and transparency in the other three states that received municipal funds through the Decentralization and Regional Development project. The state governments of Guerrero and Chiapas, for example, showed a strong preference for large urban pork barrel projects.[20]

The patterns of distribution of municipal funds *within* poor municipalities are crucial for determining their antipoverty impact. The municipal solidarity council is responsible for dividing the funds among localities. The council could allocate up to 15% of the funds to projects of its choosing, including those outside the program guidelines. Of the remaining 85% or more, only 25% could be spent in the town center, with 75% going to outlying localities. In those municipalities where more than two-thirds of the population lived in the town center, the ceiling rose to 40%. If the entire population lived in the center, then the municipalities could channel all of the resources there. This unusual intramunicipal targeting formula only applied to those states where municipal funds were supported by the World Bank Decentralization and Regional Development project. The formula was developed in response to

World Bank staff concerns that funds were being spent on projects that benefited the residents of town centers more than outlying areas (authors' interviews with World Bank staff 1994).

Our field study confirmed that project funds were actually delivered to most local committees. The mayor delivered cash or checks directly to the project committees in 82% of the cases sampled. These results suggest a major shift away from the traditional centralization of local power in the hands of the mayor. Moreover, because of powerful village-level accountability mechanisms in rural Oaxaca, once in local hands the resources were likely to be allocated to public works projects. Only in 18% of the cases were project materials delivered in kind, which increased the likelihood that resources would be lost or that project materials would be inappropriate, of low quality, or delayed.[21]

In theory, local communities could choose from a wide range of possible projects, as long as they fit under the budget ceiling and could be completed within the annual project cycle. Since the grants for each municipality were quite small to begin with, however, village-level subproject budgets were often negligible (after they were divided among the communities within the municipalities). These very low budgets led many community leaders to suggest that municipal funds be applied to somewhat more ambitious, higher-impact projects that could be carried out in stages over several years. Though this was the long-standing practice of community self-help public works projects in Oaxaca, it was explicitly prohibited by the Municipal Funds program guidelines.[22] The combination of subdivided project funds combined with fixed year-long project cycles sharply narrowed the ostensibly wide range of possible community choices to a short menu of projects that could actually be completed within a few months with a few thousand dollars (even taking into account counterpart contributions from the communities, which were consistently far above the program's 20% minimum).

The funds were successfully dispersed to remote rural areas, but a significant minority of projects had little impact on poverty reduction. One indicator is the number of projects that were simply not functioning. Our statewide sample of municipalities revealed that one-third of projects were nonoperational, while the more in-depth project level sample found a lower rate of one-quarter not functioning.[23] Another impact indicator is the distribution of funds by project category. For example, in the program's second year (1991), 27.8% of project funding in Oaxaca was earmarked for "urbanization." This category refers to such activities as paving the town square, building park benches, and fixing the town hall. In descending order, the other main funding categories were: school buildings (21%), drinking-water systems (18.5%), rural roads (9.9%), warehouses (6.9%), and culture and sports (basketball courts) (6.2%). Only 5.2% of Oaxaca project funds were spent on productive infrastructure, the highest rate among Mexico's four poorest states. Some residents may well have preferred to use project funds to pave their town square or to build a basketball court rather than to create or extend a drinking-water system but budget and technical requirements also influenced communities, biasing decisions toward cheaper, easier, and lower-impact projects. For example, sustainable drinking-water systems tend to be much more expensive than park benches and they certainly require much more technical assistance. The standard prototypes for urbanization-related designs and budgets are already on the desks of state government officials. In contrast, community drinking-water systems must be custom designed, requiring a significant investment of a technician's time. As a result, local project choices are likely to be influenced by the balance of power between state officials and local communities.

The prorural formula for distributing funds between town centers and outlying settlements was widely respected in Oaxaca. Municipalities created a variety of mechanisms through which to divide project funds between (potentially competing) smaller localities. Those with large numbers of out-lying *agencias* faced special challenges in finding formulas through which to distribute municipal funds. One obvious solution was to give equal annual grants for each village, but since the amounts were then often too small to provide even the most modest public goods, municipal authorities often encouraged *agencias* to take turns each year. This was not easy, since at first not all believed that the program would be sustained; therefore, those villages that waited perceived a risk of not getting their share. The funds offered were sometimes so small that villages rejected them, since they fell far short of the minimum needed for a high-impact project. The counterpart community funding required for any project considered worthwhile was perceived as a major burden. Even in the poorest communities, "volunteer" labor contributions come at a cost, especially for cosmetic projects that do not meet pressing immediate needs. This problem of too-small grants had a positive side, since it facilitated the bunching up of funds as different *agencias* took turns (e.g., Ejutla, Tenetze de Zaragoza, San Juan Cacahuatepec). In addition, some local authorities complained that the distribution of funds among rural munici-palities was not equitable, suggesting that those with many *agencias* should receive proportionately more than smaller municipalities. Overall, the Municipal Funds program tended to empower local *agencias* by giving them a sense of entitlement to development. Where central municipal authorities denied outlying *agencias* access to "their" funds, the resulting protest could be quite intense (as in Ixtlán, where village leaders held the governor captive until the problem was resolved).

The program's intramunicipal decentralization funding strategy fit well with Oaxaca's preexisting structure of local government. Officially, the municipality is the lowest level of government in Mexico, so the powers of submunicipal structures of representation are often not formalized. These diverse webs of submunicipal governance are considered quite formal by local residents, however. The capacity of these "hidden institutions" to represent the interests of outlying villages depends on whether their leaders are chosen "from above" or "from below." In most of Mexico, submunicipal agents are chosen by the mayor and therefore do not necessarily represent their constituents at all, especially since mayors usually come from the municipal center (*cabecera*). In some states these agents are even referred to as the mayor's "delegates." As one might expect, this situation leads to frequent "micropolitical" conflicts more than local autonomy.[24]

Where submunicipal leaders are chosen by the residents of the *agencia*, as in most of Oaxaca, they are usually chosen through community assemblies, though some are elected through the ballot box. Well over 400 of Oaxaca's 570 municipalities are organized along non-Western ethnic lines, with councils of elders and community assemblies rather than ballots and political parties.[25] Many midsized municipalities are in an ongoing process of transition, with electoral party politics in the town centers coexisting with community assemblies in outlying areas, as in Tlacolula (see Díaz Montes 1992).

The official program structure of municipal solidarity councils and local solidarity committees was largely folded into existing organs of local government.[26] Most rural Oaxaca communities already had long traditions of active public works committees as part of their ethnically based system of rotating community responsibilities. These positions are chosen through community consensus and are unpaid, full-time responsibilities. In the smaller villages, most Municipal Fund projects were carried out by committees led by municipal authorities, such as the town council or the local municipal *agente*.[27] In our sample, 64% of the presidents of the local solidarity committee were also municipal leaders, which usually meant that the municipal *agentes* presided. The local solidarity committee was named by assembly in 60% of municipalities. The committees were chosen by the mayor in 28% of cases and by "others" in the remaining 12%.

A slight majority of Municipal Funds project decisions were made primarily by community assemblies. The local solidarity committee played the primary role most often (38%), while the broader community assembly decided in 20% of the cases. Community groups therefore chose the projects in 58%

of the municipalities sampled. But the division of labor between municipal authorities, community assemblies, and local committees varied greatly. The mayor played the main role in choosing projects in 26% of the cases, with the state government delegate deciding in 16%.[28] The implication of this large role for mayors is ambiguous, since it combines those mayors who are accountable to their communities with less responsive leaders.[29] The data revealed a possible association between municipalities where the mayor centralized power and the use of antipoverty funds for largely cosmetic urbanization projects (e.g., San Pedro and San Pablo Ayutla, Santa Cruz Tachache de Mina). Even though Santa Cruz lacked a potable-water system, the mayor claimed, "people were pleased with the street paving because it gives the town another image. Both the teachers and folks who aren't from here like it."

While most project selection decisions were made in community assemblies, they were often influenced by the involvement of state government officials. Our statewide sample found that *state government officials significantly influenced project choices in at least 38 percent of the municipalities surveyed.* Because communities were largely dependent on state government officials for information about program options and procedures, for technical assistance (if any), and for official acceptance of project expense receipts, these higher-level officials could exercise de facto veto power over community project choices (as in San Juan Guichicovi, San Pedro Pochutla, San Pablo Huixtepec, and Ixtlán de Juárez). The governor himself personally handed the grant checks to the mayors of 86% of the municipalities surveyed. The ceremony and symbolism suggest centralized discretionary power, rather than increased municipal autonomy.

The case studies further suggest that state officials tended to encourage communities to choose less ambitious, lower-impact projects. After state government officials convened community assemblies to define local public works priorities, they would often respond to the prioritized list by indicating which projects were too expensive and which ones would take more than the time available.[30] Ostensibly, the program guidelines permitted production-support projects, but these guidelines were rarely made known to community leaders. Because these same state government officials were those responsible for providing technical assistance for design and budget planning, they had little incentive to encourage communities to choose projects that would require significant technical assistance, creative budgeting, and significant amounts of time spent in remote villages.[31] These officials, often engineers and architects operating out of the state government's regional office, tended to encourage communities to choose projects for which they had standardized blueprints and budgets (e.g., basketball courts versus sustainable drinking-water systems). Indeed, this higher-level veto power over local autonomy was deeply embedded in the official program procedures themselves all along, since the federal Social Development Ministry officials had to sign off on every local project proposal and budget (SEDESOL 1993a).

Local Project Impact

The statewide survey of municipalities was followed by more in-depth field observation of a sample of 145 projects, 76% of which were in areas outside of the municipal centers. The first indicator of project impact was whether or not they were actually completed and/or in operation. Most projects were found to be finished (86%), and 75% were actually in use. The largest category of projects *not* working involved drinking water (fourteen of the twenty water projects in the sample were not in operation).[32] The second indicator was based on each field researcher's assessment of whether a project had significant, low, or no positive social impact (based on the opinions of local residents and leaders together with direct field observation).[33] In terms of observed impact, 56% of projects surveyed were considered significantly positive (81 of 145). The rest were considered either low impact (27%) or with no positive impact at all (17%).

Notably, the more remote, outlying communities had fewer significant-impact projects and more project failures than the municipal centers.[34] Nonoperational projects were disproportionately concentrated in the outlying areas. Three-quarters of projects in municipal centers were considered successful (74%), in contrast to a 50% success rate in outlying areas. There was a strong correlation between project impact and location, with less than 3% margin of error. In contrast to these clear differences within municipalities, the total municipal population size was not correlated with project impact.

The more indigenous communities also had fewer high-impact projects and more project failures than the nonindigenous (*mestizo*) communities. Two distinct but complementary indicators were used to identify ethnicity. First was each community's predominant ethnic identity as explained by the local population (self-identification). The second indicator of ethnicity used municipal-level census data to determine the percentage of indigenous language speakers. The basic patterns were similar for both indicators. In terms of the self-identified community indicator of ethnicity, more than 70% of the projects studied were in indigenous communities. Twenty percent of these projects had no social impact, in contrast to the 10% failure in mestizo areas; similarly, 53% of projects in indigenous areas had significant impact, compared to 62% of projects in mestizo communities.

As one might expect, a relationship existed between community selection of projects and perceived social impact. Community assemblies made the project selection decisions in almost two-thirds of the cases (63%). Another 11% were chosen by community assemblies together with municipal councils. Municipal councils alone and mayors each selected 9% of projects, respectively. Subgroups within communities chose 3%, while a further 6% were selected by external actors. At the two extremes of positive versus insignificant projects, *community decision making produced disproportionately more effective projects, while those chosen by mayors and external actors tended to produce insignificant antipoverty impact.*

The local political context was also relevant for project impact, though not in the way one might expect. In the sample studied, municipalities governed by opposition parties were not discriminated against in project funding.[35] The key political factor correlated with positive project impact was whether municipalities had competitive political party systems, regardless of which party was in power.[36] The vast majority of municipalities governed by political parties were found to have successful projects: 85% compared to 56% overall. One possible explanation is that municipalities governed by political parties, whether official or of the opposition, are more likely to have clout with state authorities. They would therefore have more access to both technical assistance and supplemental state government funds.[37] Overall, *the Municipal Funds program worked well where democratic party competition was well consolidated (usually after many years of citizen mobilization and conflict), but worked poorly where civic movements had yet to achieve a stable, local-level democratic system.*

Conclusions

The vast majority of municipal leaders and project participants interviewed expressed a positive opinion of the Municipal Solidarity Funds program. For many rural municipalities, the grants were the first source of regular project funding, since conventional revenue-sharing does not favor rural areas. The Municipal Funds budgets were tiny and the projects chosen were often not the top local priorities, but the simple fact of having a project budget was widely considered to be a major step forward.[38]

One of this chapter's most important findings is that active community participation in project selection and implementation is necessary but far from sufficient to produce social impact. Some observers might expect Municipal Funds projects to be more successful in smaller, more indigenous communities, which tend to be more participatory in their local governance.

In practice, however, the most remote and most indigenous communities had disproportionately *fewer* successful projects (defined in terms of their perceived positive social impact). The most plausible explanation of this ethnic impact bias is related to the very small project amounts per outlying community and the lack of sufficient community leverage over state officials. Such leverage is important for getting the appropriate technical assistance (and discretionary counterpart funds) often crucial to high-impact projects.

In spite of the program's prorural targeting measures, municipal centers still received consistently larger budgets than outlying communities. Local project impact was constrained by the very small amounts available once budgets were divided up within municipalities.[39] To illustrate the gap between average amounts of money spent on projects in municipal centers and those in outlying areas, the budgets for a sample of 45 municipalities were broken down into 25 and 75% shares, assuming respect for the budget cap for projects in town centers. The results were examined in terms of the three full years of budget data, assuming that each locality received an equal share of its 75%. In only one-third of these cases were average per-project amounts outside the municipal center equal to or greater than the amounts spent in the town centers. The same issue was examined using actual project-level budget data, divided into averages for municipal centers and outlying settlements for each of the two years for which such data were available. In 1990, municipal centers received an average of $18,500, while projects in outlying areas averaged just over $4,300. In 1992, municipal center projects averaged over $25,000, while projects in localities averaged just over $9,000. Given this sharp per-project budget imbalance, it is not surprising that projects in outlying settlements did less well. Indeed, it is remarkable that the impact imbalance was not greater.

Local project impact was also constrained by the lack of adequate technical assistance. Only the largest municipalities in poor states have their own technical capacity or the resources to hire services from the private sector. As a result, the state government has a virtual monopoly on technical service provision for Municipal Funds projects, yet municipalities lack the leverage over state government officials needed to encourage better technical support.[40] Only the largest local governments among Oaxaca's 570 municipalities could be expected to have much leverage over state officials. Since electoral politics were not competitive at the state level (at least until 1998), the threat of joining the opposition offered little leverage. Yet, the lack of a statewide electoral challenge facilitates state government tolerance for those municipalities that do vote for the opposition. Most municipal governments therefore lack both the "exit" and the "voice" options needed to increase accountability

(Paul 1992). Increased funding for state technical assistance would not necessarily improve the amount and quality of services available, since the basic problem is lack of accountability to "beneficiary" communities.

The state government played a central role in program implementation but often did not encourage increased municipal autonomy and capacity as a development actor. Our study found no evidence that the Municipal Funds program significantly changed the federal/state/municipal balance of power; indeed, it caused more funding to be injected through the existing structure. The key institutional change encouraged by the Municipal Funds in Oaxaca occurred *within* municipalities, shifting *cabecera/agencia* relations in favor of outlying areas. In the context of the traditional centralization of power within municipalities, the requirement that most project funding go directly to outlying villages created an important opportunity to channel benefits to the poorest areas and to increase their voice within local government. Even though per capita investments in outlying *agencias* were very low, the Municipal Funds program increased these communities' capacity to manage projects and perhaps represent the interests of their constituents in other arenas. The sense of local entitlement encouraged by the Municipal Funds' prorural targeting formula is likely to have unexpected consequences in favor of community empowerment.

Because of the diversity of structures of rural local government, in Mexico as elsewhere, one cannot generalize these empirical findings beyond the state of Oaxaca. The analytical issues, however, highlight the key institutional determinants of rural decentralization outcomes elsewhere. The Oaxaca results suggest that the Municipal Funds program is likely to be folded into existing local governments and that it will reinforce existing submunicipal governance structures. The problem is that these two processes will produce completely different outcomes in states where municipal and submunicipal governance structures are neither democratic nor internally decentralized. According to a review of state laws regulating submunicipal systems of governance, only seven states allow local communities to choose their own submunicipal leaders, fourteen states allow the mayors to designate them, and eight have mixed systems, with some layers of local representatives chosen from above and others chosen from below (Fox and Aranda 1996b, 19, 64–67).

Where mayors are not chosen democratically, and where they in turn impose their delegates on local communities, there is no reason to expect that the Municipal Funds program will increase the responsiveness of local government. In these states, increased funding under the rubric of decentralization may well bolster the autonomy of local government by increasing its autonomy from its own citizens.

The Chiapas experience puts Oaxaca in context (see the chapters by Conroy and West and by Porter in this volume). Compared to Oaxaca, Chiapas municipalities are larger in terms of area and population, the class and ethnic polarization between town centers and *agencias* is much sharper, and mayors appoint submunicipal officials, rather than allowing them to be chosen by villagers. Most municipal authorities in Chiapas are imposed by state officials and do not appear to represent majority interests—as indicated by the widespread and broad-based civic movements that spread throughout the state after January 1994 (far beyond the area of military conflict).[41] Indeed, even the official version of the December 22, 1997, massacre in Acteal acknowledges that the murders were led by a state government-backed mayor who crushed a nonviolent movement for local autonomy.[42] If the Municipal Funds program worked consistently as designed, then it is likely that this same mayor bolstered his own local factional support with World Bank antipoverty funds.

In Oaxaca, the Municipal Funds' prorural, promunicipal decentralization effort strengthened *already responsive* structures of local government in most of the state. In Chiapas, the Municipal Funds program may well have strengthened authoritarian local elites. The Oaxaca-Chiapas comparison suggests that both municipal democracy and intramunicipal decentralization are necessary conditions for decentralized development programs to target the rural poor effectively. More broadly, they suggest that fundamental to the process of fighting rural poverty is Mexican civil society's capacity to influence the chain of local, state-level, and federal and multilateral policies, and to hold both the government and the World Bank accountable for their development decisions.[43]

References

Acevedo, María Luisa et al. 1993. *Etnografía y educación en el Estado de Oaxaca.* México, D.F.: INAH.

Barabas, Alicia, and Miguel Bartolomé, eds. 1986. *Etnicidad y pluralismo cultural: La dinámica étnica en Oaxaca.* México, D.F.: INAH.

Bhatnagar, Bhuvan, and Aubrey Williams, eds. 1992. *Participatory Development and the World Bank: Potential Directions for Change.* World Bank Discussion Paper No. 183, Washington, D.C.

Boltvinik, Julio. 1995. La pobreza en México 1984–1992 según INEGI-CEPAL. *Economía Informa* 237.

Burguete, Araceli. 1998. Remunicipalización en Chiapas: Los retos. *Memoria* 114.

Cabrero Mendoza, Enrique. 1995. *La nueva gestión municipal en México. Análisis de experiencias innovadoras en gobiernos locales.* México, D.F.: Porrúa/CIDE.

Carrasco Altamirano, Diódoro. 1995. Por un desarrollo más justo y equilibrado. In

Propuesta: Nuevo Federalismo, ed. Alicia Ziccardi. Special section of *El Nacional*, May 7.

Centro Nacional de Estudios Municipales. 1988. *Los municipios de Oaxaca*. México, D.F.: Secretaría de Gobernación.

Collins, Joe. 1995. *Communal Work and Rural Development in the State of Oaxaca in Mexico*. Geneva: International Labour Office.

Cornelius, Wayne, Ann Craig, and Jonathan Fox, eds. 1994. *Transforming State-Society Relations in Mexico: The National Solidarity Strategy*. La Jolla, Calif.: Center for U.S.-Mexican Studies, University of California at San Diego.

Crook, Richard, and James Manor. 1994. Enhancing Participation and Institutional Performance: Democratic Decentralisation in South Asia and West Africa. Unpublished report to ESCOR, the Overseas Development Administration.

Dennis, Philip. 1987. *Intervillage Conflict in Oaxaca*. New Brunswick, N.J.: Rutgers University Press.

Díaz Montes, Fausto. 1992. *Los municipios: La disputa por el poder local en Oaxaca*. Oaxaca: IIS/UABJO.

Domínguez Domínguez, Marcelino. 1988. Poder comunal: Instrumento de autodesarrollo. Caso de Cacalotepec Mixe, Oaxaca. *El Medio Milenio* 3.

Embriz, Arnulfo ed. 1993. *Indicadores socioeconómicos de los pueblos indígenas de México*. México, D.F.: Dirección de Investigación y Promoción Cultural, Instituto Nacional Indigenista.

Fox, Jonathan. 1994. Targeting the Poorest: The Role of the National Indigenous Institute in Mexico's National Solidarity Program. In *Transforming State-Society Relations in Mexico: The National Solidarity Strategy*, eds. Wayne Cornelius, Ann Craig, and Jonathan Fox. La Jolla, Calif.: Center for U.S.-Mexican Studies, University of California at San Diego.

———. 1995. Governance and Rural Development in Mexico: State Intervention and Public Accountability. *Journal of Development Studies* 32, no. 1.

———. 1996. How Does Civil Society Thicken? The Political Construction of Social Capital in Rural Mexico. *World Development* 24, no. 6.

———. 1997a. The World Bank and Social Capital: Contesting the Concept in Practice. *Journal of International Development* 9, no. 7.

———. 1997b. Transparency for Accountability: Civil Society Monitoring of Multilateral Development Bank Anti-Poverty Projects. *Development in Practice* 7, no. 2.

———. 1998. Thinking Locally, Acting Globally: Bringing the Grassroots into Transnational Advocacy. Paper presented at Regional Worlds—Latin American Cultural Environments and Development Debates, University of Chicago.

———. 1999. The World Bank and Mexico: Where Does Civil Society Fit In? In *Las nuevas fronteras del siglo XXI: Dimensiones culturales, políticas y socioeconómicas de las relaciones Mexico-Estados Unidos*, eds. Norma Klahn, Alejandro Alvarez, Norma Klahn, Federico Manchón, and Pedro Castillo. Mexico City: UAM/UNAM

Fox, Jonathan, and Josefina Aranda. 1994. Community Participation in Mexico's

Municipal Funds Program: The Case of Oaxaca. World Bank Workshop on Participatory Development, May 17–20.

———. 1996a. Los Fondos Municipales de Solidaridad y la participación comunitaria en Oaxaca. *Revista Mexicana de Sociología* 58, no. 3.

———. 1996b. Decentralization and Rural Development in Mexico: Community Participation in Oaxaca's Municipal Funds Program. La Jolla: University of California-San Diego, Center for U.S.-Mexican Studies Contemporary Monograph Series.

Fox, Jonathan, and L. David Brown, eds. 1998. *The Struggle for Accountability: The World Bank, NGOs, and Grassroots Movements.* Cambridge, Mass.: MIT Press.

Fox, Jonathan, and Luis Hernández. 1992. Mexico's Difficult Democracy: Grassroots Movements, NGOs and Local Government. *Alternatives* 17, no. 2.

Gershberg, Alec Ian. 1993. Fiscal Decentralization, Intergovernmental Relations, and Education Finance: Welfare and Efficiency Considerations in Educational Expenditures and Outcomes in Mexico. Ph.D. dissertation. Regional Science Department, University of Pennsylvania.

———. 1995. Fiscal Decentralization and Intergovernmental Relations: An Analysis of Federal Versus State Education Finance in Mexico. *Review of Urban and Regional Development Studies* 7, no. 2

Graham, Carol. 1994. *Safety Nets, Politics, and the Poor.* Washington, D.C.: Brookings Institution.

Greenberg, James B. 1989. *Blood Ties: Life and Violence in Rural Mexico.* Tucson: University of Arizona.

Hernández, Luis, and Fernando Celis. 1994. Solidarity and the New Campesino Movements: The Case of Coffee Production. In *Transforming State-Society Relations in Mexico: The National Solidarity Strategy,* eds. Wayne Cornelius, Ann Craig, and Jonathan Fox. La Jolla, Calif.: Center for U.S.-Mexican Studies, University of California at San Diego.

Hernández, Luis, and Ramón Vera, eds. 1998. *Acuerdos de San Andrés.* México, D.F.: Era.

INEGI-CEPAL. 1993. *Informe sobre la magnitud y evolución de la pobreza en México 1984–1992.* México, D.F.: United Nations Economic Commission on Latin America/National Institute of Geography and Statistics.

Littvack, Jennie, Junaid Ahmad, and Richard Bird. 1998. *Rethinking Decentralization in Developing Countries.* Washington, D.C.: World Bank, Poverty Reduction and Economic Management Network, Sector Studies Series.

Luevano Pérez, Alejandro. 1995. La lucha por los municipios en Chiapas. *La Jornada del Campo* 3, no. 36.

Martínez Assad, Carlos, and Alicia Ziccardi. 1987. El municipio entre la sociedad y el Estado. *Mexican Studies/Estudios Mexicanos* 3, no. 2.

Massolo, Alejandra. 1991. Decentralización y reforma municipal: Fracaso anunciado y sorpresas inesperadas? In *Procesos rurales y urbanos en el México actual,* eds. Alejandra Massolo et al. México, D.F.: UAM-Iztapalapa.

Merino, Mauricio, ed. 1994. *En busca de la democracia municipal: La participación ciudadana en el gobierno local mexicano.* México, D.F.: El Colegio de México.

Molinar, Juan, and Jeffrey Weldon. 1994. Electoral Determinants and Consequences of National Solidarity. In *Transforming State-Society Relations in Mexico: The National Solidarity Strategy*, eds. Wayne Cornelius, Ann Craig, and Jonathan Fox. La Jolla, Calif.: Center for U.S.-Mexican Studies, University of California at San Diego.

Parnell, Philip. 1988. *Escalating Disputes: Social Participation and Change in the Oaxacan Highlands.* Tucson: University of Arizona Press.

Paul, Samuel. 1992. Accountability in Public Services: Exit, Voice and Control. *World Development* 20, no. 7.

Prud'homme, Rémy. 1994. On the Dangers of Decentralization. Policy Research Working Paper No. 1252, The World Bank, Transport Division.

Putnam, Robert. 1993. *Making Democracy Work: Civic Traditions in Modern Italy.* Princeton, N.J.: Princeton University Press.

Rodríguez, Candelaria. 1995. Han sido removidos 45% de los ediles electos de Chiapas. *La Jornada,* Apr. 19.

Rodríguez, Victoria. 1993. The Politics of Decentralisation in Mexico: From *Municipio Libre* to *Solidaridad. Bulletin of Latin American Research* 12, no. 2.

———. 1997. *Decentralization in Mexico: From Reforma Municipal to Solidaridad to Nuevo Federalismo.* Boulder, Colo.: Westview.

Rodríguez, Victoria, and Peter Ward, eds. 1995. *Opposition Government in Mexico.* Albuquerque: University of New Mexico Press.

Rubin, Jeffrey. 1994. COCEI in Juchitán: Grassroots Radicalism and Regional History. *Journal of Latin American Studies* 26, no. 1.

———. 1997. *Decentering the Regime: Ethnicity, Radicalism, and Democracy in Juchitán, Mexico.* Durham, N.C.: Duke University Press.

SEDESOL. 1993a. *Manual único de operación.* México, D.F.: Secretaría de Desarrollo Social/Subsecretaría de Desarrollo Regional/Dirección General de Planeación.

———. 1993b. *Solidarity in National Development.* México, D.F.: SEDESOL.

———. 1995. *La Gaceta* (April 15 bulletin). México, D.F. SEDESOL.

Tendler, Judith, and Sarah Freedheim. 1994. Trust in a Rent-Seeking World: Health and Government Transformed in Northeast Brazil. *World Development* 22, no. 12.

World Bank. 1994a. *Mexico: Second Decentralization and Regional Development.* Staff Appraisal Report 13032-ME. Washington, D.C.: World Bank.

———. 1994b. *The World Bank and Participation.* Washington, D.C.: World Bank Operations Policy Department.

———. 1994c. *World Bank Sourcebook on Participation.* Washington, D.C.: World Bank Environment Department.

Ziccardi, Alicia, ed. 1995. Propuesta: Nuevo Federalismo. *El Nacional,* May 7.

9

The Local Matters

The Port of New Orleans Responds to Global Restructuring

Alma H. Young[1]

In the early 1980s, officials of the Port of New Orleans were clearly unprepared to meet the challenges posed by global economic restructuring. By middecade, however, new, more entrepreneurial leadership had adopted innovative policies that made the port more competitive nationally and internationally. In the setting of the local economy's acute downturn, the port's new leadership promoted an understanding within the local maritime industry that changes in the world economy required innovative ways of conducting business. This understanding enabled leadership to forge new political arrangements in response to global transformations. In doing so, the port's officials furthered the development agenda of an emerging governing coalition in New Orleans.

Local officials the world over have come to operate under much more uncertain economic and political circumstances, as global transformations have thrust upon them unexpected roles and responsibilities. Under these circumstances, a compelling question is: To what extent do local policy decisions make a difference (see Goetz and Clarke 1993)? This chapter's analysis of the Port of New Orleans demonstrates that local decisions can indeed make a difference.

Local Actors and Global Restructuring: Competing Perspectives

One influential interpretation of global restructuring portrays local actors as having little room to maneuver (Peterson 1981; Piore and Sabel 1984; Sassen 1990). In this view, the hypermobility of capital results in intense competition among communities as they seek private investment, therefore limiting their ability to carry out autonomous economic and social policies. This perspective has led some analysts to consider the actions of local actors within the national and global economies as insignificant. Others have argued, however, that local policies can be significant (see Gaspar 1992). This is true especially with regard to attempts at upgrading locality-specific aspects of production. Among these are technological innovations, worker discipline, and business-friendly policies (Henry 1992) that may improve the competitive position of localities.

What kinds of development policies may be formulated by local actors to mitigate the negative impacts and/or strengthen the positive impacts of world-scale restructuring on their communities? How, moreover, are such policies formulated? To answer these questions, we need to consider the arguments advanced by proponents of local political initiative. They emphasize that local and national political contexts are more important than the global political economy in shaping patterns of local development. The proponents claim that the global political economy is mediated through local and national political arrangements, resulting in diverse responses to global restructuring (see Logan and Swanstrom 1990).

Ross Gittell's (1992) analysis of economic revitalization efforts in four industrial cities indicates that local politico-economic intervention indeed matters. He finds that under certain conditions, "city leaders and institutions can facilitate beneficial adjustment to changing economic circumstances through 'reshuffling' and reorganization of local resources" (Gittell 1992, 158). Thus, the organization and management of local development activities can make a significant difference, with local political leadership being a key factor.

How this policy intervention takes place on the local level is still open to debate. Paul Peterson (1981) suggests that because of fierce economic competition between cities for businesses and residents, the development policies of cities tend to center on ways of improving their competitive positions and overall economic well-being. He argues that the benefits of development accrue to all members of the community, and hence that development policies tend to emerge in consensus fashion. For Peterson, then, external economic factors sharply limit the possibilities for local political maneuvering. Yet, as Gittell (1992, 27) notes, Peterson's deterministic framework is limited in explaining how development policies are formulated, why and when particular types of development policies are pursued, and why cities pursue significantly different development strategies.

On the other hand, the "growth coalition" theorists (Molotch 1976, 1990; Logan and Molotch 1987; Mollenkopf 1983) suggest that urban economic conditions and interests do not rigidly dictate the actions of local (generally conceived to be elected) officials, whose ample room for political maneuvering may involve initiatives taken against major business groups. These theorists depict how local leaders can exploit a city's political process and economic development policy making to enhance their own political interests. Thus, local policies respond to political mandates as well as economic constraints.

Regime theory argues explicitly that neither economics nor politics by themselves determine policy outcomes (Elkin 1985, 1987; Fainstein et al. 1986; Shefter 1985; Stone 1989, 1993; Swanstrom 1985). Clarence Stone, who has done much to advance regime theory, contends that structural constraints are real, but they are mediated through the local political configurations that enable a prevailing coalition, or regime, to govern a community. An urban regime is "the informal arrangements by which public bodies and private interests function together in order to be able to make and carry out governing decisions" (Stone 1989, 6). Integral to those decisions are urban development policies, which Stone defines as "those practices fostered by public authority that contribute to the shaping of the local community through control of land use and investments in physical infrastructure" (1993, 4). Hence, development policy grows out of the prevailing governing coalition and its relationship to the electorate and to those who control private investment. For Stone, therefore, politics matters—and it matters at the local level.

Stone (1989) knows that an exclusive focus on structural requirements obscures the range of efforts, strategies, and value choices made by community actors (see Fisher and Kling 1993). Governing coalitions differ both across particular communities and within them over time. Stone (1993) presents a typology of four rather distinct coalitions.

First, maintenance/caretaker regimes do not try to change established social and economic practice. Instead they focus on the provision of routine services. Such regimes do not attempt to mobilize private resources and place few demands on local elites (see Stone and Sanders 1987). Second, development/corporate regimes share the growth orientation of important private actors and often provide subsidies to encourage investment (Stone and Sanders 1987, 1993). The costs of growth are borne by the public; growth benefits such as jobs are presumed to filter down to the citizens at large, making unnecessary explicit redistributive governmental programs. Development/corporate regimes are concerned primarily with changing land use to foster the economy's growth. Since they attempt to alter established social and economic patterns, such regimes translate private investment decisions into public decisions. Development projects of this sort are often controversial. They therefore entail risks of popular disapproval and are advanced most successfully when hidden from public scrutiny and popular control. Nonetheless, jobs, contracts, and fees generated by development activities help to manage conflict and soften or divide the opposition (see Burns 1994).

Third, middle-class progressive/growth management regimes aggressively use public planning and emphasize measures such as environmental protection, historic preservation, affordable housing, and linkage funds for various social purposes (see Clavel 1986; Clavel and Kleniewski 1990; DeLeon 1992; Shearer 1989). Behind growth management policies is the argument that the costs of growth (e.g., decline in the quality of life) exceed the benefits, and consequently an activist government must regulate growth. Progressive regimes often rest on a base of active popular support, relying on citizen participation with the organizational capacity to inform, mobilize, and involve the public (Stone 1993).

Finally, lower-class expansion regimes respond to the needs of the poor. These regimes stress improved education and job training, better access to transportation, and greater opportunities for business and home ownership. The task of coordination is immense; elites usually participate only involuntarily in lower-class expansion regimes, and mobilizing a lower-class constituency may be difficult. Such regimes are largely hypothetical in the United States (Stone 1993).

Since 1986, the Port of New Orleans has pursued the agenda of an emerging local governing coalition that is assuming development/corporate traits. The orientation of the port's leadership itself is changing from that of caretaker to development/corporate actor. This change was induced primarily by the coincidence of local economic crisis with longer-range erosion of the port's competitiveness in the setting of global restructuring. These circumstances triggered the ascendance of new leadership within the port's executive staff and the governing board. The strategy formulated by the new leadership requires the tightened coordination of port policies with the private maritime industry. It also requires that port leadership interact more directly with the wider public, stressing the port's economic importance to both New Orleans and Louisiana in general. The evidence indicates that in orchestrating the local maritime industry's innovative responses to global economic restructuring, local political decisions have indeed mattered.

The New Orleans Context

Integral to the history of New Orleans has been the city's excessive reliance on its port, which is located near the mouth of the Mississippi River (see Map 9.1). The port once made New Orleans one of the leading U.S. cities. In 1840, New Orleans was the third largest city in the country, and until the 1950

Census it ranked as the South's largest city. Between 1960 and 1990, however, New Orleans lost almost 21% of its population, tumbling relative to other cities in both the nation and the South (Mumphrey and Pinell 1992). Since the 1960s, the local economy has taken on a tripartite base: oil and gas and related industries; tourism; and the port. It nevertheless remains much less economically diversified than other major U.S. cities.

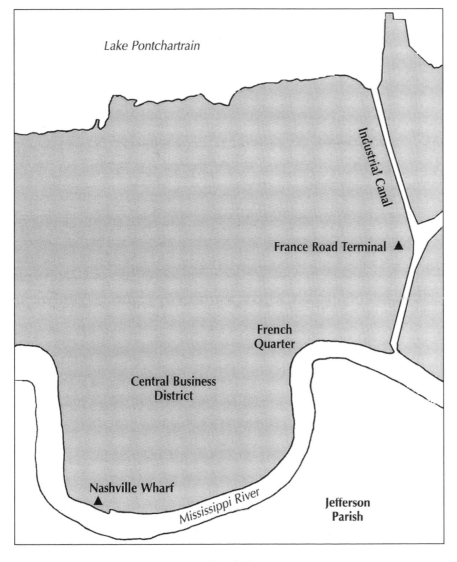

Map 9.1
New Orleans

The oil industry became an important part of the New Orleans economy after World War II with the discovery and drilling of oil off the Louisiana coast. Arguably, there emerged excessive local dependence on the oil industry. Whereas the city's total employment increased by 8% between 1969 and 1979, its mining employment, a category including the oil industry, increased by 50% (Whelan 1989). Furthermore, when oil prices collapsed in the mid-1980s, the local economy was devastated. The city had a double-digit unemployment rate for more than three years, and the oil industry's collapse led to significant out-migration. By the late 1980s, the economy began some measure of recovery. Much of that recovery has been in services, largely in the booming tourism sector.

The number of hotels, conventions, and tourists in New Orleans has risen substantially since 1975; by 1987 tourism displaced petroleum as the city's economic mainstay. By the mid-1980s, tourism was a $2.5 billion business for the metropolitan area, with much of the industry located in downtown New Orleans (Brooks and Young 1993, 262). Yet, while tourism has created many jobs, most of them are low paid.

It is against the backdrop of these transformations that in recent decades the port has faced stiffened competition from other cities. Such competition has decreased the port's tonnage of cargo and contributed to a reduction in its labor force. Since most of the dock workers are black, the effects on the black community have been especially severe, resulting in its loss of well-paid union jobs.[2] This loss of jobs occurred as blacks became the majority population group in the city.[3] Under the Port of New Orleans's new leadership, the volume of cargo (but not the number of dockside jobs) has rebounded. To become more competitive, the leadership is building new facilities away from congested downtown and closer to impoverished black neighborhoods, along the uptown riverfront where land is more plentiful (see Map 9.1). The high degree of racial segregation in New Orleans has facilitated this encroachment on black neighborhoods (but see Young and Christos-Rodgers [1995] for a discussion of one black community's resistance).

A crucial feature of the New Orleans economy is that its three major segments—the port, the oil industry, and tourism—are predominately controlled by outside interests and are highly subject to swings in the national and international economies. For instance, international shippers decide whether to make New Orleans a port of call; oil companies headquartered elsewhere decide whether to drill nearby in the Gulf of Mexico; and hoteliers from other places decide whether to operate hotels in the city. Because New Orleans is the headquarters of only one Fortune 500 company, key economic decisions concerning the city are generally made elsewhere, and much of its profits slip away. Under these conditions, the local governing coalition has been, until recently, woefully inadequate in meeting the challenges of the city's economic base. The mercantilist history of the economy, coupled with the philosophy that as long as the Mississippi River flows through the city, goods will pass through the port, has contributed to a laissez-faire attitude toward the economy, including the port.

The city's lagging economic growth and development can be attributed to the lack of local capital. This problem is compounded by the antitax posture of homeowners (including a $75,000 homestead exemption), a strong preservationist movement, and political leadership whose role has been limited to that of caretaker. Not until the mayoralty of Moon Landrieu (1970–1978) did New Orleans politics become more inclined to policies of growth and development. The new policies emphasized revitalization of the central business district and tourism promotion (see Whelan 1989; Whelan et al. 1994; Lauria et al. 1995).

Since the 1970s, the traditional caretaker approach of New Orleans government has been giving way to a development/corporate regime concerned with coordinating private investment and public action. A parallel shift has characterized the port's leadership, especially since the 1980s. Underpinning this shift was the intersection of local economic crisis and global restructuring.

The Port of New Orleans

The Board of Commissioners of the Port of New Orleans (known locally as the Dock Board) is the state of Louisiana agency charged with governing the port. The Dock Board has jurisdiction over a triparish (i.e., county) area: Orleans (including the city of New Orleans), Jefferson, and St. Bernard. The Dock Board has seven members appointed by the governor of Louisiana: four representatives from Orleans Parish, two members from Jefferson Parish (a large suburban district west of New Orleans), and one member from St. Bernard Parish (a smaller suburban district south of the city). The governor appoints Dock Board members from a list of nominees provided by a number of civic organizations; the city of New Orleans government is not a part of the nominating process. The fact that the city government has little control over the Dock Board's activities has irritated a succession of mayors, especially since the port is a vital part of the city and its economy. Thus, the port is legally independent from, but economically integrated with, the city of New Orleans (Young and Whelan 1993).

As presently constituted, the Dock Board was created in 1896, when the Louisiana legislature passed a landmark law establishing the Board of

Commissioners of the Port of New Orleans. This law, together with later amendments, gave the board authority over all water frontage (i.e., the Mississippi River and associated bodies, but not Lake Pontchartrain) in Orleans Parish and considerable portions of river and canal frontage in adjacent parishes (see Map 9.1). Within its jurisdiction, the board had "the authority to expropriate private property, to demolish and rebuild structures at will, to operate any facility that it chooses, and at its pleasure to lease portions of any facility to private operators" (Lewis 1976, 56).

Lewis (1976) argues that in most other cities at the time, such actions would have been denounced as socialist; in a city as conservative as New Orleans, one would think they would have appeared unorthodox at the very least. But New Orleanians accepted the board, because they felt that the port was too important to be left in the hands of "inept operators." Within ten years, much of the port had been totally rebuilt and facilities greatly expanded. The improvements included cotton warehouses, coal and bulk storage facilities, and one of the biggest grain elevators in the world.[4]

Despite the port's still crucial role in the city's economy, by the mid-1980s the facility was in serious trouble. Cargo tonnage and labor demand plunged. General cargo—the more highly valued of the kinds of cargo passing through the port—dropped from nearly 8 million tons in 1974 to 5 million tons in 1982, stabilizing at 6 million tons in the mid-1980s. Lower traffic flows and the substitution of container ships for breakbulk services reduced annual dockside labor requirements from 4.0 million hours in 1975 to 1.7 million hours in 1985. By the latter year the labor-intensive breakbulk general cargo traffic flowing over public wharves was one-half of its 1973 level (*Strategic Plan* 1986, 1–2).

The financial position of the Port of New Orleans also deteriorated. In 1982, port operations produced $40 million in revenue and a $3 million net surplus. By 1986, revenue declined to $31 million with a $6 million shortfall. Spending on capital facilities contracted from $23 million in 1982 to $8 million in 1986 (*Strategic Plan* 1986, 1).

The port's problems stemmed from its relation to changes in international and national markets, including the growing inadequacy of its infrastructure. Historically, the port handled relatively low-value commodities, such as agricultural products. In 1984, foreign liner imports and exports exhibited the lowest value per ton of any major U.S. port. In terms of the more highly valued general cargo, New Orleans's strengths lay in moving semifinished industrial commodities (iron and steel, aluminum ingots, natural rubber) to large corporate customers on or near the Mississippi River. In 1985, ten key commodities accounted for 70% of New Orleans's foreign general cargo tonnage.

More than two-thirds of general cargo was destined for local markets (Louisiana, Arkansas, and Mississippi) and the Mississippi valley area (*Strategic Plan* 1986, 5–8). Most products simply passed through the port, with very little value-added activity.

Changes in the world market reduced the port's trade flows, transportation competitiveness, and efficiency (including port land availability, labor costs, and equipment) (see *Strategic Plan* 1986, 7–12). By the early 1980s, Asia became the fastest-growing trade partner for the United States. New Orleans and the other Gulf Coast ports (e.g., Houston, Biloxi, Tampa) were unfavorably sited for the east-west flow of goods. Their natural trade partners were located to the north and south, but in the 1980s their southern trading partners in Latin America were experiencing a severe economic downturn. Moreover, the Gulf Coast ports encountered heightened competition for Latin American trade from ascendant Miami (see Grosfoguel 1994) and other Atlantic ports.

Another problem concerned the domestic market. Within the United States, the three states most tied to New Orleans—Louisiana, Arkansas, and Mississippi—represent a very small market. (As a point of comparison, the Texas-Oklahoma market is twice as large as New Orleans's primary domestic market.) Because its natural domestic market is so small, the Port of New Orleans must pursue distant inland markets more vigorously than ports on other coasts if major cargo volumes are to offer the same economies of scale.

A problem undercutting the port's competitiveness in both the world and domestic markets was the growing inferiority of its infrastructure. In recent decades, transport by sea, rail, barge, and truck has experienced a drive toward efficiency in order to reduce costs. This drive has had major ramifications for port facilities in the United States, as well as abroad. According to the Port of New Orleans's *Strategic Plan* (1986), the most important trends affecting the local facility are:

- Containerization, which fosters increased efficiency through labor reduction (primarily on the docks), enhanced security of carriage, and the convenience of door-to-door service;
- Vessel scale economies, in which larger ships offer lower unit costs of transportation. The average size of container ships almost doubled between 1975 and 1985;
- Feeder services, in which port "hubs" or "load centers" concentrate long-distance flows over a limited number of ports in order to build volume. Cargo is then "fed" to inland or other coastal points by rail, truck, or ocean feeder services. Feeder services have allowed the East and West Coasts to serve each other as well as points in between; and

- Integration of water and land modes, or intermodalism, in which ocean carriers provide point-to-point service to their customers by setting intermodal rates for both sea and land transit. Several ocean shipping companies have begun to own and operate both rail equipment and trucking operations.

In addition to shifts in trade patterns and the transportation industry, ports have had to contend with formidable changes in factors of production, including land, labor, and equipment. Individual ports have greater control over these factors than over trade and transportation shifts.

Land has become an increasingly valuable resource to ports as a result of two trends: increasing requirements for cargo-handling space and commercial waterfront development. First, as vessels have become more costly, the drive to minimize port time has required greater space to marshal and store cargo moving on and off ships. Land availability has therefore become a key factor in attracting ocean carriers to ports. Second, the pull toward large land areas away from congested urban centers has been supported by the push from developers seeking to utilize valuable waterfront land for commercial purposes. Retail shops, restaurants, offices, museums, and condominiums have been built on waterfront property in many U.S. cities. Thus, the value of downtown waterfront land owned or controlled by ports is rising because of new uses that are more lucrative than cargo handling.

As for labor, the transition from breakbulk to specialized cargo handling (often in containers) has involved not only a reduction in port jobs but also a shift in port jobs from the docks to other locations. Along with national growth in white-collar port jobs coordinating flows of goods and paperwork has been an acute loss of longshore jobs (see *Strategic Plan* 1986, 11). In the 1980s, some locals of the International Longshoremen's Association demanded compensation for lost work, which was paid for by assessments against cargo, placing the older, more traditional ports at a significant cost disadvantage. Furthermore, terminal operators began to use nonunion labor in ports such as Houston, Mobile, and New Orleans, bringing pressure on union labor to raise productivity and reduce wages.

Finally, ports have had to make crucial decisions concerning capital equipment and expenditures (i.e., what berths, channels, container cranes, and intermodal railyards to develop). These expenditures have been substantial as ports prepare to accommodate large, deep-draft vessels whose owners seek to minimize vessel port time. Container cranes, for example, can cost up to $10 million each. Still, port equipment is becoming more uniform across the industry. Consequently, differences in land and labor conditions, combined with the timing and level of capital outlays, have become important determinants of port competitiveness. As we will see, the Port of New Orleans has come to emphasize capital outlays and the development of physical infrastructure in attempting to regain a competitive edge.

The Port's Responses

After the port's executive director of twenty years announced that he would retire, the Dock Board responded to the gamut of challenges by commissioning a strategic planning study in 1985 to chart the port's future. An interim director was at the helm. In addition, the board's composition was changing, from almost exclusive representation of maritime interests to expanded representation of community leaders. In 1982, the first black commissioner was named to the board; in 1986, the first female commissioner (also black) was named. Leading the planning effort was a lawyer who was actively involved with several major civic organizations, and who would eventually run unsuccessfully for mayor.

The board's consultants worked with a sixty-member advisory committee, representing a diversity of community groups. The consultants identified the port's problems and strengths, most important of which was its location. They outlined a number of options to enhance the port's economic prominence in the city and the state. They recommended a shift from a traditional "landlord" role to a customer-oriented, service-providing role for maritime businesses and for users of board-owned and controlled properties. As a landlord, the board's function had been confined largely to building facilities, leasing them to private maritime companies, and maintaining the water frontage. It generally had considered the private maritime industry, not the Dock Board, to be responsible for generating cargo traffic. Port officials (and the maritime community as a whole) had assumed that given the city's location, a sufficient volume of cargo would pass through New Orleans.

In 1986, the board hired J. Ron Brinson, an energetic, young public entrepreneur, as its new executive director. A former head of the American Association of Port Authorities, Brinson had the experience to implement the strategic plan, which he wholeheartedly endorsed. He revamped the port organization to make it more entrepreneurial, bringing in new talent and better-qualified staff.[5] He adopted cost-cutting measures, carried out a capital improvements program, and made the port a more a more visible player in local economic development.

Among the first actions taken by the board under Brinson's leadership was formally to adopt the *Strategic Plan* and its recommendations. The board formulated three goals: to increase cargo volume and surpass the port's general cargo tonnage within the next decade by competing effectively with other U.S. ports; to restore financial health by generating revenue and cutting costs; and to contribute to state and regional development by expanding trade and developing port property (Young and Whelan 1993, 134).

It was agreed that in working toward these goals, the roles and responsibilities of the board and the executive staff would be distinct. The board would be responsible for setting goals and policies, while the staff would be responsible for the day-to-day management of the port. Brinson aggressively took on the role of port spokesperson. This role has become more important as the board has assumed a more active and prominent public role. In large part this is because the board has become caught up in issues such as the use of public funds for capital projects and the disposition of riverfront properties for nonmaritime use (see Young and Whelan 1993, 138).

When Brinson took over, funds available for capital improvements and maintenance were extremely limited. The state of Louisiana had historically provided a large share of the funds for port construction, amounting to $157 million between 1969 and 1985. The state's contribution to capital funding had declined, however, from 87% in 1982 to 29% in 1985. Funds remaining from past legislative appropriations (the last in 1981) were nearly exhausted, and the port had issued no bonds since 1976. Amounts generated from internal operations ranged between $2 million and $4 million a year, allowing the port to undertake only piecemeal improvements (*Strategic Plan* 1986, 22).

Unlike many ports, the Port of New Orleans lacked a dedicated revenue source to finance capital improvements. Yet, by the mid-1980s, the port needed large capital investments. In 1988, the Dock Board launched a campaign, spearheaded by then Governor of Louisiana, Buddy Roemer, to gain voter approval of a statewide referendum to increase the gasoline tax by one cent per gallon to fund infrastructure improvements throughout Louisiana. Part of the port's strategy for winning voter approval was to stress the port's importance in the local and state economies. The Louisiana legislature passed the Transportation Trust Fund on October 7, 1989. The fund provided the port with $100 million to help construct "market-driven, state of the art facilities needed to effectively compete with other well-financed ports" (Board of Commissioners 1989). The Dock Board pledged an additional $87 million of its own monies to finance a five-year Port Improvement Program (PIP), which contained key elements of the *Strategic Plan*. PIP prioritized improvements and provided the cost and schedule for the various projects.

Growing out of PIP was the master plan for the Upper Mississippi River wharves (see Map 9.1), which was adopted by the board on September 11, 1989. This stretch of wharves along the uptown Mississippi River is one of the busiest areas in the United States for breakbulk cargo. The port saw this area as the most viable arena for growth in the foreseeable future and envisioned the eventual consolidation of marine terminal operations into three superterminals. This project demonstrates the port's growing appreciation of the need to handle intermodal operations and provide facilities for general and breakbulk cargo, rather than continuing to rely on bulk cargo.

Development of the Upper Mississippi River facilities is meant to shift maritime activities away from the downtown wharves, thus permitting the long-term redevelopment of the downtown riverfront (see Map 9.1), which is vital to tourism growth. The board's plans, formulated after a series of public hearings, were to make its wharves and other downtown properties available for nonmaritime uses as they became redundant (Board of Commissioners 1990). As early as 1986, the board was entering into negotiations to turn over some of its properties to commercial developers. The Aquarium of the Americas, for example, was sited on downtown port property. After much negotiation, an agreement was ratified by the board in July 1986 that gave the quasi-public organization responsible for the aquarium the right to use of one of the downtown wharves for 50 years in return for 9% of the gross receipts of aquarium sales, up to a maximum of $25 million (Young and Whelan 1993, 140–41).

As the *Strategic Plan* called for the board to turn all of its properties into revenue-producing assets and/or to liquidate revenue-draining properties, the board entered into negotiations with the city over the title to the Rivergate, the first convention center ever built in New Orleans, owned jointly by the two bodies. Built in 1967, the Rivergate had been made redundant by the building of a new 600,000-square-foot exhibition hall nearby. After much acrimony, an agreement was signed in April 1992 giving the city full title to the Rivergate in return for a cash settlement to the Dock Board (Young and Whelan 1993, 142–43). The money received for the Rivergate has been used for infrastructural improvements at the port. The board's policy is to reinvest any funds it obtains into maritime endeavors only. Gone are the days when the port invested in nonmaritime facilities such as convention centers, office buildings, and bridges.

Results of the Port's Responses

The port's responses to the challenges of global restructuring were premised on the realization that the "Dock Board must assume a proactive role as the public authority interface for the taxpaying stakeholders and those firms and individuals who operate and use publicly-owned facilities" (Brinson 1994).

Port officials therefore worked to bring private maritime interests, elected officials, and the public into coordinated activity. Some of the results of those efforts are presented below.

Financial Stability

The Dock Board has reversed its bleak financial performance of the mid-1980s. Ad hoc decisions taken by the board in the mid-1980s to reduce certain tariffs and lease pricing in an attempt to counter the port's loss of competitiveness deprived the board of about $7 million in annual revenues. The board has overcome this reduced revenue by streamlining its workforce and applying aggressive cost control management. Steady growth of cargo tonnage has improved the revenue picture.

The port's activities are now financed and operated similar to those of private business enterprises. The intent is that the costs of providing services be financed or recovered primarily through user charges. Operating expenses before depreciation for 1995 were less than those for 1986, while long-term bonded debt dropped by almost three-quarters. Furthermore, between 1993 and 1995 the capital improvements program more than tripled in value.

These figures reflect leadership's decision to make the port leaner. Between 1986 and 1990 the number of Dock Board workers was slashed by 20%. The organization was also reorganized. Entrepreneurial talent was brought in to head the various departments, and management gained greater flexibility in the employees it could hire. Having gained a steady revenue stream for capital projects, the port has implemented a regular schedule of capital improvements and maintenance.

The port has aggressively rid itself of nonmaritime functions and facilities, as exemplified by its liquidation of the Rivergate convention facility. Finally, it is experimenting with the privatization of some of its remaining facilities. For instance, it granted primary control over one of its river terminals to a private sector terminal operator (Hall 1994).

Facilities

The board determined that "market-driven state of the art facilities [were] needed to effectively compete with other well-financed ports" (Board of Commissioners 1989). After securing $100 million in revenue from the state of Louisiana (as proceeds from the Transportation Trust Fund) and pledging to match that with $87 million of port-generated funds, the board embarked on a five-year improvement plan. The board's new financial policies raised $116 million during the five-year period for an improvement fund totaling $216 million.

Central to the plan was the modernization of the Nashville Avenue Wharf on the uptown portion of the Mississippi River (see Map 9.1), at the time "probably the busiest breakbulk terminal in the United States" and, in man hours and revenue, the most productive of the New Orleans terminals. Yet, the Nashville Avenue facilities were outmoded. The bulk of the port improvement funds has thus gone to the Nashville Avenue and adjacent facilities. These include a multipurpose terminal handling a broad range of cargo; a new terminal with more than 52 acres of marshaling yard; a heavy-duty dock with railroad tracks able to accommodate breakbulk and project cargo; and a railcar staging area to permit rapid replacement of railcars during direct discharge operations between rail and ocean carriers. The new uptown complexes provide berthing capacity to suffice until the year 2010 and include the creation of a continuous ship berth for two miles, making New Orleans the longest linear port in the world (PIP 1989). As discussed below, extensive improvements are also being made to the France Road Container Terminal in eastern New Orleans (see Map 9.1), the centerpiece of the push for intermodal (i.e., container) traffic.

Intermodalism

The Port of New Orleans made its name as the United States' leading handler of bulk and breakbulk cargo. It is now trying to become a leader in container traffic. Between 1990 and 1995 its container traffic rose by 21%. The main site of the port's intermodal operations is the France Road Container Terminal.

Because more than 80% of the cargo that moves through the port is destined for locations at least 200 miles away, good inland transportation resources are crucial for the port to work effectively. The port is served by six Class I railroads, more than any other seaport in the United States, and is well positioned on the interstate highway system in three directions. To enhance these assets, the port is investing heavily in improvements for the France Road Container Terminal, as well as for the uptown Mississippi River terminals ("Intermodal" 1994).

New Orleans's rapid progress in intermodalism resulted from concertations such as the Strategic Rail Study, which combined the efforts of the port and the railroads; and a Terminal Efficiency Task Force, which brought together the port, labor unions, the railroads, and trucking. The Dock Board seeks to coordinate its policies with such groups because their various operations and web of relations are ultimately responsible for the port's competitiveness.

Cargo

The volume of cargo flowing through New Orleans has recovered sharply. The most valued of the various kinds of cargo is general cargo, such as steel, coffee, textiles, and rubber. The amount of general cargo moving through the port increased by 34% between 1988 and 1995. In both 1994 and 1995, the port handled 10 million tons of general cargo, its highest mark in twenty-five years. General cargo now accounts for about 30% of New Orleans's total cargo. In 1995, the city ranked second to Houston in general cargo among Gulf and South Atlantic ports ("Port Cargo," 1995). The Dock Board argues that New Orleans could not have accommodated the increased tonnage without the expanded capacity provided by the $216 million capital improvements program. Bulk cargo, including oil and grain, continues at a steady pace, given the port's location at the end of the Mississippi River.

Steel is New Orleans's number one growth cargo (see Tables 9.1 and 9.2). In 1994, record-setting levels of imported semifinished slab steel were shipped through the city on their way to mills in the Midwest. In 1995, exports of steel coils from USX mills in Gary, Indiana, and Fairfield, Alabama, reached markets in Japan and South Korea ("Steel Shipments Rise" 1995). For the first nine months of 1995, rubber imports constituted 93% of the total reaching U.S. Gulf ports. Comparable figures were 76% for coffee imports, 44% for fabric exports, and 31% for steel exports ("1995: A Very Good Year" 1995, 6). These are the port's niche cargoes, attracted in part by the local maritime industry's special expertise and reinforced by the provision of upgraded facilities. Textiles are also moving through the port in increasing quantities ("Stitching It All Together" 1995, 14–17).

According to Brinson (1994), the port's upturn in general cargo coincided with resurgent trade between the United States and Latin America, particularly Mexico, in the early 1990s. New Orleans's trade with Latin America increased by 23%—roughly equal to that for Miami and Houston—compared with 14% for the United States as a whole. By the mid-1990s Latin American trade accounted for more than 30% of New Orleans's cargo volume, compared to 22% in 1988 (Table 9.2). Latin America, led by Mexico and Brazil, became the port's number one trade partner. The North American Free Trade Agreement is likely to reinforce the Mexican/Latin American surge, particularly as the port's officials are now competing aggressively with Houston and Miami in this arena. As for other foreign partners, trade with Europe has steadily declined, while that with Asia has changed little.

In his 1994 State of the Port address, Brinson suggested that one of the reasons for the port's increased cargo traffic is that the local union of the International Longshoreman's Association (ILA) has adopted the view that if the port does well, so do the workers. This seems to be holding true, as the number of ILA man-hours rose by 11% during the first nine months of 1994 (compared to the same period in 1993). ILA tonnage surpassed 6 million tons

Table 9.1
Port of New Orleans: Major Commodity Exports and Imports

	1990	1995	Change Between 1990–1995
Exports			
Steel	.33 M	.60 M	+ 82%
Forest Products	.60 M	.50 M	− 17%
Selected Bulk Cargo	.69 M	.60 M	− 13%
Imports			
Iron and Steel	1.5 M	2.27 M	+ 51%
Forest Products	.24 M	.24 M	0%
Reefer Products (meat, bananas, etc.)	.06 M	—	—
Rubber	.15 M	.26 M	+ 73%
Coffee	.28 M	.18 M	− 36%
Selected Metals	.51 M	.12 M	− 76%
Limestone Chips	.19 M	.05 M	− 74%
Cordage and Twine	.04 M	.06 M	+ 50%

Source: Ryan and Maruggi (1995).

Table 9.2
Port of New Orleans: Trade with Areas of the World,
Short Tons (by Year, Percentage of Total)

Area	1986	1988	1990	1992	1994
Europe	34.5	26.1	33.9	28.3	21.2
Asia	26.0	39.1	29.6	30.4	30.2
Latin America	25.6	22.3	26.0	28.0	36.5
Africa	11.4	10.6	8.9	12.6	10.0
Greenland and Canada	1.6	1.1	1.1	0.7	1.6
Australia and Oceania	1.0	0.8	0.5	0.8	0.6

Latin America includes South and Central America, as well as Mexico and the Caribbean.

Source: U.S. Department of Commerce. 1995. "International Accounts Data." Washington, D.C.: Bureau of Economic Analysis, U.S. Department of Commerce.

in 1994, a threshold last crossed in 1967 (Brinson 1994). In 1995, the dock-workers of ILA's Local 3000 won recognition for their productivity from two leading container ship lines—Sea-Land Service Inc. and Navieras/NPR Inc.—which cited their New Orleans terminals as the most efficient in their companies. Sea-Land singled out the New Orleans terminal from among its more than 120 terminals in eighty countries (Hall 1995a). Another positive sign came in late 1995, when Local 3000 placed an ad in the local newspaper for general dockworkers. For the first time in many years, there was increased local demand for dockworkers.

The expertise of the dockworkers and the stevedores in handling certain cargo, especially metals (mostly steel, but also copper and aluminum), has also been important. For instance, New Orleans is the only port where Chilean and Peruvian copper is discharged directly from vessels into barges midstream. This way of unloading copper cuts costs, but it requires substantial handling and expertise ("Heavy Metals" 1994, 14).

Also important has been the port's automated cargo documentation system, known as CRESCENT. Begun in 1987, CRESCENT allows users to communicate electronically with U.S. Customs, each other, and their principals around the world. It lets subscribers preclear shipments through Customs's automated commercial system up to forty-eight hours before a vessel arrives. This facilitates "just-in-time" rail and barge deliveries to customers, as has become common practice in U.S. ports. CRESCENT has given the Customs facilities in New Orleans a reputation as one of the most efficient in the country, thereby helping the port to capture additional cargo.

Economic and Fiscal Impact

The port has solidified its position as a leading economic sector in both New Orleans and Louisiana at large. It generated one of every twelve jobs in metropolitan New Orleans in 1994, a 22% increase over 1991 (Ryan 1992; Ryan and Maruggi 1995). The statewide increase was 19%. Such growth boosted employment earnings by 21% in metropolitan New Orleans and 19% in the state. The overall upswing in port-related activities expanded tax revenues for local and state governments by 19%. And in return for the state of Louisiana's $100 million investment in the port's capital improvements program, it received $216 million of asset expansion.

Conclusions

In the context of global restructuring, the crisis of the local economy in the 1980s combined with long-range decline in the competitiveness of the Port of New Orleans to push its new leadership to undertake a far-reaching program of revitalization. This program has involved port-led coordination across the local maritime industry: shipping lines; railroads; trucking companies; terminal operators; and organized labor. It has also involved the port's negotiations with the state of Louisiana to obtain more revenues for capital improvements and with city officials to divest the port of nonmaritime facilities. The program has indeed revitalized the port sector of New Orleans, making it significantly more competitive in the domestic and world markets while increasing its weight in the city and statewide economies. Moreover, the program's politics of coordination and economic development have firmly embedded the port's leadership in New Orleans's emergent governing coalition. The "development/corporate" agenda of this coalition represents a marked departure from the "maintenance/caretaker" agenda of its long-standing predecessor (see Stone 1993).

The case of the Port of New Orleans underscores the importance of local political entrepreneurship in inducing broadened participation—including the reconfiguring of the local governing coalition—in urban economic development (see Leitner and Garner 1993; Mollenkopf 1983; Schneider and Teske 1992). It likewise underscores the fact that market forces alone cannot orchestrate local economic reforms to meet the challenges posed by global restructuring (see Gittell 1992). The case demonstrates that, at least in U.S. cities, nonelected public officials can play a decisive role within a local governing coalition. That is, political entrepreneurship need not only reside within city hall but also can be found within public agencies not formally connected to city government. In addition, the case raises questions about the characteristics of local politics and society that may be favorable or unfavorable to the initiatives of political entrepreneurs. Clearly, the local matters, even within a globalizing economy.

We must be mindful, nonetheless, that the port's leadership responded to *external* pressures; namely, the intensifying global competitiveness of the maritime industry. In doing so, leadership cultivated broadened city and statewide political support by contending that economic revitalization would reap widely shared social benefits. The governing coalition of New Orleans continues to struggle over the adoption of a development/corporate political agenda. Various members of the coalition remain ambivalent about pursuing economic growth and development in such an entrepreneurial fashion, in part because it is unclear who among them will emerge as winners or losers. In fact, some of the city's economic sectors remain split between genteel, locally oriented businesses and aggressive, globally oriented ones. Furthermore, the ramifications of pronounced social and racial inequality are a troubling feature of New Orleans's ongoing political and economic transitions, in part evidenced by tensions over the encroachment of modernized port facilities into poor black neighborhoods. These and other rifts are indicative of the complexities of this case of local response to global restructuring.

References

A Horizon of Opportunity: Looking Ahead to 1995. 1994. *Port Record.* (Dec.). New Orleans, La.: Port of New Orleans.

Arnesen, Eric. 1991. *Waterfront Workers in New Orleans: Race, Class and Politics, 1863–1923.* New York: Oxford University Press.

Board of Commissioners of the Port of New Orleans. 1989. *Port Improvements Program (FY 1990–95)* [PIP]. New Orleans, La.: Port Planning and Engineering Division, Port of New Orleans.

————. 1990. *New Orleans Riverfront in Transition: A Citizens' Mandate for Planning.* New Orleans, La.: Port of New Orleans.

Brinson, J. Ron. 1994. Annual State of the Port Address. New Orleans, La.: World Trade Center, September 21.

Brooks, Jane, and Alma H. Young. 1993. Revitalizing the Central Business District in the Face of Decline: The Case of New Orleans. *Town Planning Review* 64, no. 3.

Burns, Nancy. 1994. *The Formation of American Local Governments: Private Values in Public Institutions.* New York: Oxford University Press.

Clarke, Susan E. 1993. The New Localism: Local Politics in a Global Era. In *The New Localism: Comparative Urban Politics in a Global Era,* eds. Edward G. Goetz and Susan E. Clarke. Newbury Park, Calif.: Sage.

Clavel, Pierre. 1986. *The Progressive City.* New Brunswick, N.J.: Rutgers University Press.

Clavel, Pierre, and Nancy Kleniewski. 1990. Space for Progressive Local Policy: Examples from the United States and the United Kingdom. In *Beyond the City Limits: Economic Restructuring in Comparative Perspective,* eds. John R. Logan and Todd Swanstrom. Philadelphia, Pa.: Temple University Press.

DeLeon, Richard Edward. 1992. *Left Coast City: Progressive Politics in San Francisco 1975–1991.* Lawrence: University Press of Kansas.

Elkin, Stephen L. 1985. Twentieth Century Urban Regimes. *Journal of Urban Affairs* 7.

————. 1987. *City and Regime in the American Republic.* Chicago: University of Chicago Press.

Fainstein, Susan et al., eds. 1986. *Restructuring the City.* Rev. ed. New York: Longman.

Fisher, Robert, and Joseph Kling, eds. 1993. *Mobilizing the Community: Local Politics in the Era of the Global City.* Newbury Park, Calif.: Sage.

Gaspar, J. 1992. Societal Response to Changes in the Production System. *Urban Studies* 29.

Gittell, Ross. 1992. *Renewing Cities.* Princeton, N.J.: Princeton University Press.

Goetz, Edward G., and Susan E. Clarke, eds. 1993. *The New Localism: Comparative Urban Politics in a Global Era.* Newbury Park, Calif.: Sage.

Grosfoguel, Ramón. 1994. World Cities in the Caribbean: The Rise of Miami and San Juan. *Review* 27, no. 3.

Hall, John. 1994. Port Leases Chunk of Wharf in Step Toward Privatization. *Times-Picayune* (New Orleans, La.), Apr. 1, C1.

———. 1995a. Cargo to the Max. *Times-Picayune* (New Orleans, La.), Feb. 10 1996, C1.

———. 1995b. Investment Creates Port Boom. *Times-Picayune* (New Orleans, La.) Aug. 19, C1.

Heavy Metal Success Story: Aluminum and Copper. 1994. *Port Record.* (Nov.). New Orleans, La.: Port of New Orleans.

Henry, N. 1992. The New Industrial Spaces: Locational Logic of a New Production Era? *International Journal of Urban and Regional Research* 16.

Intermodal Capability Boosts Port Tonnage. 1994. *Port Record.* (Nov.). New Orleans, La.: Port of New Orleans.

Keating, Michael. 1991. *Comparative Urban Politics.* Brookfield, Vt.: Edward Elgar.

Lauria, Mickey, Robert K. Whelan, and Alma H. Young. 1995. The Revitalization of New Orleans. In *Urban Revitalization,* eds. Fritz W. Wagner, Timothy Joder, and Anthony J. Mumphrey. Newbury Park, Calif.: Sage.

Leitner, Helga, and Mark Garner. 1993. The Limits of Local Initiatives: A Reassessment of Urban Entrepreneurialism for Urban Development. *Urban Geography* 14, no. 1.

Lewis, Peirce F. 1976. *New Orleans: The Making of an Urban Landscape.* Cambridge, Mass.: Ballinger Publishing Co.

Logan, John R. and Harvey L. Molotch. 1987. *Urban Fortunes: The Political Economy of Place.* Berkeley and Los Angeles: University of California Press.

Logan, John R., and Todd Swanstrom, eds. 1990. *Beyond the City Limits: Urban Policy and Economic Restructuring in Comparative Perspective.* Philadelphia, Penn.: Temple University Press.

Mollenkopf, John H. 1983. *The Contested City.* Princeton, N.J.: Princeton University Press.

Molotch, Harvey L. 1976. The City as a Growth Machine: Toward a Political Economy of Place. *American Journal of Sociology* 82.

———. 1990. Urban Deals in Comparative Perspective. In *Beyond the City Limits: Urban Policy and Economic Restructuring in Comparative Perspective,* eds. John R. Logan and Todd Swanstrom. Philadelphia. Penn.: Temple University Press.

Mumphrey, Anthony, and Karen Anne Pinell. 1992. New Orleans and the Top 25 Cities: Central City and Metropolitan Dualities. Paper No. 1. New Orleans: National Center for the Revitalization of Central Cities.

1995: A Very Good Year. 1995. *Port Record.* (Dec. 6). New Orleans, La.: Port of New Orleans.

Peterson, Paul. 1981. *City Limits.* Chicago: University of Chicago Press.

Piore, M., and C. F. Sabel. 1984. *The Second Industrial Divide.* New York: Basic Books.

Port Cargo Takes a Leap. 1995. *CityBusiness,* New Orleans, La., Aug. 28–Sept. 3, 1.

Rosenberg, Daniel. 1988. *New Orleans Dockworkers: Race, Labor, and Unionism, 1892–1923.* Albany: State University of New York.

Ryan, Timothy P. 1992. The Economic Impacts of the Port of New Orleans and the

New Orleans Maritime Industry. Report prepared for the Board of Commissioners of the Port of New Orleans. New Orleans, La.: University of New Orleans.

Ryan, Timothy P., and Vincent Maruggi. 1995. The Economic Impacts of the Port of New Orleans and the Maritime Industry on New Orleans and Louisiana. Report prepared for the Board of Commissioners of the Port of New Orleans. New Orleans, La.: University of New Orleans.

Sassen, Saskia. 1990. Beyond the City Limits: A Commentary. In *Beyond the City Limits: Urban Policy and Economic Restructuring in Comparative Perspective*, eds. John R. Logan and Todd Swanstrom. Philadelphia, Penn.: Temple University Press.

Schneider, M., and P. Teske. 1992. Toward a Theory of the Political Entrepreneur: Evidence from Local Government. *American Political Science Review* 86.

Shearer, D. 1989. In Search of Equal Partnerships. In *Unequal Partnerships*, ed. G.D. Squires. New Brunswick, N.J.: Rutgers University Press.

Shefter, Martin. 1985. *Political Crisis/Fiscal Crisis: The Collapse and Revival of New York City*. New York: Basic Books.

Steel Shipments Rise. 1995. *Port Record*. (Nov. 6). New Orleans, La.: Port of New Orleans.

Stitching It All Together. 1995. *Port Record*. (Sept. 14–17). New Orleans, La.: Port of New Orleans.

Stone, Clarence N. 1989. *Regime Politics: Governing Atlanta 1946–1988*. Lawrence: University Press of Kansas.

———. 1993. Urban Regimes and the Capacity to Govern: A Political Economy Approach. *Journal of Urban Affairs* 15, no. l.

Stone, Clarence N., and Heywood T. Sanders, eds. 1987. *The Politics of Urban Development*. Lawrence: University Press of Kansas.

Strategic Plan for the Port of New Orleans. 1986. New Orleans, La.: Port of New Orleans.

Swanstrom, Todd. 1985. *The Crisis of Growth Politics: Cleveland, Kucinick, and the Challenge of Urban Populism*. Philadelphia, Penn.: Temple University Press.

Whelan, Robert K. 1989. New Orleans: Public-Private Partnerships and Uneven Development. In *Unequal Partnerships: The Political Economy of Urban Redevelopment in Postwar America*, ed. Gregory D. Squires. New Brunswick, N.J.: Rutgers University Press.

Whelan, Robert, Alma H. Young, and Mickey Lauria. 1994. Urban Regimes and Racial Politics. *Journal of Urban Affairs* 16, no. 1.

Young, Alma H., and Robert K. Whelan. 1993. Strategic Planning for the Port of New Orleans. In *Comparative Studies in Local Economic Development: Problems in Policy Implementation*. ed. Peter B. Meyer. Westport, Conn.: Greenwood Press.

Young, Alma H., and Jyaphia Christos-Rodgers. 1995. Resisting Racially Gendered Spaces: The Women of the St. Thomas Resident Council, New Orleans. In *Marginal Spaces: Comparative Urban and Community Research,* vol. 5, ed. Michael Peter Smith. New Brunswick, N.J.: Transaction Publishers.

10

Employment Transformations in Mexican and U.S. Gulf Cities[1]

Bryan Roberts and Richard Tardanico

Our point of departure is the contemporary transformations of the world economy and their consequences for urban-regional patterns of development and inequality. We analyze changes in the employment patterns of Mexican and U.S. cities surrounding the Gulf of Mexico as they are broadly defined against the backdrop of economic globalization, North American integration, and domestic market-oriented reforms. This geographic focus subsumes much of the Mexican South and the U.S. South within a wider, binational region, which corresponds to The States of the Gulf of Mexico Accord signed by the zone's governors in 1995 (Zaretsky and Rosenberg 1998). The accord represents a politico-commercial initiative based on perceived trans-Gulf commonalities in relation to NAFTA. It therefore forms part of a North American wave of such cross-border, regional initiatives. Among the others are the Canadian-U.S. Pacific Northwest, Mexican-U.S. Desert Pacific, and Canadian Maritime-Northern New England accords (see Sparke 1997; Tardanico in this volume).

Proponents claim that, at least over the long run, the processes of global restructuring, North American integration, and neoliberal reform will generate prosperity across social groups and localities. We explore the short-term relation of differences among the Gulf of Mexico's urban economies to comparative changes in their industry and occupational structures of employment and their income distributions. The trends we identify serve as benchmarks for assessing the long-term relation of transnationalization and market-enhancing policies to local contours of development and social inequality.

Our strategy is to compare several Gulf cities within and between each country. We begin by documenting the diversity of the industry and occupational structures of these cities. Doing so establishes a baseline of differences for assessing the comparative impact of national and transnational restructuring, of which NAFTA is a part. We then look at comparative changes in industry and occupational patterns of employment between the 1980s and 1990s, as well as their significance for income distributions and other aspects of employment-based inequality. We pay special attention to the relevance of the shifts for gendered inequalities.[2]

The U.S. cities examined are Brownsville, Laredo, Houston, New Orleans, and Miami; the Mexican cities are Matamoros, Nuevo Laredo, Tampico, Veracruz, and Mérida.[3] The economies of these cities are characterized by pronounced diversity in local structure and supralocal relations, past and present.

Our findings are highly tentative. NAFTA is part of a larger trajectory of Mexico-U.S., continental, and worldwide integration that was accelerated by the Border Industrialization Program in the 1960s, the Maquiladora Program in the 1970s, and the GATT's tariff reductions in the 1980s (see Campos et al. 1998; Galbraith 1998, 256–62). The problem of isolating the labor market effects of NAFTA from the wider dynamics of transnationalization and promarket reform would remain even if our data extended beyond 1990 for the U.S. cases and 1993 for the Mexican cases. This is so because the data do not permit the disentangling of cyclical swings in domestic economies and short-range impacts of domestic macroeconomic policies and political conditions from secular and extranational trends.[4] These concerns remind us that urban and regional transformations are not mere derivatives of extranational dynamics, but rather are consequences of the complex interplay of local, national, and global forces.[5] Problems of cross-national data comparability, which are especially challenging because the comparison between the United States and Mexico spans both the developed and less-developed worlds, add another limitation. In light of these considerations, we emphasize broad features of comparative realignments and the conceptualization of questions for future study.

This study begins with a theoretical discussion of the interplay of urban economies and labor markets with contemporary global and national restructuring. It then briefly reviews the historical differences and transformations in the linkages of Mexican and U.S. Gulf cities to the domestic and world economies. Finally, it explores comparative changes in employment and social inequality across these cities, and concludes by raising issues for research and policy consideration.

Cities and Restructuring

Our analysis of changing employment patterns in Mexico-U.S. Gulf cities is anchored in recognition of the ongoing realignment of the world division of labor. During the post–World War II era of state-led expansion of high-volume manufacturing, this division of labor involved a national and international system of urban and rural localities grounded in their value-added importance in domestically based manufacturing production. Such organization fostered a certain convergence in the industry structure of economies across countries and cities, at least among those zones with significant manufacturing. In contrast, the accelerating trend since the 1970s or so disperses and differentiates manufacturing activities across subnational and international areas while centralizing branches of finance and specialized services of management and coordination in relatively few crucial sites at home and abroad. This process tends to lower the value-added ranking of manufacturing activities and raise that of finance and specialized services in transnational commodity chains. It also tends to devalue local and national circuits of accumulation in favor of global circuits. Complicating these trends is a gradual recentralization of manufacturing in the world's leading market zones—including North America— "with one highly integrated production complex serving a number of country markets" (Schoenberg 1994, 61). These shifts push localities into more diverse and fragile positions in an increasingly multinational-firm dominated and globalized division of labor (Dicken 1998; Sassen 1994).

What are the ramifications for the territorial contours of employment and inequality? Bound up with the previous trend of industry convergence across many countries and cities was the increased uniformity of their occupational structures, together with growth in the portion of workers holding regulated, stable, skilled, and middle-income jobs. Characteristic of contemporary restructuring, however, is the growing distinctiveness of industry and occupational structures between, as well as within, countries and cities. A consequence is the global reshaping and widening of inequalities between and within localities, industries, occupations, social classes, and ethnic and gender groups, as mitigated or accentuated by the policies and capacities of states (Roberts 1994; Sassen 1994, 1996; Tardanico and Menjívar 1997).

Regarding the cities of the most advanced national economies, some tendency toward earnings polarization now appears common to labor markets. This tendency involves shifts not only on the demand-side of production but also on the supply-side of household structure, fertility and women's labor force participation, cultural patterns of consumption, and immigration flows. Theory and research suggest that, across cities, earnings polarization varies in degree depending on local economic and sociodemographic features and their state-filtered relations to national and world market trends (ILO 1996; O'Loughlin and Friedrichs 1996; Sassen 1994). Across the most advanced national economies, such polarization appears most pronounced in the United States (Freeman 1994; Galbraith 1998; ILO 1996). Some analysts claim that widened earnings disparities are tied primarily to occupational polarization, as employment becomes more concentrated at both the high end of professionals and the low end of semiskilled and unskilled workers at the expense of the middle rungs (e.g., Harrison and Bluestone 1988; Sassen 1991, 1994). This conclusion points to policies that seek to rebuild employment's middle rungs in an age of service-oriented transformations. Other analysts claim that earnings disparities widen even as occupational structure improves, becoming more concentrated in the upper and middle rungs of professional, semiprofessional, technical, and skilled jobs (e.g., Esping-Andersen, et al. 1993; Gordon 1996; Hamnett 1994). This interpretation points to policies that consider occupational upgrading itself as inadequate for the amelioration of earnings inequalities (see Galbraith 1998; Gordon 1996).

Esping-Andersen et al. relate the latter scenario to the emergence of a "postindustrial," service-driven economy (1993, 32–57). At the core of the postindustrial economy is a decline in the importance of the traditional industries associated with Fordist, or standardized, mass production and mass consumption, primarily manufacturing and distribution services. What grows in importance are the modern services, which consist of producer, government, social, and consumer services. These shifts bring about a decrease in the percentage of employment in those occupations that are tied to the Fordist division of labor: managers, sales and clerical workers; and skilled and semiskilled production workers. Increasing in percentage are those occupations that are tied to the postindustrial division of labor: professionals, semiprofessionals and technicians, and skilled and unskilled service workers (see Gordon 1996; ILO 1996).

According to Esping-Andersen et al., there are overlaps between the industries and occupations of the new and old divisions of labor. For instance, the Fordist remnant of manufacturing increasingly incorporates the postindustrial, or post-Fordist, era's professionals and skilled service workers, while the new era's modern services absorb some of the old era's sales and clerical workers. Esping-Andersen et al. argue that such overlap adds impetus to the growing salience of postindustrial occupations, since these are nurtured by both the rapid expansion of modern services and the modernization of traditional industries. They add that the postindustrial economy is also likely to cause a fall in the percentage of unskilled manual employment, since manufacturing and services—whether producer, social, or consumer—demand less physical labor and more mental labor of low-paid workers compared to the Fordist period.

Sassen's (1991, 1994) contrasting emphasis on occupational polarization views relative decline in midlevel occupations as a variable aspect of change across the economic hierarchy of cities in developed countries. From her perspective, growth-led job shifts from manufacturing to producer services and the consequent polarization between high- and low-end occupations are most typical of "global cities." These upper-tier metropolises are focal points of the world's most important activities of management and coordination as well as powerful magnets for low-wage immigrants. Sassen anticipates that the retention of a comparatively high percentage of midlevel occupations in manufacturing and services appears most common within the especially diverse intermediate tier of urban economies. Finally, lower-tier urban economies, which tend to revolve around the provision of low-end services for surrounding agricultural production and to seek branch manufacturing and service plants on the basis of cheap and docile labor, are likely to have the greatest local concentrations of semiskilled and unskilled jobs. The occupational structure of lower-tier areas is the most vulnerable to the relocation of manufacturing and service plants to the world's less-developed countries.

Let us next consider the less-developed countries. Their tendency toward socioeconomic polarization is similar to that described above, if more pronounced and probably more variable across localities due to their generally more subordinate and tenuous relations with the world economy. Regarding employment structure, the major difference between the cities of the developed and less-developed countries is that, in the latter cases, high-end services and nonmanual occupations make up a smaller part and low-end activities a larger part of the labor force. This difference tends to be less extreme in the upper tier of their urban economies (e.g., Mexico City and São Paulo in Latin America), which have strong ties to regional-international and even global circuits, and more extreme in the lower tier. Between these poles, some specialized urban hubs of manufacturing and services have acquired particular niches in the restructured world division of labor. Thus, increasingly embedded in transnational circuits are urban centers for export manufacturing, foreign tourism, and drug trafficking, as well as border production and market nodes (Portes et al. 1997; Roberts 1995; Sassen 1994; Tardanico and Menjívar 1997).

In the less-developed countries, the restructuring of industries has boosted demand for high-earning occupations but, with the disappearance of labor-intensive manufacturing firms that cannot compete without tariff protection and state subsidies, caused the elimination of many mid-earning jobs. Some observers regard technological innovation itself as reducing the job-making capacity of both manufacturing and services and possibly fostering structural unemployment in less-developed countries, as well as on a broader international scale. Other observers regard insufficient growth of manufacturing and services as the more seminal cause of deficient job creation (see the discussions in ILO 1996; Singh and Zammit 1995). Against the background of such possibilities, employment in less-developed countries grows mainly in low-paid, often temporary or subcontracted jobs in manufacturing, commerce, and the informal economy (*CEPAL News* 1998; Portes et al. 1997; Roberts 1995; Singh and Zammit 1995; Tardanico and Menjívar 1997).

Economic activities in the cities of the less-developed world generally rank at the low to intermediate range of global commodity chains. Apart from those urban zones having the most direct transnational linkages, such ranking may temper the demand-based intensity of labor market realignments. From the standpoint of labor supply, so too may comparatively restricted gains by women in the sociocultural and political spheres, as well as comparatively modest inroads by internationalized consumerism. Other conditions, in contrast, may accelerate the local pace of labor market change. Inasmuch as statist intervention was more directly responsible for post–World War II employment upgrading in the cities of the less-developed countries, the labor-market impact of the neoliberal reforms in Latin America, Africa, and parts of Asia stands to be especially acute. This problem is compounded by the continued urbanization of labor. Much of the low-skill, low-wage economies of these countries, moreover, is quite vulnerable to displacement by the transnational mobility of capital, including its repatriation to the developed world (Oliveira and Roberts 1994; Portes et al. 1997; Roberts 1995; Singh and Zammit 1995; Tardanico and Menjívar 1997; on East Asia's distinctiveness, see Cheng and Gereffi 1994).

Clearly, then, we can expect contemporary labor-market transformations in most of the less-developed areas to involve the worsening of earnings disparities. We can also expect that, consistent with Sassen's (1994) argument, occupational composition would become more sharply divided between, on the upper end, professional, semiprofessional, and technical jobs, and, on the lower end, unskilled jobs in export-assembly production, commerce, and the informal economy. The possibility of occupational polarization, however, must be qualified in ways that suggest convergence with Esping-Andersen et al.'s (1993) perspective. For one thing, average years of education in much of the less-developed world have continued to climb, thereby reducing the fraction of labor forces with no more than primary schooling and augmenting the fraction with at least intermediate skills (ECLAC 1995; World Bank 1995). This supply-side trend, of course, is unlikely to be translated into upward occupational mobility without corresponding demand-side growth for more skilled labor in the production of goods and services. Yet such demand-side growth seems to have occurred, particularly in those countries and urban locales that have become most incorporated into either the transnationalized, service-oriented paths of accumulation or skilled segments of manufacturing (see Cheng and Gereffi 1994; ILO 1996; Roberts 1995; Tardanico and Menjívar 1997). Insofar as these supply- and demand-side shifts characterize specific locales in the less-developed countries, we can expect to document not only earnings polarization but also, to a lesser degree than in the advanced national economies, some upgrading of occupational composition.

We anticipate finding, first, earnings polarization in the Mexican and U.S. Gulf cities alike; and second, greater uniformity in the distributional patterns of occupational and earnings change among the upper versus the lower economic strata of cities in our sample. Whether we will find polarization or upgrading in occupational structure is less clear. To the extent that occupational upgrading has taken place, it should be most typical of the cities— probably Houston, Miami, and New Orleans—whose economies are the most oriented to advanced services. Our analysis of this possibility is informed by Esping-Andersen et al.'s (1993) classification of Fordist and post-Fordist occupations.

Two problems are that our data do not adequately distinguish between the Fordist and post-Fordist divisions of labor, and they crudely and inconsistently distinguish among skill categories of labor.[6] Moreover, the data do not capture trends in intracategory inequality, the heightened salience of which is widely recognized (e.g., Freeman 1994; ILO 1996). And for Mexico as well as perhaps the U.S. border cities, neither these nor other survey data convey the comparative fluidity of income-earning activities that typifies the world's less-developed areas. Given these qualifications, we reiterate that our purpose is to explore comparative patterns and changes in employment and social inequality with the objective of raising issues for research and policy consideration.

Mexican and U.S. Gulf Cities: An Overview

National Contrasts in Development

What is the relevance of this framework to Mexican and U.S. Gulf cities? Mexico and the United States cross paths with global restructuring from highly disparate levels of national development. Indicative of their disparities is that although the Mexican population's degree of urbanization has converged with that of the United States, its per capita income is some eight times lower. Hence, whereas services are the predominant form of employment in both countries, there are sharp national differences in the types of service jobs. In Mexico, most service work is in distributive and personal services and in self-employment; in the United States, most service work is in government, social, and producer services, with self-employment being a very small component. Manufacturing remains a much more important source of employment in Mexico than in the United States. Further, the structure of manufacturing is more traditional in Mexico. For example, 33% of value added in Mexican manufacturing corresponds to basic goods industries such as food, beverages, textiles and clothing, compared with only 18% of value added in U.S. manufacturing (World Bank 1994, Table 6).

There is consensus over the sharpening of U.S. inequalities between and within industry and occupational categories since the 1970s. Debates on one level concern the extent to which the concepts of "polarization" and "duality" accurately capture the complexities of change in occupational and earnings distributions. On another level they contest whether accentuated inequalities primarily represent changes on the supply side of labor forces (e.g., household-linked feminization, immigration of unskilled workers, a younger labor force, inequalities of educational attainment, and behavioral aversions to employment), on the demand side of production (e.g., globalization, domestic relocation, deindustrialization, technological innovation, deskilling, organizational change, and subcontracting), or at the intersection of the two (e.g., the weakening of labor unions). Also contested is the relative influence of secular or cyclical shifts in economies and state policies.

Turning to Mexico, we confront a basic difference between the literatures on social inequality in developed and less-developed countries: while the former stresses matters of equity, the latter stresses matters of survival (Benería 1992; Chant 1991; Selby et al. 1991; Escobar and González de la Rocha 1995; see Schteingart 1997). The matter of equity, however, is becoming increasingly important in the Mexican literature as well (Escobar 1996; Schteingart 1997). Mexico's income distribution—which already ranked among the most unequal in the Western Hemisphere at the beginning of the 1980s—became much more polarized during the decade's economic crisis. Between 1983 and 1989, the average real wages of Mexican workers plummeted by a reported 40 to 50% (Lustig 1992, 61–95; see also Cortés and Rubalcava 1991 and CEPAL 1998). By comparison, between 1979 and 1989 the average real wages of U.S. workers increased by an estimated 5.9% among men and 26.2% among women (U.S. Bureau of the Census 1996: Historical Income Tables, P15; see Galbraith 1998).

Poor and middle-class Mexican households mitigated the abrupt drop in living standards by placing more of their members in the labor force and by taking various cost-cutting initiatives (González de la Rocha 1994; Oliveira and García 1997). Several ensuing years of modest, socially uneven recovery gave way in 1994–1995 to yet another crisis with severe economic impact on labor and households. Given the undermining of Mexico's comparatively minimal edifice of government welfare programs, U.S.-style debates over state-induced behavioral causes of social inequality and poverty are notably absent from the Mexican literature. The latter does consider other supply-side dimensions of the workforce, such as rural-urban migration, shifts in household composition, the labor force impact of internationalized consumerism, and a secular rise in female labor force participation. Consistent with Latin America-wide scholarly and policy analysis is the Mexican literature's twofold emphasis. The first is the attempt to relate supply-side changes in the labor force to demand-side changes in production, such as the explosion in export manufacturing since the 1960s, the sector's ongoing transformation, and the ramifications of neoliberal policies for other branches of manufacturing and for agriculture. The second is the documentation of circumstances under which economic formality or informality (i.e., state regulation or deregulation) stand to impede or promote growth and development (Lustig 1992; Oliveira and García 1997; Rendón and Salas 1992; Spener 1995; Wilson 1992).

The Cities

Against this backdrop of dramatic national contrasts, our approach is to compare selected Gulf cities within and between each country. New Orleans was far and away the leading city of the international Gulf region until World War II, when fast-growing Houston surpassed it in key ways. The economic commonalities of the two cities include their foundations in pre–Civil War slavery, cotton, sugar, and port commerce, along with the twentieth-century additions of petroleum and petrochemicals, petroleum-related manufacturing, shipbuilding, the space industry, medical services, and tourism. Yet, whereas the end of the Civil War and the expansion of railways signaled the eclipse of New Orleans's commercial preeminence in the U.S. South, the same factors launched Houston into vigorous growth as a commercial node for the rapidly expanding Southwest (Feagin 1988). Following World War II, federal government policies and the transnational restructuring that underlay the economic and demographic boom in parts of the U.S. Sunbelt catapulted Houston ahead of New Orleans. The decisive advantages of state-built economic infrastructure also helped Houston rank, in terms of value added, as the fourth largest manufacturing city in the United States by the late 1970s (Feagin 1988; see Glasmeier and Leichenko in this volume). Although New Orleans was not excluded from the Sunbelt's economic transformation, the city's muted growth marked its definitive fall from the upper echelon of U.S. southern metropolises (Lauria et al. 1993; Smith and Keller 1983).

By the mid-1980s, the plunge in world oil prices and the negative impact of an overvalued dollar on Gulf Coast exports hurled Houston and New Orleans into the upper level of recession-battered U.S. cities. The severity of the downswing—including major outflows of population—was worse for Houston in the short run and for New Orleans in the long run. By the late 1980s, Houston's economy entered a new stage of slow, tenuous growth, grafted upon restructuring both within the shrunken petroleum sector and beyond to the city's notable offerings in high-tech industry and advanced producer services (Feagin 1988; Saussey 1988; *U.S./Latin Trade* 1995a). For New Orleans, any semblance of recovery was later in coming and remains less palpable. Recovery in New Orleans focuses on tourism and the vigorous modernization of the port economy, as the city's government attempts to reverse a tide of losses to the ports of Houston, Miami, and other cities of the Gulf and beyond (Bussey 1997; Hoeschen 1995; Kalmback and Shuler 1996; Lauria et al. 1993; Saussey 1993; *U.S./Latin Trade* 1995a, 1995b; Young in this volume). Between 1980 and 1990, the metropolitan population rose by a net 11.6% in Houston—to 3,731,000—but dropped by a net 1.5% in New Orleans—to 1,285,000 (U.S. Bureau of the Census 1993, Table 42).

Miami, of course, sits on the Atlantic Ocean rather than the Gulf of Mexico. Yet, as the principal commercial and cultural intermediary for Caribbean and Latin American relations with the United States and the wider world, its international web of competition increasingly overlaps with those of Houston and New Orleans. Miami was a mere trading post when northeastern speculators began cultivating it as a tourism center in the 1890s. The growth of tourism opened a stream of predominately northeastern migration to the city, which after World War II encouraged the diversification of its service-oriented economy. What shattered Miami's ambience as a provincial southern city with northern overlays was massive immigration from Cuba triggered by that country's revolution in 1959, the failure of the Bay of Pigs invasion in 1961, and the Mariel boatlift in 1980. The initial waves of Cuban immigration accelerated Miami's economic and demographic transitions as a Sunbelt city. In addition, thanks to the class composition of the Cuban exiles and major federal subsidies, a substantial portion of the early immigrants moved into entrepreneurial, professional, and managerial slots, thereby transforming the city's labor market. The Mariel generation, in contrast, entered

Miami's labor market at the low end, where Cubans joined growing numbers of Haitians in economic competition with African Americans.

Political strife, the oil boom, economic crisis, and transnational restructuring in Latin America and the Caribbean have brought flight capital and people—above all the less-skilled, but remarkable numbers of professionals and entrepreneurs as well—from throughout the region to Miami. Between 1980 and 1990, its metropolitan population grew by a net 20.8%—to 3,193,000 (U.S. Bureau of the Census 1993, Table 42). By the latter year, the metropolitan area's percentage of foreign-born residents had become the highest in the United States. And while Miami's economy has not been immune to national business cycles, its ups and downs have been synchronized with those of its neighbors to the south. Indeed, the city's most dynamic economic activities represent an agglomeration of business and consumer services for Latin America and the Caribbean (Grosfoguel 1994; Nijman 1996; Portes and Stepick 1993; *U.S./Latin Trade 1994*). Diversifying this Latin American/Caribbean base during the late 1990s were two governmental additions: the relocation of the U.S. military's Southern Command headquarters from Panama to Miami; and the selection of Miami as the temporary headquarters for the negotiation of a hemispheric free-trade zone. Nevertheless, Miami's economy finds itself at a growing disadvantage relative to other U.S. cities in the South and elsewhere as a result of various local problems. These include deficient economic and social infrastructure; a comparatively low-skilled workforce; excessive reliance on declining industries (tourism, apparel/textiles); competitive weakness in banking (including international banking); and a cultural and business orientation toward Latin America that, together with an outlying geographic position, restricts the city's access to important national market networks (Fields 1997a, 1997b; Fields and Whitefield 1997a 1997b; Whitefield 1997b).

The cities of the Gulf region most directly affected by changes in U.S.-Mexico economic relations are those of the Texas-Mexico border. The "twin cities" of Brownsville and Matamoros, and of Laredo and Nuevo Laredo, are located in Texas's lower Río Grande valley and the Mexican Gulf state of Tamaulipas. Texas's Río Grande valley came to revolve around cotton and similar commodities after the introduction of extensive irrigation in the 1930s. Commercial agriculture generated large-scale demand for seasonal labor, which in great part was supplied from the interior of Mexico. The Mexican cities of Matamoros and Nuevo Laredo became ports of entry to the United States for labor from Mexico's interior and provided a permanent home for part of this workforce, which was partly sponsored by the Bracero program (1942–65). The Texas cities located across the border—Brownsville and Laredo—grew as service nodes for their own agricultural hinterlands. The two Laredos, moreover, acquired importance as customs points for Mexican-U.S. trade. A major land route extends from Monterrey, Mexico, to the two Laredos, and in turn to interior Texas cities such as San Antonio and to the U.S. Midwest.

In 1965, the initiation of the Border Industrialization Program (BIP), which authorized the establishment of in-bond assembly plants (maquiladoras), began to alter the economic linkages between the U.S.-Mexican border cities. Low-cost Mexican labor and the proximity of the Mexican border cities to the U.S. interstate transportation network enticed many U.S. firms, particularly those specializing in electronics and garment assembly, to locate there. By the late 1980s Matamoros had become a major site of maquiladora activity, with approximately 90 plants employing more than 36,000 workers (INEGI 1980–1998). Such activity was slower to develop in Nuevo Laredo, largely because the city's business elite, which revolved around customs brokerage and complementary endeavors such as short-haul transport, sought to curb potential challenges to its local influence. This stance stemmed from the fact that the two Laredos are important customs points, in the early 1990s accounting for 62% of the dollar value of surface imports to the United States (Spener 1995, 1996). By the mid-1980s, however, maquiladora expansion in Nuevo Laredo gathered steam, and by the decade's end the city housed fifty-six plants employing some 15,000 workers (INEGI 1980–1998; see Sklair 1993).

Many of the maquiladoras in Matamoros and Nuevo Laredo maintain offices in their twin U.S. cities. At the same time, firms located elsewhere in the United States supply the Mexican plants with manufactured inputs and provide maintenance, financial, and professional services. Increased cross-border trade, both local and long-distance, has created specialized businesses on both sides of the Río Grande. Texas residents cross the border for tourism and to obtain low-cost medical and dental services; Mexican residents cross the border to shop in malls and to purchase specialized inputs for their businesses. While the managers of maquiladoras tend to live on the Texas side, Mexicans from Matamoros and Laredo commute to their twin U.S. cities for employment as domestic workers and construction workers. In this context, a possible counterpart to the specialization of Matamoros and Nuevo Laredo in manufacturing has been that of Brownsville and Laredo in professional, financial, and technical services, as well as in hotels, restaurants, and shopping. Since 1970, population has grown rapidly in each of these locales, especially in the Texas cities, including an influx of migrants from the Mexican interior. Between 1980 and 1990, metropolitan population increased by a net

24% in Brownsville—to 260,000—and a net 34.4% in Laredo—to 123,000 (U.S. Bureau of the Census 1993, Tables 42 and 46; see Gilbreath 1998).

Annual population growth in Matamoros, the twin city of Brownsville, was 3.4% between 1980 and 1990, the highest growth rate of the Mexican Gulf cities in our study. Matamoros's population reached 266,000 by 1990. Nuevo Laredo, in contrast, scarcely increased in population over the same years, reaching a high of 218,000 (INEGI 1994). This difference in population growth between the two Mexican border cities reflects Nuevo Laredo's late arrival as a maquiladora center. By the late 1980s, however, Nuevo Laredo's rate of job growth was probably greater than that of Matamoros, as maquiladora production expanded in newer locales (see Gilbreath 1998; Kopinak 1996; Oliveira and García 1997; Sklair 1993; Wilson 1992).

Moving southward along Mexico's Gulf coast, the contemporary economic base of Tampico rests on the city's twentieth-century importance to the nation's petroleum industry. Some of the nation's richest oil wells before 1960 were located in the coastal fringe around Tampico, which became a port for refining, storing, and exporting petroleum. Until the more recent development of Mexico's southern-Gulf petroleum complexes, Tampico, together with the adjoining city of Ciudad Madero, contained the nation's largest concentration of unionized oil workers. The political and economic clout of the oil workers translated into material benefits for Tampico, as the union invested funds in oil-related manufacturing and service enterprises. Tampico's most dynamic expansion was during the 1960s. Thereafter, the petroleum industry became displaced southward to the Chicontepec basin comprising the states of Veracruz, Tabasco, Chiapas, and Campeche. In this setting, Tampico's population growth between 1980 and 1990 was a modest 1.8% a year, reaching a total of 560,000 by 1990. The port remains important, handling 9% of the total cargo handled by Mexico's Gulf-Caribbean ports, compared with Veracruz's 5.5%. Both Tampico and Veracruz, though, are dwarfed by the petroleum-industry ports of Cayo Arcos, Pajaritos, and Dos Bocas (in the states of Campeche, Veracruz, and Tabasco, respectively), which collectively handle some 70% of the zone's cargo volume. The significance of the ports of Tampico and Veracruz now lies much less in exports than in imports, as they are Mexico's major entry points for seaborne cargo.

Veracruz emerged as Mexico's leading port during the colonial era. Historically, it has been pivotal to the country's network of internal and external transportation. Mexico's first railroad was built from Veracruz to Mexico City in the late 1860s. Trade was the catalyst to the industrialization of Veracruz and its surrounding region, where a significant amount of textile, paper, and other basic-goods manufacturing developed at the end of the nineteenth century. Stagnation ensued in most of these activities during the twentieth century as the nation's central region consolidated its hegemony in infrastructure, manufacturing, services, and markets. Yet Veracruz did benefit from two twentieth-century phenomena: the petroleum industry and tourism. It became the principal supplier of pipelines and ships for Mexico's state-owned oil company, Pemex, and an important site for the middle-class tourism of Mexican nationals. As a crucial link in Mexico's petroleum industry, Veracruz, like Tampico, became a center of labor union power. By the 1980s, however, the radical restructuring of both the port economy and Pemex undercut the political leverage of organized labor. Pemex's role in the Veracruz economy has shrunk, as it has in Tampico. Even so, the city and state of Veracruz have been left with serious environmental problems related to the petroleum industry, particularly the contamination of rivers and lagoons (Rodríguez Herrero 1996). Between 1980 and 1990, the city's population grew to 472,000, with a relatively high growth rate of 2.5% annually. This increase probably stemmed from an upturn in the port's activity and associated service diversification (see Salmerón 1994).

Located on the Yucatán Peninsula, Mérida is the only state capital among this chapter's cross-national group of cities. In the nineteenth century Mérida's economic importance derived from the henequen industry. The city served as the industry's organizational hub and the place of residence of the plantation elites, as the nearby Port of Progreso became the regional economy's export node. Among Mexico's Gulf cities, Mérida is the most stratified by class and ethnicity (Ramírez 1993). Historically, social stratification in Mérida and its adjacent areas was based on an urban-rural divide in which the "white" plantation elites, their indigenous servants, and the mestizo commercial and craft workers inhabited the city, while the rural population remained almost exclusively indigenous. In recent decades, migration from the countryside has considerably broadened the indigenous layer of the city's population.

Mérida's growth since World War II has revolved around three elements (see Wilson and Kayne in this volume). The first is the presence of state and federal government agencies, both of which expanded rapidly during Mexico's post-1940 era of state-centric economic development. The second is Mérida's role in servicing the tourist industry along Mexico's Caribbean coast, which burgeoned after the 1960s. Although the zone's main tourist locales (Cancún and Cozumel) lie some distance from Mérida, the city provides inputs for the industry and lures tourists from the coastal areas to its surrounding archaeological sites. Lastly, Mérida has attracted some maquiladora plants thanks to its proximity by sea and air to the U.S. South. Between 1986 and 1993, its population rose by an annual rate of 2.7 percent to reach 595,000 (INEGI 1994b).

Employment Transformations[7]

Industry Structure

By the end of the periods we are considering (1990 in the United States, 1993 in Mexico), manufacturing represented a larger percentage of employment in the Mexican than the U.S. Gulf cities. As part of a worldwide pattern, expansion of service-oriented employment has been the secular trend in the United States and Mexico alike. Nonetheless, a much larger percentage of employment in the U.S. than Mexican Gulf cities is located in the strategic sector of producer services (Table 10.1).

In general, the industry pattern of employment in the Mexican Gulf cities hardly changed during the period considered. By comparison, in the U.S. Gulf cities there was, for men and women, a marked decline in the employment share of manufacturing and a marked increase in the share of services. Thus the trend toward a postindustrial economy, as measured by the relative growth of jobs in producer, social, and consumer services, was less advanced in the Mexican than the U.S. cases, particularly among women.[8]

The Mexican Gulf cities do not include any of Mexico's largest metropolises. Nevertheless, their shift in the industry distribution of employment

Table 10.1
Industry Structure of Employment

| | Mexican Gulf Cities | | | | U.S. Gulf Cities | | | |
| | Males % | | Females % | | Males % | | Females % | |
	1986	1993	1986	1993	1980	1990	1980	1990
Agriculture & Mining	8.0	3.3	1.7	0.5	4.6	4.6	2.5	2.0
Manufacturing	18.9	18.7	18.3	17.2	21.1	15.6	11.9	8.4
Construction	10.8	9.5	0.8	1.2	13.8	12.4	2.1	1.7
Trade	17.6	19.7	23.2	24.6	18.8	19.5	18.9	17.9
Transport	9.8	9.4	1.8	2.4	9.2	8.7	5.4	5.4
Producer Services[a]	3.6	5.2	4.8	5.2	12.3	14.3	16.8	18.9
Social Services[b]	6.0	6.5	19.1	19.0	6.6	7.9	25.0	27.7
Consumer Services[c]	18.9	21.3	27.2	25.8	9.7	12.6	14.1	14.5
Government	6.4	6.4	3.1	4.1	3.9	4.4	3.3	3.5
Total	100	100	100	100	100	100	100	100

Sources: INEGI (1986, 1993), second quarters; U.S. Bureau of the Census (1980, 1990).
[a]Producer services include financial, insurance, real estate, and professional services.
[b]Social services include education and health.
[c]Consumer services include hotels, restaurants, entertainment, repair, and domestic services.

broadly conformed to that of Mexico's largest cities, including Mexico City.[9] Structural adjustment policies, which led to a certain retrenchment of government employment and to diminished growth in social services, restrained national growth of a service-based economy during this period. A large portion of Mexico's new service jobs was concentrated in low-skilled, low-paid work in consumer services (Oliveira and García 1997; Rendón and Salas 1992). We shall see, however, that the pattern reported in Table 10.1 for the Mexican Gulf cities conceals substantial variation among them—much more than among the U.S. Gulf cases.

The trajectory of the Mexican border cities, Matamoros and Nuevo Laredo, diverged sharply from that of the other Mexican cities in the study. Only in the border cities did the proportion of jobs in manufacturing rise, due to the mounting importance of maquiladoras. Manufacturing's share of employment in Matamoros rose from 29.7 to 34.4%, and in Nuevo Laredo from 14.1 to 19.2%. Diminishing in employment share were trade and producer services. From the mid-1980s onward, the growth of U.S. and Japanese investment along Mexico's northern frontier enabled Matamoros to consolidate itself as a major site of export-assembly manufacturing and Nuevo Laredo to enter the ranks of notable export producers. Consequently, Nuevo Laredo jumped from fourth—behind not only Matamoros but also Mérida and Veracruz—to second place in percentage of local employment in manufacturing. Linked to Nuevo Laredo's transformation was its dramatic job growth in modern services, primarily government and social services. Nuevo Laredo rose to become second only to Mérida in the local fraction of employment in modern services.

The other Mexican Gulf cities followed a more pronounced trend of employment deindustrialization and service growth. Mérida and Veracruz underwent declines in the relative weight of manufacturing jobs. By this measure, Mérida tumbled from second place to middle rank, and Veracruz from third place to last, among the five Mexican cities. Tampico is likely also to have lost ground in manufacturing employment. Of the Mexican Gulf cities, relative job growth in consumer services was fastest in Tampico and Veracruz. This resulted, in part, from their improvement in real incomes, particularly in the top 10% of earners. It is also a sign, though, that substantial parts of their economies and labor forces were becoming marginalized. At the other end of the spectrum, Mérida had the fastest relative job growth in producer, government, and social services.

Hence, manufacturing became a larger part of employment only in the border cities of Nuevo Laredo and Matamoros. Increased job concentration in modern services indicates some postindustrial dynamism in Mérida, possibly tied to the growth of international and domestic tourism in the Yucatán Peninsula. For the entire sample of Mexican Gulf cities, however, a measure of economic underdevelopment is that producer services formed a small part of employment (2–7%) and that in the nonborder cities almost half of employment remained in trade and consumer services.

The shift to a service-oriented employment structure was clear in all the U.S. Gulf cities sampled, as it is in other U.S. cities as well.[10] As the share of producer service jobs climbed everywhere except Brownsville, their relative weight remained highest in Miami and Houston and lowest in Laredo and Brownsville. The share of employment in government and social services rose everywhere except Laredo, with Houston and Miami ranking at the bottom in this category. The local weight of binational consumerism's surge in Brownsville and tourism's surge in New Orleans, along with the relative weakness of producer service growth in these cities, pushed them ahead of Miami in the percentage of local jobs in consumer services. This took place despite Miami's rapid ascent as a hub for Latin American and Caribbean consumer activity.

There is little evidence that the complementarities of Brownsville and Laredo with the Mexican market have led to specialization in their industry compositions of employment. Producer services—whose employment would be expected to expand as a complement to maquiladoras on the Mexican side—remained proportionally less important in Brownsville and Laredo than in the other U.S. cities. In general, though, Brownsville and Laredo conformed to the U.S. Gulf-city trend of postindustrial transition.

Occupational Structure

The data on change in occupational structure reveal a clearer trend across countries and cities in postindustrial economic organization, although such change was merely incipient (Table 10.2). For the U.S. Gulf cities at large, the mainly service occupations that Esping-Andersen et al. (1993, 24–25) categorize as postindustrial gained in relative importance for men and women. The fastest growing occupations among men were manual services; among women, professional positions, managers, and skilled manufacturing workers. For the Mexican Gulf cities, the aggregate data show a comparable shift away from Fordist occupations for men, but just a marginal shift for women. Compared with the U.S. cities, however, the Mexican decreased fraction of unskilled service jobs likely reflects the erosion of not an industrial but a *preindustrial* category. That is, Mexico's unskilled service jobs are residues of a less-developed economy in which, for example, domestic service was prevalent. Consistent with the U.S. and Mexican industry data, the pattern of occu-

Table 10.2
Occupational Structure

Occupational Structure[a]	Mexican Gulf Cities				U.S. Gulf Cities			
	Males %		Females %		Males %		Females %	
	1986	1993	1986	1993	1980	1990	1980	1990
Fordist								
Managers & Administrators	4.0	4.2	2.1	1.6	15.8	14.3	8.8	12.3
Clerical	6.4	6.5	19.5	17.1	6.3	6.6	33.2	28.0
Sales	10.3	12.5	18.1	18.8	9.1	9.1	12.0	11.7
Skilled Manuf.	35.5	33.0	8.6	8.2	24.9	24.9	3.3	4.4
Semiskilled Manuf.	14.2	10.5	5.9	7.8	18.0	16.1	7.1	5.1
Postindustrial								
Professionals	3.9	5.4	2.1	3.9	8.1	8.4	2.3	3.6
Semiprofessionals	7.8	11.6	14.9	16.5	8.5	8.7	16.8	18.1
Skilled Service	11.0	11.6	8.4	9.5	4.5	6.2	7.6	8.2
Unskilled Service	6.9	4.7	20.4	16.6	4.8	5.7	8.9	8.6
Total	100	100	100	100	100	100	100	100

Sources: INEGI (1986, 1993), second quarters; U.S. Bureau of the Census (1980, 1990).
[a]See Esping-Andersen et al. (1993, 24–25) and note 6.

pational change in the binational Gulf cities appears similar to that of other, including larger, cities in the two nations.

The aggregate data for the binational Gulf cities do not suggest occupational polarization. In line with the evidence cited by Esping-Andersen et al. (1993), the fastest growing occupations tended to be the professions, while the sharpest declines in growth were at the bottom of the ladder: the semiskilled and unskilled occupations in manufacturing and services. An exception was the rapid rise in semiskilled and unskilled manufacturing work among women in the Mexican cities, which reflects burgeoning maquiladora activity. In the Mexican and U.S. cities alike, there was some increase in the employment share of middle-range occupations, with the categories of this shift differing between men and women. For example, clerical work fell in importance for women, but rose slightly for men.

Each of the U.S. Gulf cities conformed to the profile described above, as the fraction of postindustrial employment grew. But there were intercity differences in, first, the extent of shift into postindustrial occupations, and second, the distribution of jobs within the postindustrial structure. Arguably a sign of significant decline in the relative standing of New Orleans and Laredo in the national and world economies is that they were the only U.S. Gulf cities where Fordist occupations grew as a percentage of total employment. Fordist occupations rose from 57 to 62.6% of total employment in New

Orleans and from 67.6 to 69.3% in Laredo. In contrast, the Fordist share dropped abruptly in Brownsville (from 72.1 to 51.8%) and Houston (from 70.5 to 56.9%), and minimally in Miami (from 69.5% to 67.7%). By itself, however, decline in Fordist share may be deceiving as a signal of a city's economic vitality. What matters most is the skill and pay structure of a city's postindustrial occupations relative to both the industrial era of the past and the standards of today.

Let us note that even as Miami ranked highest in job concentration in producer services, its postindustrial occupational momentum was surprisingly slow, as it skidded from second to fourth among the U.S. Gulf cities in postindustrial job share. This is consistent with evidence that, given Miami's economic and social niche as a way station between Latin America, the United States, and the world, the city's offerings in advanced services are comparatively narrow and poorly meshed with the rest of its economy (see Fields 1997a, 1997b; Fields and Whitefield 1997a, 1997b; Nijman 1996).

As for the structure of postindustrial occupations, the importance of professional and semiprofessional employment varied considerably among the U.S. Gulf cases. Houston retained its lead in the concentration of male professional and semiprofessional jobs (19% in 1990), followed closely by New Orleans (18.6%) and distantly by Miami (15%), Brownsville (13.3%), and Laredo (10%). In Houston and New Orleans, most male jobs at this rung were in the professions, whereas in Miami and especially the border cities most of these jobs were semiprofessional. Among women, New Orleans retained its lead in the relative weight of professional and semiprofessional jobs (25.1% in 1990), followed by Houston (23.2%), Brownsville (20.7%), Laredo (20.3%), and Miami (19.4%). Such female employment was overwhelmingly semiprofessional. This was most true of Brownsville and Laredo, as the job share of female professionals was largest in Houston, ahead of New Orleans and Miami. The large fraction of female professional and semiprofessional employment in New Orleans appears linked to its labor market's comparatively large sectors of government and social services. Miami's paucity of upper-stratum jobs relative to the other major cities reinforces our speculation on the weaknesses of its advanced services economy.

Judging by net growth in the employment share of upper-rung jobs (professional, managerial, and semiprofessional), occupational structure improved most in Brownsville (18.5%) and New Orleans (15.8%), trailed by Houston (12.2%) and Miami (7.1%). Laredo experienced a net loss (3.7%) in this category. Judging by net contraction in employment share at the lower rung (semiskilled manufacturing and unskilled service), the leaders were New Orleans (16.6%) and Brownsville (14.6%), ahead of Miami (11.2%), Houston (11.1%), and Laredo (8.4%). These measures imply that the upward push in occupational composition was strongest in Brownsville and New Orleans and weakest in Laredo. For New Orleans, this conclusion provides bitter irony in that the city suffered an absolute net loss of jobs (20.8% for men, 0.2% for women). The city's high level of reliance on government and social service employment means that reductions in such jobs through austerity and privatization programs could significantly weaken its occupational mix.

The greatest variation among the Mexican Gulf cities was between the most dynamic manufacturing site, the maquiladora frontier city of Matamoros, and the others. Only in Matamoros did the Fordist share of total employment rise, albeit marginally (from 69.3% in 1986 to 70.1% in 1993). In none of the Mexican cases did the Fordist share drop nearly as much as in the U.S. cases of Brownsville and Houston;[11] it dropped most in Veracruz (from 62.4 to 56.9%) and Mérida (from 65.2 to 61.3%), trailed by Tampico (from 64.0 to 62.0%) and Nuevo Laredo (from 65.9 to 64.0%).

Consistent with this intercity variation is that the category of manual manufacturing jobs was largest for males and females in Matamoros, the only city in the binational set where such jobs rose as a percentage of total male employment. By 1993, 49.8% of Matamoros's employed men and 45.8% of its employed women were skilled or semiskilled manufacturing workers. At the other pole was Mérida, where the layer of manual manufacturing jobs was smallest and where its importance shrank. By 1993, 38.6% of Mérida's employed men and 11.6% of its employed women were skilled or semiskilled manufacturing workers.

Despite the rapidity of Nuevo Laredo's recent maquiladora growth, and despite its having the second highest share of female workers in skilled and semiskilled manufacturing work (18.8%), this border city had the Mexican sample's fastest female growth in the upper occupations, above all semiprofessional jobs. These occupations comprised 22.3% of Nuevo Laredo's female employment in 1993, short of Mérida's level (24.6%) as the continued leader but much higher than that of the other Mexican cases. This coincides with Nuevo Laredo's increased role in brokering and managing cross-border trade, which expanded the city's workforce in professional services and customs activities, including government employment. It also coincides with Mérida's importance in business and government activities linked to tourism. The local fractions of male upper employment remained highest in Mérida (21.6%) and the port city of Veracruz (18.4%), followed by Nuevo Laredo (14.7%). Such jobs in the Mexican cities were almost exclusively semiprofessional, except for males in Veracruz and Mérida and, to a much lesser degree, females in Mérida.

In none of the Mexican Gulf localities do we detect occupational polarization in the sense of growth at the top and bottom at the expense of the middle. A different sort of polarization occurred in Matamoros, where, as maquiladoras expanded the portions of both upper and middle occupations fell as the portion of lower occupations rose. In contrast, Nuevo Laredo, Tampico, Veracruz, and Mérida experienced relative job increases in the upper tier and decreases in the lower tier. As measured by net growth in the share of upper-tier employment, improvement in occupational structure was much sharper in Nuevo Laredo (63.7%) and Mérida (51.4%) than in Tampico (14.9%) and Veracruz (12.9%). As measured by net decline in the share of lower-tier jobs, Mérida was the leader (46.0%), with Nuevo Laredo (24.6%), Veracruz (22.4%), and Tampico (16.1%) lagging far behind. These indicators point to Mérida, ahead of Nuevo Laredo, as the case of greatest upward job shift among the Mexican Gulf cities, with Matamoros being the sole site of downward shift in the entire binational set.

Industry and Occupational Transformations: A Summary

As expected, differences in employment structure and change revolved around the large, developed cities versus the small, less-developed cities, and around the range of economic niches among the latter cases. The industry mix of employment in the largest cities—Miami and Houston—was, as predicted, most inclined to producer services. Yet the commonalities of occupational structure and change among Houston, Miami, and even New Orleans overshadow their differences. The binational shifts in occupational composition are generally nascent. The pattern of change, however, is strikingly at odds with predictions derived from Sassen's work (1991, 1994) on restructuring. In every U.S. Gulf city and almost every Mexican Gulf city, occupational composition became not more, but less polarized, a finding that echoes the arguments of Esping-Andersen et al. (1993) and others (e.g., Hamnett 1994; O'Loughlin and Friedrichs 1996). The one apparent exception, Matamoros, underwent not polarization per se but rather a downward compression of its entire occupational structure. Occupational upgrading, then, seems to have characterized cities independently of their comparative positions in the national and transnational economies. Greater intercity variability in occupational change within the framework of improved composition does seem linked to weaker economic positions.

Identifying the underlying causes of the overall trend is difficult since it probably reflects the play of different forces, both between countries and between cities. Take, for example, the decreased share of skilled manufacturing jobs in the Mexican frontier city of Matamoros, where the percentages of middle and upper employment fell. It is plausible that skilled manufacturing jobs, which are located in small craft workshops, offer worse labor conditions and lower gross pay (including benefits) than do "semiskilled" jobs in maquiladoras. The relative decrease in skilled jobs may partly involve transfers into the semiskilled jobs, which may represent occupational upgrading rather than downgrading. Conversely, in cities such as Veracruz in Mexico and New Orleans in the United States, the proportional fall in skilled manufacturing jobs tended to reflect job loss in the face of worldwide techno-organizational transformations, together with some local growth of middle and upper services employment. Moreover, improved occupational composition in New Orleans was based much less on economic buoyancy than on a serious loss of employment, together with the countercyclical impact of the city's high share of employment in government and social services. Economic growth in Miami and postcrisis recovery in Houston were much more responsible for their improved occupational structures. This fact is especially clear when considering their sizable infusions of unskilled immigrants into bottom-layer jobs over the same period.

Some caveats must be added. Worldwide evidence (e.g., Freeman 1994; ILO 1996) indicates that inequalities in job conditions have tended to widen not only between industries and occupations but also as much or more so within them. Our data do not address within-category shifts that could complicate our reading of occupational upgrading. Further, upward occupational reclassification need not necessarily correspond to improvement in the position of workers in the social relations of production, whether in manufacturing or services. This is so as under emerging techno-organizational, geographic, and state-society arrangements, the bargaining leverage of not only manual workers but also a broadened sweep of semiskilled and skilled nonmanual workers as well as professionals tends to become weakened (see Galbraith 1998; Gordon 1996). Methodologically, moreover, the actual content of the occupational classifications is not easy to compare binationally. For instance, in Mexico the ostensibly middle-echelon occupation of "sales" includes a range of employment conditions (though street vending was excluded), and the occupation of "skilled services" includes workers such as self-employed shoe repairers, tortilla makers, and seamstresses. As documented so far, we can expect that neither occupational gains nor losses were distributed evenly by gender, nor by ethnicity. An overriding question is the degree to which the tendencies discussed amount to cyclical or secular changes.

Earnings Trends

Average real earnings grew in both the U.S. and Mexican Gulf cities during the periods studied. The rate of net growth was higher in the Mexican cities (17%) than the U.S. cities (4%).[12] This aggregate difference, though, conceals a key cross-national similarity: on both sides of the border, women's average earnings rose faster than men's. The average rate of net growth was the same (22%) for U.S. and Mexican women. In contrast, average earnings grew slower for Mexican men (17%) and contracted slightly (−0.6%) for U.S. men.

Intercity variation in earnings growth was marked on both sides of the border. On the U.S. side, net growth was fastest by far in Miami (13.6%), followed by Houston (3.9%) and Laredo (2.0%). It did not reach even 1% in Brownsville and New Orleans. On the Mexican side, the most rapid earnings growth was in Mérida (41.8%), far ahead of runner-up Tampico (23.2%). At the low end were Nuevo Laredo (8.9%), Veracruz (7%), and Matamoros (−2.9%). Only in Matamoros, then, did average real earnings drop.

These data reinforce most of our earlier observations on employment trends by industry and occupation. Among the U.S. cases, average earnings growth was strongest in the two leading postindustrial cities, Miami and Houston, especially the former. Among the Mexican cases, such growth was most robust in the service and tourism hub of Mérida, although the performance of Tampico, a port and petroleum-industry center, was strong. Border industrialization in the twin cities of Brownsville and Matamoros brought little or no income benefit. Average earnings rose more in the twin Laredos, but this rise was weak compared with the wider U.S.-Mexican field.

Earnings Inequality

We have seen little evidence of occupational polarization in the U.S. and Mexican Gulf cities. Will we therefore find that, also in contrast to the predictions of research on contemporary restructuring, the earnings distributions became more equitable? Average earnings were seven to nine times higher in the U.S. cities than the Mexican cities. There is, however, a striking U.S.-Mexican similarity in the trend of inequality. The cases for both countries reveal clear polarization in overall male and female earnings. That is, between the 1980s and 1990s, the earnings ratio of the top 10% to the bottom 40% became more unequal overall, as well as among men and among women (Table 10.3).

So far, then, the evidence on change in earnings inequality is broadly consistent with the expectations of the restructuring literature. Is the polarizing trend most acute in the cities that rank highest in the national and world divi-

Table 10.3
Earnings Distribution

	Mexican Gulf Cities				U.S. Gulf Cities			
	Males		Females		Males		Females	
	1986	1993	1986	1993	1980	1990	1980	1990
Earnings 40th percentile[a]	$1,359	$1,344	$972	$946	$12,005	$10,386	$6,205	$7,250
SD Bottom 40th %[b]	$75.3	$72.6	$61.3	$57.8	$3,975	$3,308	$2,089	$2,340
Earnings 90th percentile[a]	$3,601	$4,645	$2,179	$3,053	$33,005	$34,448	$16,475	$20,612
SD Top 10%[b]	$754.2	$1,901	$458.7	$807	$17,063	$30,774	$9,573	$14,732
Ratio of Earnings Top 10%/Bottom 40%	1.7	2.8	1.8	2.3	2	2.8	1.8	2

Source: INEGI (1986, 1993), second quarters; U.S. Bureau of the Census (1980, 1990).
[a]Yearly earnings in dollars of workers in this category.
[b]The standard deviation from the mean earnings of workers in this category.

sions of labor, as Sassen (1991, 1994) anticipates? This would be so because the labor markets of such cities have come to focus on producer services, which she regards as the most sharply bifurcated, while also serving as the most powerful magnets for low-wage immigrants.

Contrary to Sassen's perspective, there is little intercity variation in the degree of earnings polarization. Among the U.S. Gulf localities, the real earnings of men at the 40th percentile diminished everywhere except Miami, where they remained constant. Even so, in Miami there was a substantial widening of male earnings inequality (from a ratio of 2.1 to 3). The real earnings of women at the 40th percentile decreased in the small, border economies of Brownsville and Laredo, but they increased in Houston, Miami, and New Orleans.

On the Mexican side, Matamoros and Nuevo Laredo had the least growth in male earnings inequality, as male earnings rose more at the 40th than 90th percentile. This occurred as Matamoros's fraction of manual manufacturing jobs expanded while that of professional and managerial jobs shrunk. Male inequality worsened in Mérida, as earnings grew less at the 40th than 90th percentile. The instance of most severe male earnings polarization was Veracruz, where earnings declined at the 40th percentile but surged at the 90th percentile. While retaining its lead among the Mexican cities in local portion of upper-level employment, Veracruz plunged from the middle to last in local share of manufacturing jobs and tied with Tampico for fastest proportional growth of consumer service jobs.

With regard to women, earnings polarized least in Matamoros and Nuevo

Laredo, where pay rose at the 40th percentile. The context was Matamoros's position as the regional node for skilled and semiskilled manufacturing jobs while Nuevo Laredo became the regional site of most rapid female upward occupational mobility. Mérida, the city most favorable to middle and upper postindustrial employment for women, was the only other Mexican case where female pay rose at the 40th percentile. Female earnings polarized most in Tampico and Veracruz, for reasons mentioned above.

The Mexican and U.S. border cases, especially Matamoros and Brownsville, shed light on the effects of transnational integration on the territorial earnings distribution. The Mexican border cities have created jobs in modern manufacturing that, although classified as semiskilled, pay relatively well. Yet the most industrialized city in our Mexican sample, Matamoros, sustains a thinner layer of professional and managerial occupations than do the other Mexican cities. In addition, earnings in these high-tier occupations in Matamoros are stagnant. Meanwhile, the U.S. border cities in our study, particularly Brownsville, derive few benefits from the Mexican side's industrialization in the form of high paying jobs in professional services and spin-off occupations. Such job growth may be more likely to occur in the largest, interior cities of Texas such as Dallas and Houston, where the principal firms that supply and service the maquiladora industry are located. Mexican and U.S. frontier cities appear to be integrated precariously into national and transnational channels of accumulation (see Kopinak 1996; Roberts 1994; Spener and Staudt 1998).

We can further explore these issues by considering longitudinal shifts in earnings by occupation (Table 10.4). The pattern of change is consistent across the U.S. and Mexican sites. Not only was there a greater percentage of professionals, managers, and semiprofessionals by the end of the period, but this stratum's earnings advantages widened over the other occupations. At the same time, the earnings share of mid- and low-rung jobs lost ground faster than their occupational share. With few exceptions, the negative trends in earnings were as steep among the midrung occupations (clerical, sales, and skilled manual jobs) as among the semiskilled and unskilled occupations.

Examining these patterns clarifies why, in spite of the virtual absence of occupational polarization, there was earnings polarization. The percentage of employment shifted from low to mid- and upper-rung jobs, yet the earnings drop was equally steep for mid-rung and low-rung workers. Earnings inequality widened at all levels: between lower and middle occupations, lower and upper occupations, and middle and upper occupations.

The data partially confirm the expectations derived from studies on contemporary restructuring. Consistent with the expectations and with U.S. and

Table 10.4
Earnings Structure by Occupation

| | Mexican Gulf Cities | | | | | | | | U.S. Gulf Cities | | | | | | | |
| | Males | | | | Females | | | | Males | | | | Females | | | |
Occupational Structure	(A) Mean Real Income 1993a US$	(B) Share of Total Income 1993	(C) Shift in Income Share 1986–1993	(D) Shift in Occupations 1986–1993	(A) Mean Real Income 1993a US$	(B) Share of Total Income 1993	(C) Shift in Income Share 1986–1993	(D) Shift in Occupations 1986–1993	(A) Mean Real Income 1990b US$	(B) Share of Total Income 1990	(C) Shift in Income Share 1980–1990	(D) Shift in Occupations 1980–1990	(A) Mean Real Income 1990b US$	(B) Share of Total Income 1990	(C) Shift in Income Share 1980–1990	(D) Shift in Occupations 1980–1990
Fordist																
Managers & Administrators	7,373	13.8	50.0	4.6	4,302	4.8	24.6	-23.9	28,521	22.6	-4.3	-9.7	15,571	18.2	39.9	39.6
Clerical	1,762	5.1	-11.2	1.5	1,513	18.1	-27.2	-12.2	12,590	4.6	-4.3	4.6	9,757	25.9	-22.1	-15.6
Sales	1,983	11.0	6.4	21.9	963	12.7	-4.2	4.1	18,782	9.5	-3.2	-0.1	7,790	8.6	-8.1	-2.7
Skilled Manufacturing	1,942	28.5	-18.6	-6.7	1,019	5.9	-21.8	-4.4	15,704	21.8	-4.6	0.1	10,813	4.5	29.5	32.4
Semiskilled Manufacturing	1,381	6.5	-35.0	-25.6	1,401	7.7	11.6	32.6	10,335	9.3	-22.0	-10.5	6,515	3.2	-39.2	-27.8
Postindustrial																
Professional	4,957	12.0	75.5	41.9	3,094	8.5	104.2	87.3	35,674	16.6	26.8	3.4	19,603	6.8	75.0	56.8
Semiprofessional	2,677	13.8	50.1	48.7	2,312	26.8	28.6	10.5	19,045	9.2	4.7	2.6	13,864	23.8	10.3	7.9
Skilled Service	1,389	7.1	-17.0	11.6	1,027	6.8	-7.5	12.6	11,989	4.1	35.6	37.5	6,264	4.9	-12.1	8.0
Unskilled Service	1,052	2.2	-57.4	4.7	746	8.7	-22.3	-18.9	7,131	2.3	9.5	19.5	5,063	4.1	-11.4	-3.6
Total	100			100				100				100				

Sources: INEGI (1986, 1993), second quarters; U.S. Bureau of the Census (1980, 1990).

a Mexican yearly earnings for 1986 and 1993 are standardized to the values of the second quarter of 1988, using the Mexican Monthly Consumer Price Index and converting the data into dollars (at about 2.99 pesos to the dollar).

b 1990 U.S. yearly earnings are standardized to 1980 values.

Mexican national evidence, earnings did become more polarized in each of the U.S. and Mexican Gulf cities (see Levine [1996] on national samples of U.S. and Canadian cities). The degree of earnings polarization, however, was much less variable than anticipated in view of the unequal positions of cities in the domestic and transnational divisions of labor (as Stopper 1997 reports for U.S. metropolitan and nonmetropolitan areas in general; see Levine 1996 on U.S. and Canadian cities). This implies that during a period of abruptly reduced and redefined state intervention in economy and society in both Mexico and the United States, the local variants of economic and social composition counted much less than national promarket policies and transnational dynamics in molding change in earnings inequality.

Gender Inequality

Gender differentiates the binational area's employment on several dimensions, which, despite marked intercity variation in economic development, take the same basic shape in each locality. Men are less likely than women to work in services and are more likely to work in manufacturing and especially construction. Men are more likely than women to be professionals, managers, and skilled or semiskilled manufacturing workers and are less likely to be semiprofessionals and unskilled service workers.

These gender inequalities bring us to the matter of female versus male earnings. Table 10.4 shows that in the Mexican and U.S. cities women earn less than men on average. This gap holds true across occupations, with the exception of semiskilled manufacturing workers in Mexico. (Maquiladora workers, who are mainly women, are probably responsible for raising the average earnings of semiskilled female manufacturing workers higher than that of their male counterparts, who are more likely to work in small craft workshops.) The male/female earnings distribution is similar in the Mexican and U.S. cases (see Table 10.3).[13]

This pattern raises the question of the extent to which change in occupational earnings inequality is a result of changes in the gender composition of employment in Mexico and the United States. This question has two components. One is whether advantages or disadvantages of gender increase or decrease over time. The other is whether growth in the labor force's portion of women, who on average are low paid, is responsible for the occupational cases of reduced earnings.

Women's share of employment rose from 42.9 to 45.4% in the U.S. cities and from 33.5 to 37.9% in the Mexican cities. Women's annual rate of job growth was fastest in Mexico (5.3 versus 1.4%). This is consistent with evidence underscoring the marked acceleration of Mexico's secular trend of expanding female labor force participation against the background of economic crisis, austerity policies, and restructuring (Oliveira and García 1997). Coinciding with the industry and occupational mixes already described, there was greater intercity variation on the Mexican than U.S. side in women's share of employment.

In the Mexican group, women's share of jobs rose most in the deindustrializing port cities of Tampico (25.3%) and Veracruz (17.6%), ahead of Nuevo Laredo (15.5%), Mérida (7.0%), and Matamoros (3.3%). In this context, Veracruz moved from second to first, and Tampico from fourth to second, in the Mexican sample's degree of employment feminization. This occurred as Matamoros slid from first to third and Nuevo Laredo, despite its midlevel expansion in women's share of jobs, remained the least feminized of all. A reason for this surprising lag of the frontier cities is that during the 1980s men began to obtain more employment in maquiladoras as their production became more diversified (see Oliveira and García 1997; Sklair 1993; Wilson 1992).

In the U.S. group, women's portion of employment also increased fastest in a deindustrializing port city, New Orleans (13.7%). Far behind it were Brownsville (7.1%), Houston (5.5%), Laredo (4.4%), and Miami (2.9%). In the U.S. group, therefore, women's share of employment rose most rapidly in those local economies with the most sluggish earnings growth, New Orleans and Brownsville. New Orleans leaped from third to first in the group's extent of job feminization, as former leader Miami fell to third. Brownsville remained second, Houston fourth, and Laredo fifth.

In sum, increases in the female share of jobs were greatest in three port cities (Tampico, Veracruz, and New Orleans) and two frontier cities (Nuevo Laredo and Brownsville). For all the sampled cities, this trend seems to have expanded women's portions of upper occupations and earnings (Table 10.5). Thus the labor market disadvantage of being a woman evidently decreased. In the Mexican cities, women's fraction of total earnings rose by an average yearly rate of 2.6% versus a yearly gain in job share of 1.9%. This apparently means that women increased their earnings power relative to men. In the U.S. cities, women's fraction of total earnings rose by virtually the same annual pace, 2.5%, while their average annual gain in job share, 0.6%, was much slower than that of the Mexican women. This seems to mean, though, that U.S. women took even faster strides to narrow the gender gap in earnings power.

Table 10.5 tells us that, regarding upper occupations, women in the Mexican cities considerably expanded their percentage of employment in the professions but lost ground as managers and semiprofessionals. Even in the

Table 10.5
Shares of Earnings and Occupations

| Ocupational Structure | Mexican Gulf Cities | | | | U.S. Gulf Cities | | | |
| | Males | | Females | | Males | | Females | |
	% Change in Share of Income 1986–1993[a]	% Change in Share of All Occups. 1986–1993[a]	% Change in Share of Income 1986–1993[b]	% Change in Share of All Occups. 1986–1993[b]	% Change in Share of Income 1986–1993[a]	% Change in Share of All Occups. 1986–1993[a]	% Change in Share of Income 1986–1993[b]	% Change in Share of All Occups. 1986–1993[b]
Fordist								
Managers & Administrators	−0.4	2.3	3.4	−9.1	−14.1	−17.3	71.8	41.2
Clerical	−1.4	−3.2	1.0	2.1	−7.5	9.5	3.0	−2.4
Sales	−3.4	−1.9	8.7	2.2	−7.0	−3.6	20.7	3.7
Skilled Manufacturing	−1.2	−2.6	18.7	21.7	−4.2	−4.0	77.9	40.3
Semiskilled Manufacturing	−16.9	−16.9	78.6	80.8	−0.9	2.6	5.6	−8.6
Postindustrial								
Professionals	−6.7	−11.6	35.8	42.5	−7.8	−10.7	73.9	49.6
Semiprofessional & Technical	−2.9	4.8	4.1	−5.0	−17.1	−8.9	19.5	5.9
Skilled Service	−7.6	−7.6	28.8	19.7	4.7	8.0	−7.2	−6.3
Unskilled Service	−34.1	−21.4	50.4	14.3	−4.5	6.7	5.6	−4.9
Total Change	−5.6	−6.7	18.1	13.3	−8.8	−4.3	24.7	5.7

Sources: INEGI (1986, 1993), second quarters; U.S. Bureau of the Census (1980, 1990).
[a] Change in male earnings and male share of occupational category relative to females.
[b] Change in female earnings and female share of occupational category relative to males.

latter categories, however, women's portion of total earnings grew. On average, therefore, those Mexican women who gained a foothold in managerial and semiprofessional jobs advanced in earning power relative to their male counterparts, while women's relative earning progress in the professions is explained by their equivalent growth in job share. Women's portion of employment rose in the remaining occupations, especially in semiskilled and skilled manufacturing and skilled and unskilled services, the latter categories being the sites of most dramatic advances in female versus male earnings power. Women's relative earnings gains in manufacturing are attributable, as in the professions, to their widened employment share. So, from the standpoint of earnings per worker, the progress of women versus men in the Mexican cities appears greatest in unskilled and skilled service jobs and in semiprofessional and managerial jobs. Otherwise, such progress appears based on women's increased fraction of employment.

The pattern in the U.S. cities is different in that women gained in job share in the upper strata and lost in the lower strata, and that in all occupations women's earnings share expanded faster or contracted less than their job share (Table 10.5). Consequently, even in clerical work, semiskilled manufacturing, and services, where women's portion of employment declined, men's earnings superiority tended to weaken. Only in skilled services did men maintain their previous degree of earnings dominance.

The sweep of employment transformations in the Mexican and U.S. Gulf cities is clearly differentiated by gender. Given a baseline of women's subordinate position in labor markets—and keeping in mind the mounting burdens of combining women's primary responsibility for the daily lives of households and communities with their expanded role as earners—these transformations have generally improved the employment standing of women relative to men (see ILO 1995, 1996).

Conclusions

The predominant features of change in the industry structure of employment across the binational sample of Gulf cities are the decreased weight of manual labor and the increased weight of service labor. There is almost no evidence of occupational polarization, but there is substantial evidence of earnings polarization combined with advances in female versus male earning power. The data concerning the employment impact of transnational integration are ambivalent. Employment figures for Miami and Houston, the cities most securely embedded in transnational markets, reveal both the highest increases in average real earnings and the strongest orientations to advanced services. In contrast, employment in the frontier cities, whose economies are based on the complementary integration of the U.S. and Mexican markets, displays few benefits relative to the other cities. Important differences in the structure and growth of employment and earnings are indeed evident not only between but also within the U.S. and Mexican sets of cities, a sign of important variation in the nexus of local, national, and global conditions. Nevertheless, the most basic trends—the improvement of occupational composition coupled with earnings polarization—hold true in virtually every case, regardless of the comparative relations of cities to the national and world economies. The sole exception was the worsening of occupational composition in the Mexican frontier city of Matamoros.

How much of these regional trends is cyclical or secular is a fundamental question. Whatever the answer, the trends suggest that as government plays a diminishing role in cushioning localities from the impact of accelerating transformations in the wider world, local labor markets in developed and less-developed countries may in some ways be converging toward a common new form, characterized by greater precariousness and inequality (see Rodrik 1997; Singh and Zammit 1995). The winners stand to be some transnational mix of those occupational, class, ethnic, gender, and territorial fragments that, within the framework of the techo-organizational and spatial restructuring of firms, interfirm networks, employment practices, and state-society relations, emerge from the era of high-volume manufacturing with two sets of advantages: political advantages of state protection and subsidy, as renegotiated under domestic and transnational policies of market liberalization; and market advantages of financial, producer, and buyer dominance, including innovativeness, flexibility, and location. The world-scale losers stand to grow in proportion and to fall farther behind than during the heyday of the previous era. Workforce anxieties and discontent will swell insofar as social access to political capital shrinks and the connection of occupational advancement to earnings gain becomes unhinged. Both the formulation of compensatory policies and their chances of implementation in a globalizing world are matters of considerable debate. Central to the research agenda are the long-range ramifications of the current trends for sociogeographic forms of collective identity, organization, and action, as well as for domestic and transnational political alignments.

References

Benería, Lourdes. 1992. The Mexican Debt Crisis: Restructuring the Economy and the Household. In *Unequal Burden: Economic Crisis, Persistent Poverty, and Women's Work*, eds. Lourdes Benería and Shelley Feldman. Boulder, Colo.: Westview.

Bussey, Jane. 1997. New Orleans Is Looking South, Too. *Miami Herald Business Monday*, Jan. 13, 15–16.

Campos, Mónica Verea, Rafael Fernández de Castro, and Sidney Weintraub, coords. 1998. *Nueva agenda bilateral en la relación México-Estados Unidos.* México, D.F.: Fondo de Cultura Económica.

CEPAL News (Santiago, Chile). 1998. Feb.

Chant, Sylvia. 1991. *Women and Survival in Mexican Cities: Perspectives on Gender, Labour Markets, and Low-Income Households.* Manchester, Eng.: Manchester University Press.

Cheng, Lu-Lim, and Gary Gereffi. 1994. The Informal Economy in East Asian Development. *International Journal of Urban and Regional Research* 18, no. 2.

Cortés, Fernando, and Rosa María Rubalcava. 1991. Autoexplotación forzada y equidad por empobrecimiento. *Jornadas* 120. México, D.F.: El Colegio de México.

Dicken, Peter. 1998. *Global Shift*, 3d ed. rev. New York: The Guilford Press.

Economic Commission for Latin America and the Caribbean (ECLAC). 1995. *Statistical Yearbook for Latin America and the Caribbean.* Santiago, Chile.

Escobar, Agustín. 1996. Mexico: Poverty as Politics and Academic Disciplines. In *Poverty: A Global Review*, eds. Else Oyen, S. M. Miller, and Syed Abdus. Oslo: Scandinavian University Press.

Escobar, Agustín, and Mercedes González de la Rocha. 1995. Crisis, Restructuring, and Urban Poverty in Mexico. *Environment and Urbanization* 7, no. 1.

Esping-Andersen, Gosta, Zina Assimakopoulou, and Kees van Kersbergen. 1993. Trends in Contemporary Class Structuration. In *Changing Classes: Stratification and Mobility in Post-Industrial Societies*, ed. Gosta Esping-Andersen. London: Sage Publications.

Feagin, Joe R. 1988. *Free Enterprise City: Houston in Political-Economic Perspective*. New Brunswick, N.J.: Rutgers University Press.

Fields, Gregg. 1997a. Draining Away in Dade: Five Industries Fading Away in the 90s. *Miami Herald Business Monday*, Aug. 11, 25, 27.

———. 1997b. Dade Must Enhance Its Role in International Trade, Report Finds. *Miami Herald*. Oct. 14, 1A, 10A.

Fields, Gregg, and Mimi Whitefield. 1997a. Work Force, Economy Don't Fit. *Miami Herald*, Aug. 10, 1A, 22A.

———. 1997b. L.A., Dade: Two Paths to Jobs. *Miami Herald*, Aug. 12, 1A, 15A.

Freeman, Richard B., ed. 1994. *Working Under Different Rules*. New York: Russell Sage.

Galbraith, James K. 1998. *Created Unequal: The Crisis in American Pay*. New York: The Free Press.

Gilbreath, Jan. 1998. La relación México-Texas: redefinición del regionalismo. In *Nueva agenda bilateral en la relación México-Estados Unidos*, coords. Mónica Verea Campos, Rafael Fernández de Castro, and Sidney Weintraub. México, D.F.: Fondo de Cultura Económica.

González de la Rocha, Mercedes. 1994. *The Resources of Poverty: Women and Survival in a Mexican City*. Oxford: Blackwell.

Gordon, David M. 1996. *Fat and Mean: The Corporate Squeeze of Working Americans and the Myth of Managerial Downsizing*. New York: Martin Kessler Books.

Grosfoguel, Ramón. 1994. World Cities in the Caribbean: The Rise of Miami and San Juan. *Review* 17, no. 3.

Hammermesh, Daniel S., and Frank D. Bean, eds. 1998. *Help or Hindrance? The Economic Implications of Immigration for African Americans*. New York: Russell Sage.

Hamnett, Chris. 1994. Social Polarisation in Global Cities: Theory and Evidence. *Urban Studies* 31, no. 3.

Harrison, Bennett, and Barry Bluestone. 1988. *The Great U-Turn*. 2d ed. New York: Basic Books.

Hoeschen, Brad L. F. 1995. N.O. Thrown for a Loop as Casino Folds. *New Orleans City Business*, Nov. 27.

International Labour Office (ILO). 1995. Women Earn Less than Men in Comparable Jobs. *ILO Washington Focus* (fall).

ILO. 1996. *World Employment 1996/97: National Policies in a Global Context*. Geneva.

INEGI. 1980–1998. *Estadísticas de la industria maquiladora de exportacíon.* Aguascalientes, AG: INEGI.

———. 1986, 1987, 1993, 1994. *Encuesta nacional de empleo urbano.* 2d quarters. Aguascalientes, A.G.: INEGI.

———. 1994b. *Censo general de población y vivienda.* Aguascalientes, A.G.: INEGI.

Kalmbach, Fred, and Marsha Shuler. 1996. Board Sues Harrah's to Force Casino Completion. *The Advocate* (Baton Rouge, La.), Jan. 24.

Kopinak, Kathryn. 1996. *Desert Capitalism: Maquiladoras in North America's Western Industrial Corridor.* Tucson: University of Arizona Press.

Lauria, Mickey, Robert K. Whelan, and Alma H. Young. 1993. Urban Revitalization Strategies and Plans in New Orleans, 1970–1993. Working Paper No. 10, College of Urban and Public Affairs, University of New Orleans.

Levine, Marc V. 1995. Globalization and Wage Polarization in U.S. and Canadian Cities: Does Public Policy Make a Difference? In *North American Cities and the Global Economy,* eds. Peter Karl Kresl and Gary Gavpert. Thousand Oaks, Calif.: Sage.

Lustig, Nora. 1992. *Mexico: The Remaking of an Economy.* Washington, D.C.; The Brookings Institution.

Nijman, Jan. 1996. Ethnicity, Class, and the Economic Internationalization of Miami. In *Social Polarization in Post-Industrial Metropolises,* eds. John O'Loughlin and Jurgen Friedrichs. Berlin: Walter de Gruyter.

Oliveira, Orlandina de, and Brígida García. 1997. Mexico: Socioeconomic Transformation and Urban Labor Markets. In *Global Restructuring, Employment, and Social Inequality in Urban Latin America,* eds. Richard Tardanico and Rafael Menjívar Larín. Coral Gables, Fla.: The North-South Center at the University of Miami; Boulder, Colo.: Lynne Rienner Publishers.

Oliveira, Orlandina de, and Bryan Roberts. 1994. Urban Growth and Urban Social Structure in Latin America, 1930–1990. In *The Cambridge History of Latin America,* vol. VI, pt. 1, ed. Leslie Bethell. Cambridge: Cambridge University Press.

O'Loughlin, John, and Jurgen Friedrichs, eds. 1996. *Social Polarization in Post-Industrial Metropolises.* Berlin: Walter de Gruyter.

Portes, Alejandro, Carlos Dore, and Patricia Landolt, eds. 1997. *The Urban Caribbean: Transition to the New Global Economy.* Baltimore: Johns Hopkins University Press.

Portes, Alejandro, and Rubén Rumbaut. 1996. *Immigrant America.* 2d ed. Berkeley and Los Angeles: University of California Press.

Portes, Alejandro, and Alex Stepick. 1993. *City on the Edge: The Transformation of Miami.* Berkeley and Los Angeles: University of California Press.

Ramírez, Luis A. 1993. Sociedad y población urbana en Yucatán, 1950–1989. *Cuadernos del CES.* México, D.F.: Centro de Estudios Sociológicos, El Colegio de México.

Rendón, Teresa, and Carlos Salas. 1992. El mercado de trabajo no agrícola en México. In *Ajuste estructural, mercados laborales y tratado de libre comercio.* México, D.F.: Centro de Estudios Sociológicos del Colegio de México, Fundación Friedrich Ebert, and El Colegio de la Frontera Norte.

Roberts, Bryan. 1994. Urbanization, Development, and the Household. In *Comparative National Development: Society and Economy in the New Global Order*, eds. A. Douglas Kincaid and Alejandro Portes. Chapel Hill: University of North Carolina Press.

———. 1995. *The Making of Citizens: Cities of Peasants Revisited*. London: Arnold.

Rodrik, Dani. 1997. *Has Globalization Gone Too Far?* Washington, D.C.: Institute for International Economy.

Rodríguez Herrero, Hipólito. 1996. Movilidad social y espacio urbano en dos ciudades del Golfo de México. Unpublished doctoral dissertation. Guadalajara: CIESAS/Universidad de Guadalajara.

Rubery, Jill, ed. 1988. *Women and Recession*. London: Routledge & Kegan Paul.

Salmerón, Fernando I. 1994. El trabajo en Veracruz: ¿Qué hay de nuevo? Paper presented at the meetings of the Latin American Studies Association, Atlanta, March.

Sassen, Saskia. 1991. *The Global City: New York, London, Tokyo*. Princeton, N.J.: Princeton University Press.

———. 1994. *Cities in a World Economy*. Thousand Oaks, Calif.: Pine Forge Press.

———. 1996. *Loss of Control? Sovereignty in an Age of Globalization*. New York: Columbia University Press.

Saussey, Gordon A. 1993. New Orleans and Houston Metro Economies: Some Features the Same, Others Decidedly Not the Same. *Louisiana Business Survey* 24, no. 2.

Sayer, Andrew, and Richard Walker. 1992. *The New Social Economy: Reworking the Division of Labor*. Cambridge, Mass.: Blackwell.

Schoenberg, Erica. 1994. Competition, Time, and Space in Industrial Change. In *Commodity Chains and Global Capitalism*, eds. Gary Gereffi and Miguel Korzeniewicz. Westport, Conn.: Praeger.

Schteingart, Marta. 1997. Pobreza y políticas sociales en México y Estados Unidos de Norteamérica: un estudio comparativo. *Revista Mexicana de Sociología* 59, no. 2.

Selby, Henry A., Arthur D. Murphy, and Stephen A. Lorenzer. 1990. *The Mexican Urban Household: Organizing for Self-Defense*. Austin: University of Texas Press.

Singh, Ajit, and Ann Zammit. 1995. Employment and Unemployment, North and South. In *Managing the Global Economy*, eds. Jonathan Mitchie and John Grieve Smith. New York: Oxford University Press.

Sklair, Leslie. 1993. *Assembling for Development: The Maquila Industry in Mexico and the U.S..* La Jolla, Calif.: Center for U.S.-Mexican Studies, University of California at San Diego.

Smith, Michael Peter, and Marlene Keller. 1983. Managed Growth and the Politics of Uneven Development in New Orleans. In *Restructuring the City: The Political Economy of Urban Redevelopment*, eds. Susan S. Fainstein, Norman I. Fainstein, Richard Child Hill, Dennis Judd, and Michael Peter Smith. New York: Longman.

Sparke, Matthew. 1997. Emergent Transnational Regions in the Context of NAFTA:

The Case of Cascadia. Paper presented at the Meetings of the Association of the American Academy of Science, Seattle, April.

Spener, David. 1995. Entrepreneurship and Small-Scale Enterprise on the Texas-Mexican Border. Unpublished doctoral dissertation. University of Texas at Austin, Department of Sociology.

———. 1996. Small Firms, Commodity Chains, and Free Trade: Some Lessons from the Tex-Mex Border Region. In *Latin America in the World-Economy*, eds. Roberto Patricio Korzeniewicz and William C. Smith. Westport, Conn.: Greenwood Publishers.

Spener, David, and Kathleen Staudt, eds. 1998. *The U.S.-Mexico Border: Transcending Divisions, Contesting Identities.* Boulder, Colo.: Lynne Rienner Publishers.

Storper, Michael. 1997. *The Regional World: Territorial Development in a Global Economy.* New York: The Guilford Press.

Tardanico, Richard, and Rafael Menjívar Larín. 1997. Restructuring, Employment, and Social Inequality: Comparative Latin American Patterns. In *Global Restructuring, Employment, and Social Inequality in Urban Latin America*, eds. Richard Tardanico and Rafael Menjívar Larín. Coral Gables, Fla.: The North-South Center at the University of Miami; Boulder, Colo.: Lynne Rienner Publishers.

U.S. Bureau of the Census. 1980, 1990. *5% Sample of the Public Use Microsample.* Washington, D.C.: U.S. Bureau of the Census.

———. 1993. *Statistical Abstract of the United States, 1993.* Washington, D.C.: U.S. Bureau of the Census.

———. 1996. *Online Information: Housing and Household Economics Statistics Division, Historical Income Tables.* Washington, D.C.: U.S. Bureau of the Census.

U.S./Latin Trade. 1994. Miami: Gateway to the Americas. Special Report. December. Coral Gables, Fla.

———. 1995a. Houston: Partner for Latin America. Nov. Coral Gables, Fla.

———. 1995b. New Orleans: New Goals, New Focus. July. Coral Gables, Fla.

Wallerstein, Immanuel. 1995. *After Liberalism.* New York: The New Press.

Whitefield, Mimi. 1997a. Poised to Percolate. *Miami Herald Business Monday,* June 23, 22–24.

———. 1997b. Atlanta's Corporate Hustle Fuels Job Growth. *Miami Herald,* Aug. 12, 15A.

Wilson, Patricia A. 1992. *Exports and Local Development: Mexico's New Maquiladoras.* Austin: University of Texas Press.

World Bank. 1994. *World Development Report, 1994.* New York: Oxford University Press.

———. 1995. *World Development Report, 1995.* New York: Oxford University Press.

Zaretsky, Nancy, and Mark B. Rosenberg. 1998. *Thinking Globally and Acting Locally: NAFTA, Globalization and the Gulf Governors' Accord.* Miami: Latin American and Caribbean Center, Florida International University.

CONCLUSION

Map 11.1
Gulf Coastal Plain of North America

11

Poverty or Development?

Richard Tardanico

Debate remains intense regarding the short- and long-range effects of NAFTA. Two basic points, though, have become widely conceded. The first is that NAFTA itself is not the principal catalyst to deepening ties between the Mexican, U.S., and Canadian economies, but instead represents a neoliberal institutionalization and acceleration of a long-range "silent integration." The second is that, in North America as on a world scale, cross-border integration creates a distinctive set of winners and losers relative to the preceding era of more nationally organized economies.[1]

Focusing on the Mexican South and the U.S. South, this volume has conceptualized winners and losers in North America's continental-global shifts from the standpoint of a world division of labor whose inequalities are both politico-economic and territorial. In the introductory chapter to this volume, Richard Tardanico and Mark Rosenberg describe territorial positions of dominance and subordination within the world division of labor as encompassing not only nations but more fundamentally the domestic and transborder regions upon which nations and blocs of nations are built. Tardanico and Rosenberg define regions as hierarchically arranged, territorial ensembles of relations, interests, values, identities, resources, and capacities. They argue that, in addition to reflecting comparative-historical interplays of local and supralocal forces, the characteristics of the ensembles improve or diminish the prospects of their constituent economic sectors, social groups, government entities, and localities in a changing world division of labor. They conclude that the structural inequalities and policy ramifications of contemporary global realignments are most tellingly revealed at the level of subnational and transnational regions, rather than nations.

Tardanico and Rosenberg note that a growing research literature explores this premise by comparing features of territorial-global realignment across rich and poor countries. The volume has compared many such features of the U.S. South and the Mexican South from two angles. The first concerns the convergent histories and legacies of the U.S. South and the Mexican South as labor-repressive producers of primary commodities, which dispose each of the regions to particular degrees and forms of contemporary socioeconomic exploitation and displacement. The second concerns a crucial divergence: since the mid-twentieth century a wide array of the U.S. South's activities, groups, and places has advanced into the middle and upper tiers of the world division of labor, while, without denying its own quite variable characteristics, the Mexican South has remained profoundly underdeveloped. What policy ideas might be derived from examining not only convergence but also divergence between the regions, especially with respect to economic and social transformations since World War II? What are the ramifications for the neoliberal claim that deregulated and denationalized market competition is superior to state-centric programs as a path to development?

This approach represents one step toward a comprehensive comparison of North American regions under global restructuring and NAFTA. Such a comparison would involve Mexican, U.S., and Canadian regions whose political economies leave them acutely vulnerable to global and continental shifts, as well as regions whose macroperformances under the new conditions seem disposed to range from breakeven to strong (see Britton 1996; Conklin 1997; Noponen et al. 1993; Otero 1996). The central questions include the ones that integrate this volume's chapters on the Mexican South and the U.S. South:

- What politico-economic and social characteristics of regions—including links to wider distributions of wealth and power—are associated with their upward and downward mobility or resistance to displacement in the changing global division of labor?
- What are the consequences of such mobility or resistance for sectoral, social, and geographic inequalities within regions?
- What are the implications of these baseline characteristics, patterns of mobility or resistance, and changing inequalities for the longer-range, comparative prospects of regions in the new global order?

The remainder of this chapter synthesizes the volume's findings on the U.S. South and the Mexican South in view of these questions and applies the synthesis to further discussion of regional-global comparisons in North America as well as the wider world. It begins by summarizing the findings on the U.S. South. It then does the same for the Mexican South while also addressing the significance of the U.S. South's post–World War II policy foundations for development politics in southern Mexico. The chapter concludes by considering North America's regional-global inequalities in terms of emerging transborder politico-commercial accords between particular regions of Mexico, the United States, and Canada.

Two Souths in Global-Continental Perspective

The U.S. South

Amy Glasmeier and Robin Leichenko describe a U.S. southern trajectory from the Great Depression onward bearing little resemblance to the neoliberal portrayal of unbridled market competition as the catalyst to economic and social development. The "New South," they document, is a product of vigorous federal government intervention—economic, political, and social—since the Great Depression. Glasmeier and Leichenko point out, moreover, that during the 1950s and 1960s the New South—or more precisely, the U.S. South's modernizing, upwardly mobile sectors, institutions, and localities—rode the coattails of U.S. national hegemony[2] in a world economy that differed substantially from the current version. The post–World War II version was characterized not only by the anchoring presence of a hegemonic, rather than merely powerful, U.S. government and economy, but also by the institutional legitimacy of inward-oriented economic policies, smaller proportions as well as a much looser weave of cross-national investment, production, and commerce, and a clearer reliance of underdeveloped economies on primary commodity exports (see Dicken 1998, chap. 3; Kitson and Michie 1995, 9–31).

According to Glasmeier and Leichenko, the proximate foundations for the U.S. South's post–World War II urban-industrial advancement were laid by federal government intervention during the Great Depression. The establishment of a federal minimum wage raised the cost of southern labor relative to national standards. Very low pay, virulent racism, a vast labor reserve, and union bashing remained integral to the southern status quo. Nonetheless, the federal minimum wage compelled southern manufacturers to deemphasize the lowest-wage-earning activities, improve productivity, and seek capital from the industrially formidable North. This trend coincided with the beginning of large federal outlays for southern economic infrastructure and manufacturing subsidy. The outlays strengthened the region's economic undergirdings and access to industrial capital in the short run. In addition they forged regional-federal political bonds that opened the channels for a flood of federal interventions and northern capital infusions during subsequent decades.

It was under these regional-federal arrangements that World War II's militarized economy triggered a surge in southern manufacturing production, as Glasmeier and Leichenko observe. Complementing this surge was the postwar campaign of federal highway construction, which made the rural South more accessible to northern-based industrialization. Within the framework of U.S. hegemony in the world economy and cold-war military competition with the Soviet Union, the new southern arrangements were consolidated by the federal government's massive military-industrial investments, civil rights legislation, and vigorous economic and social programs in general. Glasmeier and Leichenko emphasize that racially centered inequality and poverty overlapped with glaring deficits of human and social capital on the whole to restrict the U.S. South's transformation. Even so, the region's military-industrial complexes, business services in principal urban hubs, and tourism-retirement locales were on their way to major advances. Whether much of the rural economy made significant advances is debatable. By the 1970s, the appearance of cracks in the edifice of U.S. hegemony and its postwar politico-social contract made the rural South, with its legacies of minimal government and low wages, a more important site for northern industries seeking less-regulated production and cheapened costs. A matter for consideration is how much southern agricultural modernization did or did not generate authentic gains for rural economy and society, both internally and in its linkages with the region's urban agglomerations of manufacturing and services.[3]

To summarize, Glasmeier and Leichenko document the confluence of global, national, and regional conditions, including the critical importance of federal government intervention, in generating the New South's highly uneven transformations. Their emphasis on not only social but also territorial unevenness directs attention to diversity in southern local conditions as well. Glasmeier and Leichenko stress that no longer can the South's lagging territories and social groups count on U.S. hegemony, heavy federal spending, or trade protection to boost their prospects, as military-industrial and social programs have been slashed and trade is being liberalized. Displacing the bulwarks of the South's postwar ascent is intensified competition, both national and international, to attract territorially mobile manufacturing and service activities. This competition increases the economic and politico-social costs of public incentives to entice investors while simultaneously exposing the South's vulnerability as a haven for low-cost operations.

Gary Gereffi's discussion of the U.S. South's apparel industry complements Glasmeier and Leichenko's chapter. Gereffi's portrayal of the transnationalization of the apparel production complex underlines the present-day dilemmas of developed as well as underdeveloped countries. Apparel manufacturing becomes increasingly cost-competitive as it continues to drop in functional importance within the global division of labor. Accelerated by the various political initiatives of trade and investment liberalization, leading textile and garment producers in the developed national economies are consequently subcontracting routine production activities to low-wage, low-cost firms at home and abroad. At the same time, they are bolstering their position on the sector's global commodity chain by refocusing on technology-intensive production and on the coordination of transnational production networks. Gereffi asserts that North American garment production is poised for rapid expansion, as much subcontracting by U.S. firms is becoming transferred from Asia—which, led by China, is the main producer of apparel for the United States—to the Western Hemisphere. Nonetheless, branch plants and low-skilled textile and apparel workers in the U.S. South, where many leading textile companies are headquartered, continue to be principal losers in the process of global and hemispheric reorganization. Their losses occur, Gereffi observes, as some U.S. manufacturing operations are being both redefined and relocated to the Texas border and Miami as well as abroad, while attention at headquarters shifts to advanced-technology production and to business services. Hence, the modernization of headquarter activities in parts of the U.S. South exacts it own regional cost in economically displaced workers and locales. Complicating this picture is the solidification of "retailer-centered" apparel networks. These revolve around megaretailers such as Arkansas-based Wal-Mart and Dallas-based J.C. Penney, which are forging partnerships with central Mexico-based counterparts such as Caffra. According to Gereffi, this trend likely contributes to retail concentration, employment dislocation, and income bifurcation across the U.S. South and the United States in general, as well as Mexico. Implicitly, promarket government policies loom large in Gereffi's chapter as facilitators of supranational spatial-economic and social restructuring. His analysis is not sanguine concerning the neoliberal premise that near-term socioeconomic displacements will yield to long-term, market-driven recuperation for most of the U.S. South's people and places.

David Griffith changes the topic from manufacturing to agriculture by examining transnationalization, ethnicity, and labor relations in South Florida's winter vegetable farming. South Florida's farm owners are predominately white. Most of its workers, however, are Mexican/Mexican American, Guatemalan, African American, and Caribbean. Griffith informs us that Mexicans/Mexican Americans have come to represent the largest part of the workforce, a feature in the making since at least the 1960s, when Florida's urbanization and tourism growth intersected with federal civil rights legislation to lure most of the then-predominant African American workers into nonagricultural activities. South Florida farmers turned for much of their labor to South Texas, tapping into a swelling cross-frontier stream of low-wage-earning Mexican/Mexican American workers. The makeup of the Mexican-based stream has changed as indigenous groups from southern Mexico have increasingly entered it and as many of the Mexican farmworkers have become U.S. citizens. Griffith regards NAFTA as reinforcing the Mexicanization of the agricultural workforce in not only South Florida but also the United States as a whole. In the meantime, political strife and economic weakness in the wider Caribbean Basin have intersected with the region's U.S. political and socioeconomic linkages to further diversify the South Florida workforce's transnational and ethnic makeup.

Griffith depicts farmwork in South Florida as encompassing a wide diversity of job positions, conditions, and earnings. The latter, he says, are often high relative to low-skill earnings in sectors such as food processing, hotels and restaurants, and landscaping—into and out of which farmworkers increasingly circulate—and is certainly high relative to earnings in the sending countries. Yet, according to Griffith, NAFTA contributes to socioeconomic polarization in South Florida, as well as elsewhere across the U.S. South and the United States. It does so, he claims, by displacing medium- and small-scale farmers and by consolidating a segment of the labor market typified by exploitive wages and work conditions. The labor patterns are interlocked with such factors as the changing ethno-national profile and geopolitical embeddedness of farm labor. Not least of this relationship are the expanded significance of the agricultural workforce's Mexican Americans (that is, the workforce's members who are U.S. citizens as well as ethnically tied to its noncitizen Mexicans) and the increased diplomacy of the Mexican government on behalf of remittance-sending Mexican workers.

Alma Young's chapter on port restructuring in New Orleans refocuses attention on the urban arena. Her chapter reinforces the conclusions of Glasmeier and Leichenko on U.S. southern transformations by underscoring the crucial importance of government action to defend and advance the positions of specific sectors, groups, and localities in a globalizing economy. The New Orleans economy—whose pillars are the port, petroleum, and tourism—has inclined to the margins of the South's federally led modernization since World War II. The city's racial status quo, old-boy politics, decrepit infrastructure, bloated poverty, and insular ways express clear continuities with the region's old regime. As late as the 1980s, moreover, changing trade flows as well as local deficiencies of capital, infrastructure, and labor-management relations were diminishing the port's competitiveness. Given both this constellation and petroleum's plunging fortunes, Young examines the ascent of local "political entrepreneurs" bent on reversing the port's decline, together with the decisive maneuvering by which they rebuilt the port's institutional underpinnings and reignited its prosperity.

Young links the ascent of local political entrepreneurs within the Dock Board—the state of Louisiana agency charged with governing the New Orleans port—to a conjuncture of citywide (as well as state-level) economic crisis and politico-administrative transition within the board. Its position as a state-level agency governing a city port appears to have broadened the board's leeway for political initiative. The board's leadership appointed a young new executive director who combined modernizing, technocratic expertise with a drive for careerist political advancement in an age of economic reconfiguration and market-oriented reforms. Young lays out the politics of how the newly constituted board carried out an ambitious program of capital raising, cost cutting, facilities improvement, and management-labor reform, all of which served to reinvigorate the port economy. She describes the importance of this reinvigoration to the wider economies of New Orleans and Louisiana. She also describes how the modernizing program pitted the port's leadership against other factions of the New Orleans governing coalition, as well as—in a city of pronounced racial segregation and poverty—against poor black neighborhoods surrounding valuable sites of port-facility expansion and improvement.

As part of a binational analysis, Bryan Roberts and Richard Tardanico compare transformations of employment and social inequality among several U.S. southern cities that more or less rim the Gulf of Mexico. This geographic band is subsumed within a U.S.-Mexico regional consortium, The States of the Gulf of Mexico Accord. As discussed later in this chapter, the consortium is one example of the North American emergence of cross-national, regional politico-commercial responses to NAFTA. Roberts and Tardanico situate the comparative urban changes in employment and social inequality within, on the one hand, promarket and supranational shifts and, on the other hand, theoretical debates over the consequences of these shifts for urban labor markets. Roberts and Tardanico find that each of the sampled U.S. Gulf cities has undergone employment deindustrialization. As students of restructuring would generally expect, the key sector of producer services is largest in the job markets in Houston and Miami, the sample's most securely internationalized economies. Yet, consistent with one pole of the theoretical debate, the authors find improvement in, rather than polarization of, occupational structure. Accompanying this improvement, however, is a polarization of income inequality. Hence, the upward reclassification of occupations in the sampled cities tends not to improve the standing of workers in the social relations of production in either manufacturing or services. In this context, the income gap between male and female workers has not widened but rather diminished, due to some mix of greater male losses and greater female gains (coupled with widened intragender inequalities). These patterns vary to some extent among the U.S. Gulf cities. What predominates, though, are intercity similarities. This suggests commonalities of socioeconomic restructuring and eventual compensatory policies irrespective of the unequal positions of the cities in the domestic and global divisions of labor.

How do the conclusions of these chapters pertain to the volume's overarching questions? Glasmeier and Leichenko emphasize far-reaching federal government intervention as having established the economic and social infrastructure as well as provided the military-industrial subsidies that underpinned and launched the New South. This intervention occurred during a world-historical era that legitimated state-centric policies of national development, including their overlap with exigencies of international military rivalry. Glasmeier and Leichenko also emphasize that the New South's ascent was tied not simply to the federal government and the national economy but more precisely to their hegemony in the post–World War II international order. Nevertheless, Glasmeier and Leichenko chart a postwar regional ascent that while impressive for many sectors, groups, and places, left others considerably behind. Moreover, it left much of the upwardly mobile South beholden to external powers, whims, and fluctuations.

According to Glasmeier and Leichenko, exacerbating the South's intraregional inequalities since the 1980s has been the eclipse of the midcentury domestic and international conditions that underlay the New South's emergence. Thus, jeopardizing the prospects of the South's marginalized sectors, groups, and places has been a complex of shifts. These include escalating global competition; the decline of U.S. government and economy from hegemony to mere dominance in the world; the dissolution of the postwar politico-social contract; the rise of market-centric government policy; and military-industrial cutbacks. Does the new matrix warrant a distinctive and coherent southern policy of regional development? The volume's chapters on the U.S. South dovetail with other writings (e.g., Bremer 1997; Griffin and Doyle 1995; MDC 1995, 1998; Wilson and Ferris 1989) to suggest a two-pronged answer. On one side, vitiating any rationale for such a policy is the convergence of much of the South with the mainstream United States, together with the South's increasingly diverse and unequal relations with the nation and the world. On the other side, much of both the rural and urban South remains hamstrung by old-regime continuities. Among these are underdeveloped public infrastructure and social services; excessive percentages of undereducated people, low-wage workers, branch manufacturing plants, and undercapitalized business firms relative to national standards; still substantial legacies of deeply rooted racial exploitation; and economic subordination to external ownership, linkages, and control. It is therefore arguable that, as in other regions of the United States and the world, distinctive conditions in the contemporary U.S. South call for some extent of regional (and intraregional) specificity in development policy.[4]

The chapters raise myriad other issues in regard to the set of questions presented in the volume's introduction. For example, Gereffi directs attention to the intersection of the U.S. South's portion of the global apparel-commodity chain with its portions of other chains—in manufacturing, agriculture, and services—that likewise are sinking in strategic importance and becoming intensely cost-competitive. Additional research could explore which southern segments of the chains do or do not ascend to higher-value activities such as technology-intensive production, product innovation, and transnational coordination.[5] It could also explore whether product markets, techno-social organization, interfirm and business-government relations, geography, or other features differentiate ascending and descending segments. And it could examine the local and regional consequences of such ascent and descent for interfirm linkages, agglomeration economies, employment structures, political configurations, and fiscal patterns.

With respect to NAFTA, Griffith's chapter points to research on the U.S. South's emerging class and ethno-national changes across subsectors of agriculture, lines of connection with urban economies, and intraregional geographic zones. His discussion of such changes during the 1960s, when Mexicans began to replace African Americans in Florida's agricultural workforce, provides a midcentury example of labor markets for comparison with today's situation (see Lieberson 1980; Portes and Rumbaut 1996). Of interest would be research on similarities and differences in the economic, sociocultural, and political features of the two migratory waves. This could include analysis of their similarities and differences in the spatial and gendered organization of employment, earnings, households, savings/expenditures, communities, cultural identities, and the politics of citizenship and labor rights (see Portes 1996; Wallerstein 1995, 203–5).

Young provokes questions about the local/extralocal conjunctures that permit political entrepreneurs not only to gain authority but also to implement their agenda. Her study prods us to consider the interrelations of local, state, and federal government policies with global restructuring. For New Orleans, it leads us to ask about the local politics of sectors other than the maritime industry, such as rising tourism and falling petroleum. Young demonstrates that local political responses to globalization have quite tangible significance for class and racial/ethnic divisions. Among the contested matters are fiscal, land-use/environmental, and labor policy. In this regard, Young discusses the port's centrality to the economies of New Orleans and Louisiana at large. Beyond the scope of her chapter is whether the politics of port revitalization since the 1980s represents a boon to the wider economy and society or else a narrowing of sociosectoral subsidy and prosperity. So too is whether, during the current era of intensified competition, revamping the institutional organization, facilities, and market strategy of any stagnant port would necessarily trigger its resurgence.

Roberts and Tardanico call for further research on the nexus of local labor markets and social inequality with government policies and globalization. This complements the studies by Gereffi on commodity-chain transformations; Griffith on immigration, race/ethnicity, and rural/urban labor circuits; and Young on political intervention and urban restructuring. For the U.S. South and elsewhere, Roberts and Tardanico invite inquiry into facets of convergence and divergence, both between and within tiers of cities in the world economy. Among the pertinent issues are changes in intrasectoral and intraoccupational inequalities as they crisscross with social class, race/ethnicity, gender, age, and immigration. Patterns of inequality in small urban areas would seem to merit particular attention. This is so given the apparently pronounced socioeconomic vulnerability of and variability among small cities. Possible inter-urban differences in class, racial/ethnic, and gendered household practices of income-earning and social reproduction intersect with these concerns, as do consequences for the contestation of urban realignments.

The Mexican South

Michael Conroy and Sarah Elizabeth West link impoverishment and rebellion in contemporary Chiapas to southern Mexico's historically entrenched underdevelopment, which in turn they link to the political economy of Mexican regional inequalities. Integral to the present-day unfolding of such inequalities, they emphasize, are Mexico's territorially unequal relations with NAFTA and globalization. According to Conroy and West, the midcentury baseline for such relations represented essential continuity with the history of southern Mexico's subordination to the national, as well as international, political economy. Whereas the U.S. South made dramatic gains within the federal government and national economy of the world-hegemonic United States, most of the Mexican South stood at the edge of the post–World War II upswing in Mexico's federal expenditures and manufacturing economy. The region simultaneously became locked into the subordinate role of supplying low-cost primary commodities (such as electricity, petroleum, timber, meat, henequen, coffee, beans, and corn) and cheap reserve labor for central and north-central Mexico's import-substitution ascent. Only a few parts of southern Mexico—such as the petroleum and petrochemical zones of Campeche and Veracruz, the port of Veracruz, the light-industrial urban corridor of Orizaba-Córdoba (Veracruz), and administrative and tourism nodes in Veracruz, Yucatán, and Oaxaca—partook significantly in the postwar national economic upswing. This problem has since been compounded by neoliberal reforms and northern Mexico-U.S. economic integration. Conroy and West emphasize the considerable variability in development conditions across southern Mexico, with parts of the Yucatán Peninsula ranking highest and the indigenous strongholds of Oaxaca and Chiapas ranking lowest. The long-term marginalization of southern Mexico stands in stark contrast to the postwar experience of most of the U.S. South, if alongside the experience of many, predominately rural, U.S. southern areas.

Conroy and West see no chance for any approximation in southern Mexico of the national-regional shifts that undergirded the U.S. South's economic takeoff. They do acknowledge signs of restricted opportunity in southern Mexico, mainly for the most urbanized and accessible locales such as the city of Mérida in Yucatán, for a smattering of tourism sites, and for certain locations and sociopolitical forms of primary commodity production. Foremost among the signs, they assert, is Mexico's ongoing political decentralization, which may provide some latitude for new regional growth poles. Conroy and West predict, however, that without major government programs to develop infrastructure, skills, and social equity, southern Mexico will derive little benefit from any national gains attached to economic globalization and NAFTA. (On extranational aspects of such programs, see Fox and Brown 1998; Galbraith 1998; Hollingsworth and Boyer 1997; Michie and Smith 1995). They therefore imply that, under prevailing arrangements, the region's economic role will increasingly be that of impoverished exporter of cheap labor to the transnationalized growth poles in northern and central Mexico and the United States.

Gary Gereffi's analysis of the Mexican share of the transnational apparel industry is perhaps even more pessimistic about southern Mexico's future. Gereffi describes Mexico's textile/garment producers as divided into three segments: central Mexico's large but internationally uncompetitive textile companies; northern Mexico's highly competitive export-assembly garment producers; and, hewing to the geographic contours of the nation's population, small firms producing cheap and substandard clothing for the domestic market. Gereffi writes that the weakness of the U.S. apparel commodity chain, garment production, is precisely the strength of the Mexican chain. Yet there are two important qualifications to this statement, he observes: first, Mexico's booming export-assembly production has minimal linkages to the domestic economy; and second, Mexican production for the home market has been abruptly pushed aside by foreign competition, above all U.S. producers and U.S. distributors of Asian-made goods. The ramifications for national economic and social development are adverse, as likewise are those of Mexican alliances with U.S. megaretailers. Seemingly ambiguous, on the other hand, are the domestic effects of the central Mexican textile sector's formal integration with U.S. firms. Given its competitive vulnerability under NAFTA, partially compensating for the Mexican textile sector's deepening subordination to U.S. partners are its gains in technology and product innovation. This includes its potential role in anchoring a more integrated and techno-organizationally modernized, albeit more denationalized, apparel industry in Mexico. A clear loser, in any event, is southern Mexico. A marginal participant in the import-substitution era's national apparel chain, it finds itself shunted even further aside under the new political economy.

Patricia Wilson and Thea Kayne delve into this aspect of southern Mexico's marginalization from the vantage point of Yucatán. For roughly a century, the export of henequen, used in making twine and rope, formed the core of Yucatán's economy. By the 1970s, however, foreign competition and synthetic fibers triggered a marked decline in local henequen's export market. In part as a response, federal and state government agencies sought to take advantage of the Yucatán Peninsula's comparative advantages in tourism and low-wage manufacturing. Government intervention prompted a boom in international tourism in coastal locales of Cancún and Cozumel, with substantial spillover to the interior city of Mérida and its surrounding archaeological sites. The area's tourism economy remains prosperous, if diminished by heightened competition from Mexico's west coast, the Caribbean Basin, and U.S. southern locales such as Florida. Whatever the social impact of tourism may have been, far less successful in the aggregate has been export-assembly manufacturing, which, as Wilson and Kayne explain, is premised on Yucatán's proximity to the U.S. South and an ample supply of cheap, predominately female labor.

Yucatán's number of export-assembly plants, which are overwhelmingly concentrated in metropolitan Mérida, has indeed grown significantly. Even so, the zone's maquiladora economy pales by Mexico's northern and national standards. Its industrial parks and transportation facilities are not competitive. Furthermore, it disproportionately involves the production of apparel as opposed to more technology- and skill-intensive commodities such as electronics and vehicle parts. Finally, its factories are typically deficient in capital, organization, technology, and market networks. Still another problem is that local maquiladoras have been unsuccessful in achieving a key objective of the export-promotion campaign: the absorption of displaced henequen workers. Wilson and Kayne describe strong ties between Yucatán's export-assembly plants and enterprises located in the U.S. Gulf and Upper South. They conclude, nevertheless, that Yucatán will remain a very weak player in the export-assembly economy of Mexico and the Caribbean Basin without major improvements in local conditions. They call for advances in infrastructure, skill, and the density and breadth of local economic linkages, and for astute action to carve out unique, quality-oriented niches in the supranational manufacturing production chain.

The topics of commodity chain and government policy remain at the center of attention in Robert Porter's chapter on restructuring, coffee, and small farmers. Although coffee has been a Mexican export since the late 1800s, since the 1980s it has become a high-quality ingredient of U.S. gourmet coffee and ice cream. The region's coffee production has therefore attained a competitive edge that, according to the chapters by Conroy and West and by Wilson and Kayne, most of southern Mexico's exports lack. Porter's study of Chiapas, Oaxaca, and Veracruz underlines the variable relations of small farmers—the predominant producers of Mexican coffee—to surrounding webs of power. Contrary to the overgeneralizations that riddle much of the literature on global restructuring, Porter documents considerable range in the effects of the process's economic and political changes on small coffee farmers. To be sure, he stresses that small farmers are the primary losers in the coffee economy's reorganization. He shows, however, that a sizable fraction of the small farmers, primarily in Oaxaca, has managed to enhance its control over key links in the commodity chain and thus to bolster its competitive position in the new export niches. He argues that underlying their success, and the failure of other small farmers, is southern Mexico's variation in four spheres: the social organization of coffee production; the distribution of political power between small and large producers; the policy dispositions of state governments; and the organizational characteristics of small-producer unions.

In short, state and local politics loom as critical for southern Mexico's coffee producers, as both grounded in and partially independent from territorial socioeconomic conditions. Porter outlines possible lessons from this case for small producers of other agricultural commodities. His discussion suggests comparison with other agricultural commodity chains in southern Mexico and beyond to assess the relative capacities of other small farmers to increase their politico-social leverage over, and their share of the profits from, the activities of production, distribution, and retailing (see Goodman and Watts 1997; McMichael 1994).

The focus on politics continues in the chapter by Jonathan Fox and Josefina Aranda, who, like Porter, emphasize patterns of rural development policy. Consistent with the other volume contributors on both the Mexican South and the U.S. South, Fox and Aranda stress a basic contradiction of pro-market reforms: while the state's machinery withdraws from some arenas, its intervention is simply redefined in other arenas, or both redefined and deepened in still others. Within this framework, Fox and Aranda concur with Porter in underlining the political and social embeddedness of Mexico's rural market restructuring. They observe that political risks of popular disaffection and opposition in the countryside led the federal state's managers to pursue a mix of market-enhancing reforms and compensatory interventions. The federal managers have sought to skirt the obstacles to targeted antipoverty measures posed by the patronage hierarchy of the official Partido Revolucionario Institucional. Fox and Aranda write that rural local governments potentially provide the most direct access to the very poor and thus would seem to warrant decentralized programs. Have the decentralized, targeted programs indeed promoted rural grassroots development and responded to local public priorities, as the federal managers have promised?

Fox and Aranda's analysis of the Municipal Solidarity Funds program in Oaxaca contextualizes the case within the federal National Solidarity Program and the World Bank's financing of Mexican development projects. Municipal Solidarity Funds, which the World Bank financed, channel federal funds for small-scale, participatory development to rural localities, with state governments allocating the monies among local governments. In regard to Oaxaca, Fox and Aranda find that the program—whose project budgets were minuscule—was generally effective in supporting incremental, grassroots projects. The program did not notably alter the balance of power between federal, state, and local government. However, it did alter the intralocal balance of power, as the outlying, poorest communities increased their access to local funding and decision making. Fox and Aranda restrict their empirical conclusions to the case of Oaxaca, whose state and local governments they, like Porter, describe as democratic and responsive relative to others in southern Mexico. Based on a preliminary comparison with Chiapas, they speculate that the Municipal Funds program reinforced government's preexisting responsiveness in Oaxaca but authoritarianism in Chiapas. Fox and Aranda tell us that from the perspective of effectiveness in poverty mitigation, programs of decentralized, grassroots rural development, such as those gaining some favor within the World Bank, must take into account the diversity of local conditions of government and citizenship. They also tell us that the empowerment of citizens is fundamental to holding both the multiple tiers of government and the international agencies accountable for their actions.

Discussion shifts to the urban realm as, in their chapter on labor market inequalities within the binational Gulf of Mexico zone, Bryan Roberts and Richard Tardanico examine changes in a sample of Mexican cities. Given their more subordinate and tenuous positions in the world economy, the Mexican Gulf cities evince greater variability than their U.S. counterparts. Overall, though, their comparative underdevelopment and poverty make them much less geared to advanced services and to professional and skilled employment than the U.S. Gulf cities. Indeed, the Mexican border cities of Matamoros and Nuevo Laredo are the only instances in the binational sample where manufacturing rose as a percentage of local jobs, based on surges in low-wage, export-platform activities. On the whole, the Mexican Gulf cities adhere to the binational trend of not degraded but upgraded occupational composition, combined with polarization of earnings inequality. The sole deviation provides neither relief nor optimism: as maquiladoras grew rapidly in Matamoros, the city's upper and middle occupations actually dropped as a fraction of its total employment. On the Mexican Gulf's positive side, the earnings of women increased versus those of men. As in the United States, though, this encompasses worsened intragender gaps, plus case-by-case differences in the degree to which it reflects authentic female gains versus deterioration for males. Notwithstanding the impoverishment of the Mexican cities and their greater variation than the U.S. cities in seemingly all respects, both the Mexican and U.S. samples are characterized on balance by the same labor market shifts: improved occupational structure; worsened earnings disparities; and diminished gender inequality.

What do these writings on the Mexican South have to say about the volume's integrating questions? And what insights are provided by the case of the twentieth-century U.S. South for development policy in the Mexican South? Conroy and West stress the importance of the federal government's midcentury interventions in propelling the import-substitution industrialization of central and north-central Mexico, while for the most part merely modernizing the traditional subordination of southern Mexico. The latter's pockets of relative prosperity—such as seats of state government, tourism sites, and the Gulf's petroleum and petrochemical areas, ports, and manufacturing nodes— prove this rule, since integral to their regional exceptionalism were post–World War II inflows of federal expenditure. Such inflows underpinned southern Mexico's minimal gains from the U.S.-dominated, postwar international order. Its dissolution has unleashed a scramble among sectors, groups, and places to protect or redefine their positions of domestic and global engagement. Not only parts of the U.S. South but also most of the Mexican South exemplify the scramble's losers in rich and poor countries alike.

The case studies on southern Mexico describe aspects of this scramble. Together with the chapter by Conroy and West, they indicate that the pronounced and widening development gap between southern Mexico and the nation at large warrants a much more distinctive and coherent, government-led regional development policy than would be advisable for the U.S. South. For example, the chapters by Gereffi and by Wilson and Kayne point out that southern Mexico is at a considerable disadvantage for export-platform manufacturing relative to not only the country's northern region but also the impoverished nations of the Caribbean Basin. Like Conroy and West, Wilson and Kayne cite the imperative of pursuing competitive niches in the international market. This is what, according to Porter, Oaxacan farmers have done in coffee exports (and, according to Young, the U.S. port of New Orleans has done in shipping). Gereffi discusses how, as the U.S. South's textile firms come to concentrate on innovative forms of production and on supranational coordination, they are transferring routine production activities to central Mexico by teaming up with its textile firms. These, in turn, are climbing up the apparel commodity chain by obtaining U.S. technology and product innovations. Simultaneously they are taking advantage of Mexico's extensive export-platform operations to create a more integrated and advanced, if more externally controlled, domestic apparel industry. Under what conditions could Mexico's federal and provincial governments, whether on their own or as part of a North American consortium, eventually guide some share of both the garment-assembly operations and their input linkages to southern Mexican sites such as Mérida and Orizaba-Córdoba, which already have industrial bases? Effecting a significant degree of garment-assembly relocation could be a notable component of a comprehensive regional development program. This would be so if, as follows from the chapters by Wilson and Kayne and by Roberts and Tardanico, it were conjoined with major regional-local development undertakings.

Such an approach calls for new, more agile and targeted development policies, both within and across national boundaries (Brohman 1997; Fox and Brown 1998; Galbraith 1998; Hollingsworth and Boyer 1997; Michie and Smith 1995; Otero 1996). Notwithstanding the above example, the appropriate policy focus in southern Mexico would be not the cities but the countryside. The chapters by Fox and Aranda and by Porter tell us that a key ingredient of the development programs, both rural and urban, would be their nexus with state and local governments. They imply, moreover, that independent grassroots organization and democratic, responsive state and local governments are vital to the chances of implementing decentralized, participatory reforms in the first place, as well to any long-range possibilities for orchestrating sustainable agrarian development (see Fox 1998, 1999; Fox and Brown 1998). Porter depicts the geoinstitutional terrain of market opportunities and obstacles for small coffee farmers. In doing so, he identifies sites and circumstances of potential facilitation, intervention, or withdrawal by government, nongovernmental organizations, and multilateral agencies. This approach complements Wilson and Kayne's study of export-assembly manufacturing in Yucatán.[6] It likewise pushes us to consider the relevance for other agricultural commodities and farmers, plus nonagricultural indigenous cases such as crafts and their producers (e.g., Bray 1995; Brohman 1997; Cook and Binford 1990; Murphy and Stepick 1991; Schmidt et al. 1999).

Concerning the politics of participatory rural development, Fox and Aranda end their contribution by referring to grassroots empowerment as crucial to the establishment of accountability at the various rungs of the transnational policy ladder. Elsewhere, Fox (1999) asserts that Mexico has tangibly greater leeway in negotiating and deploying World Bank loans than is typically supposed. This, he writes, reflects several factors: the size and complexity of Mexico's economy; the sophistication of its governing class; its geopolitical importance; political rifts within both Mexico's federal government and the World Bank; and the bank's restricted monitoring and supervisory capacities. He claims that, in Mexico as well as other poor countries, additional leeway could be leveraged if grassroots constituencies, which are hampered by resource limitations and security threats, could more strategically join with nongovernmental organizations in pressing for both national democratization and transnational advocacy. Fox (1998, 1) calls for an approach epitomized by Brazil's "Network on Multilateral Institutions": the building of multi-issue, participatory

> subnational and national level networks, federations and umbrella groups that *link and bridge the local and international arenas.* These "bridging organizations" can help local actors to work transnationally in ways that broaden their coalitions horizontally, creating the possibility of influencing the local and national balance of power at the same time [emphasis in original].

The construction of a viable ensemble of such networks across Mexico, the United States, and Canada would seem essential to the cause of sustainable development in the Mexican South. Appropriately modified, it would seem no less important for marginalized peoples and places in the U.S. South, as well as other regions of the NAFTA bloc (see Chalmers et al. 1997; Cook 1997).

NAFTA and Transnational Regions: The Case of The Mexico-U.S. Gulf

Reinforcing this volume's rationale for comparing southern Mexico and the southern United States is the fact that a regional band of Mexican and U.S. government leadership has undertaken a politico-commercial initiative on the basis of perceived commonalities in relation to NAFTA and globalization (see the chapter by Roberts and Tardanico). On May 13, 1995, the governors of the Mexican and U.S. states bordering the Gulf of Mexico signed an agreement premised on the sharing of a "well defined geographic region" that subsumes the Gulf's waters as well as much of southern Mexico and the southern United States.[7] The States of the Gulf of Mexico Accord asserts that this binational set of states has "many areas of common interest including the support of private sector development between our regions, and the implementation of the articles of the North American Free Trade Agreement." The document pledges the governors' support for "partnerships, joint ventures, bilateral and other agreements" on behalf of "trade, investment, transportation, communication, tourism, health and environmental issues, agriculture, educational and cultural exchange." So far, the principal endeavor has been to convene binational working groups on Gulf-wide integration. The groups have proposed several projects. These include the completion of a road network from Florida to Quintana Roo (see Map 11.1); the creation of new maritime routes, the improvement of Mexican port infrastructure, and the implementation of distance learning programs (Zaretsky and Rosenberg 1998).

The Gulf Accord is part of a proliferation of multicentric formal connections—both governmental and nongovernmental—traversing not only North America's national frontiers but also other such frontiers worldwide under post–cold war globalization, regionalization, and fragmentation. As Robert Boyer and J. Rogers Hollingsworth write:

> a multifaceted causality runs in virtually all directions among the various levels of society: nations, sectors, free trade zones, international regimes, supranational regions, large cities, and even small but well-specialized localities interact according to unprecedented configurations.... [N]o single authority, let it be supranational, continental, national, or local, has the power to monitor and to regulate such a complex system. (1997, 470)

James Rosenau observes that "regional contiguities have become increasingly salient because their numerous problems impact on each other with sufficient force to create processes that cannot be accounted for, much less managed by, standard perspectives and strategies" (1993, 8). He adds that the locus of policy-making responsibilities for cross-border issues and problems is therefore likely to become "dispersed among an unfamiliar array of interactive local subdivisions and nongovernmental actors" (see Cook 1997).

Two conditions surrounding the Gulf Accord are of particular comparative and global relevance. First, since the age of European colonial competition, never have the Gulf's territorial commonalities and connections more than minimally approximated the density and strength of countervailing political, sociocultural, and economic tugs; thus never has the area more than minimally approximated any reasonable standard for defining a region. Second, relative to the other emergent cross-frontier, regional groupings, the Gulf consortium in general is only marginally competitive under global-continental restructuring. It thus is acutely vulnerable to market-based policies.

In fact, significant continuity characterizes much of the physical geography and natural resources of the binational states rimming the Gulf of Mexico (McCoy 1997). Along with the commonality of the Gulf's shores and waters, the states are part of a "geological province" called the Gulf Coastal Plain of North America, which stretches from Florida in the United States to the Yucatán Peninsula in Mexico (Map 11.1). The climate is generally hot, rainy, and humid, and the most important natural resources are the Gulf's Mexican and U.S. petroleum deposits, waters, and marine life. Significant continuity therefore characterizes the Gulf's binational commodity profile as well. Key regional commodities and economic activities include petroleum and petrochemicals; forestry; fishing; citrus, sugarcane and winter fruits and vegetables; maritime shipping; and tourism. Moreover, some elements of historical and cultural commonality are evident along much of the Mexico-U.S. Gulf rim (e.g., from Campeche, Mérida, Veracruz, and Tampico to Corpus Christi, Beaumont, New Orleans, and Mobile [Map 1.1]).

These continuities notwithstanding, the history of Spanish, French, and British colonial competition in North America and the circum-Caribbean did not permit the modern Gulf basin to cohere as a politico-economic or sociocultural region (McCoy 1997). Neither did the subsequent, often head-to-head dynamics of Mexican and U.S. nation building. It is nevertheless striking that, in response to both threats and opportunities emanating from transnational and domestic realignments, a set of government and business interests—whose composition and relations await in-depth study—has appealed to largely dormant, generally weak territorial ties and identities to orchestrate this cross-border initiative.[8]

There are major questions concerning the economic prospects of the zone's sectors, groups, and places. In this respect, another striking feature of the Gulf Accord is that the zone's economic activities seem more oriented to staving off or minimizing displacement from the new order's continental and global commodity chains, or to making marginal advances, than to latching onto more upwardly mobile links. This appears most true for activities that cut across the Mexican Gulf area, but it corresponds to much of the U.S. Gulf rim as well. At least three other agreements of this kind have been established in North America: the Pacific Northwest Economic Region, the Desert Pacific Region, and the New Atlantic Region[9] (CSIP 1997, 1–2). Advantages of industry mix and/or market geography seem to give the Pacific Northwest and Desert Pacific consortiums the best economic prospects, while the Gulf consortium may face the worst. Furthermore, we can expect that disparities of market advantage and political influence characterize the inner workings of each consortium. This means that, whatever its comparative prospects and eventual effectiveness, a consortium's policies will not deliver equal benefits to the business interests housed within its territorial confines, not to mention to its array of social groups and localities.

These external and internal relations call attention to the roles and objectives of those layers of state and local government that are involved in organizing such cross-national initiatives. It stands to reason that such layers of government join with certain business factions to reinforce, recover, or redefine the reach of their local economies, which may involve attempts to capture expanded or alternative hinterlands at home and abroad[10] (see Sassen 1994, 39–52; Wackerman 1997). The initiatives may seek mainly to protect and advance the positions of regional and local firms that, while operating to some extent outside national boundaries or possessing potential to do so, are losing out to more competitive enterprises with sizable national and transnational reach.[11]

In sum, integral to the unfolding of sectoral, social, and territorial categories of winners and losers in North American restructuring are the interventions of the local, state, federal, and supranational echelons of government. Indeed, a growing literature emphasizes that globalization, regionalization, and market-boosting reform are not truly undercutting government authority as many observers claim. Rather, depending on the world-area and country, the trends are rebalancing the weight of government from an agenda of more or less inclusionary social policies and inward-oriented accumulation, to one of more regressive or mass-marginalizing and exclusionary social policies along with transnationalized accumulation[12] (e.g., Dicken 1998; Hollingsworth and Boyer 1997; Sassen 1996; Stallings 1995). This shift includes state and local governments, as slashed federal protections and subsidies combine with autonomous subfederal pressures to push government, business, and other sociopolitical interests at these rungs into an intensified scramble to avoid being swept aside.[13] Research might fruitfully address the comparative prevalence, inter- and intragovernment dynamics, government-society relations, and varieties and actions of transfrontier, business-promoting consortiums. It might do so across the rising, stagnant, and falling links and territories of commodity chains in North America and the world, as well as across distinctive politico-economic and cultural contexts.

It is anyone's guess how numerous, varied, and influential such consortiums and related groupings will become across North America and the world. Their roles will be shaped in concert with changes in national and supranational political economies. Hence their roles will also depend on changing socio-geographic forms of contestation, including bureaucratic forces within the evolving domestic/supranational fabric of governmental and multilateral bureaucracies (Chalmers et al. 1997; Cook 1997; see Fox 1998, 1999; Fox and Brown 1998; Hollingsworth and Boyer 1997). In any event, the units for comparison in the study of worldwide inequality are becoming more fluid and varied. Among the myriad new possibilities is comparative research from the perspective of nascent entities such as North America's territorial politico-commercial accords, and their implications for peoples and places in the Mexican South, the U.S. South, and beyond.

References

Amin, Ash. 1998. Globalisation and Regional Development: A Relational Perspective. *Competition & Change* 3, nos. 1 and 2.

Boyer, Robert, and J. Rogers Hollingsworth. 1997. From National Embeddedness to Spatial and Institutional Nestedness. In *Contemporary Capitalism: The Embeddedness of Institutions*, eds. J. Rogers Hollingsworth and Robert Boyer. Cambridge: Cambridge University Press.

Bray, David Barton. 1995. Peasant Organizations and "The Permanent Reconstruction of Nature": Grassroots Sustainable Development in Rural Mexico. *Journal of Environment & Development* 4, no. 2.

Bremer, Jennifer. 1997. Positioning the South in the New Global Economy. *Southern Growth* (spring).

Britton, John N. H., ed. 1996. *Canada and the Global Economy: The Geography of Structural and Technological Change*. Montreal and Kingston: McGill-Queen's University Press.

Brohman, John. 1996. *Popular Development: Rethinking the Theory and Practice of Development*. Oxford: Blackwell.

Chalmers, Douglas A., Scott B. Martin, and Kerianne Piester. 1997. Associative Networks: New Structures of Representation for the Popular Sectors? In *The New Politics of Inequality in Latin America*, eds. Douglas A. Chalmers, Carlos A. Vilas, Katherine Hite, Scott B. Mortin, Kerianne Prestor, and Monique Segarra. Oxford: Oxford University Press.

Chase-Dunn, Christopher. 1998. *Global Formations*. 2d ed. rev. Lanham, Md.: Rowman & Littlefield.

Cheshire, Paul C., and Ian R. Gordon. 1996. Territorial Competition and the Predictability of Collective (In)Action. *International Journal of Urban and Regional Research* 20, no. 3.

Clarke, Susan E., and Gary L. Gaile. 1997. Local Politics in a Global Era: Thinking Locally, Acting Globally. In *The Annals of the American Academy of Political and Social Science*, Issue on Globalization and the Changing U.S. City, ed. David Wilson. May.

Clearinghouse on State International Policies (CSIP). 1997. Research Triangle, N.C.: Southern Growth Policies Board. April.

Conklin, David W. 1997. NAFTA: Regional Impacts. In *The Political Economy of Regionalism*, eds. Michael Keating and John Longlin. London: Frank Cass.

Cook, María Lorena. 1997. Regional Integration and Transnational Politics: Popular Sector Strategies in the NAFTA Era. In *The New Politics of Inequality in Latin America*, eds. Douglas A. Chalmers, Carlos M. Vilas, Katherine Hite, Scott B. Martin, Kerianne Piester, and Monique Segarra. Oxford: Oxford University Press.

Cook, Scott, and Leigh Binford. 1990. *Obliging Need: Rural Petty Industry in Mexican Capitalism*. Austin: University of Texas Press.

Cox, Kevin R. 1995. Globalisation, Competition and the Politics of Local Economic Development. *Urban Studies* 33, no. 2.

Dicken, Peter. 1998. *Global Shift*, 3d ed. rev. New York: The Guilford Press.

Fox, Jonathan. 1998. Thinking Locally, Acting Globally: Bringing the Grassroots into Transnational Advocacy. Paper Presented at the Conference on Regional Worlds—Latin America: Cultural Environments and Development Debates, University of Chicago.

———. 1999. The World Bank and Mexico: Where Does Civil Society Fit In? In *Las nuevas fronteras del siglo XXI: Dimensiones culturales, políticas y socioeconómicas de las relaciones México-Estados Unidos*, eds. Norma Klahn et al. México, D.F.: UAM/UAM.

Fox, Jonathan, and L. David Brown, eds. 1998. *The Struggle for Accountability: Grassroots Movements, NGOs, and the World Bank*. Cambridge, Mass.: MIT Press.

Galbraith, James K. 1998. *Created Unequal: The Crisis in American Pay*. New York: The Free Press.

Goodman, David, and Michael Watts, eds. 1997. *Globalising Food: Agrarian Questions and Global Restructuring*. London: Routledge.

Griffin, Larry J., and Don H. Doyle, eds. 1995. *The South as an American Problem*. Athens: University of Georgia Press.

Hansen, Gordon H. 1998. Regional Adjustment to Trade Liberalization. *Regional Science and Urban Economics* 28, no. 4.

Harrison, Bennett. 1994. *Lean and Mean: The Changing Landscape of Corporate Power in the Age of Flexibility*. New York: Basic Books.

Hollingsworth, J. Rogers, and Robert Boyer, eds. 1997. *Contemporary Capitalism: The Embeddedness of Institutions*. Cambridge: Cambridge University Press.

Kitson, Michael, and Jonathan Michie. 1995. Trade and Growth: A Historical Perspective. In *Managing the Global Economy*, eds. Jonathan Michie and John Grieve Smith. Oxford: Oxford University Press.

Lieberson, Stanley. 1980. *A Piece of the Pie: Blacks and White Immigrants since 1880*. Berkeley and Los Angeles: University of California Press.

McCoy, Terry L. 1997. The Gulf of Mexico: A Regional Overview. *LACC Occasional Papers*. Miami: Latin American and Caribbean Center, Florida International University.

McMichael, Philip, ed. 1994. *The Global Restructuring of Agro-Food Systems*. Ithaca, N.Y.: Cornell University Press.

MDC. 1995. *The State of the South*. Chapel Hill, N.C.: MDC.

———. 1998. *The State of the South*. Chapel Hill, N.C.: MDC.

Meyer-Stamer, Jorg. 1998. Path Dependence in Regional Development: Persistence and Change in Three Industrial Clusters in Santa Catarina, Brazil. *World Development* 26, no. 8.

Michie, Jonathan, and John Grieve Smith, eds. 1995. *Managing the Global Economy*. Oxford: Oxford University Press.

Murphy, Arthur D., and Alex Stepick. 1991. *Social Inequality in Oaxaca*. Philadelphia, Penn.: Temple University Press.

Noponen, Helzi, Julie Graham, and Ann R. Markusen, eds. 1993. *Trading Industries, Trading Regions: International Trade, American Industry, and Regional Economic Development*. New York: The Guilford Press.

Otero, Gerardo, ed. 1996. *Neoliberalism Revisited: Economic Restructuring and Mexico's Political Future*. Boulder, Colo.: Westview.

Portes, Alejandro. 1996. Transnational Communities: Their Emergence and Significance in the Contemporary World System. In *Latin America in the World-Economy*, eds. Roberto Patricio Korzeniewicz and William C. Smith. Westport, Conn.: Praeger.

Portes, Alejandro, and Rubén Rumbaut. 1996. 2d ed. *Immigrant America*. Berkeley and Los Angeles: University of California Press.

Rosenau, James N. 1993. Coherent Connection or Commonplace Contiguity? Theorizing about the California-Mexico Overlap. In *The California-Mexico Connection*, eds. Abraham F. Lowenthal and Katrina Burgess. Stanford: Stanford University Press.

Sassen, Saskia. 1994. *Cities in a World Economy*. Thousand Oaks, Calif.: Pine Forge Press.

———. 1996. *Loss of Control? Sovereignty in an Age of Globalization*. New York: Columbia University Press.

Scott, Allen J. 1998. *Regions and the World Political Economy: The Coming Shape of Global Production, Competition, and Political Order*. Oxford: Oxford University Press.

Schmidt, Ralph, Joyce K. Berry, and John C. Gordon, eds. 1999. *Forests to Fight Poverty: Creating National Strategies*. New Haven, Conn.: Yale University Press.

Sparke, Matthew. 1997. Emergent Transnational Regions in the Context of NAFTA: The Case of Cascadia. Paper presented at the Meetings of the Association of the American Academy of Science, Seattle, Washington, April.

Stallings, Barbara, ed. 1995. *Global Change, Regional Response: The New International Context of Development.* Cambridge: Cambridge University Press.

Wackerman, Gabriel. 1997. Transport, Trade, Tourism and the World Economic System. *International Social Science Journal* 151(March).

Wallerstein, Immanuel. 1995. *After Liberalism.* New York: The New Press.

Wilson, Charles Reagan, and William Ferris, eds. 1989. *Encyclopedia of Southern Culture.* Chapel Hill: University of North Carolina Press.

Zaretsky, Nancy, and Mark B. Rosenberg. 1998. *Thinking Globally and Acting Locally: NAFTA, Globalization and the Gulf Governors' Accord.* Miami: Latin American and Caribbean Center, Florida International University.

Notes

Chapter 1

1. We thank Douglas Kincaid for his critique of an earlier draft. We bear sole responsibility for any remaining deficiencies.
2. *Neoliberal* refers to ostensibly laissez-faire policies centering on the shrinkage of government bureaucracy, the privatization of state enterprises, the deregulation of markets, the liberalization of trade, and the reduction of government social programs. On the contradictory and variable features of neoliberalism, see Fox and Brown (1998); Galbraith (1998); Hollingsworth and Boyer (1997); Stallings (1995); and Wallerstein (1995).
3. The European Union (EU) contains a tier of relatively poor nations: Spain, Greece, Ireland, and Portugal. In terms of the various indicators of economic and social development, however, these nations rank as midlevel compared with Mexico. For instance, the World Bank (1996, 189) reports purchasing power parity per capita (U.S.=100) as 27.2 for Mexico versus 53.1 for Spain, 52.4 for Ireland, 46.3 for Portugal, and 42.2 for Greece.

   On both the valid and overdrawn distinctions between today's formal and "market-led" blocs, see Cable (1994) and Galbraith (1998, 256–62). Cable observes that, whether formal or market-led, today's trade and investment blocs are more clearly premised on transnational corporations, capital flows, and financial services than were their predecessors of the 1960s and 1970s, which were geared to import-substitution objectives (Cable 1994, 2–3).

   According to Anderson and Blackhurst (1993, 4–5), there are five gradients of the contemporary world's formal structures of regional-international market integration. From weakest to strongest, the gradients are: (1) preferential trade agreement; (2) free-trade agreement; (3) customs union; (4) common market; and (5) economic union (see Cable 1994; El-Agraa 1997). What these have in common, write Anderson and Blackhurst (1993, 5), is the "reciprocal nature of the preferential treatment." In its various forms, such geographically organized reciprocity is taking shape as a basic characteristic of politico-market competition and relations of power, dependency, and marginality in the new global order. Strictly speaking, Anderson and Blackhurst exclude from consideration as formal market-integration regimes the one-way preferences conceded by the EU and individual member-countries to former colonies and other underdeveloped countries. The same can be said of U.S. policies such as the Caribbean Basin Initiative and assorted one-way preferences to Asian-Pacific countries (see Cox and Skidmore-Hess 1999). Anderson and Blackhurst (1993) and Winters (1993, 115) portray such one-way preferences as institutional legacies of a previous world order characterized by more nationally centered political economies and cold-war international rivalry, and/or as ways of addressing delimited, present-day international concerns of constellations of interests traversing selected rich and poor countries. These concerns include fostering political stability in poor countries, maintaining First World geopolitical spheres of influence, subsidizing and protecting particular economic sectors in rich and poor countries, ensuring poor-country access to First World aid, and controlling immigration flows from poor to rich countries. Indicative of the roots of one-way preferences in the previous, largely eclipsed order is that they have become vulnerable to the mandates of the new global order's incipient institutions, such as the World Trade Organization (WTO) and the proposed Multilateral Agreement on Investment (MAI). Such mandates impose new dimensions of vulnerability on poor countries (Cox and Skidmore-Hess 1999; Hollingsworth and Boyer 1997; McMichael 1994; Raynolds 1997; Sassen 1996).

The Asian Pacific Economic Cooperation (APEC) forum, established in 1989, represents a potential parallel to NAFTA's combination of advanced and under-developed national economies. APEC was founded by ASEAN (presently consisting of Brunei, Indonesia, Malaysia, the Philippines, Singapore, Thailand, and Vietnam) together with Australia, Canada, Japan, New Zealand, South Korea, and the United States. As described by El-Agraa (1997, 31), "in 1994 APEC declared its intention (vision) to create a free trade and investment area by the year 2010 by its advanced members, with the rest to follow ten years later." (See also Bhalla and Bhalla 1997, chap. 5).

4. As McMichael (1990) puts it, conventional comparative methodology assumes that cases are unrelated to each other in time and space. In contrast, as described above, an alternative approach underlines the "emergent totality" of the world order, which is studied by means of "comparative analysis of 'parts' as moments in a self-forming whole" (McMichael 1990, 386, 391). Richard Locke and Kathleen Thelen describe an overlapping approach that, although seeming to compare "apples and oranges" (1995, 344), emphasizes both "unexpected parallels across cases that the conventional literature sees as very different" and "significant differences between cases typically seen as most similar" (338).

5. Barnes and Ledebur (1998, 3) quote Robert Reich as defining a national economy as simply "the region of the global economy denominated by a nation's political borders," and Jane Jacobs as observing, "most nations are composed of collections or grab bags of very different economies." According to Scott, global trends "have not only *not* undermined the region as a basis of dense and many-sided human interactions (though they have greatly affected many of the qualitative attributes of such interactions) but in many respects have actually reinforced it" (1998, 4). See Hollingsworth and Boyer (1997); Scott (1998); Tilly (1992); Wallerstein (1974, 1995); and Wolf (1982) on historical and contemporary conflicts over the melding of regions into national and supranational markets.

6. Pertinent to this matter is Charles Tilly's (1975, 62–65) elaboration of a methodology for studying political contention among social groups. Based on the work of Harrison White, Tilly conceptualizes social groups from the standpoint of degrees of strength along two conceptual axes: "category," as defined both by members and by others; and "networks," as defined by level of integration across the various

kinds of interpersonal ties. This approach is well suited to the study of regional political economies (e.g., Tilly 1984, 1992).

7. ISI was a state-centric program intended to decrease imports of manufactured goods, and thus dependence on foreign capital and markets, by producing such goods at home. Integral to the program was the state's economic and social intervention to expand domestic market demand with the objective of building industrial economies of scale (see Gereffi 1994).

Chapter 2

1. See Map 1.1, which, in conforming to the commonplace distinction, omits Delaware, Maryland, the District of Columbia, and Oklahoma.

Chapter 3

1. The content of this chapter represents the professional opinion of the authors alone; it explicitly does not represent the perspective of the Ford Foundation. Significant portions of this chapter are drawn from Sarah Elizabeth West's unpublished professional report for the MA degree in Latin American Studies at the University of Texas at Austin, entitled *PRONASOL and Poverty in Mexico: Regional Changes in Federal Spending, 1980–1982* (August 1994).

2. The nine indicators are: illiteracy; percent of homes without septic or sewer systems; percent of homes without electricity; percent of homes without piped water; percent of homes deemed "overcrowded"; percent of homes with dirt floors; percent of population in localities of less than 5,000; and percent of labor force earning less than twice the minimum wage (CONAPO 1990).

3. See, for example, Collier (1995), Parra Vásquez and Díaz Hernández (1996); Urbina Nandayapa (1994); Russell (1995); Hernández Navarro (1998); and Burbach and Rosset (1994).

4. There were, unfortunately, no data in the studies released that day to support the secretary's estimates of the impact of NAFTA.

Chapter 4

1. In 1990, the hourly wage in Mexican textile and apparel maquilas was estimated at $0.70, compared to real hourly wages for U.S. apparel workers of nearly $7.00 (OTA 1992, 189).

2. In terms of market share, "basic" products sold year-round account for about 20% of U.S. apparel sales, "seasonal" products with a twenty-week shelf life make up 45% of the market, and "fashion" products with a ten-week life account for the remaining 35%. About two-fifths of the industry, whether measured by employment or sales, is sensitive to fashion, and one-fifth focuses on basic, commodity garments (OTA 1992, 176n).

3. A good illustration of the constraining role of quotas is China's declining share of U.S. cotton trouser imports between 1983 and 1994 (see Tables 4.6 and 4.7), a period when China's overall apparel exports to the United States were booming.

4. Each segment represents a different kind of industry. Synthetic fibers is a highly capital-intensive industry, with large vertically integrated firms and sophisticated technology; textiles is a moderately capital-intensive industry with medium to

large factories; and garment production tends to be labor-intensive, often carried out in small firms with simple technology.

5. My account of the evolution of Mexico's garment industry is based on the excellent study by Hanson (1991).

6. There is considerable price competition within this group. For cotton underwear (MFA category 352), Jamaica ($1.02 per pair) and Mexico ($0.98) are relatively high-cost suppliers, Costa Rica ($0.60) and the Dominican Republic ($0.69) are low-cost producers, and El Salvador ($0.73), Guatemala ($0.74), and Honduras ($0.81) are in the middle.

7. Other vertically integrated U.S. apparel companies that make a substantial portion of their own fabrics include VF Corporation, Kellwood Company, Phillips-Van Heusen Corporation, Russell Corporation, and Tultex Corporation (see Finnie 1995b, 85).

8. In local accounts, this was conceptualized as a shift in the role of the state from "un estado regulador y controlador" to "un estado promotor y concertador."

9. Author interview with Norma Rodríguez Orozco, Gerente de Comercialización, Banco Nacional de Comercio Exterior, Mexico City, Mexico, July 22, 1994.

Chapter 5

1. At the largest apparel maquiladora in Yucatán, signs above the assembly line showing a jubilant worker proclaiming, "I'm happy because I check my quality!" appear to be the extent of worker involvement in quality control.

2. Business incubators are programs that provide assistance to small, fledgling firms. The assistance includes subsidized access to consultants, to office and manufacturing space, and to complementary services and equipment.

Chapter 6

1. Pertinent to this volume's focus on southern Mexico and the southern United States is that much of the former's coffee exports enter the United States through the southern ports of New Orleans, Port Everglades (Ft. Lauderdale), and Miami.

2. Author's calculations based on Mexican Coffee Council (1994) and ICO (1996) data.

3. Author's interview (April 1997) with David Griswold, president of Sustainable Harvests and cofounder of Aztec Harvests.

4. Each of these concepts has multiple indicators, which are not included here because of space (Porter, forthcoming).

5. Richard Snyder (forthcoming) makes a similar argument about the kinds of policy regimes that resulted in different coffee-producing states. My argument focuses instead on the actual outcomes for small producers and their unions.

6. The actual sales office of CNOC is called the *Promotora Comercial de Cafés Suaves Mexicanos, S.A. de C.V.*

7. Author's interviews with regional INI officials in Oaxaca, summer 1995 and June–November 1996.

8. This producer union is called the Union of Indigenous Communities from the Isthmus Region of Oaxaca (UCIRI).

9. Participant observation at CNOC Second Congress, Chiapas, September 1996, and interview with CEPCO and CNOC officials.

10. Compiled from CNOC and CNC documents.
11. The Inter-American Foundation, an agency funded by the U.S. Congress to fight poverty in Latin America, aided many independent coffee producer unions during the Salinas and Zedillo administrations.

Chapter 7

1. Quiché is one of more than twenty Mayan languages spoken by Guatemalan people, who also refer to themselves by this term. Most of the Quiché in South Florida come from Guatemala's northwestern departments, where the heaviest fighting occurred during the civil wars of the past twenty years. Other Guatemalan ethnic groups in South Florida include X'anjobal, Jacaltec, and Chuj.
2. I prefer the term *neighborhood* to, say, community, because these areas often consist primarily of clusters of housing units where individuals have little history in common. *Communities,* by contrast, share historical experiences as well as functioning institutions such as schools, churches, police forces, and so forth.
3. Many of Miami's public schools have experienced increased competition over public space in the form of sporadic incidents of fighting and mass violence between students of different ethnic and national backgrounds.
4. During discussions of fast-track authority in November 1997, for example, economists routinely dismissed anecdotes about Florida farmers going out of business with observations that the nation was at full employment. Such rhetoric glosses over quality of life attributes of various occupations, particularly those, such as farming and fishing, where independent operators are willing to undervalue their own labor power and work long hours with little pay, because they are unwilling to work for others.
5. Most of the research for this chapter was conducted in the late 1980s and early 1990s, prior to the implementation of NAFTA. Additional data were collected from 1992 to 1995. Here I focus on the labor relations that have developed within the winter vegetable industry, the roles of culture brokers and labor contractors in such relations, and the implications of increasing numbers of indigenous U.S. workers in the industry's labor force. The 1989–1991 research was funded by a grant from the Commission on Agricultural Workers, and the 1992–1995 research was funded by grants from the Howard Heinz Endowment and the National Science Foundation (DBS-9211620). Associate investigators on the latter project included Alex Stepick, Karen Richman, Jerónimo Camposeco, Ed Kissam, Guillermo Grenier, and Allan Burns. Many thanks to these individuals and the supporting agencies.
6. Many of these workers come from peasant communities that either have been negatively impacted by NAFTA or have received few or no benefits from freer trade. Gereffi's article (this volume) suggests that while northern Mexico and the United States are becoming more integrated because of NAFTA in terms of the "apparel commodity chain," northern and southern regions of Mexico are becoming less integrated. It is often these southern regions that supply new indigenous workers to the U.S. farm labor market (see Conroy and West in this volume).
7. H2a refers to a visa issued to an individual for temporary labor in the United States. The H2a program is also known as the British West Indies Temporary Alien Labor Program, which from 1943 to 1991 allowed sugar growers in South Florida to import workers to cut sugarcane from November to April every year.
8. The single most important development in this area was the success of labor

organizing among the citrus workers of central Florida as, in December 1971, the Coca-Cola Company signed a contract with the United Farm Workers. As remarkable as this early breakthrough in Florida farm labor relations seemed then, even more remarkable is that it has remained confined to Coca-Cola, a company that is particularly sensitive to its public image.

9. The revolution boosted Florida sugar production in particular: after gradual increases of around 3–5,000 acres per year between 1954 and 1959, sugar acreage leaped from 47,100 acres in 1959 to 137,935 in 1962 (Salley 1983).

10. These problems have become more common as the farm labor market becomes more ethnically complex and more individuals are needed who can translate between indigenous languages and Spanish, enforce compliance with labor rules, and so forth.

11. Names used in these illustrations are pseudonyms.

Chapter 8

1. The authors are grateful to Professor Fausto Díaz Montes of the Universidad Autónoma Benito Juárez de Oaxaca and the members of the field research team: Alejandro Arrellano, Luis Miguel Bascones, Manuel Fernández, Salomon González, Fernando Guardarrama, and Luis Adolfo Méndez Lugo. Thanks also to Pablo Policzer for assistance with the statistical analysis. Jonathan Schlefer, Ronald Dore, Andrea Silverman, and Aubrey Williams provided useful comments on earlier drafts. We also remember Martin Diskin for his inspiration and support early in this project. Our study was funded by the World Bank's Internal Participation Learning Group, with support from the Swedish International Development Agency (see Bhatnagar and Williams 1992; World Bank 1994b, 1994c). The Ford Foundation's Mexico City office provided additional support via the Universidad Autónoma Benito Juárez de Oaxaca. The first stage of this study was presented as Fox and Aranda (1994). An earlier version of this chapter was published in Spanish as Fox and Aranda (1996a). For more extensive detail and case studies, see Fox and Aranda (1996b). The data and analysis presented here are the exclusive responsibility of the authors.

2. Institutional development aside, rural local governments may be at a special disadvantage for carrying out development activities that involve economies of scale. Prud'homme (1994) discusses many of the risks involved in indiscriminate decentralization. Similarly, Gershberg (1993, 1995) found that the empirical evidence from developing countries for increased service delivery effectiveness through decentralization is actually quite weak. The World Bank's faith in rural decentralization can therefore be characterized as rather underinformed. For a partial reassessment, see Littvak et al. (1998).

3. For one of the most prominent recent studies of the outcomes of decentralization and the impact of prior social legacies, see Putnam (1993). Crook and Manor's (1994) cross-national comparison looks at completely different cases but comes to similar conclusions. Fox (1996) assesses Putnam's argument in the rural Mexican context.

4. This is consistent with Gershberg's (1993, 1995) comprehensive analysis of Mexico's educational system, which found that decentralization without accountability is unlikely to produce improved service delivery.

5. Graham (1994, 12) makes a similar observation, citing experiences in West Bengal and Nepal: "unless local power structures are also reformed, decentralization

may merely allow the local elites to become more powerful." Few researchers have grappled with the question of which level of government is most appropriate for decentralization of which activity. When should responsibility be devolved to state governments, and when to local governments? There is a widespread implicit assumption that "more local is always better," but Tendler's findings in northeastern Brazil suggest that reformist health and agricultural extension programs succeeded there largely because a democratized state government did not cede control to clientelistic municipalities (Tendler and Freedheim 1994).

6. For the 1989–1993 period, municipal funds accounted for 14% of PRONASOL spending (SEDESOL 1993b, 26). For background on PRONASOL, see Cornelius et al (1994). It should be noted that the highest levels of per capita PRONASOL spending were in the middle-income rather than the poorest states, at least for the 1990–1992 period (detailed data presented in Fox 1995). This is consistent with Molinar and Weldon's findings that spending levels were determined in part by state electoral calendars (1994).

7. Note that this study covers only the Salinas period.

8. For the most comprehensive official data on changing urban and rural poverty levels, see INEGI-CEPAL (1993), discussed in Fox and Aranda (1994, 1996b). This survey found that 16.1% of Mexico's population was considered to be in extreme poverty in 1992, slightly less than in 1989 (18.8%) but still a larger percentage than in 1984 (15.4%)—two years into the post-1982 crisis. Two-thirds of those in extreme poverty lived in rural areas, increasing from 8.4 million in 1989 to 8.8 million people in 1992. Boltvinik's methodological critique of the survey suggests that levels of extreme poverty were significantly higher (1995).

9. For broader discussion of the World Bank's antipoverty strategy in Mexico, see Fox and Aranda (1996b); Fox (1999); and www.laneta.apc.org/trasparencia.

10. The census defines more than 52% of Oaxaca's population as indigenous, tied for first place with Yucatán. Oaxaca also accounts for 18.3% of Mexico's total indigenous population, more than any other state (Embriz et al. 1993, 38). For descriptive data, see Centro Nacional de Estudios Municipales (1998). On Oaxaca's ethnic diversity, see Barabas and Bartolomé (1986), and Acevedo (1993). For Oaxaca state government "pro decentralization" discourse, see Carrasco Altamirano (1995). For a comprehensive analysis of local government in Oaxaca, see Díaz Montes (1992). On local political conflict, see Dennis (1987); Greenberg (1989); Parnell (1988); and Rubin (1994, 1997).

11. For a comparison of PIDER, Conasupo-Coplamar, and INI-Solidaridad, see Fox (1994, 1996). For an overview of the rise of diverse citizens' movements, see Fox and Hernández (1992).

12. On municipal reform in Mexico, see Cabrero Mendoza (1995); Martínez and Ziccardi (1987); Massolo (1991); Merino (1994); V. Rodríguez (1993, 1997); Rodríguez and Ward (1995); and Ziccardi (1995); among others.

13. According to the World Bank (1994a), the pre-1990 federal revenue sharing formula gave poorer states, on average, one-third the per capita amount received by richer states. The 1989 Ley de Coordinación Fiscal's new formula reduced the ratio of transfers to the three richest entities (Nuevo León, Baja California, and the Federal District) as compared to the six poorest states from 3:1 in 1989 to 2:1 in 1992. The imbalance in capital investments was much greater, with a few states and the Federal District receiving three times the average level of investment per capita of the rest of the states combined.

14. The sample of fifty municipalities was divided according to the state's eight dis-

tinct regions, covering four to eight municipalities of diverse sizes within each region. The study covered projects funded during three annual cycles (1990–1992). In terms of the rural population distribution, in thirty-eight of the fifty cases the entire population lived in localities with less than 6,000 inhabitants. After assessing this broad sample of municipalities, field researchers focused on specific projects, collecting data on one hundred and forty-five (76% of which were located outside of municipal centers). For details on sample selection and methodology more generally, see Fox and Aranda (1994, 1996b).

15. The names used to describe the principal submunicipal jurisdictions vary greatly; in other states they are called *delegaciones* or *comisarías*. Some municipalities have even smaller subdivisions, such as *agencias de policía* or *rancherías*.

16. Two main reasons make it inherently difficult to put these resource allocation guidelines into practice. First, project funding decisions are supposed to be "demand-driven." This implies that the most vocal beneficiaries are most likely to win project approval, not necessarily the poorest. Second, there may be conflicts between benefiting the poorest and the largest number of residents. Public goods are attractive to local leaders because most residents presumably benefit, though they may not have much social impact. For example, a basketball court may benefit most local families, whereas more "high-impact" projects, such as a drinking-water system, electricity, or a crop warehouse, may only reach part of a community.

17. Types of eligible infrastructure include rural roads, bridges, electricity transmission lines, town marketplaces (only under the 25% cap for the town center), warehouses, radiotelephones, and social infrastructure, including piped water, sewerage, neighborhood electricity installation, waste treatment and collection, street and sidewalk paving (only where piped water and sewerage already exist, and under the 25% ceiling for the town center), parks (only if residents contribute 50%), improvement of schoolhouses and health centers, construction of "telesecondary" schools, sports fields (if beneficiaries contribute 50%, and not including wire or fences), pedestrian paths, and headquarters for local farmers' groups (*casa ejidal*, if members contribute 50%). Projects that fit this menu of options must also: cost less than $30,000, include a contribution of at least 20% from the solidarity committee (in cash, materials, or labor), not take place where land tenure conflicts might interfere, be a new project (works in progress cannot be covered), be completed in less than one fiscal year, and not be divided into stages. In the case of schools and health centers, the other respective government agencies must previously commit staffing and equipment (this provision is widely ignored). Municipal funds are not to be spent on projects involving town halls or churches.

18. The Municipal Funds program was preceded by a similar community development effort that focused on one of the state's poorest regions, the Mixteca, with support from the International Labour Office and the United Nations Development Program. See Collins's (1995) evaluation.

19. Oaxaca's intermunicipal allocation criteria were clear-cut from a state point of view, but the allocation logic was often confusing from the point of view of grassroots communities. Since municipal populations vary greatly within rural areas, and the number of *agencias* does not vary proportionately, municipal funds investment per capita differed sharply from one municipality to another. More recently, after the 1992 change in governor, Oaxaca's municipal distribution formula changed, increasing the weight of the "population size" criteria and therefore

the portion of funding assigned to urban areas. Since overall funding did not increase, some rural areas lost out. Federal Social Development Ministry officials involved in the program suggested that this shift was probably electorally motivated, since urban areas have more voters and are more electorally competitive.

20. Authors' interviews with World Bank officials 1994. A member of the World Bank's resident mission staff charged with evaluating spending by the first Decentralization Project estimated that he was able to block only 40% of the "white elephant" projects proposed by state and federal officials (e.g., a beltway highway for the Chiapas state capital). The Second Decentralization and Regional Development loan, which includes four other states and emphasizes municipal funds, was designed to take this issue into account. The $500 million loan limits World Bank support for municipal funds to rural communities with less than 5,000 inhabitants. Funds are not to be disbursed to individual states until state governments spell out their intermunicipal distribution criteria. See the project description in World Bank (1994a). This document is available through the World Bank's Public Information Center (pic@worldbank.org).

21. The question of who handles the funds is not the only relevant indicator of control, however. In terms of who decided where to purchase construction materials, in 70% of the cases it was the local committee, in 16% the mayor, and in 10% the state government representative. A generalized pattern of manipulation of material purchases was found in only one of the state's eight regions (Sierra Norte), but this pattern ended when the state government's regional *delegado* became a state congressman in 1992.

22. In practice, the project cycle tended to be less than half a year, once red tape, travel time to government offices, and lead time for project design was factored in. Due to these delays, the funds usually arrived during the rainy season, greatly complicating construction efforts.

23. All projects were officially considered "finished," but that category included schools without teachers or furniture, similarly empty clinic buildings, or corn mills locked up for lack of local access to electricity. Notably, drinking-water projects were among the most likely not to be in operation. Some of these investments may eventually become useful; for example, having a schoolhouse increases a community's bargaining power to request assignment of a teacher.

24. Local movements calling for the democratization of submunicipal government have included the 1992 Xi' Nich march from Chiapas to Mexico City, as well as more recent protests in rural Guerrero and Veracruz. Small as these local offices may be, some local bosses prefer to use violence rather than submit to majority rule. Note, for example, the murder of two Mixteco activists in Tlacoachistlahuaca, Guerrero's democracy movement (*La Jornada* June 6, 7, 15, and 22, 1995), or Cutzamala, Guerrero, where the local boss's loss of the *comisaría* election triggered a wave of assassinations (*La Jornada*, July 1995). In contrast, democratically chosen submunicipal officials can end up leading broader social movements, as in the case of the Tabasco Chontales movement for oil pollution compensation (*La Jornada*, June 4, 1995). On state-by-state differences in structures of submunicipal governance, see Fox and Aranda (1996b, Appendix 3).

25. For example, Domínguez (1988, 28) presents a clear self-description of the Mixe people's system of "communal power," which is based on: "the land, the language, the assembly, the *cargo* [rotating authority system], the *tequio* [community self-help] and the festival.... The highest authority is the communal assembly."

26. The municipal solidarity committees, which include the town council *(cabildo)*

and the heads of local solidarity committees, met in only 54% of cases. They were much more likely to have met in the larger municipalities. In the more urban areas of the medium-sized and larger towns, the solidarity committees tended to be organized as block committees (as in Juchitán and Nochixtlán). In one large municipality, Miahuatlán, the municipal council was surpassed by an even more decentralized structure that emerged prior to the program: successive cycles of citizen mobilization to democratize local government created a council of *agencias* to act as a counterweight to the mayor's office.

27. As one municipal official put it: "Listen, here in our community we have the custom of doing it this way: we all have the commitment to give services to the community, and for free. When the assembly names us, we are obliged to comply with the responsibility [*cargo*] and we must sacrifice our own small personal jobs during the year and a half that the community commissions us for [note: the period of service varies by community]. This means that we each have our responsibility, just as each other citizen has.... That's why if we wanted to name an additional committee to deal with a project, no one would accept. Everyone already has had their task, whether it's in the municipality, the agrarian authorities, the church, the school, or the village fiesta, or it'll be their turn in the future. So if there are any tasks to deal with during our turn as municipal authorities, it's our job, that's why they named us. That's our custom. The government has its way of doing things, but here we do things our own way, as we always have, and it's not going to change now because some new government program asks for it. That program will end sooner or later, and some other one will come along and will ask for something different. But here, we aren't going to change our form of work" (Santiago Comaltepec).

28. In contrast to one of our initial hypotheses, the presence of strong grassroots organizations, especially producer groups, had little impact on the project decision-making process, playing a role in only 8% of cases reported. This was not only the result of the lack of dissemination of the fact that productive projects could be included in the project menu; it also seemed due to the widely held conception of the division of labor between the duties of local government and the role of producer and other social organizations. Local government is widely seen to be responsible for service provision, while producer groups are expected to focus on economic activities. Moreover, even where producer groups are strong, not all citizens belong (such as those who do not produce a marketable surplus). In municipalities where social organizations are strong, however, their members did participate actively in local Municipal Funds projects as individual citizens. In fact, where social organizations were strong they seemed to provide much larger contributions to the local service provision than the Municipal Funds did, as in the case of the Sierra Norte community forestry organizations.

29. Professor Díaz Montes of the Autonomous State University of Oaxaca estimates that only approximately 10% of Oaxaca's more than four hundred indigenous municipalities are dominated by authoritarian local bosses. The mayors in the smallest communities tend to be chosen in community assemblies, either through voting or rotating *cargos*. Legally, the term is for three years, but in the smallest municipalities and in most rural *agencias* the term is usually only one year (because of the opportunity cost of giving up income-generating activity).

30. As one municipal official put it: "The truth is that, even though we are very clear about what our most pressing needs are and what projects we'd like to carry out, we always have to adapt our proposal to the government's conditions and the

small amount of money they give us. For example, the program rules do not accept incomplete projects, which means that we can't do a project in stages. So we have to do little tiny projects, which—even though the community doesn't really need them—we can finish in the same year, since they want the final paperwork delivered. In the end, we go on without resolving our larger problems and we end up just the same as when we started" (San Pedro y San Pablo Ayutla). Another common refrain from municipal officials was: "The budgets come already decided in Oaxaca [City]. They don't even take us into account, nor do they consider the real costs of building the project we propose. It's we who have to adjust our proposal to the money they give us" (San Pablo Macuiltianguis and Tenetze). It should also be noted that many of Oaxaca's mayors and municipal agents lack literacy skills and/or fluency in Spanish, which greatly limits their bargaining power with the state government officials who are their main points of contact with the Municipal Funds program.

31. Local authorities reported that technical assistance was either unavailable to most small, rural municipalities or was of poor quality. For example, as one municipal official observed: "We would've liked to use metal pipe in our [water] project, but there wasn't enough money and we had to buy plastic. But plastic doesn't work for this kind of project, it breaks right away under high water pressure, while the metal pipe can handle it. But we had to accept the project as it came, since they didn't give us any more money. We have to do poor quality projects, and there's no other way. . . . The technicians know that the project they're advising isn't going to work, but there's no more money to do something better" (Santiago Zacatepec). In another case the state technicians' project design required water to flow uphill, so it was never built. The materials purchased remained in storage.

32. This finding underscores the high social and economic cost associated with the lack of reliable technical assistance needed for appropriate and sustainable water system designs, as well as the apparent lack of sufficient local "ownership" of water projects to sustain adequate maintenance.

33. Because of the great diversity of types of project, no one "objective" indicator would have produced comparable results. The impact categories used were simply "*bueno, regular, y malo.*"

34. Correlations were measured using the Chi Square, which tests the hypothesis that the variables are independent. Results are considered statistically significant with a less than 5% margin of error. Because of the size of the data set, the results are much less reliable when more than two dichotomous variables are correlated. A much larger data set would be necessary for more sophisticated multivariate tests.

35. The sample included several well-known municipalities governed by the opposition, including Juchitán (COCEI-Party of the Democratic Revolution) and Huajuapan de León (National Action Party). There was no direct relationship between opposition government and level of community participation, however. For example, levels of community participation were rather low in Huajaupan and San Pedro Pochutla (Party of the Authentic Mexican Revolution). In Huajuapan, the mayor chose the projects and which streets to pave. Residents tended to contribute money rather than labor. Community participation was particularly high in Juchitán, where the governing regional sociopolitical organization has long encouraged block organization. The municipal government is also one of the few with its own autonomous technical team, which provides technical assistance to neighboring municipalities. Municipal fund resource allocation was politicized in those municipalities where political competition was relatively new and the legit-

imacy of the electoral process was widely questioned. In these cases, local polarization often led to a stalemated "dual power" situation of parallel municipal authorities after the state government used municipal funds to support the ruling party faction (as in Tlacolula). For background on Juchitán, see Rubin (1994, 1997). On Tlacolula, see Díaz Montes (1992).

36. As background information on how these municipal governance systems worked, in the majority of cases studied (52%) local authorities were chosen by *usos y costumbres*, rather than through elections. Researchers examined this issue by asking whether local authorities were chosen by assembly or through political party competition. Only 14% of the localities chose their authorities through party competition, implying that the community assembly method includes both open voting and the customary rotating community responsibility systems. It should be mentioned that on paper, virtually all Oaxaca mayors chosen by *usos y costumbres* are subsequently listed as victors for the ruling party. Local civic movements are beginning to challenge this practice. For example, the regional Comité de Pueblos Chatinos recently criticized the ruling party for "taking the names of our authorities, elected in assembly, and registering them as their list" (*La Jornada*, June 16, 1995). More recently, Mixteco lawyer Francisco López Barcenas has pointed out that the term *usos y costumbres* does not adequately communicate the sense in which these "traditions" are actually legal-normative systems and should be referred to as such.

37. Many Municipal Funds projects were only completed thanks to extra project funds from the state government. Distribution of such funds was completely discretional and dependent on local-state political bargaining. Comprehensive data were unavailable.

38. In some regions, however, the tiny size of the grants added to existing resentment of government neglect: "Now it seems that the government is very interested in paying attention to the peasants with this program because before the community did its little projects with its own sweat and no help at all. . . . Some say it's a very good program [but] we think it is a tactic to improve the image of the PRI, since it's gone downhill. . . It's a way for the government to get the peasants to keep quiet so they don't complain, but we already know the way we can get the government to do what it says, by pressuring it, [because] that's what they don't like. If the government wants folks to be quiet it's going to have to help the peasants even more" (Tanetze).

39. One problem with measuring this phenomenon is that the data on outlying settlements are quite uneven. Oaxaca has four different government catalogs of "localities" (submunicipal settlements); if one adds all four lists and subtracts for repetitions, then there are more than two thousand more localities than are listed in the single largest catalog.

40. Such projects are too small to be profitable for the private sector, and Oaxaca's nongovernmental organizations are not strong in the area of infrastructure services, such as water system design.

41. By the end of 1994, pre-rebellion mayors had been overthrown by indigenous civic protests in 45% of the state's municipalities (49 of 110). In thirty-four of these municipalities, politically and ethnically pluralistic town councils were created in their place (C. Rodríguez 1995). For a recent account of municipal issues in Chiapas, see Burguete (1998). The need to democratize indigenous municipalities, including municipal authorities, was specifically addressed in the 1996 San Andrés Accords signed by the federal government and the EZLN. The agreements were

supported by both the national indigenous movement and the multiparty congressional peace commission (COCOPA), but were later rejected by the Zedillo government. For the full text and analysis, see Hernández and Vera (1998). For the text and analysis in English, see *Cultural Survival Quarterly*, March 1999.

42. See the various articles in *La Jornada* (December 22 and 23, 1998).

43. On the issue of World Bank accountability more generally, both in Mexico and internationally, see Fox (1997a, 1997b, 1998, 1999); and Fox and Brown (1998).

Chapter 9

1. The author was a member of the Board of Commissioners of the Port of New Orleans from 1986 to 1991 and chaired the board in 1989–90. She was also a professor of urban and regional planning at the University of New Orleans and was active in planning issues, especially when she served as the board's chair. She was the first woman to serve on the board in its ninety-year history.

2. For a historical account of the role of black dockworkers in New Orleans, see Arnesen (1991) and Rosenberg (1988).

3. In 1990, blacks made up 61.4% of the population; in 1960, whites constituted 62.6%.

4. These facilities, all built at about the same time, would eventually become obsolete as a unit.

5. In doing so, Brinson obtained civil service exemption for twenty-one key positions.

Chapter 10

1. We share equal responsibility for the contents of this chapter. Our thanks to Marcela Cerrutti and David Spener for preparing some of the analysis of the Mexican and U.S. data, and to Agustín Escobar for his help in characterizing the Mexican Gulf cities.

2. The fact that the Mexican data do not report on ethnicity precludes analysis of this key issue, including its pertinence to the key topic of migration and labor inequalities (see Griffith in this volume; Hammermesh and Bean 1998; Portes and Rubault 1996; Sassen 1994).

3. Miami, of course, is located on the Atlantic coast, while Laredo and Nuevo Laredo are located in the U.S.-Mexico interior. Miami is pertinent to our comparative analysis in that, as the "capital of the Caribbean Basin," it increasingly competes with Houston and New Orleans in commercial relations with Mexico, the Caribbean, and Latin America at large (see Tardanico in this volume; *U.S./Latin Trade* 1994, 1995a, 1995b). Laredo and Nuevo Laredo are relevant as small but fast-growing sites of export-assembly manufacturing, which government and business groups in Mérida have sought to attract (see Wilson and Kayne in this volume).

     Due both to space limitations and to our interest in exploring changes in "twin cities" along the U.S.-Mexican frontier, we cannot include the U.S. Gulf cases of Mobile, Alabama, and Tampa, Florida. Moreover, problems of data availability, quality, and computer readability preclude analysis of the same time periods in the United States and Mexico. Our data analysis therefore covers 1980–1990 for the United States and 1986–1993 for most aspects of the Mexican case.

4. For the sampled U.S. cities 1980 fell in the midst of relative prosperity, including the petroleum-based booms of Houston and New Orleans. In contrast 1990 fell in

the midst of national recession. For these U.S. cities, then, the data exaggerate downturns in the labor market. As for Mexico 1986 was a time of economic stabilization and slow recovery from the crisis of the early decade, while 1993 was a time of continued aggregate upswing, including NAFTA-linked optimism. Hence the data for the sample of Mexican cities emphasize labor market changes linked to some amount of macroeconomic rebound. For discussions of the impact of economic cycles on labor-market inequalities, see Galbraith (1998); Portes et al. (1997); and Rubery (1988).

5. Concerning determinants of urban labor market change, we can expect that, under any given conditions in the world market, the roles of domestic economy and politics become more influential under the following circumstances: more strategic national and local positions in global commodity chains; greater size and/or diversity of national and local economies; geopolitical relations that strengthen national and local markets and government negotiating leverage; and, combining the preceding elements with national and local state-society structures, stronger interventionist and regulatory capacities of national and regional/urban government machinery.

6. In our scheme, production, craft, and repair occupations in the service industries, such as electrician, are classified as skilled under the Fordist occupational structure. Likewise, occupations such as guard, police, and cook, are classified as skilled under the post-Fordist structure, even though they may be located in manufacturing.

7. Space limitations permit us to present only selected city-specific data, as opposed to the aggregate data for the samples of both Mexican and U.S. cities.

8. We use the terms *postindustrial* and *post-Fordist* simply to refer to Esping-Andersen et al.'s (1993) perspective on sociooccupational restructuring. For critiques of the terms, see Sassen (1994) and Sayer and Walker (1992).

9. The sixteen-city data were not available to us for 1986, so to place our five-city data in context we use the Mexican urban labor force surveys for the second quarters of 1987 and 1994 (INEGI 1987, 1994a). The data for sixteen of Mexico's largest cities indicate that manufacturing and government services declined as employment shares. On the rise were shares in trade, producer, and consumer services.

10. We say this based on a review of 1980–1990 data for New York City and Los Angeles, which epitomize Sassen's definition of "global cities," as well as for a notable range of large and medium cities, including the southern cases of Atlanta, Birmingham, Charlotte, Dallas, and Nashville (see, e.g., Storper 1997, 225–26).

11. The fact that the data cover seven years for Mexico versus ten years for the United States does not appear to account for much of the difference.

12. Remember that the U.S. data begin at a time of economic upswing and end at a time of downswing, while the Mexican data reflect recovery from the economic crisis of the early 1980s. The earnings trends for the five U.S. cities are broadly similar to those reported earlier for U.S. workers nationally (males 3.3%, females 15.6%) (U.S. Bureau of the Census 1996). The earnings trends for the five Mexican Gulf cities are less positive than those for the 16-city sample of Mexican workers (males 37%, females 35%) (INEGI 1987, 1994a).

13. Gender earnings inequality appears higher in the U.S. than Mexican cities in most occupational categories (Table 10.3). This contrast may be misleading since it does not take account of variables such as the relative human capital of men and women, age distribution of male and female workers, and hours worked by men and women.

Chapter 11

1. Observers across the political spectrum tend to agree that neoliberal reform, continentalization, and globalization produce winners and losers. They tend to disagree on the balance of winners and losers in the near and long terms, as well as on the ramifications for government policy. Some points of commonality, however, traverse the political spectrum. For example, on both the political left and right there are opponents of market integration who underscore its dislocating and polarizing effects.

2. *Hegemony* refers to unchallenged military-diplomatic, production, financial, and commercial supremacy in the world political economy (see Chase-Dunn 1998).

3. The post–World War II southern citrus, lumber, and tobacco industries are among the relevant cases.

4. For comparative discussion, see Amin (1998); Britton (1996); Conklin (1997); Hansen (1998); Harrison (1994); Meyer-Stamer (1998); Noponen et al. (1993); and Scott (1998).

5. As noted before, pertinent examples include the southern citrus, lumber, and tobacco industries.

6. In addition, it complements Young's discussion of port restructuring in New Orleans. Pertinent to the two chapters is the question of whether, under tightening market competition, the successful strategies documented would necessarily prove successful for other sectors, commodities, or places.

7. The agreement defines the Gulf of Mexico area as consisting of the Mexican states of Tamaulipas, Veracruz, Campeche, Tabasco, Yucatán, and Quintana Roo and the U.S. states of Texas, Louisiana, Mississippi, Alabama, and Florida (Map 1.1). Of the area's some 50 million people, 26% live on the Mexican side and 74% on the U.S. side. The Mexican contribution to the area's total yearly economic output is minuscule: at possibly as high as $30 billion, it equals about one-third that of Miami-Dade County, Florida.

8. Relevant to the Gulf Accord is Matthew Sparke's (1997) discussion of Pacific Northwestern boosterism's endeavor to organize the U.S. states of Washington and Oregon and the Canadian province of British Columbia as a transnational economic zone called Cascadia. Sparke (1997, 2) questions whether the baseline "degree and character of transnational economic integration in the region" justifies the initiative. He writes that its government and business proponents attempt to rally support on the basis of geocultural identity. They emphasize "an ecotopian-turned environmental concept of a bioregion defined by the temperate rainforest, the Cascade mountain ranges, and the waterfalls after which they were named" (1997, 4; see Clarke and Gaile 1997, 42–43).

9. The Pacific Northwest Economic Region includes the U.S. states of Washington, Oregon, Idaho, Montana, and Alaska and the Canadian provinces of British Columbia and Alberta. The Desert Pacific Region includes the U.S. states of Arizona, Nevada, and Utah and the Mexican states of Sonora, Sinaloa, and Baja California. The New Atlantic Region includes the U.S. states of Maine, New Hampshire, and Vermont and the Canadian Provinces of New Brunswick, Nova Scotia, Prince Edward Island, and Newfoundland.

10. Of course, such attempts are unlikely to be confined to any one geographic zone, however defined. For instance, business and government representatives of the port of New Orleans are attempting to recoup and extend its reach within the Americas beyond the Gulf and Caribbean basins, and likewise beyond the Amer-

icas to the wider world economy (see Young in this volume). Port interests in Veracruz are also looking beyond the more proximate geographic areas to, among others, the European Union. The geographic breadth of such initiatives would probably vary according to the strategic importance and the diversity of their underlying economic, political, and territorial entities.

11. Relevant here is Harrison's (1994) empirical critique of the view that small firms are amassing a larger share of innovations, markets, and employment in advanced national economies.

12. Recall Fox and Aranda's discussion of commonly downplayed or disregarded social policy demands of market-centric (and, implicitly, export-oriented) reforms, a point that Fox and Brown (1998), Hollingsworth and Boyer (1997), and Stallings (1995) explore in worldwide perspective.

13. Cheshire and Gordon (1996) and Cox (1995) make cautionary remarks on the pitfalls of overly abstract, linear, and generalized discussions about the forces at play and the consequences of intensified competition with regard to local transformations. Among their arguments is that such competition does not necessarily lead to coordinated and/or effective local political responses, and that the forms and sociospatial beneficiaries of local political responses vary greatly. We can anticipate that substantive economic and even social gains may occur in some localities despite weak and/or inappropriate political responses. They may also occur as an unintended outcome of policies enacted previously under different conditions and with different objectives and/or as an intended or unintended result of social and political opposition to specific policies or policy regimes.

Contributors

Josefina Aranda is a researcher in the Institute for Sociological Research at Benito Juárez Autonomous University in Oaxaca, Mexico.

Michael E. Conroy is an economist and program representative at the Ford Foundation in New York City.

Jonathan A. Fox, a political scientist, is an associate professor in the Latin American and Latino Studies Program at the University of California at Santa Cruz.

Gary Gereffi is a professor of sociology at Duke University.

Amy K. Glasmeier is a professor of geography at Pennsylvania State University.

David Griffith is an associate professor of anthropology and a senior scientist at the Institute for Coastal and Marine Resources at East Carolina University.

Thea Kayne is an international development planner with Catholic Relief Services in Baltimore, Maryland.

Robin M. Leichenko is an assistant professor of geography at Rutgers University.

Robert Porter is a Ph.D. candidate in the Political Science Department at the University of California at Santa Barbara. He teaches at Ventura College.

Bryan Roberts is the C.B. Smith Senior Centennial Chair in U.S.–Mexican Relations and a professor of sociology at the University of Texas at Austin.

Mark B. Rosenberg is provost and a professor of political science, as well as founding director of the Latin American and Caribbean Center, at Florida International University.

Richard Tardanico is an associate professor of sociology at Florida International University.

Sarah Elizabeth West is a Mellon post-doctoral fellow at Macalester College.

Patricia A. Wilson is a professor of community and regional planning at the University of Texas at Austin.

Alma H. Young is the Coleman A. Young Professor of Urban Affairs at Wayne State University.

Index